Protestant Concepts of

Church and State

Thomas G. Sanders

Protestant Concepts

Historical

Backgrounds and

Approaches for

the Future

# of Church

and State

Holt, Rinehart and Winston

New York   Chicago   San Francisco

First Edition

This volume is the first to appear in the series:

Studies of Church and State

Published in co-operation with
The Department of Religious Liberty of the
National Council of Churches of Christ in the U.S.A.

The Department of Religious Liberty of the National Council of the Churches of Christ in the United States of America has recommended the publication of this study as a contribution to better understanding of relations between church and state in America.

The content of this work is the responsibility of the author and does not necessarily reflect the official position or the opinion of the National Council of Churches, the Department of Religious Liberty, or their constituent communions.

Designer: Ernst Reichl
87705-0114
Printed in the United States of America

Acknowledgments

THIS CLARIFICATION of Protestant views on church and state would not have been possible without the interest and co-operation of many people and institutions. To the Center for the Study of Democratic Institutions of the Fund for the Republic, and its director, John Cogley, I am especially grateful for encouragement and financial assistance.

The helpfulness of the staffs of the following libraries was indispensable: Brown University, Union Theological Seminary, Harvard Divinity School, Swarthmore College, and Haverford College. I appreciate very much the time and co-operation given me by officials of the Baptist Joint Committee on Public Affairs, The Council for Christian Social Action of the United Church of Christ, the Office of Church and Society of the United Presbyterian Church, the National Lutheran Council, the Department of Public Relations of the Lutheran Church-Missouri Synod, the American Friends Service Committee, the Friends Committee on National Legislation, the National Association of Evangelicals, and the Department of Christian Social Relations of the Protestant Episcopal Church.

At various stages the following people examined what I had written and made useful suggestions, for which I am grateful: Dean M. Kelley of the Department of Religious Liberty, National Council of Churches; Professor Wendell S. Dietrich of Brown University; and Professor M. Searle Bates of Union Theological Seminary. One of my students, Stanley O. Yarian, and my wife were invaluable aids in reading proofs for me.

I would like to dedicate this book to my father, whose interest in church-state problems from a somewhat different perspective than my own first drew my attention to this extremely complex field.

Grateful acknowledgment is also made to the following publishers who have so generously granted permission to reprint from their publications:

George Allen & Unwin Ltd., London, for the Halley Stewart Trust, for excerpts from *The Works of Robert Harrison and Robert Brown*, by Albert Peel and Leland H. Carlson. Copyright 1953 by George Allen & Unwin Ltd.

George Allen & Unwin Ltd., London, for passages from *Between God and History*, by Richard K. Ullman. Copyright © 1959 by George Allen & Unwin Ltd.

Augsburg Publishing House, Minneapolis, for excerpts from *What Lutherans Are Thinking*, edited by E. C. Fendt. Copyright 1946 by Augsburg Publishing House, copyright owners by assignment from the Wartburg Press.

Hugh S. Barbour, for excerpts from his unpublished Ph.D. dissertation at Yale University, 1952, *The Early Quaker Outlook Upon "the World" and Society, 1647–1662*.

The Carey Kingsgate Press Ltd., London, for excerpts from "Christ and Freedom," by Walter P. Binns, *Official Report: Baptist World Alliance*, Ninth Baptist World Congress, London, 1955.

W. A. Cole, for passages from his unpublished Ph.D. dissertation at Cambridge University, 1955, *The Quakers and Politics*.

Concordia Publishing House, St. Louis, for excerpts from "Church and State," by Theodore Hoyer, in *The Abiding Word*, Vol. II, edited by Theodore Laetsch. Copyright 1947 by Concordia Publishing House.

Council for Christian Action of the United Church of Christ, New York, for passages from "The American Tradition of Religious Freedom," by Luther A. Weigle, in *Social Action*, Vol. XIII, November 15, 1947.

J. M. Dent & Sons Ltd., London, and The University of Chicago Press, for excerpts from *Puritanism and Liberty*, by A. S. P. Woodhouse.

Fortress Press, Philadelphia, for excerpts from the *Works of Martin Luther*, Vols. I–V. Copyright 1943 by the Board of Publication of the United Lutheran Church in America.

Fortress Press, Philadelphia, for excerpts from *The Dilemma of Church and State*, by Elston Ruff. Copyright 1954 by Muhlenberg Press.

Harper & Row, Publishers, Incorporated, for passages from *Church and State in the United States*, Vols. I and II, by Anson Phelps Stokes. Copyright 1950 by Harper & Row, Publishers, Incorporated.

Harvard University Press, for excerpts from *The Development of Religious Toleration in England;* Volume I, 1534–1603; Volume II, 1603–1640; by Wilbur K. Jordan. Copyright 1932 and 1936 by Harvard University Press.

Herald Press of the Mennonite Publishing House, Scottdale, Pennsylvania, for excerpts from *The Doctrines of the Mennonites*, by John C. Wenger. Copyright 1950 by Mennonite Publishing House.

Herald Press of the Mennonite Publishing House, for excerpts from *War, Peace, and Nonresistance*, first edition, by Guy F. Hershberger. Copyright 1944 by Herald Press.

Herald Press of the Mennonite Publishing House, for passages from *The Complete Writings of Menno Simons*, edited by John C. Wenger. Copyright © 1956 by Mennonite Publishing House.

Library Committee of the Society of Friends, London, and Cambridge University Press, London, for excerpts from *The Journal of George Fox*, edited by J. L. Nickalls. Copyright 1952 by the Library Committee of the Society of Friends, London.

The Mennonite Historical Society, Goshen, Indiana; The Philosophical Library, New York; and Random House, Inc., for excerpts from *Great Voices of the Reformation,* edited by Harry E. Fosdick. Copyright 1952 by Random House, Inc.

Mennonite Quarterly Review, Goshen, Indiana, for excerpts from the following articles: "The Pennsylvania Quaker Experiment in Politics, 1682–1756," by Guy F. Hershberger, X (October, 1936); "Christianity and the State," by Edward Yoder, XI (July, 1937); "A Mennonite Critique of the Pacifist Movement," by Don E. Smucker, XX (January, 1946); "The Theological Basis for Christian Pacifism," by Don E. Smucker, XXVII (July, 1952); "The Anabaptists and Religious Liberty in the Sixteenth Century," by Harold S. Bender, XXIX (April, 1955); "The Pacifism of the Sixteenth-Century Anabaptists," by Harold S. Bender, XXX (January, 1956); "The Anabaptist View of the State," by Hans J. Hillerbrand, XXXII (April, 1958).

National Lutheran Council, New York, and Dr. Franklin Sherman, for excerpts from "Christian Love and Public Policy Today," by Franklin Sherman, *The Lutheran Quarterly,* XIII, 3 (August, 1961).

Charles Scribner's Sons, for passages from *Christians and the State,* by John C. Bennett. Copyright © 1958 by John C. Bennett.

The Sunday School Board of the Southern Baptist Convention, for excerpts from *Champions of Religious Liberty,* by Rufus W. Weaver. Copyright 1946 by The Sunday School Board of the Southern Baptist Convention.

The University of Chicago, for excerpts from the following articles from *Church History*: "Quakerism and the End of the Interregnum: A Chapter in the Domestication of Radical Puritanism," by James F. Maclear, XIX (December, 1950); "American Protestantism During the Revolutionary Epoch," by Sidney Mead, XXII (December, 1953); "The Rule of the Saints in American Politics," by Jerald C. Brauer, (September, 1958); " 'The True American Union' of Church and State: The Reconstruction of the Theocratic Tradition," by James F. Maclear, XXVIII (March, 1959).

The Westminster Press, Philadelphia, for excerpts from *Calvin: Institutes of the Christian Religion,* Vols. I, XX, LCC. Copyright © 1960 by W. L. Jenkins.

The Westminster Press, Philadelphia, and Student Christian Movement Press, Ltd., London, for passages from *Spiritual and Anabaptist Writers,* Vols. XXV, LCC, edited by George Hunston Williams, 1957.

Contents

Introduction   1

Toward a Definition of Protestantism   3
The Christian Political Heritage   6
Protestantism and the Modern World   11
Issues Contributing to a Typology   17
Five Representative Protestant Answers   19

I   God's Regiments and Man's Vocation:
    Luther and Lutheranism

Luther's Radical Theocentrism and the Two Regiments   23
Lutheran Developments in Europe and America   48
The Modern Period   52
Revisionism in American Lutheranism   59
The Missouri Synod   67
Lutheran Contributions to a Protestant Church-State Theory   70

II   Christian Life Without Political Compromise:
    The Anabaptists and Mennonites

Anabaptism   75
Persecution of the Anabaptists   91
Historical Developments Among the Anabaptists   94
Contemporary Developments   97
The Mennonite Witness   109

III   From Theocracy to Pacifism:
    The Quakers

The Origins   113
The Beginning of Quietism   130

Governmental Experiments in America   132
Quietist Characteristics   137
The Decline of Quietism   141
Contemporary Quaker Interests in the State   144

IV   Separationism:
Defenders of the Wall

The Development of Modern Separationism   161
The Origins of Separationism   165
Revivalism and Separationism   183
Separationism in the Nineteenth Century   191
Separationism and the Social Gospel   196
The Baptists as Separationists   198
Separationist Revisionism   216
The Significance of Separationism   220

V   Moderation and Pragmatism:
The Transformationists

The Calvinist Origins of Transformationism   225
Puritan Beginnings   234
The Revival of Transformationism in the Nineteenth Century   248
Modern Transformationism and Church-State "Separation"   257
An Evaluation of Transformationism   276

Conclusion

The Relevance of Protestant Diversity   281
Sources of Protestant Diversity   284
Protestantism and the Christian Political Motifs   287
Vocation   289
Church-State Problems as Ethical Problems:
   A Protestant Perspective   292

Notes
                                                                    301

Index
                                                                    331

Protestant Concepts of
Church and State

Introduction

Church and state: We think immediately of conflict, of opposing demands for man's loyalty. Man's dedication has often been torn between God and country, religious faith and patriotism. Church and state have been the most significant institutions within which Western man has lived, but struggle has ensued between them because each has tended to make absolute claims.

In the Greek world an Aristotle could hold that civic life effectively fulfilled the needs of human nature, but Christianity, inheriting the insight of the Old Testament prophets that political interest did not necessarily correspond to God's will, undermined the classic assumption. In Revelation and I Peter, the New Testament reflects the first Christian conflict with the state, when the primitive church denounced as idolatry the claim of the post-Augustan Roman Empire that final authority lay in an apotheosized emperor.

This first conflict illustrates three aspects of all subsequent church-state problems: 1. The religious institution is evaluated by the political authority in terms of its own responsibilities for order and justice. 2. The church's view of the state is affected by its consciousness of a divine mission within history. 3. Law and power are used as instruments, and the church's response varies between resistance and acquiescence.

The first years of Christianity witnessed examples of all these elements. Pliny and Celsus, for example, both interpreted the new religion in terms of imperial interest—the former as a responsible and dispassionate bureaucrat, the latter as a polemical apologist for pagan philosophy. As for Christians, Paul thought of government as the instrument of God, but the author of Revelation saw it as the handiwork of the devil. While Nero initiated a policy of persecution, a later emperor, Commodus, moderated it. In the twentieth century, with its Nazi and Communist persecutions of Christianity, and increased church-state tension in America, the same fundamental elements have played important roles: the attitude of government toward religion, the attitude of religion toward government, and the policy of harmony or conflict.

Many studies of church-state relations have tended to emphasize the first element. All Western political theorists, for example, have regarded the place of religion in society as an unavoidable issue; and the modern era has produced such solutions as the subordination of religion to political interests in Machiavelli and Hobbes, its hoped-for disintegration in Marx, and its acceptance as an integral part of society in the pluralism of Laski, Barker, and Figgis.[1]

Other church-state studies have stressed the third element—the constitutional, legal, customary, or unreflective ways in which the relations of church and state have been adjusted. These vary from country to country,[2] the legal institutions often reflecting an underlying political view of religion held by society or by the government.

This book seeks to illuminate the second of these elements— the attitude of the church toward the state, especially as it appears in American Protestantism.[3]

When questions are raised about the attitudes of religious groups toward the state, attention most frequently focuses on the Roman Catholic Church. Since the time of St. Augustine, Roman Catholicism has sought to include the political order within a comprehensive philosophical and theological perspective, on the assumption that every aspect of reality should be seen as under the control of a creative, sovereign, and redemptive God. Since World War II, Roman Catholic scholars and theologians have significantly re-evaluated their traditions on church and state, an enterprise that has attracted non-Catholic attention as well.[4]

Many Protestants have also developed theories of the political order and their relationship to it, though they have not always clearly articulated their presuppositions. The variety of such theories in Protestantism is usually not recognized: John C. Bennett, in his recent *Christians and the State,* though discerning a Baptist view, says that there is "no Protestant doctrine concerning Church-State relations."[5] Of course, there is no official Protestant position, but the Baptists are not the only Protestant group that has developed a distinctive view. Whenever there has been a conflict between a Protestant church and the state—and such situations have been virtually unavoidable—an implicit perspective on the church's relations to the state has emerged. Such a perspective draws heavily on the authority of the Bible, but also makes use of the historical and cultural circumstances of the conflict. Most of the thinkers who articulated such perspectives considered their positions self-evident in the light of Protestant convictions, but we can see that they selected certain biblical and traditional elements rather than others, in part because of social, political, and other nonreligious causes.

Toward a Definition of Protestantism

Following Paul Tillich, many interpreters of Protestantism hold that its distinguishing characteristic is the "Protestant principle": an emphasis on the sovereignty of God, in contrast with the finiteness of human expressions, which leads to a focus on divine judgment. But clearly, most Protestants would not agree.[6]

What does the term "Protestant" mean? During its rather brief history, Protestantism has embraced nearly every type of religious outlook in the West. The search for a guiding principle remains unsettled; in fact, one may expect even more novel expressions of Protestantism in the future. Because any definition has clear shortcomings, Protestantism, in this study, will be viewed as an historical and sociological phenomenon, and will refer simply to the thought and institutions of those who claim to be Protestant.

It should now be possible to discuss the different types of Protestantism. Despite variations in a given historical period, one can classify expressions of Protestantism according to selected criteria. Of course, the groups or individuals involved differ, depending on whether one is classifying views on God or views on church organization. Denominational distinctions in America, for example, while giving little insight into differences of belief, help differentiate one system of church government from another; but even differences of belief can be classified if one realizes that ideas cross denominational boundaries. Except for strongly confessional churches, beliefs vary radically within American denominations, and some Baptists agree more closely with the theological views of Episcopalians than with their fellow Baptists. Even churches that adhere to a rigidly traditional position experience difficulty maintaining theological continuity in the American melting pot, which confronts them with new religious and secular ideas and values.

For our purposes, it is helpful to recall the five views on the relationship of Christian faith and culture that were described by H. R. Niebuhr: Christ against culture, Christ and culture in essential conformity, Christ above culture, Christ and culture in paradox, and Christ transforming culture.[7] A classification of Protestant perspectives on church and state encounters the same problems that Niebuhr faced, for certain thinkers seem to have characteristics of more than one type, or some thinkers do not fit into a typology at all. Whereas some reflective Christians feel ill at ease with classifications because they see the freedom of the human spirit as too great and the perspectives with which men view reality as too diverse, other equally thoughtful Christians feel a sense of kinship with their fellow believers that demands articulation.

The Sources of Protestant Diversity

The obvious reason for such diversity of viewpoints is that, unlike Roman Catholicism, Protestantism lacks an authority to maintain relative order in theological and ethical statements, an agent to choose from Bible and tradition and distinguish essential elements of faith and practice from problems on which disagreement may continue. The leaders of the Reformation did not anticipate such a chaotic condition; in opposing the authority of the church with the Bible, they assumed that Scripture spoke for itself, that the gospel was self-evident. All the Reformers of the sixteenth century held that the principles of church-state relations as well as of theology lay incontestably in the Bible, and they rejected alternative views with a passion almost beyond comprehension today. However, not only did sixteenth-century theorists reflect the outlooks of their particular nations and positions within the political and social structure, but the presumed sources of authority opened by Protestantism offered wide possibilities of interpretation. The Bible, for example, ranges from a prescription for a religiously guided government in Israel to admonitions for a struggling group of Christians under persecution. Written over a thousand years and representing traditions that stretch back even farther, the Bible can better be regarded politically as a description of the changing temporal circumstances of the people it discusses than as a source for a consistent church-state theory.

In addition to the Bible, Protestant denominations have also depended upon tradition as an authority. Protestants usually reject or minimize this fact because of the centrality of the Bible among the Reformers and their conscious polemic against tradition as an equal authority; American Protestant thought, especially its sectarian forms, often tends to justify positions solely by reference to the New Testament. Kenneth S. Latourette has commented on the disposition of American Protestantism in the nineteenth century "to ignore the developments which had taken place in Christianity in the Old World after the first century."[8] Tradition appears in two forms in Protestantism: the residue of experience and conviction from medieval Catholicism, and the conscious attempt of Protestant groups to follow their sixteenth- and seventeenth-century founders. The first type of tradition is found in the thought of the Reformers. Even when they claim to be returning to the Bible, some Reformers can be labeled "medieval" in various aspects of their thought. The second kind of tradition has frequently appeared in Protestant attempts to relate religious convictions to the state. Even though they faced new historical, geographical, cultural, and psychological conditions, church-state theorists have often adhered uncritically to a view held in the time of the Reformation. The authority of a Luther or a Calvin has inhibited fresh inquiry into the Bible or a genuine wrestling with existent problems.

By applying the tradition to contemporary circumstances in this fashion, the tradition itself has often seemed strikingly unreal. A theory formulated in terms of a sixteenth-century confessional state cannot deal very well with the American tradition of separation of church and state; a theory which speaks of the one true church must take into consideration the divided character of American Protestantism. Convictions about church and state held by Protestants derived, like their other theological beliefs, from the Bible, from tradition, and from the pattern of living in the sixteenth and seventeenth centuries, have passed through centuries of further experience. In their contemporary forms they bear the marks of this experience and can be understood fully only through an examination of this history.

The Christian Political Heritage

Protestantism shares with Roman Catholicism and Eastern Orthodoxy three fundamental elements of all Christian political theory: the dualism of church and state, the sovereignty of God over church and state, and the evaluation of the state as both good and evil. One must also point out that the understanding of these principles in the three great branches of Christendom is not uniform, but often the very source of disagreement. However, the origin of these common elements lies in the Bible, and their persistence in church-state discussion makes them an inescapable part of Christian tradition.

Dualism

Dualism should not be confused with the American system of church-state separation. Of course, there are some who would read Jesus' distinction between the things that are Caesar's and the things that are God's as a flat endorsement of the American arrangement, but in Christian history, dualism has meant an independence of the religious and political orders that has expressed itself in many different legal forms.

This understanding of dualism grew out of the struggles of the church to maintain its integrity against intrusion by the Empire. Among the polytheistic and syncretistic religions of the Hellenistic period, the inclusion of the Emperor among the deities was considered appropriate, but Christianity resisted this form of idolatry; against the assumption of the ancient world that the political order could control religious expression, the primitive church argued for some degree of freedom. The Christian was subject to the political powers, to be sure, in the dimensions of life that lay in their responsibility, but the church insisted that in religious matters one must obey God rather than man. Oscar Cullmann, in a careful examination of the New Testament references to the political order, has shown the consistency of the primitive church in accepting the Empire when it functioned in purely political matters but rejecting it when it presumed to determine religious obligations and truth.[9]

The great authority of St. Augustine, who described the citizens of the heavenly and earthly cities as those who love God and those who love the world, made the dualistic outlook normative for both Protestants and Catholics. Augustine's "two cities" do not correspond, nevertheless, to church and state. The church *represents* the heavenly city, but false Christians may be found within the church and lovers of God outside it. Similarly, though its founder was Cain, who turned away from God, and its present ruler is Satan, the earthly city is not the same as the political order; in direction, the citizens of the earthly city are turned toward themselves in defiance of God. The Empire bears the marks of this human egoism and strife, but in effecting peace, order, and a relative degree of justice, it serves a divine function.[10]

As many historians have pointed out, Augustine's successors undermined his distinction between the "cities," as societies based on the objects of their citizens' wills and loves, and the ecclesiastical and political institutions that merely represented the cities. Roman Catholic views on dualism stem especially from Pope Gelasius I, who informed the Emperor Anastasius I in A.D. 494 that there are "two powers . . . by which this world is chiefly ruled: the sacred authority of the Popes and the royal power."[11] Though chief emphasis lies on papal authority, the dualistic implication is clear. The Emperor in this instance had interfered in a matter considered subject to religious determination, and the Pope, as the agent responsible for religion, criticized him.

The dualistic principle underlay the unitary *corpus Christianum* of the Middle Ages, though the loose manner in which it was defined gave occasion for the well-known struggles between popes and emperors. The principle, by pointing to different purposes and instruments of the ecclesiastical and political authorities in the Middle Ages, guaranteed a relative integrity to each against the intrusions of the other. As a principle, dualism was accepted by both, even in times of its violation by one or the other.

Dualism finds expression in Protestantism in the notion of the two kingdoms and the emphasis on religious liberty and separation of church and state as theological concepts. The notion of two kingdoms usually arose in the context of established and privileged churches, while the concern for religious liberty and separation of church and state points to a sectarian, nonestablished background.[12] In a politically and religiously unified society, an established church sought to define the two great dimensions of life, with their sanctions and limitations, as dual expressions of God's activity. Religious freedom and separation of church and state, on the other hand, grew from the protests of minority groups against restrictions on their religious activity or against the privileges of an established church.

Separation and liberty may be understood, not merely as a legal arrangement, but as theological elements dealing with church and state. Within Protestantism, separation has sometimes conveyed merely the tradition of dualism. Often, however, it has indicated that God does not want his followers to have any official connection with or support from the state, or that a particular church-state structure, frequently the American, represents the will of God and is of universal applicability.

In this context, similarly, liberty differs from the classical view of the freedom of the Christian man emphasized in the thought of Paul and Luther. Pauline freedom is closely associated with the doctrine of justification by grace. It defines the condition of the Christian who is no longer enslaved to sin, but living freely in accordance with the Spirit. Such freedom refers to man's status in the eyes of God and to his direction in living the Christian life. Unsophisticated Protestant thinkers have sometimes equated this theological view of freedom with the liberty of the religious individual and institution from political interference. Both freedom and liberty have a long tradition in Christianity, but the latter usually indicates a Protestant way of arguing for the independence of religious life from the functions of the state—in other words, dualism.

Dualism, by distinguishing the realms of religious and secular activity, thus implies the liberty of religion to engage in its legitimate concerns, and a theoretical separation of church and state. The ideas of liberty and separation of church and state are reminders of the dual loyalties in men's personal and corporate lives; both have become associated with particular legal frameworks for guaranteeing these principles, one of which is the First Amendment to the United States Constitution and its subsequent judicial interpretations.

The Sovereignty of God

The second element shared by all Christian political thought is the sovereignty of God over both church and state. Christianity, as an historical religion, sees its God acting in the lives of men and institutions, both religious and secular. The absolute distinction between sacred and profane, in spite of popular tendencies to think in such terms, was abhorrent to the prophets of the

Old Testament and the great voices of Christian theology. They argued instead for the relationship of all creation to the creator by upholding the biblical judgment: "God saw everything that he had made, and behold, it was very good." The tendency to separate the temporal and material from the control of God— either by positing two gods, one a creator and the other a re- deemer, or by placing a realm of matter or of Satan outside the sovereignty of God—has appeared persistently in Christian his- tory: in Marcionism, Gnosticism, and Manichaeism. In each instance the church has unequivocally judged it heretical, argu- ing that God is creator as well as redeemer, that the material as well as the spiritual dimensions of creation are good, that the body of man is not at war with his soul.

What implications does the concept of divine sovereignty hold for the state? First, it indicates that the state may serve as an instrument of God's historical activity. Whether in the form of a Pharaoh for Moses, a Babylon for Jeremiah, a Roman Empire for Augustine, or a Turk for Luther, the elusive meaning of secu- lar political events and figures cannot be abstracted from God's purposes. The association of historical events with divine activity has greatly declined in the modern world, but throughout Chris- tian history thoughtful men have tried to discern what lay behind the occurrences about them.

Second, the concept implies that the political order is estab- lished for particular abiding purposes. Government may stem from the essential nature of man or from the Fall, but it has been ordained by God for the purposes that it ordinarily fulfills. Both Christian and secular thought have defined these purposes as order, peace, prosperity, and justice. Christianity has rarely re- garded the state as something accidental, but rather as in some way grounded in God's creative and ruling activity.

Third, if God is active in political and social institutions, he has a purpose for them which can to some extent be learned. The appeals of the Old Testament prophets to the rulers and popu- lace of their day should be understood in this light. In an historical religion, men see their ethical responsibilities through their involvement in history; in everyday personal relationships and institutional participation, they try to ascertain God's inten- tions. Christians in all periods of history have refused to separate the various political vocations—statesman, subject, soldier, voter, and so on—from their religious convictions. Often, of course, they reflected too closely the social and political structures in which they lived, but at other times an awareness of tension with these structures was made evident. The classical Reformation, radically theocentric, tried in principle to question, judge, and renew all dimensions of life through adherence to God's will.

The Moral Ambivalence of Government

Consciousness of God's sovereignty has implied both sanction and judgment of political activity. This leads to the third element in the Christian political tradition, the morally ambivalent character of the state, which Herbert Butterfield emphasizes in his *Christianity and History*.

> There has come down in the Christian tradition a profound paradoxical system of teaching on the subject of the origin of government. On the one hand government is regarded as being due to the Fall of Man, a consequence of human sin, while at the same time it is looked upon as being of Divine institution, the creation of Providence. . . . Though government does not cure men of sinfulness any more than the institution of the idea of property eliminates human selfishness, the evil is mitigated by institutions that are the gift of God, and it is brought under regulation by the orderings of society. And so Providence produces a world in which men can live and gradually improve their external conditions, in spite of sin. . . .[13]

The state persistently threatens the intention of God for political society by seeking its own interests. Augustine observed that the city of the world resembles a band of robbers who serve selfish ends, but that out of the struggle of competing interests comes a degree of order, an armed truce under which men can live a tolerable life.[14] He attributed the suffering of civic life to men's sin, its blessings to God's grace. Other Christian thinkers have held higher or lower estimates of the political sphere of life, but Christians in all periods have tried to balance interpretations of the state which have accounted for it in terms of both good and evil. Christians believe in the sovereignty of God, the goodness of creation, and also sin: this is the heart of our paradox. Even the most optimistic liberal Christians did not deny imperfections in political and social life, though their explanations of them differ from earlier Christian theology.

In their effort to obey God's will, Christians sometimes have invoked divine sanction of the political order. Perhaps men give greater sanction to political than to other institutions because of the strength of political loyalty: We often uncritically assume a special blessing by God on such political structures as democracy or church-state separation. Such absolutizing of particular political forms is an extension of the traditional Christian acceptance of government as ordained by God, without simultaneous emphasis on the divine judgment. Often Christians have unquestioningly accepted a high degree of injustice and tyranny because they could at the same time point to the personal and religious activity guaranteed by the mere presence of government.

On the other hand, awareness of the sovereignty of God has also produced criticism of sinful and idolatrous tendencies in the state, with a variety of responses asked of Christians in such a situation. In spite of great pressure for unconditional sanction of the state, Christianity has never lost sight of the tradition of criticism transmitted by the prophets and the demonic description of the earthly city by Augustine. Sensitive men have pointed out violations by the state of both human and religious welfare; from the primitive church through Augustine, the medieval popes, the Anabaptists, the Puritans, Wilberforce, Channing, Rauschenbusch, and Bonhoeffer the tradition of judgment has continued. The basis of this criticism rested in the awareness of God's sovereignty. In providing political institutions, God had established a normative pattern as well as a continuing intention for them, and violation of his will demands protest and action even to the point of rebellion. In future chapters it will be shown that every Protestant tradition has wrestled with the problem of when one must serve God rather than men, and the corollary, *how* one serves God in opposition to the demands of men.

Protestants have interpreted diversely the three common Christian elements—dualism, divine sovereignty, and the moral ambivalence of political institutions—but disputes have also developed from a variety of other problems of church and state, as will be seen from a discussion of the different Protestant positions.

Protestantism and the Modern World

First, however, we should indicate the historical forces alongside which Protestantism has grown. Protestantism is a phenomenon of the modern world, though it has inherited much from the classical, Christian, and Germanic synthesis of the Middle Ages. Both Protestantism and Roman Catholicism have helped shape the modern world, but the distinctive characteristics of modernity have given a special cast to the former, since Protestantism—at least, after its formative period—has been more closely associated with secular thought and institutions.

Political Absolutism

The most prominent characteristic of the modern political world is the development of governmental sovereignty or absolutism. Where Protestantism functioned effectively, a complete political absolutism was impossible, because religion encompassed a dimension of private life outside the bounds of political determination. Nevertheless, most forms of Protestantism have had to deal with political societies tending toward absolute sovereignty. This is because both nationalism and Protestantism in the sixteenth century shared a common enemy, the papacy (and the Holy Roman Empire). The former resisted papal limitations upon and criticism of national development, the latter attacked what it understood to be a distorted interpretation of Christianity. The radical difference between nationalistic-Renaissance political rulers and theologically concerned Reformers did not prevent their alliance, and the Reformers did not foresee its unhappy consequences.

American Protestants often assume erroneously that Protestantism from its beginning promoted political and religious liberty and separation of church and state; but in England and on the Continent, Protestantism parroted the claims of the rulers, sanctioned their wars against the Catholic powers, and accepted their protection in the form of establishment. Looking at the total sweep of Christian history, it would seem that Protestant establishments lost the vigorous political criticism frequently found in the medieval papacy. They continued to adhere to the traditional dualism, but the strength with which they upheld ecclesiastical independence declined. Roman Catholicism, especially the Jesuit theorists, rather than Protestantism, most effectively opposed modern nationalism.[15] In a number of European nations the Protestant church became subservient to the state under the structure usually called Erastianism,[16] in which the privileges of the established church and the toleration of sects were left to the benevolence and prudence of government.

Protestantism contained, however, another tendency: by undermining the unity of Christendom and failing to find an adequate replacement for papal authority, it opened the way for a proliferation of sects. Whereas the bulk of Protestantism initially clung to the new national states for protection against papacy and Empire, other Protestant groups rejected Erastianism, either to guarantee their survival or from theological convictions. Sociologists have called these two impulses "church" and "sect," a terminology which fits the Reformation period quite well and points to the differences between established and nonestablished religious groups. The sectarian struggle for survival and the resulting church-state theories stimulated modern movements toward toleration, religious freedom, and separation of church and state. The vigor of the sects compelled governments to adopt these policies for prudential reasons, as in America, where sectarian Protestantism was the most influential form of Christianity.

Unfortunately, many American Christians have a highly provincial outlook toward the nature of Protestantism and the sources of church-state separation. For one thing, they fail to realize that from the sixteenth century to the present, Protestantism has reflected both established and separatist tendencies and has existed as both "church" and "sect": it can lead as well to the established churches of England and Scandinavia as to the nonestablishment of the United States. It should also be pointed out that church-state separation, though advocated by sectarian and rationalist groups in the eighteenth century, derives principally from prudential decisions by the Founding Fathers of the nation. This is best shown by the continuation of established churches in certain states until the final disestablishment in Massachusetts in 1833.[17] In some of the former colonies single churches continued to have privileges while others were merely tolerated, whereas in the nation as a whole the lack of a majority religion dictated nonestablishment or separation. As time passed, however, the growth of nonestablished groups within the states led to disestablishment there as well.

Whereas Protestantism in its churchly form tended toward acceptance of political absolutism, sectarianism, by combating the religious disabilities imposed upon it by confessional states, contributed to a criticism of the new nationalism.[18] One finds in the seventeenth century, for example, papacy and sectarianism as the chief advocates of limitations on the power of the state. In this way the struggle between church and sect helped develop alternative political forms in the modern world, so that Protes-

tantism has promoted political absolutism and also criticism of
absolutism, both deriving from the Protestant encounter with
absolutism throughout its history.

Secularism

A second feature of the modern age, of great importance to
Protestantism and religion in general, was the replacement of a
homogeneous religious society by secularism. In the Middle Ages,
according to Paul Tillich, society could be called "theonomous."[19]
Although stress upon reason gave human autonomy a high evaluation, nevertheless all of culture was in principle directed toward
actualizing commonly accepted religious and ethical norms. In
a society that conceived of itself as *respublica Christiana,* the association of citizenship with Christianity was clear, and Jews, for
example, were not considered real members of society.

Beginning with the Renaissance, men with a genuinely skep-
tical outlook appeared on the intellectual scene, while religious
indifference among the common people increased. There is evidence, for example, that Luther alienated a considerable segment
of the peasantry by his attitude toward their uprisings, and in
many countries of Europe we have testimonies of increasing
estrangement from religious life. The climax of this process came
in nineteenth-century Europe, when the industrial workers concluded that the churches were on the side of their oppressors and
the new Socialist movement consciously opposed religion.[20]

The situation was somewhat different in America, although
signs of the breakdown of Christian society appeared even earlier
than in Europe. Cast off on the shores of the new world, with
inadequate attention from the churches of their national origins,
the immigrants showed little inclination to religion. In the colonial period, and especially after the Revolutionary War, church
membership was very low—in 1790, perhaps 5 to 10 per cent. The
revivalist movement helped counter the dissipation of Christian
faith, and later decades have witnessed a steady increase of membership in the American churches.

Nevertheless, secularism as a modern expression has considerably influenced Protestantism. One form of this has been the
presence of a conscious intellectual and popular nonreligion that
has challenged the Christian churches—especially of the established variety, which have taken for granted the religious unity
of society. Another form has been a direction of culture, reflected
in the interests even of people associated with the churches,

which has helped mold the life and thought of the churches. American churches offer particularly helpful examples, for along with the religious vitality they have expressed, one constantly finds inroads of thought and interests that are patently non-religious. One must view Protestantism in the light of the con-current secularism of the modern era, either in reaction to it or absorbing it, for its relatively recent origin prevents it from look-ing back nostalgically, as Roman Catholicism can, on an earlier "age of faith." The history and destiny of Protestantism have coincided with autonomous secularism.

Associated with this secularism have been the rise of modern science and the development and decline of capitalism as an economic system. Both of these grew from the critical impulses within the Middle Ages, though neither consciously tried to be nonreligious. Nevertheless, the Catholic synthesis could not con-tain such independent expressions of the modern spirit, and their relationship to Protestantism, because of an increasing inclina-tion to autonomy and even criticism of religion, has been a tenuous one. Protestantism sought to mold and was often itself molded by these forces.

American Influences

When we discuss the church-state theories of American Protes-tantism, it is hard to do justice to the obvious fact that the Protestant groups being dealt with are American. We have a difficult problem of historical interpretation, because if it is said that the American milieu tends to produce a certain outlook to-ward church-state problems, it must be immediately added that this same milieu has been and continues to be informed by the attitudes of its constituent religious groups. Americanization does not consist simply in the legal structure called church-state separation, though this is part of it. Religious groups immigrating to the United States must adjust to the variety of denominations and the lack of structural relation to the state. Sometimes this means that church-state separation, American-style, becomes a fundamental religious premise, to the surprise of denominational brethren in other countries where religion functions successfully under quite different circumstances. At other times, it means that views of the state formulated under different political circum-stances must undergo some adjustment in the new situation.

In addition, the issues of concern to churches in America have not been the same as those in Europe. Whereas separation of church and state in America is predicated on a pluralistic philosophy by which churches participate with other corporate groups in molding public policy, separation in parts of Europe has often implied an alienation of religion from public life, a relegation of churches to worship alone.[21] Such attempts to subordinate religion to national interest illustrate absolute sovereignty in the modern state. In the twentieth century, especially, the chief problem of the European churches has been political totalitarianism, especially Nazism and Communism; and the most significant recent political writings among both Protestants[22] and Catholics[23] have stressed this.

In America, on the other hand, the problem of totalitarianism occupies little attention, except among writers strongly influenced by European thought, whose discussion often seems strangely irrelevant. American writers display interest in problems of religious influence on society and politics. To be sure, the American churches recognize the necessity of limitations on the authority of the state, but the American Constitution distinctly confines the state within certain bounds and only under special circumstances can it restrict the churches.

If, however, overt totalitarianism is not at issue, in recent years religious writers have recognized a somewhat related problem in America. The historian Christopher Dawson, for example, argues that in democratic countries Christians need not fear:

> . . . violent persecution but rather . . . the crushing out of religion from modern life by the sheer weight of a State-inspired public opinion and by the mass organisation of society on a purely secular basis. Such a state of things has never occurred before because the State has never been powerful enough to control every side of social life. It has been a State with limited functions, not a Totalitarian State. . . . To-day the conflict is a deeper and a wider one. It goes to the very roots of life and affects every aspect of human thought and action.[24]

This means that conformity to an American way of life, strengthened by an omnipotent public opinion, constitutes a distinct threat to the integrity of religion.[25] Because Americans, especially laymen, take democracy and separation of church and state to be political arrangements specially favored by God, critics like Will Herberg argue quite cogently that the American way of life is in fact the operative faith in this country. Even if one does not find the American influence so all-pervasive, the questions asked and the answers given about church and state frequently tend to reflect the American political circumstances.

We must recognize, therefore, the way in which American Protestant emphases on church-state questions differ from denominational traditions, particularly in other parts of the world. One could expect attention to be given in America to such issues as the validity of religious pluralism in American society, the attitude toward public nonsectarian education, representative democracy as a form of government, the responsibilities of Christians as citizens for the common good of society, the attitude toward "rulers" who are in effect simply representatives of the citizenry, governmental support of religion in a society committed to "separation" of church and state, and the role of religious symbols in a neutral society. Within a religious framework these issues do not represent mere matters of policy, but, rather, adaptations of conviction and tradition to new social situations.

Issues Contributing to a Typology

We may now begin developing a typology of Protestant church-state views on the basis of interpretations and responses to the elements of Christian tradition and of modern Western and American life, as well as answers to certain questions that perennially appear when the norms of Christian thinking encounter the political order.

A prime question concerns the nature of the state. It has been noted that Christians regard the state as ordained by God, but at the same time imperfect. Protestant answers have varied from emphasis on the perfectibility to the virtually demonic character of the state. A related problem is that of holding public office. Some writers have argued that officeholding contradicts the integrity of Christian living, while others have given it essentially the same kind of approval bestowed upon government in general. Others have drawn a distinction between sanction of the office and of the individual who holds it. An additional area of discussion centers on the problem of coercion and warfare, with responses ranging from acceptance of these as essential characteristics of government to hope for their elimination. Finally, the question arises: Why has God established government at all? —to maintain a minimal order, to achieve justice, or as a vehicle for advancing the kingdom of God? All of these questions involve the nature of the state or government.

A somewhat different area is the response of the individual to government. In the authoritarian political systems of the Reformation period, citizens did little but obey. This emphasis is still relevant, for successful government even today presumes an essential obedience to its dictates on the part of citizens. In nearly all Protestant traditions, however, obedience has not been absolute; men have felt the tension between being "subject to the governing authorities, for there is no authority except from God" (Romans 13:1) and "we must obey God rather than men" (Acts 5:29). The issues revolve around the conditions that require disobedience and the form of disobedience. Can a citizen do something unjust? Can he engage in war? Shifting emphasis to a more positive but related area, the opportunity of American citizens to participate politically has posed the issue of criticism and change of society as a Christian responsibility. What role does the Christian play in a society where he can influence policy?

Contrary to the popular understanding of Protestantism, most of its spokesmen have never regarded Christianity as completely individualistic, but have looked on the church as a fellowship of believers and as the institution by which doctrine and grace have been mediated. Some Protestants have distinguished between the invisible church—those who are genuinely Christian—and the visible church—the members of specific church associations. The problem of church and state deals with the role of the visible, institutional church in a particular body politic; this is not the same as the problem of the individual Christian and the state. Especially in the early decades of the Reformation, discussion centered on church and state, but the impact of individualism, a product of the Enlightenment, has caused a significant shift to such issues as the freedom of the individual religious conscience.

The relation of church to state as a theological concept should be seen on a different plane from the particular solutions to this problem in various public laws. Thus, even though American law has normalized the relations of church and state, within this structure various churches see their role in more ultimate terms. Some Protestant traditions emphasize an almost cosmic sense of the demonic, provisionally frustrating the will of God. Whatever role the state determines for the churches in a society, Christians must still make an evaluation for themselves, and their secondary loyalty to the state might be expressed in terms of divine ordination or demonic perversion.

In any case, the questions are persistent: Does the church have the responsibility to resist state oppression or to define national goals, or is this merely a problem for individual Christians? Does the state have a responsibility to support or protect the church, to give a certain symbolic sanction to religion—as is done to some extent in the United States—or to base its law on Christian morality? How does the state view ecclesiastical claims of a particular or even exclusive interpretation of Christianity? If the state is ordained by God, in what way do its ordination and function differ from those of the church? In areas of joint interest, does state or church have the right to authoritative determination? What is—or should be—the relation between minister and ruler, the principal officials of church and state?

Five Representative Protestant Answers

These are the kinds of questions Protestants have asked, and the answers given defy simple categorization. In examining five typical answers, one should insist that they by no means represent all Protestants. Rather, they are illustrations, selected because of long traditions within Protestantism, and voiced by thinkers and movements regarded by historians as significant expressions of Protestantism.

Three of the positions have been especially associated with denominations and will be so considered: Lutheran, Mennonite (Anabaptist), and Quaker. Unfortunately, one cannot absolutize their denominational character; especially in the twentieth century, members of other denominations have adopted these views. All three are minority positions in American Protestantism. Lutheranism and the Anabaptist-Mennonite tradition reflect a strong theological emphasis and a pronounced desire to adhere to the position of their sixteenth-century forebears, although today both are clearly in a process of transition along new lines defined by American culture. In his *Christ and Culture*, H. R. Niebuhr included these two, respectively, under "Christ and Culture in Paradox" and "Christ against Culture." Such terms convey only a limited understanding when the issues concern church and state, so the denominational labels will be used. In Lutheranism one finds the theological formulation of a classical church; in Anabaptism, that of a classical sect. Whereas Lutheranism was principally concerned, as an established religion, to help maintain society, Anabaptism sought to live the full dimensions of the

Sermon on the Mount within small religious conventicles. The Lutheran emphasis on sin and justification by grace through faith had implications for its view of the state, as did the Anabaptist stress on discipleship, even though both shared in theory the same basic religious principles. Both believed in the sovereignty of God and the energetic activity of the devil, but they drew different implications about the nature of church and state from them.

In contrast with Lutheranism and Anabaptism, Quakerism has undergone radical changes since its formation. The basis for isolating it as a distinct position lies in the historical involvement of Quakerism with political events and the centrality of pacifism as its basic principle of activity. Its political interests distinguish it from Anabaptism, though the two groups agree in upholding pacifism. Whereas Anabaptism expressed its pacifism by withdrawing from worldly responsibilities, Quakerism tended to regard pacifism as a goal and method of political action. Both approaches have profound implications for a larger view of the state. This study will trace the foundations of the difference between the Anabaptists, who derived from Luther and Zwingli a sense of the demonic and of biblical authority, and Quakerism, which appropriated the spiritualism and millenarianism of later English Puritanism.

These three denominational types, however, do not exhaust Protestant church-state theories in America. Most of the major denominations include adherents of two sharply divergent attitudes that may be expressed in the following dichotomies: Is there a wall of separation between church and state, or is separation a relatively defined structure for guaranteeing mutual independence of church and state? Is separation of church and state a fundamental principle of Protestantism, or is Protestantism associated with a variety of institutional relations to the state? Does Christian ethics center around the conversion of individuals and their influence on society and politics, or is the church as a corporate body also to influence public policy? Is Roman Catholicism a major threat to American freedom and church-state separation, or should Protestants seek close co-operation with Roman Catholics for common objectives? The nuances between these positions may seem slight, but their effects in terms of policy are very great.

The second alternative in each of these distinctions seems more relativistic: separation of church and state is not absolute but is rather a set of laws whose implications are not yet fully drawn, a policy designed to guarantee the freedom and integrity of political and religious institutions amid many overlapping concerns and issues. On the matter of conflicts between Roman Catholicism and American life, the latter position stresses the variety of Catholic expressions in the world, many of which are directed toward democracy and religious freedom, as well as the violation of the boundary between church and state by Protestant groups in America and in other countries. It emphasizes influence by the church upon the state as a fundamental element of Protestantism, without which Protestantism would be truncated, individualistic, and altar-bound, without moral influence on the important institutions of society.

The best representatives of this position are John C. Bennett of Union Theological Seminary and the policy of the journal he edits (with Reinhold Niebuhr), *Christianity and Crisis*. Reflections of this outlook also appear in other writers and in some denominational statements. Representing the other side, one finds especially active the organization, Protestants and Other Americans United for Separation of Church and State (P.O.A.U.) and its publication, *Church and State Review*, as well as a number of denominations especially of Baptist or evangelical heritage.

Both sides represent long-prevalent impulses in Protestantism. The more relativistic view resembles to some extent a modernized form of the theocentric and conversionist outlook of Calvinism, the other, the quest for detachment from formal association with the state of the seventeenth-century English sects. Because denominational terms are clearly inadequate, the former position will be called transformationist (from H. R. Niebuhr); the latter, separationist. Historically, the two movements, especially in American life, have worked together and intertwined, and the impulses of each have attracted the other. Both have contributed to American religion, which in its earlier stages drew principally from Calvinism and sectarianism, and both have grown together, influencing and influenced by American society. This study will attempt to show, however, that denominational and ecumenical statements today indicate some movement toward transformationism.

The three denominational positions will appear in a chronological order based on their origins in the sixteenth and seventeenth centuries: 1. Lutheran. 2. Anabaptist-Mennonite. 3. Quaker. Quakerism sprang from developments in transformationism and separationism, but as a continuous and isolable denominational tradition it corresponds to Lutheranism and Anabaptism. Both transformationism and separationism represented forms of Calvinism in the seventeenth century, but because modern transformationism has developed to some extent as a response to separationism, they will be discussed in the following order: 4. Separationism. 5. Transformationism.

1 God's Regiments
and Man's Vocation:
Luther and Lutheranism

Luther

Martin Luther not only initiated the movement that developed into Protestantism, but he formulated a theory of church-state relations upheld relatively faithfully by the denominations bearing his name. His influence, naturally, went far beyond the Lutheran Church, and twentieth-century European theological movements, uniting Christians of Lutheran and Reformed (Calvinistic) backgrounds, have drawn heavily on his work.[1] In America, however, non-Lutheran Christians interested in the history of political thought generally blame him for what they conceive of as defects in the political and social attitudes of Lutheran churches.[2]

Luther's
Radical Theocentrism and the Two Regiments

The authority of Luther in the Lutheran churches is rather ambiguous. For the great Reformer and his followers, Scripture provides the norm of the Christian faith, but in practice the statements of Luther himself have gained virtual canonical status in the Lutheran churches. Lutherans do not equate his revelatory wisdom with that of the Bible, but they feel that in the final analysis Luther was the consummate biblical theologian.

23

The voluminous contemporary writing on church and state in European and American Lutheran circles frequently constitutes a form of Luther research, criticisms and revisions springing from rediscovered facets of his thought. Reservations are expressed, but the inspiration for reinterpreting the church's relation to the state is clearly grounded on Luther.[3] Nazi domination during World War II provided an obvious occasion for this response in Europe. The late Bishop Eivind Berggrav, primate of Norway, illustrated this when he said: "In 1941-1942 Luther was one of our chief weapons in the struggle. It was imperative that the apostolic rule come to the fore: 'We are to obey God rather than men.' It was in this spirit that Luther spoke."[4] In America, although there has been no comparable ideological challenge, there has also been considerable rethinking, influenced by contemporary European Luther research[5] and participation in the ecumenical movement.[6] The contemporary Lutheran church is vigorously reassessing its heritage, but because of the role played by Luther even in American Lutheranism, his thought on church and state is still crucial, even four and a half centuries after the events that shaped his thought.

To those schools of historical analysis for which religious factors play little role, the Reformation was principally a social, political, and economic movement. Luther's political thought usually provides one of the most important arguments for such a position, because on the surface Luther seemed to represent German nationalism and the feudal aristocracy against the challenges of papacy, Holy Roman Empire, and lower classes. Luther, to be sure, cannot be extracted from the events of his time and his own social loyalties, but examination of his writings indicates that his views on the state were fundamentally religious.[7] Luther, like most of the Reformers, was still a citizen of the Middle Ages, in the sense that like the Scholastics he tried to bring his ideas on all of reality within a theological framework whose beginning, end, and direction were God. The modern tendency to separate various phases of life from theological presuppositions and norms was foreign to him; unlike the leaders of the Renaissance who wanted to free the political, economic, and cultural enterprises of man from religious orthodoxy, Luther tried instead to strengthen the relationship of man and his activities to God. He was convinced that the proper nature of these relations had been obscured by defective theological and institutional structures.

Luther should properly be interpreted as radically theocentric or God-centered. The theologians of the Middle Ages were similarly oriented: through Church, sacraments, *respublica Christiana*, and a Christian philosophy, they tried to symbolize the faith of Western society that God reigned everywhere in life. Luther knew the danger of this attempt: symbols may become absolutized and the ultimate no longer be seen through them. Nevertheless he sought, despite the inescapably partial conditions of human life, to bring man once again into an uncorrupted relationship with God. Whether man acknowledged God or not, Luther hoped to show how God exercised his divine sovereignty over all phases of existence, including the political order.

The realism of the Reformer lay in his recognition of the tension between the authority of God and man's perversions of that authority—particularly manifested, he felt, in the theology and hierarchy of the Roman Catholic Church. But in his attempts to let God be God, he himself succumbed to influences that allow some historians to interpret him as an uncritical opportunist. Even an admirer may readily discern a high degree of rationalization in his theological defense of the German political authorities against the claims of Emperor, Pope, and peasant.[8] Nevertheless, from Luther's own point of view, he integrated his political thought and decisions with a theology through which he genuinely sought to avoid the errors of the papacy and to grasp the actions of God in history. Luther himself would probably admit his failure to live up to this program of theocentricity, for he knew that man's partial perspectives always distort the will of God. But in the face of what he felt were patent corruptions, Luther believed himself called to a new illumination of the nature of God's rule, to a reformation. His evaluation of the political forces of his time had as fulcrum either biblical authority or a theological principle derived from the Bible. Even if the partiality of his vision colored his judgment, it is unfair to abstract his political views from the rest of his thought.[9] And just as faith in God's sovereignty has implications for the relationship of church and state, similarly Luther's views on justification by faith, vocation, eschatology, and the demonic provide a context for a formal approach to the religious and political "regiments" through which God acts in church and state.

For a theocentric Christian like Luther—and this is generally true for Protestant leaders in the sixteenth century—one does not begin a discussion of church-state relations by asking about the nature of church and state; one does not even follow the existentialist method of centering attention on the individual's function in the church and state. The prior issue is: Why did

God, sovereign and acting in history, institute church and state, and what is he doing in them? Once the answer to this question is known, the Christian who is in relationship with God will know how to co-operate with the God who uses both Christians and non-Christians to effect his will in history.

The Two Regiments

The presupposition of God's sovereign rule explains Luther's analysis of the church-state problem in terms of two kingdoms or regiments. Jesus spoke of a contrast between the kingdom of God and the kingdom of the world, a heavenly and an earthly kingdom, and the things of Caesar and of God; but Luther saw in Jesus' use of the pairs of symbols a convenient and inclusive representation of the two sides of life over which God reigned. Even though Jesus, especially in the Sermon on the Mount, intended to disparage the way of life not associated with the kingdom of God, Luther, with his strong views of divine sovereignty, could not allow even the kingdom of the world to escape the love and wrath and rule of God. The Sermon on the Mount, as Jesus presented it, was an evangelical message, designed to contrast the ways of the faithful and the unbelievers, but in Luther's thought it became a description of the purposeful action of God: those not related to God as members of his kingdom of salvation were related through his wider kingdom of creation and sovereignty.

Luther recognized, however, that in God's eyes the principal distinction in the status of men is whether or not they are justified and reconciled by grace through faith. All men are divided into two classes:

> . . . the first belong to the kingdom of God, the second to the kingdom of the world. Those belonging to the kingdom of God are all true believers in Christ and are subject to Christ. For Christ is the King and Lord in the kingdom of God. . . . Now observe, these people need no secular sword or law. And if all the world were composed of real Christians, that is, true believers, no prince, king, sword, or law would be needed.

> All who are not Christians belong to the kingdom of the world and are under the law. Since few believe and still fewer live a Christian life, do not resist the evil, and themselves do no evil, God has provided for non-Christians a different government outside the Christian estate and God's kingdom, and has subjected them to the sword, so that, even though they would

do so, they cannot practice their wickedness, and that, if they do, they may not do it without fear nor in peace and prosperity.[10]

Government originates, therefore, from the unfaithful and unsaved condition of mankind. Luther has been justly criticized for inconsistency in attributing the sin which necessitates government only to non-Christians, whereas his theology also recognizes a comparable degree of sin in Christians, whose salvation depends not on their sinlessness but on their trust in God's grace. One would assume that the Christian who is *justus* (justified), but also *peccator* (a sinner), would likewise contribute to the anarchy that necessitates action by government. This contradiction may be ascribed to Luther's apparent striving for a simple schema of two kingdoms and two governments along the lines of Augustinian thought, for he pointed out later in this same passage that "the law is given for the sake of the unrighteous . . . [but] since . . . no one is by nature Christian or pious, but every one sinful and evil, God places the restraints of the law upon them all. . . ."[11] Government, then, is a direct consequence of the sin which dominates men's lives, particularly among those whose disorientation from God would lead them into unrestrained aggression without the restrictions of law and compulsion. Mankind cannot dispense with government, for "if there were no worldly government, no man could live because of other men; one would devour the other, as the brute beasts do."

God has established in both the worldly and the spiritual kingdoms instruments through which he governs, the state and the church. The word that Luther most commonly used to refer to these is "regiment," literally "power" or "government." Gustaf Törnvall has noted that Luther probably chose this particular word deliberately because it expresses in a dynamic and concrete way the manner in which God actualizes his rule in history.[12] It denotes an *active* sovereignty, consistent with Luther's view that God is intimately involved in all life and events. Luther has often been criticized for separating too sharply the spheres of church and state, but one may conclude that here, at any rate, is no absolute dualism, for the two find a unity in the creating and reigning God. In his treatise, "Whether Soldiers, Too, Can Be Saved," Luther emphasized this unity in describing the function of the two types of government:

For He [God] has established two kinds of government among men. The one is spiritual; it has no sword, but it has the Word, by means of which men are to become good and righteous, so that with this righteousness they may attain everlasting life. This righteousness He administers through the Word, which he has committed to the preachers. The other is worldly government, through the sword, which aims to keep peace among men, and this He rewards with temporal blessing. *For He gives to rulers so much property, honor, and power, to be possessed by them above others, in order that they may serve Him by administering this righteousness. Thus God Himself is the founder, lord, master, protector, and rewarder of both kinds of righteousness. There is no human ordinance or authority in either, but each is altogether a divine thing.*[13]

Luther regards the ruler unequivocally as a servant of God, bringing about a type of civic righteousness (*iustitia civilis*), which not only confers temporal benefits on the ruler but also constitutes a divine blessing to humanity.[14]

Although the state governs for God in the secular kingdom, political authority alone does not encompass all the dimensions of worldly life. Rather, government is the apex of a series of relationships called "orders," in which people hold "offices." These orders may be natural or biological, such as the family; or cultural, such as one's work and schooling.[15]

Luther looked at the world with an authoritarian and hierarchical outlook and consequently interpreted these relationships in terms of those who commanded and those who obeyed. For example, the paterfamilias should make decisions for his family, and wife and children should obey. Inasmuch as men participate in these orders, they are instruments by which God, as if through a mask, expresses his love in human life, even to men who are not Christians and do not understand that they are serving God. The ruler by wielding the sword enables political society to continue and represses the evil tendencies of men in the same way that the father by his rod corrects the recalcitrance of his child, for without authority in all the stations of life chaos would ensue and men could not live. The various forms of control in the temporal world compel an outward righteousness, and by keeping sin within limits, manifest the providence of God.

When Luther discussed the validity even of unwilling participation in the offices of the temporal world, he usually used the state as his example, distinguishing its functions from those of the church. Gustaf Törnvall has emphasized the correlation of civil justice and religious justice under the aegis of God's sovereignty.[16] The created world belongs to God and is sanctified by the *iustitia civilis* achieved through the state, just as *iustitia Christiana* is the means of salvation mediated by the church. But it is noteworthy that the individual cannot claim any merit from his civil justice in relation to God, for the justice lies in the office as part of creation, and not in the person for whose salvation only the justice merited by Christ has validity.

Church and state, the spiritual and temporal governments, are unified by the sovereignty of God and the loyal submission of the believer to both. Luther speaks of the worldly regiment as the left hand of the kingdom, and the spiritual regiment as God's right hand;[17] both belong to God. He felt, however, that the most serious problem of political thought in his own time lay in confusing the functions of the two regiments. His polemic against the papacy and the Anabaptists largely grew out of his conviction that they were violating the divinely established distinction between the two governments. Although God is the efficient and final cause of both, they are different in nature, they have different commissions, stand in different relationships to God, and give expression to his sovereignty with completely different instruments. Unlike the Roman Catholic distinction between a lower and a higher order, a realm of nature and a realm of grace, Luther thought of the two as related but separated modes of God's activity.[18] They correspond to Luther's view of law and gospel. The law, though good as a part of creation in enabling natural man to live a tolerable life, is ineffectual for achieving salvation, for which the church holds responsibility. The gospel does not invalidate the law, but one must never confusedly regard the law as a legitimate means of saving man.

The political order, representing the worldly kingdom, is the foremost and controlling agency over man's temporal enterprises, "restraining the unchristian and wicked," and enabling men to participate in such things as family life and economic activity. These other aspects of existence, all of which are encompassed by the kingdom of the world, are subordinate to the state, for only the state has concrete power to guarantee their continuation. On the other hand, God has established the church "by the Holy Spirit under Christ [to make] Christians and pious people. . . ."[19] The state achieves its purposes through the ruler's use of law and the sword, the church its purposes through the word of the Bible and its preaching by the minister; the nature of the state is force and coercion, of the church, love and humility. All of these aspects must be kept sharply separated. The political ruler should not interfere in the religious life of his nation; similarly, ecclesiastical officials distort their function and violate God's will when they undertake political activity. Luther adamantly denied the use of law and the sword for the furtherance of the church's objectives, or humility and love for political purposes, since the state cannot preserve stability without coercion.

Ideally speaking, each regiment helps the other, for the state enables the church to carry out its work under orderly conditions, while the church furnishes pious and co-operative citizens. Unfortunately, however, this ideal structure rarely exists. A hostile force ravages the world, seeking to thwart God's will, not least by confusing the religious and political realms of life. This force is the devil. The Swedish school of Luther interpretation has emphasized the role of the demonic as a clue to the dynamic and fluid character of Luther's thought.[20] Just as Luther's view presumes a God who is involved in history, so also man's religious, moral, social, and political life is under continuous attack and distortion. In the words of Aulén:

> The solidary interrelationship of sin concretizes itself in inscrutable and obscure powers, a mysterious complex which cannot be accurately delimited and defined, and which slips away and becomes shadowy as soon as one tries to grasp and comprehend it. Nevertheless it shows its power in the most fearful manner and by the most cruel oppression of human life. . . . Man is placed in a vast conflict between the two powers: the Kingdom of God and the Kingdom from below. The divine will contends with the hostile spiritual powers which tyrannize man.[21]

History derives its ambiguity from an evil reality active in all phases of life, against which God has provided means of defense in the form of the two regiments.

Neither church nor state is immune from satanic distortion, and nowhere is the influence of the devil more apparent than when one regiment neglects its function or trespasses on the prerogatives of the other. Inasmuch as scarcely "one among thousands" is a true Christian, the vast majority of mankind serve the

devil, and he so successfully leads political and ecclesiastical officials astray that both regiments, which are supposed to be *larvae*
(masks) of God, actually mirror the demonic. Thus the state presents an ambivalent countenance to the man of faith.[22] Nevertheless, God uses his two regiments as instruments in the battle
against the devil, until the last day will signal God's final triumph. But as long as *this* era continues, the devil struggles
against God by promoting revolutions and wars and by tempt-
ing judges and rulers to arbitrariness.[23] Where disorder and
unfaith, caesaropapism and papal caesarism reign, they represent
the triumph of the demonic and a corruption of God's intention.
Luther gives great emphasis to the extent of this unhappy situation: "God has cast us into the world, under the power of the
devil, so that we have here no paradise, but are to expect all
kinds of misfortune to body, wife, child, property, and honor
every hour; and if ten misfortunes do not come in an hour, nay, if
you can live for an hour, you ought to say, 'Oh, how great is the
kindness which my God shows me, that in this hour every misfortune has not come.' "[24] Consequently, when a Christian supports
political stability by rendering obedience to the governing authorities, he strengthens the hand of God against his cosmic opponent.

During his lifetime, Luther encountered two groups which, he
felt, were especially flagrant in violating the design of God—the
papacy and the Anabaptists. The former sought to use political
instruments for religious objectives, and the latter tried to apply
the norms of the gospel directly to politics.

In the sixteenth century, the popes were political as well as
spiritual rulers on a large scale. The maintenance and furtherance of their temporal interests required participation in wars
and alliances, and considerably compromised their spiritual integrity, especially as they justified political expansion with religious reasons. Throughout much of Luther's life, Christendom
also lived under the threatening shadow of the Turks, who pene-
trated to Vienna in 1529. The problem of the Turks gave Luther
the occasion to criticize the political activity of the papacy, because the popes had for some years been urging a new crusade to
rid Christendom of the Muslim danger. In his treatise "On War
Against the Turk,"[25] Luther denied that the war against the
Turks was being fought by an army of Christians against the
enemies of Christ. He held that by claiming to act in the name of
Christianity the papacy was violating the Sermon on the Mount,

and that God was being blasphemed because most of the people in the army were not really Christians. Looking on the pope and bishops as particularly guilty in taking up the sword instead of the Bible and prayer, he sarcastically commented: "Oh how gladly would Christ receive me at the Last Judgment, if when summoned to the spiritual office, to preach and care for souls, I had left it and busied myself with fighting and with the temporal sword!"

Luther actually did not oppose a defensive war by the proper political authorities against the Turks, but he objected to the idea that a religious purpose was being served by the proposed crusade. Such an enterprise represented only one more in a long series of distortions by the Catholic Church which led him to the conclusion that the pope was really the Antichrist. Just as Rome had abandoned the gospel and substituted a form of meritorious legalism, so it had forsaken its spiritual functions for the more lucrative rewards of worldly rulers. If the Turks were peaceful, no one had any right to fight against them, though in their current aggressions, each ruler was obliged to defend his territory against them. The church should try to persuade the Turks of the validity of Christianity by means of the Word alone.

Beginning early in the Reformation period, the movement associated with Luther was joined by a variety of groups, usually claiming to go beyond the measures Luther himself undertook. More about the left wing or Anabaptists will appear in the next chapter, but it is worth saying at this juncture that Luther was profoundly suspicious of what he understood of their intentions, however mistaken he might have been in his over-all evaluation of the movement. As early as 1523, he directed one of his strongest objections against the alleged Anabaptist tenet that, in the new religious era which seemed to be dawning, the gospel would be substituted for the sword in the administration of temporal affairs. Luther knew that theological and institutional changes could not hide the fact that even if everyone were baptized and a member of the state church, "the world and the masses are and always will be unchristian, although they are all baptized and are nominally Christians."[26] To try to rule the world according to the gospel would unleash egoistic and destructive tendencies always present in human hearts, so that under the guise of Christian action men would subject their neighbors to unrestrained savagery.[27] This was Luther's answer to utopians who believed that mankind would reach such a point of grace or virtue that the necessity of coercion would terminate. For Luther such a time would come only beyond this historical era. The unity of church and state in a common source and will, and their separation of function, thus proceeded from the theological concepts of creation and sovereignty.

Christian Participation Through Love and Vocation

Similarly, an inquiry into the response of the Christian individual as ruler, minister, or subject reveals not merely acquiescent participation in a cosmically given reality, but a dynamic reaction to a living religious experience. As God reveals his righteousness in creation by ordaining structures of spiritual and temporal government, he shows his righteousness in salvation by the grace with which he justifies men apart from their own worthiness. The attitude with which the Christian approaches his role in the institutions of the temporal order—family, work, and state—is intimately associated with his experience of God's mercy. The individual who does not live by faith adjusts himself to the familial, occupational, and political authorities out of compulsion; but the justified Christian does good works out of grateful love, conscious that he no longer needs to make himself acceptable to God by his works. The supposed good works of the unbeliever do not please God, but Christian acts of love are accounted as good works because they are done in faith.[28] In his "Treatise on Christian Liberty" Luther strikingly described the mode of action by the justified man:

> Although the Christian is thus free from all works, he ought in this liberty to empty himself, to take upon himself the form of a servant, to be made in the likeness of men, to be found in fashion as a man, and to serve, help and in every way deal with his neighbor as he sees that God through Christ has dealt and still deals with himself. And this he should do freely, having regard to nothing except the divine approval. He ought to think: "Though I am an unworthy and condemned man, my God has given me in Christ all the riches of righteousness and salvation without any merit on my part, out of pure, free mercy, so that henceforth I need nothing whatever except faith which believes that this is true. Why should I not therefore freely, joyfully, with all my heart, and with an eager will, do all things which I know are pleasing and acceptable to such a Father, who has overwhelmed me with his inestimable riches?

I will therefore give myself as a Christ to my neighbor, just as
Christ offered Himself to me; I will do nothing in this life except what I see is necessary, profitable and salutary to my
neighbor, since through faith I have an abundance of all good
things in Christ."[29]

With such a response the Christian engages in the structures or
orders by which God provides channels for responsive love so that
man will not constantly face the anxiety of making new decisions.
Christian participation in the orders, Luther called "vocation"
(*Beruf, vocatio*). Roman Catholic thought had limited this term
to the monastic or priestly calling alone, implying a less significant evaluation of the ordinary positions of life, but Luther extended and altered the term by applying it to temporal as well as
spiritual offices. Vocation finds its essential meaning in the Christian attitude of one who acts in a particular calling.[30]
    Christian love takes a different form when applied to temporal
government by ruler or subject. There is a wrong way and a right
way to act in one's order, and Luther undertook to instruct "the
princes and the secular authorities in such a way that they shall
remain Christians and that Christ shall remain Lord, yet so that
Christ's commandments need not for their sake be changed into
counsels."[31] Luther accepted compromises in Jesus' ethic as necessary to maintain stability and justice in a political society, for
Jesus taught an ethic abstracted from all problems of social order
and coercion. Roman Catholic ethics had solved this problem by
reserving the teachings of the Sermon on the Mount for those
called to enter the monastic life, while others followed the natural law, an ethical system which takes into consideration the
conditions of conventional life in society. Luther insisted that
Jesus' ethic applies to all Christians, but that one's responsibility
in an order must be carried out in a spirit of love as a vocation.
This applies, strangely, both to the political office, which coerces
through its instrument, the sword, and to the position of the subject, who must obey and may have to kill to help preserve the
state.
    Although Luther tried to outline the proper way for rulers to
govern, he knew that contemporary rulers, instead of accepting
their office as a vocation from God and seeking the welfare of
their subjects in love, usually acted for their own interests.
Judged even by minimal standards of justice, the monarchs of the
sixteenth century were quite deficient. In that age of political

authoritarianism, safeguards against their arbitrary action were almost totally lacking, and they readily took advantage of the power in their hands. It was clear to Luther that rulers are "usually the greatest fools or the worst knaves on earth; therefore one must constantly expect the worst from them and look for little good from them. . . ."[32] Nevertheless, because of the goodness of the created order, even the unjust and egocentric prince serves God when he maintains security and peace in his realm. At the very minimum, the rulers are "God's jailers and hangmen, and His divine wrath needs them to punish the wicked and preserve outward peace."[33] In protecting their own selfish interests rulers at the same time shield their people against the depredations of those who would unsettle normal life.

But the ruler can be more than this. In his treatise "On Secular Authority," Luther raised the question whether political officials can be good Christians. His affirmative answer rests on two assumptions central to his whole outlook—that the state and the sword are a divine service by which the wicked are punished and good defended, and that one performs one's duties out of concern for the neighbor and not for oneself. Society could not survive if no officials existed whose work in arresting and executing apparently contradicts the Sermon on the Mount; but when done for the sake of the common good, such functions become works of love.[34] In fact, Christians should leap at the opportunity to serve God and the neighbor in this way, as something beneficial to society.

> Therefore, should you see that there is a lack of hangmen, beadles, judges, lords, or princes, and find that you are qualified, you should offer your services and seek the place, that necessary government may by no means be despised and become inefficient or perish. For the world cannot and dare not dispense with it.[35]

Luther held the office of prince, next to that of the preacher, to be the highest and most useful on earth.[36]

The norms of the Sermon on the Mount apply in questions of personal interest. If one should happen to suffer personal injustice, he should turn the other cheek and give up his mantle with his cloak. But Christians in authority satisfy "God's kingdom inwardly and the kingdom of the world outwardly, at the same

time suffer evil and injustice and yet punish evil and injustice, at
the same time do not resist evil and yet resist it."[37] In the first
case, one's own interest is involved, in the other, the interests of
society—but in both, Christian love expressed as selflessness serves
as guide.

Luther defined the virtuous prince according to the absolutist
but paternalistic standard of his time. In addition to preserving
the security of his realm, the ruler should fulfill his Christian vocation by supporting the preaching of God's Word and by reigning justly. The former task requires the protection of the godly,
the suppression of the godless, and measures for freely teaching
and learning the gospel; the latter refers to the care of the poor,
orphans, and widows, just and good laws and customs, and righteous works.[38] Here Luther represented the standard views of the
Middle Ages, by which the ruler patronized the religious life of
his subjects and upheld recognized norms of justice. In an authoritarian age the governing officials naturally played a significant role in guaranteeing the health of a society. Although Luther knew that a truly Christian prince was rare, he appreciated
even the limited stability and justice he found, for it guaranteed
the continued transmission of the gospel and the opportunity for
men to live quietly and piously in family, work, and church.
Peace and order seemed to be the most that one could ordinarily
expect.

It behooves Christian subjects to help maintain this limited
good, which through the eyes of faith represents a divine blessing.
Even though governments may be unjust and corrupt, the fundamental response of all subjects, Christian or non-Christian, is
unconditional obedience to the authorities. At times Luther
seemed to think that Christians do not need law and coercion to
be good citizens: a person motivated by love does not commit aggression; and because of concern for his neighbor and awareness
of the beneficent effects of even a tyrannical government in contrast with no government at all, he will willingly bear the sword,
pay taxes, and honor the authorities. Like the ruler, the Christian citizen fulfills his vocation in love: "He serves the State as
he performs all other works of love, which he himself does not
need . . . but because others need it."[39] In this way the citizen
bolsters God's dike against human wickedness, setting a good example for others who would not submit to authority willingly,
and maintaining the good reputation of the gospel. Obedience to

the law and submission to authority define the manner in which the Christian acts as a citizen.

The subject who is not a true Christian, on the other hand, obeys the government for a reason consistent with his depraved nature—fear of the consequences. God instituted government to check the pernicious aggressiveness of natural man. Luther's view of sin profoundly influenced his description of social men as "brute beasts" who would render society chaotic if they could. Many have criticized Luther for his depreciation of man and his understanding of government in terms of coercion, but such criticism has generally stemmed from ignorance of the political circumstances of the sixteenth century. Modern Americans usually think of government principally as a vehicle of free expression and a source of justice and welfare; but such an attitude overlooks the fact that these benefits presuppose order. In fact, freedom on too grand a scale, without order, would probably lead to an intolerable chaos in which both freedom and justice would perish.

Luther shared with his contemporaries a horror of revolution, based on the assumption that in an age of insecurity and injustice the fundamental purpose of government was peace and order. Because revolutions tended to destroy even those minimal benefits, the capstone of all sixteenth-century political thought was that if men were to live tolerably, legitimate government must continue. Luther argued that "it is better to suffer wrong from one tyrant . . . than from unnumbered tyrants, that is, from the mob."[40] His view was not unusual for his time, especially since the feudal authorities had quickly suppressed several previous peasants' revolts.

Luther had a precedent for his insistence on obedience in Paul's influential admonition to the Romans to "be subject to the governing authorities" whom God has instituted to punish the wrongdoer. Both Paul and Luther lived in periods of injustice and potential disorder, when the propagation of the Christian message owed much to the relative political stability they enjoyed, and both regarded their lifetimes as final moments before the end of history would signal the last judgment and resurrection of the faithful.[41] Accusations of political conservatism against Luther must take into consideration the influence on him of New Testament eschatology. Eschatology can take many directions, but with Luther's pessimistic view of man's capacities it led to acceptance of the existent order.

The same suppositions about the necessity of effective authority govern Luther's conclusion that war is a legitimate activity for
both prince and subject if undertaken to preserve the security of
the political society. Luther did not uncritically accept war, but
rather indicated with some care the characteristics of an acceptable war. As already mentioned, he did not justify a crusade
against the Turks because war is a political, not a religious, activity. To say that war in itself is wrong, however, is to say that it is
wrong to use the sword in assuring domestic peace. Just as love
leads Christians to obey the political authorities, it encourages
them to fight in defense of their neighbors. Although as Christians they do not defend themselves and acknowledge no worldly
rulers over their souls, as members of the state they must fight to
enable rulers to carry out their divine commission.[42] It is "a
Christian act and an act of love confidently to kill, rob, and pil-
lage the enemy, and to do everything that can injure him until
he has conquered him according to the methods of war. Only one
must beware of sin, not violate wives and virgins, and when victory comes, offer mercy and peace to those who surrender and
humble themselves."[43] To the contention that Jesus did not bear
the sword, Luther argued that Jesus' vocation was the establishment of his own kingdom. In doing so, Jesus did not reject other
vocations, for just as he did not abolish matrimony, even though
he was himself not married, he did not forbid the sword to those
who were required to bear it.[44]

The burden of responsibility for undertaking a war ordinarily
lies with the ruler, since his subjects usually will follow him. Luther was strongly influenced by the concepts of a "just war"
handed down from the Middle Ages;[45] fundamentally, whoever
starts a war is wrong and by justice should be defeated and punished. Hence, a morally valid war between nations can only occur
with the conscientious conviction that one is fighting against his
will; in other words, the just war is one of protection and self-
defense. Every governor should avoid war except to defend his
country; but if attacked, he is duty-bound in accordance with his
office to punish the aggressor and protect his subjects, "for a lord
and prince is not a person to himself, but to others; he has to
serve them, that is, protect and defend them. . . ."[46]

The subject must in principle obey his ruler when battle en-
sues, but not unconditionally. The problem of war provided an
occasion for the first of several reservations by Luther regarding
the attitude of the citizen toward the authorities, inasmuch as a

conflict might arise between participation in an unjust war and one's duty to obey his superiors. Since Luther referred to this example at least three times,[47] he apparently regarded it as an important dilemma of the Christian conscience. When a prince wrongly undertakes a war, his people should not follow him, for one must obey God rather than man, and to engage in an unjust war causes suffering to the innocent neighbor in the other nation. If a Christian can heed Jesus' admonition to leave father and mother for the sake of God, then he can leave his ruler for the same reason. Luther did not justify rebellion or active resistance, but only man's commitment to suffering through a conscience obedient to God, come what may.

Inasmuch as Luther assumed that most rulers were wicked and self-seeking, their wars being no exception, it is surprising that he and his followers did not exploit the implications of this position. Perhaps the vigor of German nationalism and the consciousness that the wars of the sixteenth century were struggles for Protestant survival led Lutherans to support their rulers unquestioningly in these conflicts.

Because one's perspective is shaped by the corporate group to which he belongs, in some wars the Christian will not know what to do. He may think that his ruler is acting unjustly, but he may not be sure. In this case the demands of temporal obedience take precedence over one's doubt; God will not hold an individual responsible because he obeyed his lord in a time of uncertainty. In summation, then, Luther allowed both rulers and subjects to wage a just war according to their station, even though conflict contradicts the admonitions of Jesus in the Sermon on the Mount; but he predicated such action on the view that Christian ethics is not a new form of legalism based on the laws of Jesus, but a response of love and concern in a world where human sin obviates the use of the gospel ethic in political relationships, and coercion of human egoism becomes a genuine Christian work.

Even though citizens and rulers may defend themselves as a society against unjust attack, resistance to injustice is valid only between equal authorities, that is, between nations. Luther vehemently denied the right of an inferior to revolt against a superior, such as subjects attacking nobles, nobles their princes, or princes the Emperor. He associated tyrannicide with paganism and felt that Christianity—especially the Reform movement which, unlike the papacy, did not interfere in politics—gave stability and sup-

port to temporal authority by its injunction of obedience. Luther
applied this principle even when a king had promised his subjects
to rule according to certain laws and then violated them. Vengeance is not the responsibility of the citizens, but of God, who has
commanded the king to be righteous and will punish violations
in this life or the next. If this principle were not upheld, men
would feel free to deny authority in all phases of life, and God's
beneficent providence throughout the temporal world would be
undercut—servants would rise up against their masters, children
against their parents, pupils against their teachers. To the charge
that he was playing up to the princes, Luther cited his frequent
condemnations of the rulers and insisted that he was simply trying to show how everyone should obey God by submitting to his
superiors. However, the Reformer had little confidence that the
norms he outlined would be taken seriously; the authorities
practiced injustice, and their subjects would not hesitate to throw
society into chaos rather than endure suffering: "For if today or
tomorrow a people rises up and deposes their lord or slays him,
—well, that will happen, and the lords must expect it, if it is
God's decree;—but it does not follow that for that reason it is a
right and just act. I have never known a case of this kind that
was just, and even now I cannot imagine one."[48]

In the famous Peasants' Revolt of 1524-1525, the invalidity of
insurrection and the confusion of the regiments were at stake.
Luther acted on the basis of strong convictions about the proper
role of God and man in history, even though from a twentieth-
century perspective one can see how his own sympathy for
authority led him into virtual hysteria against the peasants. The
historical conflict between God and the devil provided constant
occasions for a message of God to man, and in this instance
Luther saw the action of the devil.[49] In every situation man can
react either in faith or unfaith. Luther relied on free obedience
and trust in God's guidance, not on an autonomous law. He was
not quietistic or passive in dealing with social issues, but constantly acted in the social and political controversies of his day,
appointing himself guide and critic of prince and peasant.[50]
But he was conservative and hierarchical, and his directions to
people of all classes assumed the continuation of the existent
structure and the effectiveness of moral appeal to the consciences
of his hearers as his legitimate instrument.

The causes for peasant unrest are mirrored in the economic
and religious reforms suggested in the "Twelve Articles,"[51] one

of several manifestoes promulgated by the revolutionary movements in many parts of German-speaking Europe. The economic proposals were not really changes, but demands for retention of the traditional privileges of the serfs, such as fishing, hunting, and cutting wood on the common lands, which were abrogated by the greed of sixteenth-century nobles. The religious features in the first, third, and twelfth articles, called for local selection of pastors, denounced serfdom as a violation of Christian freedom, and expressed the willingness of the peasants to remove any articles not consonant with the Word of God. The religious articles indicate that the peasants regarded their movement as an expression of the current religious reform.

Luther's attitude changed as the insurrection developed, but his theological principles remained the same. In the early stages he wrote an "Admonition" replying to the "Twelve Articles," in which he castigated both nobles and peasants.

Against the former he said that we "have no one on earth to thank for this mischievous rebellion except you princes and lords . . . [who] do nothing but flay and rob your subjects in order that you may lead a life of splendor and pride, until the common people can bear it no longer."[52] Luther contended that the injustice of the aristocracy would lead God to destroy Germany by the peasants or some other means. Referring to the "Twelve Articles" as "fair and just," he reminded the rulers that they "are not instituted in order that they may seek their own profit and self-will, but in order to provide for the best interests of their subjects."[53]

The peasants, on the other hand, by threatening revolution in the name of Christ, were taking the name of the Lord in vain, for Christ explicitly forbade the sword to Christians for their own sake. "Suffering, suffering; cross, cross! This and nothing else, is the Christian law!"[54] If they were defending themselves against wrongs, they should leave the name of Christian out of it. Besides, the Bible and natural law do not justify rebellion on the grounds of injustice; the authority of the rulers is the foundation of property and even life; without it, there would be anarchy. Even though the rulers were unjust, the party that attacked initially should not adopt the name of Christian, for they could not possibly be Christian. The peasants should seek their objectives by patience and prayer, not by violence.[55]

Luther attempted to mediate between the peasants and lords, pointing out that no Christian issues lay between them, that both parties were acting against God and were under his wrath. He urged that representatives be chosen to settle the matter in a friendly manner by a compromise in which the lords would recognize their tyranny, while the peasants would give up their more extreme articles. When the peasants' movement developed into widespread destruction, Luther concluded that they were more obviously acting against the will of God than the rulers were.

In Luther's catalogue of the peasants' errors he cited their resistance to rulers, their robbing, plundering, and murdering, and their blasphemy in calling themselves "Christian brethren." In his often quoted treatise "Against the Robbing and Murdering Hordes of Peasants" he called on the rulers to fulfill God's will in Romans 13 by smiting the rebels and thus thwart the devil's attempt to destroy order. The actions of the rulers should be tempered, however, by fear of God and confession that their own sins had led to these disastrous consequences. Luther frankly felt that the final judgment had come, that the revolt was one of the signs of the end.[56]

Luther was generally blamed for the cruelty of the nobles toward the defeated peasants, and although he tried to justify himself, the Lutheran reform lost much popular support. Luther argued that the blame should not fall on him, because he had called on the lords to be merciful.[57] In not showing consideration to both innocent and guilty, the "bloody dogs"[58] were wallowing in blood, subjects of their master, the devil. Nevertheless, critics should not ordinarily expect mercy, a Christian virtue, in the earthly kingdom, the realm of wrath and severity, "the servant of God's wrath upon the wicked . . . a real precursor of hell and everlasting death."[59]

This final quotation provides a key to the understanding of Luther's position in the Peasants' Revolt. Profoundly pessimistic about the boiling situation, Luther hoped for a compromise, but since both sides were wrong, the peasants committed a double sin by attacking first and defying authority. The severity of the nobles revealed their estrangement from God as well, but given the world as it is one cannot expect order to be maintained in any other way. By crushing the peasants, life could go on. If the peasants had succeeded in their revolution, society would have collapsed, and a group of fanatics would have blasphemed God by assuming that their movement was his kingdom.

While offering no excuse for revolution in principle, Luther did sanction the opposition of the Elector of Saxony against the Emperor; this was done on the basis of an imperial law providing for such resistance in case of "notorious injury." In this particular instance, when the Emperor refused to call a council and tried to suppress the Lutheran movement by proceeding against the Protestant princes, Luther after much hesitation found a means in the traditional law to circumvent the prohibitions against resistance by an inferior.[60]

The Church as Critic of the State

The exposition so far has stressed the role of obedience to authority in Luther's thought, and although this provides the fundamental response of man to the reign of God in the temporal government, Luther's reservations against unrestricted activity by the worldly regiment are important, if neglected, aspects of his thought. This neglect has contributed to the stereotyped view that Luther uncritically supported the political authorities. Just as his emphases in support of established authority were grounded in his theology, similarly his objections were not capricious, but integral to the picture of God's governance and man's response in faith. God wills more for temporal authority than maintaining peace and order, and he has provided hints on how to ascertain this will.

Luther's early (1523) treatise "On Secular Authority" is subtitled, "To what extent it shall be obeyed," implying limits. Near the outset he says that he is going to "write concerning the secular authorities and the sword they bear; how it should be used in a Christian manner. . . ."[61] Two limits on secular authority have already been noted: the state cannot interfere in the domain of the spiritual authorities, and the ruler cannot compel a Christian to engage in an unjust war.

God has also provided for an institution to admonish the temporal authorities, namely, the spiritual regiment, the church. The prince does not subordinate himself to the churchly hierarchy, and Luther was quite conscious that he had rescued the integrity of the political order from control by the papacy;[62] at the same time the ruler must acknowledge the authority of the Word and heed it. The minister of the church guards the Word, serving as adviser of both ruler and ruled; since men are blinded by the cunning of the devil and refuse to see the law of their lives, the minister must inform them. He must publicly respond when the sword is misused or when people suffer injustice, although this duty is an *opus alienum* in addition to his *opus proprium* of preaching the gospel.[63] If the minister does not ease the sufferings of the oppressed, he contributes to the likelihood of a revolution. This is essentially how Luther acted when he offered to arbitrate between the peasants and the nobles before the Revolt became a reality. One could learn a great deal about Luther's concept of the pastoral office in relation to the temporal power simply by observing his lifelong engagement in the vital issues of his day.

Luther's clearest views on this subject are found in his exposition of the Eighty-second Psalm. Since God has established rulers, they should not be tempted by pride, for God stands in the congregation and judges them. It is God's will that rulers be subject to his Word or suffer misfortune, for "God's Word appoints them, and makes them gods, and subjects everything to them. Therefore, they are not to despise it, for it is their institutor and appointer; but they are to be subject to it, and allow themselves to be judged, rebuked, made, and mastered by it."[64] One knows God's Word through his priests and preachers, who hold a responsible office, even when they are knaves, to judge and rebuke rulers. Too often, unfortunately, through unfaithfulness, laziness, or cowardice, ministers neglect their function.

> So, then, this first verse teaches that to rebuke rulers is not seditious, provided it is done in the way here described; namely, by the office to which God has committed that duty, and through God's Word, spoken publicly, boldly, and honestly. To rebuke rulers in this way is, on the contrary, a praiseworthy, noble, and rare virtue, and would be far more seditious, if a preacher were not to rebuke the sins of the rulers, for then he makes people angry and sullen, and strengthens the wickedness of the tyrants and becomes a partaker in it, and bears responsibility for it. Thus God might be angered and might allow rebellion to come as a penalty.[65]

In spite of Luther's questionable exegesis of this psalm, in which he takes the word "gods" to mean "rulers," this exposition has far-reaching implications.

The place of justice as a determinant of ministerial criticism of the political order should be emphasized because it has aroused so much attention in contemporary Lutheranism. His *Table Talk* reported that Luther, when asked concerning the line at which the rights of man are transgressed, replied, "The church's front line is wherever there are those who suffer unjustly."[66] Elsewhere he argued:

> Christ has instructed us preachers not to withhold the truth from the lords but to exhort and to chide them in their injustice. . . . We recognize the authority, but we must rebuke our Pilates in their crimes and self-confidence. . . . We should suffer. We should not keep still. The Christian must bear testimony for the truth and die for the truth. But how can he die for the truth if he has not first confessed the truth? Thus Christ showed that Pilate did exercise authority from God and at the same time rebuked him for doing wrong.[67]

When Luther spoke of justice, he represented the medieval view based on natural law and the customary understanding of rights and duties for each segment of society. Injustice referred not to inequality, but rather to gross oppression or violation of the natural law. Luther acted in much the same way as the prophet Amos, sensing gross miscarriages of function by the political authorities and reprimanding them.

Christian Disobedience

When the worldly regiment violates its responsibilities, Christians may have to disobey. One may legitimately disobey in the name of God because government is an aspect of God's rule and possesses validity only insofar as it serves God. In fact, Christians obey political authority as a form of obedience to God and his Word, so that when the prince orders a Christian to sin, he is no longer obliged to obey. If a prince tells one to follow the pope, to believe an heretical doctrine, or to give up certain books such as the Bible, then Lucifer, not God, is acting through him, and to follow him denies God.[68] Luther went one step further and urged opposition to injustice.

> Here we must provoke to anger father, mother, and the best of friends. Here we must strive against spiritual and temporal powers, and be accused of disobedience. . . . And although this is especially the duty of those who are commanded to preach God's Word, yet every Christian is also obliged to do so when time and place demand. . . . Here we must first of all resist all wrong, where truth or righteousness suffers violence

or need, and dare make no distinction of persons. . . . For the greater portion of the powerful, rich and friends do injustice and oppress the poor, the lowly, and their own opponents; and the greater the men, the worse the deeds; and where we cannot by force prevent it and help the truth, we should at least confess it, and do what we can with words, not take the part of the unrighteous, not approve them, but speak the truth boldly.[69]

This quotation is valuable in recognizing both ministerial and lay obligations to civil disobedience, but also in indicating what Luther meant by injustice. Placed alongside Luther's actions and words in the Peasants' Revolt, some idea of the dialectic in his thought becomes apparent. Conceivably he might have supported the peasants in passive resistance or if they had claimed to act, not for themselves, but for their neighbors. But in launching a violent attack for their own betterment, they showed the questionable quality of their Christian spirit and thus fell under condemnation. The radical call to dedication against injustice in this quotation refutes any charges of social passivity in Luther's view of church and state.

In no case, however, was a Christian permitted to offer violent resistance. He is to suffer in love and self-sacrifice according to the pattern of Christ; in extraordinary cases of oppression he may flee into another country.[70] One exception may be found to this rule, for God sometimes raises up *Wunderleute*, "supermen," and gives them a special call to overthrow an unjust authority. *Wunderleute*, who serve as instruments of God and act not for their own interests but for others, must have a call from God and possess charismatic gifts. Luther cited the example of Samson, who freed the Israelites from Philistine bondage.[71] Otherwise, one must rest in the hope that God will kill the tyrant by some means or raise up a foreign ruler to depose him.[72]

Jews and Heretics

One final point in Luther's outlook should be considered in this study, namely, his attitude toward Jews and heretics. A typical view of the Middle Ages, that of St. Thomas Aquinas, permitted toleration of Jews in a Christian society only in the manner that harlots were tolerated; heretics were accepted in the hope of their eventual conversion, but in the event of continued recalcitrance, they should be killed.[73] Luther's attitude toward the Jews changed over the years.[74] In 1523 he was hopeful of bringing them to Christianity, since the papacy, which had sporadically persecuted them, was being undermined by the Reform.

But for various reasons, such as the Jews' economic practices and religious exclusiveness, but also because of their continued refusal to become Christian, by the 1540's Luther had developed an almost pathological hatred of them. He advocated rigorous restrictions against them, lest God be blasphemed and Jesus defamed. The responsibility for this repression rested, he held, on the temporal authority, which cannot interfere in an issue of conversion, but should prevent blasphemy in its realm. This unfortunate example reveals a practical way in which the worldly regiment expresses its dependence on the sovereignty of God.

In a long and helpful article Roland Bainton has traced the development of Luther's attitude toward heretics.[75] In the early years of the Reformation, feeling that heresy as a spiritual matter was strictly a responsibility of the ministers and the Word, Luther emphasized the inappropriateness of political force to compel people to certain beliefs. In "On Secular Authority" he insisted that "heresy can never be prevented by force,"[76] and only becomes stronger because people sense that force is being used for a wrong cause.

In April, 1529, the Diet of Speyer produced an imperial edict by which Anabaptists were condemned to fire and sword without ecclesiastical examination. Luther, who even then seemed to oppose the death penalty, remained quiet, but in March, 1530, he consented to the edict on the ground that Anabaptists were seditious as well as blasphemous. In his exposition that same year of the Eighty-second Psalm, he attempted to articulate his views more clearly. There are many kinds of heretics. One group, those who deny that a Christian can be a ruler or hold property, and are seditious, are not simply heretics, but rebels and should be punished accordingly. Another group, who deny such a fundamental doctrine as the divinity of Christ, are blasphemers. Rulers should not tolerate such individuals and should punish them, unless they move to a place where there are no Christians to lead astray. Luther said nothing in this treatise about the form of punishment, but the death penalty is assumed. Finally, on conflicts between Catholics and Protestants, the ruler of a realm should decide which group is consistent with Scripture and banish adherents of the other view, for two religious faiths in a realm would lead to intolerable dissension.[77]

By 1536 any subtle distinctions between heresy and blasphemy

had disappeared, and Luther called upon magistrates to suppress
heresy actively. This represented, in effect, a radical change in
Luther's view, influenced to a large extent by political circumstances and the tenacious popularity of the Anabaptists among
the lower classes. In the sixteenth century there were few places
in the Western world, Protestant or Catholic, where a given
society would allow more than one religious confession. It was
also a time when men justified cruelty against other religious
groups in the name of the integrity of God, to whom blasphemy
and heresy were insults.

Lutheran Developments in Europe and America

From the time of Melanchthon, Luther's colleague and suc-
cessor, the theological content of Luther's church-state views was
altered and the political order was regarded as an independent
dimension. It lost its relation to God's sovereignty, justification,
love, and vocation. In the so-called orthodox period, the discussion of temporal justice became a form of natural theology, similar to the Roman Catholic view of an independent nature subordinate to grace, a lower stage to be supplemented by Christian
justification communicated by revelation. As Ernst Troeltsch has
pointed out, the political ethic became secularized. The attempt
to associate persistent historical problems such as war, authority,
force, and law with the Christian ethic foundered on the independence of the political order, and men boasted that the Lutheran doctrine gave a divine sanction for any political enterprise.[78]

The cause of this neglect of Luther's theological dialectic lay
to a large extent in the political circumstances upon which the
Reformation depended for its survival. Luther himself supported
the political determination of religious faith in particular territories, and the Peace of Augsburg in 1555 made this principle
of *cuius regio, eius religio* normative in Western Europe. It was
preceded in Germany by a series of developments by which the
independence of the ecclesiastical order was undermined. As
early as 1520, for example, Luther called on the nobility to reform the church, since the papacy was unwilling to reform
itself.[79] Luther admitted that this task more properly belonged
to the clergy, but because of their indifference he hoped that
God might save his church through the laity.

Prior to 1526 Luther seemed to have envisioned a polity centered on the local congregation, which would choose its pastor and administer its own financial affairs, bound to other Christian congregations only by a common faith and love; but in that year Luther asked the Elector of Saxony to appoint a committee to make recommendations for the spiritual welfare of the realm with the Elector himself serving as a *Notbischof,* an "emergency bishop." In 1528 Melanchthon's "Instruction of the Visitors to the Pastors" set the pattern for the German states, although Luther's preface argued that the system was a temporary measure and that the prince should interfere only to prevent anarchy. The core of the system was a superintendent who advised the ruler regarding church issues on which he should act. In 1529 a consistory developed, composed of two theologians, two lawyers, and other officials who exercised control over the clergy; it punished gross immorality among the populace, promoted religious conformity, and determined ecclesiastical organization. Until Luther's death the political officials of Saxony consistently bowed to the wishes of the theologians on religious matters. Throughout his life Luther continued to insist on the temporary character of the consistories, but with his death they became the accepted instrument by which the political authorities exercised close control over the religious life of their realms.[80] In theory, the church was ruled by Christ and the Word; in practice it was governed by the ruling princes and the pastors. By accepting political control over the church as an emergency measure, the German Reformation deprived itself of the opportunity to establish structures by which it would maintain its full independence.

With the critical aspects of Luther's view of the state nullified by the incapacity of Lutheran theologians to understand the dynamic of his thought and by the structures of control maintained by the princes, Lutheran piety came to express itself in the form of inward spirituality, a tendency reinforced by the growth of Pietism in the late seventeenth and eighteenth century. In effect, Lutheranism abdicated responsibility for political and social problems and adjusted itself to whatever political regime happened to be in power. Troeltsch correctly recognized that Lutheranism had no theoretical tendency toward monarchy or absolutism. It was only because absolutism and the manorial estates existed in Central and Northern Germany that this became associated with Lutheranism, but because of its development, Troeltsch argued, Lutheranism "adapts itself most easily to political conditions of a monarchical and aristocratic kind, and to an economic social situation which is predominantly agrarian and middle class."[81] In practice this meant that Christian political responsibility centered on unquestioned obedience to all government officials, who represented God. It was assumed that the civil order would direct its activities according to the natural law and the Word of God, but the responsibility of the church to define these disappeared. To cite Troeltsch once again, " . . . the idea of moulding Society according to Christian ideals certainly existed; but it was left entirely to the Government, to be carried out in accordance with natural reason, which harmonized with the Gospel and was adapted to the fallen state."[82]

By the nineteenth century, the separation of religious and political realms opened the way for a variety of non-Lutheran, nonbiblical, authoritarian interpretations of church and state, all designed to advance the interests of the state and utilize the church as a tool of the nation. One such theory was that of Friedrich Julius Stahl, who exercised great influence among conservatives amid the social unrest of the mid-nineteenth century. Both state and church, he argued, are authoritarian instruments of God toward which men respond in obedience, and political and social issues by no means interest the church.[83]

Such Lutheran passivity cannot be justified on the basis of what Luther really thought and did, although one side of his thought provided the impetus for such a position. Edgar M. Carlson has pointed out that the church in Sweden neither adhered to the principle of *cuius regio, eius religio,* nor allowed the monarch to gain the control over the church typical of Germany. In 1593, when the Augsburg Confession was adopted as the doctrinal position of the Swedish Church, the king was Roman Catholic and the regent a Calvinist. During the seventeenth century a series of effective bishops built an ecclesiastical structure of such independence that the monarchy never was able to control it in the German pattern. One of the Swedish bishops, Johannes Rudbeckius, saw the difference: "In Germany, since the Reformation, it has gone badly with religion, for the province has patterned itself after the ruler. But we, praise God, have hitherto managed well. If the magistrate has wanted to do what he ought not to do, the clergy has held the magistrate in check; the magistrate has also kept the clergy in mind during these one hundred years."[84] The failure of Swedish Lutheranism to conform to the German political and social quietism, a fact overlooked by many interpreters, indicates that Luther's thought does not lead inevitably to an agrarian, absolute monarchy. It is also worth noticing that the American form of the Swedish church, the Augustana Synod, has led in the contemporary "re-interpretation" of Luther, as well as in social and political interests.

In the United States, Lutheranism responded positively to church-state separation, but with a few exceptions the church did not analyze the social and political possibilities of independence from state control. The General Synod, comprising the more Americanized Lutherans, in contrast to the General Council, encountered the Social Gospel through its membership in the Federal Council of Churches. The Social Gospel movement emphasized Christian activity in society and state to alleviate social evils, but as an historian of Lutheranism in the period has remarked, "its participation in that movement was more talk than action."[85] Disagreement with the Social Gospel led many in the General Synod to emphasize the distinctive outlook of Lutheranism and to draw closer to other Lutherans in the General Council.

During this period the *Lutheran Church Review,* an influential theological journal, reflected little interest in church-state matters, except for the relation of religion to education.[86] Writers advocated Bible reading in the public schools and experiments with governmental support of parochial schools and released-time religion classes. Theologically, they attempted to set off traditional Lutheranism from the new liberal currents. For example, a classical view of the two regiments based on the seventeenth-century orthodox theologian, Gerhard, outlined the duties of the citizen to the state as follows: to be subordinate to government, to obey it, to support it financially and personally, to hold office if elected, and to pray for it. In return the state should protect the church without interfering in its doctrine and discipline.[87] The interrelation characteristic of Luther's outlook is notably absent.

In opposition to the Social Gospel, several articles emphasized Christian concern for the individual, rather than for the group; the church's basic evangelical and redemptive mission; the stubborn persistence of sin in men which defies simple solutions; and the fundamental responsibility of the state, rather than the church, for social matters. They pointed out, however, that the Christian citizen linked church and state. Individual responsibility, rather than churchly engagement in politics, appears in the following statement:

Nor can she [the Church] officially throw her forces, which are the Lord's, under a political leadership which is not herself under her Lord. Politics is external human control, religion is internal divine control. The Church is not in politics. She is not here to establish God's will by political means. . . . But every member of the Church on earth is also a member of the natural order. It is his privilege and his duty . . . to carry his Christian character and principles and to exercise his Christian judgment and action in the natural order. . . . As he has opportunity and wisdom, he must make his Christianity effective in politics.[88]

Structurally, the contrast between outer political and inner religious life and a sharp dichotomy and noninterference between the two regiments prevailed in American Lutheranism.

The Modern Period

The Effect of World War II on Lutheran Church-State Views

The catalyst that produced the contemporary rediscovery of Luther's views on church and state was the Second World War. Lutheran churches in Germany and Norway faced in a particularly severe way the threat of a totalitarian state which tried to reconstruct the organization and, at times, the beliefs of the Christian church. Luther did not foresee totalitarianism in this form; he frequently witnessed political meddling in religious affairs, but not a powerful national ideology designed to replace Christianity. Luther was far more concerned about the problems of the Christian church which had neglected its proper place in the divine plan than he was about the state. Contemporary Lutherans, even with the demise of Nazism, have continued to face this problem in Communism. In the words of Bishop Otto Dibelius: "The problem of the state today is—the totalitarian state; nothing else, absolutely nothing else than this one problem—the totalitarian state."[89] This change in situation has led to a more careful exploration of the aspects of Luther's thought which contradict an uncritical reverence for authority. American Lutheran writers have also noted a tendency in the United States toward national idolatry, reflected in the uncritical neglect of religion and morality in wartime, secularism, and the religion of social adjustment and conformity to American mores.[90]

In Germany the struggle against Nazism centered on the freedom of the church against attempts by the Hitler government to control appointments and to propagandize for a highly nationalistic interpretation of Christianity. In 1934 the nucleus of a group which later became the "Confessing Church" met at Barmen and affirmed its loyalty to Christ against the distortions introduced by the state. These clauses, the most important of the Barmen Declaration, reveal the tenor of the German concern.

> Jesus Christ, as the Holy Scripture witnesses to him, is the one Word of God whom we must hear, whom we must trust and obey in life and death. We reject the false teaching that the church, alongside this one Word of God, can and must acknowledge as the source of its proclamation other events and powers, structures and truths, than God's revelation.
>
> Just as Jesus Christ is God's consolation in the forgiveness of all our sins, so with the same seriousness he is also God's powerful claim upon our whole life; through him to us flows joyous freedom from the godless ties of this world to free, thankful service to his creation. We reject the false teaching that there are areas of our life, in which we acknowledge other lords and not Jesus Christ, areas in which we do not need the justification and sanctification through him.[91]

The emphasis clearly falls on the right of the church to interpret the meaning of Christ for itself, to regard the Bible as its sole source of authority, and to reject the restriction of Christianity to certain spheres of activity. Although avoiding the question of justice in Lutheran doctrine, the German resistance contributed one of its major figures, Dietrich Bonhoeffer, to the attempted assassination of Hitler. The claim of Christian vocation in an extraordinarily attenuated situation led to the introduction of the hitherto unacceptable concept of tyrannicide into Lutheran ethics.

In Norway, on the other hand, the struggle focused upon justice and the integrity of accepted legal institutions, with moral support from the writings of influential theologians in neutral Sweden. The two regiments, which are separated to the extent that the state cannot interfere in the church, but so related that the church is the conscience of the state, became the basis for their position. Bishop Berggrav, who personally directed the resistance of the church, articulated his views in a book, *Man and*

State,[92] written while he was imprisoned by the Nazis. Although influenced by Luther's views of the two regiments, the respective functions of each, the necessity of civil obedience, and the demonic perversion of the orders, Berggrav made a distinctive contribution through his emphasis on violation of law as a rationale for disobedience.

Referring to Romans 13, the keystone of Luther's political views, Berggrav contended that Paul advocated submission to authority because authority was subject to law. "In the mind of Paul it is *the Law* and not the state that is supreme. Consequently where he writes 'power' we ought sometimes read 'Law.' . . . There is no power except that which is of the Law."[93] In its ideal form law reflects the freedom and dignity of man and represents a mode by which relations among men are adjusted without discrimination. The political power is subject to this law—it cannot act independently in the sense of arbitrariness. Berggrav noted that Luther, in his *Table Talk,* said that the emperor "must remain in the second table [of the Ten Commandments]. He cannot rise higher (unless the devil leads him astray). He is subject to the second table."[94] Legitimate authority is, therefore, lawful authority, and to obey unlawful authority involves submission to the devil. The Christian citizen gives his loyalty in actuality to the law, so that just as one would not obey a murderer, one does not obey when a ruler acts violently and contrary to the law. In this manner Berggrav pointed out that Luther justified the resistance of the Schmalkald League to the Emperor.

The presence of a doctrine of revolution in the Calvinist tradition also made an impression on Berggrav, although such drastic action must proceed in fear of the judgment of God. Christianity must condemn a revolt based on personal interest, but where "God's orders are trodden under foot and the right of one's fellow man to live is threatened at the very outset, there the Christian must be willing to go the way of *sacrifice,* even if it involves revolt against illegal authority."[95]

It is doubtful that Berggrav's interpretation of Romans 13 and the right of revolution are fully true to Luther,[96] and perhaps his motives were somewhat determined by his patriotism, but the Norwegian Church under his leadership took extremely seriously Luther's understanding of the church as the critic of government and the necessity for disobedience by Christian citizens. The experiences of the Norwegian Church provoked a series of studies, particularly in Sweden and Germany, to see exactly what Luther did say. Although Lutheran church members at large remain relatively unaffected by these discussions, throughout the Lutheran world scholars and church leaders have tried to face the implications of their faith for political and social problems.

The Problem of Authority

The first step, an assessment of the traditional sources of authority, has had two directions: one, the recognition that Luther differed in flexibility and activity from traditional Lutheranism; the other, that Luther himself was limited by his political circumstances and his thought may need to be criticized and supplemented. In addition to the contemporary encounter with totalitarianism and the separation of church and state, one finds at least three new developments. One is the assumption of political power by ordinary citizens. The distribution of authority in America among the people, the governing representatives, and the law makes discussion in terms of rulers and subjects not fully relevant; obedience as an obligation continues, but a far more complex issue concerns the contribution of a concept like vocation to the citizens' role in justice, social morality, and the formation of public policy. Second, Luther addressed himself to a few individuals who held power of life and death over their subjects in the name of commonly accepted views of human integrity, natural law, and justice; but today political authority has an impersonal nature and there is no commonly shared system of values. The church must rethink Luther's association of political power with parental power, analyzing instead the nature and norms of modern political authority. Third, Luther tended to think of the state as a dike against sin with limited responsibilities, but today the state has assumed widespread welfare functions, in the process, insinuating itself deeply into the personal lives of the citizens. What dangers and opportunities does this hold? And what shall the church say to it?

Lutheran leaders are beginning to feel that to function creatively the church must assess the circumstances in which it finds itself and then evaluate Luther accordingly. An American writer makes this point clearly, insisting that "Lutherans of today do not presume that Luther has done all of their theological and political thinking for them, or that his teachings are a necessary rule and guide for them. Where Luther is wrong or archaic in terms of today, he is relegated to a historical curiosity because Lutheranism, for the most part, has tried to be objective and critical about Luther."[97] The altered political circumstances even lead to a questioning of the Lutheran norm that lies even higher than Luther, the Bible. The Swedish scholar, Hillerdal, asks whether "the texts in Rom. 13:1-7 and elsewhere, demanding subjection to authority in principle, can be an absolute obligation in the complicated situations of our modern states. The modern state knows no longer merely passive subjects, but assumes instead an active common responsibility of the citizens for what happens in the state."[98]

Properly understood, however, Luther remains a valuable resource for all Protestants, and his basic framework a helpful method of approach to modern church-state problems.[99]

Interpretation of the Orders

In theologically conscious Europe, the discussion of a proper political ethic for Lutheranism focuses on a few rather involved issues. In 1937, when Nils Ehrenström surveyed various theologies of the state for the Oxford Conference, he found that the chief problems lay in the interpretation of the "orders," particularly the relationship between the church and the Nazi state.[100] At that time preoccupation with the orders represented a rejection of liberalism and individualism. The problem continues, but in a somewhat different form,[101] and representatives of a strong "order theology," such as Werner Elert, resist the speculations among Lutheran theologians on the right of resistance. Elert criticizes those who are constantly trying to apply "Peter's clause," to obey God rather than men, in order to dissociate themselves from the obligation of obedience to the state. He argues that New Testament Christians continued to obey the state despite persecution—because the authorities fulfilled their natural responsibility of preventing chaos in other parts of life. Paul, the author of the admonition to submission, lived during the time of Nero. One may not actively resist injustice, Elert insists, but must accept martyrdom; if tyrants attempt to destroy the church, then it must look to the end, understanding its situation in light of God's promises to redeem his church.[102]

Hillerdal, on the other hand, maintains that Elert's interpretation of the orders is more legalistic than Luther intended, that Elert has made the guiding principle of Christian action the rational determination of what is required to maintain the order, rather than motivation by love. Hillerdal charges that in Elert the orders cannot be broken even when love demands it.[103]

Lutheran ethics today in general is marked by emphasis on flexibility and the need to decipher God's will in particular situations, a process obscured by too much stress on principles, laws, and structures.[104] Swedish thought in particular has sought to bind together the concepts of love, vocation, and order:[105] the justified sinner surrenders to the will of God, which is love. The orders serve merely as occasions and structures for love: in fulfilling one's role in an order, a man serves God and his neighbor by contributing to the interconnected activities that make life possible.

Christ and the Devil in the World

Another dispute with important consequences for church-state relations concerns the relationship of the state to the redemption of Christ and to the struggle between God and the devil. Karl Barth, although a member of the Swiss Reformed Church, represents the position, strong in German Lutheran circles, which insists on the already accomplished redemptive victory of Christ, so encompassing creation that even the state is included.[106] This concept does not produce illusions about the virtue of the political order, but it contradicts rather strongly the dualism emphasized in Swedish interpretations of church and state. The latter explain the constant engagement of the Christian as a struggle for the will of God against the forces of the demonic. Barth subordinates the existential godlessness of the surrounding world to the triumph of Christ's redemption. Bonhoeffer, one of Barth's followers, argued that the only way to avoid using natural law as an explanation for government is to derive government from Christ: "Jesus showed that government can only serve Him, precisely because it is a power which comes down from above, no matter whether it discharges its office well or badly. Both in acquitting Him of guilt and in delivering Him up to be crucified, government was obliged to show that it stands in the service of Jesus Christ. . . . So long as the earth continues, Jesus will always be at the same time Lord of all government and Head of the Church, without government and Church ever becoming one and the same."[107]

Critics of this position insist on Luther's view that in some way the kingdom of the world, while ultimately subject to the sovereignty of God, represents existentially the rule of the devil, and that Christ will not consummate his redemption until the end of time.[108] Meanwhile, the struggle between God and the forces of evil in individuals and social institutions provides the dynamic of existence in this era. The latter position seeks to relate the state to the divine through the creation and sovereignty of God rather than through the redemption of Christ. Despite the dominion of the demonic and the frustration of Christian aims, the Christian knows that government is God's *larva* (mask).

Iustitia Civilis

A third important Continental emphasis concerns the validity of *iustitia civilis*. Given the traditionally strong view of original sin in Lutheranism, it was assumed that by following the law man could do no virtuous act in the eyes of God; but Gustaf Törnvall[109] insists that civil righteousness as well as the righteousness of justification has its ground in God, and that like the latter, *iustitia civilis* is really righteous. The foundation of this virtue lies, however, in the office itself, which actualizes God's will, rather than in the person who holds the office. The decisive righteousness for the individual is the righteousness of justification, but just as the law retains its validity, the political structures of a society are good because of their role in God's sovereignty. Thus, the concept of *iustitia civilis*, derived from what Luther called the first use of the law, strengthens the association of the political order with the reign of God. Original sin does not abrogate the *iustitia civilis*, for actions which serve the will of God by producing order and justice are legally good, though they do not contribute to salvation.[110] Luther did not deny that man can do things in the natural world that are useful and relatively good, although he polemicized against the assumption that these works could bring salvation.

Edgar Carlson says that this concept has "far-reaching implications. It means that Luther acknowledges a positive value to social action."[111] Joined with Luther's sense of vocation and his understanding of the pastoral duty to admonish the temporal authorities, *iustitia civilis* does help justify social involvement for Christians, who act in the situation according to the capacities that they have.

Bonhoeffer, unlike Törnvall, merely contrasted *iustitia civilis* with *iustitia Christiana*, though he admitted that the first use of the law gives a special dignity to government in contrast with the Roman Catholic exaltation of monasticism.[112] In general, Bonhoeffer's presentation emphasizes the ascription of value to government, not from its natural functions, but "in maintaining by the power of the sword an outward justice in which life is preserved and is thus held open for Christ. . . . Indeed, it is only in protecting the righteous that government fulfills its true mission of serving Christ."[113]

This seemingly esoteric difference of opinion determines whether the political order has its goodness because it accomplishes goals of a nonredemptive sort in God's continuing guidance of history, or whether God created it as an agent in the redemption of man by Christ. Gustaf Aulén argues for the former position: "Christianity looks upon the State primarily from the viewpoint of justice; it is the function of the State to create and uphold order instead of chaos in the human community. This function belongs to the State in conformity with the will of God: the State is thus acknowledged to have a divine function."[114]

The respective emphases of German and Scandinavian scholarship on this issue reflect their objectives in the battle with Nazism. Because the Germans struggled for the freedom of the church, they see the state as an instrument by which God protects the church in bringing men to Christ. For the Scandinavians, God has founded the state to achieve justice, the justification of the Norwegian opposition. In the Scandinavian interpretation the Christian seeks justice, not only because God wills it, but because Christian love expresses itself by achieving the well-being of the neighbor.

Revisionism in American Lutheranism

American Lutheranism has not produced outstanding scholarship, nor has it had to face the issues of Nazism and Communism in the way its European brethren have, but perhaps more than any other American Protestant group, Lutheranism responds to the impulses of its European associates. American Lutheranism faces the problem of applying the reanalysis of the Lutheran tradition to the unique circumstances of America, with its separation of church and state and its institutions of representative government.

Among American Lutheran revisionists the older passivism is now an embarrassment. As Elson Ruff, editor of *The Lutheran*, an official magazine of the Lutheran Church in America, puts it:

It is true that Lutherans have been quietists and have stayed out of politics and that Germans were not properly shocked when an evil man became their leader in 1933. But in Luther's own teaching there was a corrective to this abject submission to the leader, and it was this which was largely forgotten. He never agreed that the world should be surrendered to the devil or that the church should not concern itself with public affairs. This essential in Luther's thought did not come back to life until a dozen years ago, when men such as Bishop Eivind Berggrav in Norway said, "We flung Luther in the face of the Gestapo."[115]

The same author cites approvingly the activities of the German Confessing Church and ascribes the failures of the pre-Hitler church to history and not to Luther.

Lutheranism and Church-State Separation

How do American Lutherans view separation of church and state? "In America the Church has for the first time been separated from political subordination and is still seeking a way to maintain itself within the life of the people without being controlled by governmental powers of that people."[116] The amorphous character of American separation symbolizes a tension within Lutheran thought between the foundation of the political order in creation and the separation of spiritual and temporal functions.

This tension is further revealed in the affirmation of T. A. Kantonen that God expects of the state "the acknowledgment that absolute sovereignty belongs to God himself."[117] Carlson goes further in insisting that the church make clear to the state that its authority is subject to God; without this admonition, the state might think of its power and authority over citizens as its natural prerogatives.[118] If these voices typify the church, Lutherans seem grateful for the various symbols that the American government uses to acknowledge a power lying beyond the state and implying a divine limitation on political sovereignty.

Consistent with this position, Lutherans have criticized alleged increases in secularism. Both Ruff and Kantonen attribute this to a seed within the very foundations of American democracy, the views of the Founding Fathers.[119] Thoughtful Lutherans realize how the rationalism and optimism that motivated such men as Jefferson and Madison diverge from the Lutheran tradition; and

while American Lutherans fully accept the principle of separation of church and state, they question such rationalist assumptions as the separation of economic and political institutions
from religious criticism and the apprehension of truth by reason
alone. The threat seems to lie in America's noblest virtues: its
spiritual ideals and its passion for freedom.[120]

To some extent the affirmation of spiritual values in American
life obscures the exertions of acquisitive interests upon government and public media for their own selfish interests. Lutherans
have not ignored the contention of Karl Barth that American
capitalism as well as Russian Communism threatens the integrity
of Christianity.[121] Just as the commitment to spiritual values may
become corrupted, similarly freedom may be either creative or
destructive. Positively, political freedom fortifies the Christian
view of the dignity of man, but freedom absolutized becomes
alienation from God and is consequently demonic. Kantonen correctly points out that Luther struggled for a free conscience unfettered by the Roman Catholic Church in order to subject it to
a truer freedom, subject it to God as discovered in the gospel.
Luther did not view human equality as egalitarianism, but as a
common state of original sin and the necessity of God's grace.[122]

The tendency to deny the divine ground of life, as the leaders
of the French Revolution did, always lurks under the surface of
American political ideals. At its worst, this would mean the sub-
stitution of a religion of democracy for the Christian faith. The
secular public school is an arena for this conflict: "Shall the political order in a democratic community acknowledge the sovereignty of God and seek to promote the kind of character and attitudes that grow out of this acknowledgment or shall it accept the
cult of democracy as its religion? This is the issue in the present
controversy concerning the teaching of religion in public schools.
Some kind of common faith is obviously needed, if only to prevent the complete demonization of youth."[123] Ruff insists that
separation of church and state should be maintained, but should
not lead to public neutrality toward God. Instruction in the
Christian faith cannot be part of the public school curriculum,
but neglect of religion, in other disciplines, implying its unim-
portance, makes the schools "servants of No-God." Ruff, for one,
advocates some means of permitting religious instruction in the
public schools, but under the direction of the church.[124]

Although acknowledging the value of Paul Blanshard's criticism of Roman Catholic power in American life, Ruff contends

that the warm response to Mr. Blanshard also reveals the lack of understanding by the American public of the danger of secularism. Describing Blanshard as a "secularist who wishes to banish all churches from public affairs," Ruff also criticizes the organization, Protestants and Other Americans United for Separation of Church and State, for "adopting the secularist position on exclusion of religion from the public schools."[125] Given the important issues in American life today, "Protestants are allies of the Catholic Church in resisting the devouring totalitarian state, whether it is communist or secularist. The Roman Catholic Church has maintained a Christian faith center at the heart of much of Western civilization."[126] Ruff seeks to make clear, however, that persuasion, not pressure, must be the means used by Protestants.

Although the separation of church and state cannot be absolutized by Lutherans, the principle has helped prevent totalitarianism in America. The state, whether guided by a political or economic center, tends to seize power over the subordinate groups in society. Ruff ascribes the quest by the state for control of the church to its need for religious sanction of absolute power. The political leader "takes possession of the church as the ultimate necessity in maintaining himself in power. There must be a power center to prevent anarchy and achieve justice."[127] In Europe, totalitarianism has taken blatant forms, but in America the principle of separation of church and state has often spearheaded a totalitarian leveling in the name of conformity and secularism. If there is any pernicious tendency in Lutheranism, present-day theologians agree, it has been the apparent willingness to support state absolutism in return for the guaranteed spiritual life of the church, but they are now determined to resist it.

Separation of church and state also harmonizes with Lutheranism against the alleged theocratic tendencies of Roman Catholicism and the Calvinist tradition. Whereas Lutheranism yields to the ruler under ordinary circumstances the right to determine policy for a just social order, Roman Catholicism in medieval Europe and Puritanism in colonial America regarded themselves as divinely appointed guardians of political affairs. The latter derived its theocratic ideal from the Old Testament, but for Lutherans this confused the law and the gospel, the earthly and spiritual regiments. Though no hard and fast rule on the relation of church and state exists, they must "be in constant tension, neither subduing the other. There is no way out of this competition for authority as long as we are children both of the slave and of the free woman, and live in the city of God and also the city of the world. This is the dilemma of church and state. Americans have worked a long time at this problem, and at one time were nearer a solution than people had ever been before. Big problems don't usually stay solved. We must be aware that increasing danger looms ahead in the American separation of church and state."[128]

American Lutheran thinkers recognize the ambiguity of church-state separation and distinguish themselves by their critical attitude toward it.

Lutheranism and Political Responsibility

The most significant aspect of revisionist Lutheran thinking on church-state matters lies in the responsibility of the church for modern society. The complexity of today's problems often demands activity in the political order if the church is to achieve its objectives. Most Lutherans looked negatively at the original Social Gospel, because the theological presuppositions of Liberalism so patently contradicted the religious views of Lutheranism; but the contemporary theological movement called Neo-Orthodoxy in its American form advocates strong social concern, while appropriating views of God, man, and salvation more consistent with those of the Reformation.[129] Lutherans open to ecumenical influences no longer fear that a social concern will neglect the basic evangelical task of the church. Lutheran thinkers have even influenced current attempts outside the confession to provide a rationale for social action springing from justification by faith, individual and social sin, and the concept of vocation,[130] considered by their advocates an antidote to the vestiges of legalism, individualism, and rationalism remaining from Liberalism.

Two significant contributions have been the symposia, *What Lutherans Are Thinking,* by theological professors from all but one American synod, and *Christian Social Responsibility,* by theologians of the United Lutheran Church. Both reflect the changed and concerned outlook under discussion. The former volume justifies this attitude in the following words:

> The obligation of the church to the state is part of its total obligation to society. As the church stimulates thinking in the area of Christian ethics as applied to practical, everyday life as the way of applying the leaven to society, the problems of state will also be affected. The gospel enunciated from the pulpit and the Bible *has* a place in the market place and the halls of

government. The legislator sweating under the tug and pull of pressure groups in a democracy needs the clear light of Christian ethics and the best scientific knowledge available in the areas of politics, economics, and sociology to determine how to cast his vote so that the state might serve the best interests of its people.[131]

If American Lutherans have evaded the opportunity to exercise Christian guidance in the political order, both symposia sound a vigorous call to rectify the matter.

One of the most important interpreters of both Luther and the new Lutheran ethic is President Edgar M. Carlson of Gustavus Adolphus College. The only American to give a major address at the meeting of the Lutheran World Federation in 1957, Carlson used his forum to expound the ethical implications of the Lutheran concept of the two regiments.[132] Obviously influenced by the Swedish emphasis on the demonic, justice, vocation, and love, Carlson insists that the state not only coerces the unruly, but no less pertinently maintains a just order, the power for coercion providing the means for achieving justice. In fact, the real end of the instruments of coercion is justice, punishment of the wicked constituting a defense of the law that defines justice. Carlson is convinced that the church should play a significant part in defining the laws by which justice is expressed, for the church "is the custodian of the law as well as of the gospel. The church alone knows the Lawgiver because it alone knows the Father of our Lord Jesus Christ."[133] Such activity by the church must be generalized, however, for differences arise even among men genuinely committed to justice. The church cannot identify itself with any particular program or party, or pretend to give them divine sanction. On an issue where the government has violated or threatens civil freedom, the church may take clear and positive action, such as passive non-co-operation or an active effort to substitute order and freedom for oppressive domination. Such action occurs in the name of true order and honest government and in behalf of the common welfare, not as a private action.[134]

A. D. Mattson, a professor at the Augustana Theological Seminary, finds that the social pronouncements of the ecumenical bodies provide legitimate guidance for Christian action. He points to the 1932 Social Creed of the Federal Council of Churches as illustrating "what it means to apply Christianity to the social order. It points to the kind of world which is possible if the Christian faith were seriously applied to the problems of society."[135] The Lutheran Church, he argues, has rescued many victims from sin, but it has done far less to prevent people from falling into sin. Because environment helps influence character, society can tear down more than the church can build up unless the church exerts its influence to better social conditions.[136]

In a paper read before a seminar of the National Lutheran Council, Franklin Sherman summed up a typical American appropriation of the Swedish concern for justice.

> Thus justice is the form love takes in the public order . . . [Christianity] does not overlook the context of community which makes . . . freedom meaningful, nor does it forget that social action frequently is needful precisely in order to secure or to protect the freedom of the individual. Conversely, Christianity views positively the role of government in promoting public welfare, and it acknowledges the necessity in a society such as our own for large-scale social organization. . . . Thus we may sum up the Christian's pathway of approach to questions of public policy in terms of two formulations: *faith active in love*, and *love seeking justice*. But what, more precisely is justice?

> Thus for the Protestant Christian, the search for justice is precisely that—a search, a process of inquiry which must be forever carried on. The Christian is impelled by love to be concerned with public policy. His faith contributes certain broad perspectives, and it does rule out extreme alternatives. . . . Within these boundaries, the Christian stands on the same footing with those who share his passion for the public welfare, participating in the great debate on social philosophies and political programs. The Christian should be able to bring to discussion of policy questions considerable wisdom about man; but he has no set of detailed answers packaged in advance.[137]

This concern has gained practical expression through the increasing tendency of Lutheran bodies, led by the Augustana Synod and the United Lutheran Church, to speak on issues with political implications. The most effective force in promoting this kind of interest has been the National Lutheran Council, which includes in its membership all but the most conservative synods.

Recognizing the hesitation on theological grounds of many Lutherans to associate too closely with non-Lutheran bodies, the NLC has attempted to provide an agency through which Lutherans can learn from each other and speak with a united Lutheran voice on problems of common concern. The leadership of the NLC is strongly influenced by the criticisms of traditional Lutheranism. Its Committee on Social Trends, which meets annually, formulates statements for approval by the NLC on such issues as foreign policy, the social consequences of industrial development, advertising, and the role of religion in American life. While recognizing the potentially partisan implications of taking positions, the NLC feels obligated, nevertheless, to speak out of a context of ethical conviction.

Lutheranism and Roman Catholicism

In recent years the attitude toward Roman Catholicism, which is usually reflected in certain church-state problems, has moved from opposition to ambivalence in Lutheran circles. In a study of the United Lutheran Church, Harold Haas points out that the literature of the denomination was almost unanimous in its opposition to a Roman Catholic for the presidency of the United States in 1928, an American ambassador to the Vatican, and federal aid to parochial schools, because of "the dangerous and false teaching of the Roman Catholic Church concerning the relationship of Church and State."[138] One finds little or no change on the latter two issues, but in the compaign of 1960, twenty Lutheran theologians, apparently concerned over the uncritical residue of anti-Catholicism, as well as the association of many Lutherans with the Republican Party, publicly endorsed Mr. Kennedy.[139] Fredrik A. Schiotz, president of the Evangelical Lutheran Church, questioned this action, saying that a pastor's "concern for righteousness in the community may be better exercised by speaking out on questions of human rights and on moral and ethical issues," rather than unduly influencing his parishioners by publicly supporting candidates for office.[140]

The significance of such a dispute within Lutheranism lies in its potential effects on a reorientation of attitude toward certain church-state issues, where the church's stand was once obvious —such as, opposition to Roman Catholicism. The abandonment of outworn stereotypes of Catholicism was strengthened in Lutheranism by the appointment of a commission within the Lutheran World Federation to study the nature of modern

Catholicism, led first by the distinguished Danish scholar, K. E. Skydsgaard,[141] and subsequently by George Lindbeck of Yale University.

Lutheran leaders influenced by recent currents of thought continue to lack clarity about the precise directions of the church's relation to the state, though they agree on the over-all theological framework for approaching this area. But on an official level the most noticeable development is the consciousness that questions should be raised which point toward action by individuals or by the denomination, alone and in co-operation with the ecumenical movement. The traditional passivity in Lutheranism toward the political order is changing more rapidly than at any time in American history.

The Missouri Synod

In the Missouri Synod, one of the most conservative branches of American Lutheranism, signs of change are not as apparent. This basically German group has escaped the Scandinavian interest in problems of justice and law, and, not belonging to ecumenical groups, it does not accept any of their social pronouncements. An article by Theodore Hoyer illustrates the views of the Missouri Synod quite well.[142] Like the denomination as a whole, Hoyer attributes considerable authority to the Lutheran confessions, as well as to Luther's views themselves. While tending to describe government in terms that better apply to the Hellenistic or Reformation world than the twentieth century, he deeply appreciates one aspect of American life, separation of church and state; had Luther been able to do so, "he would have organized a Church like ours. . . . The freedom of the Church, lost under Constantine, was not even regained in the Reformation. The Church of Germany—and of all Protestant countries of Europe—became, and to this day has remained, a part of the State's machinery. Not until the United States of America was established did the world see a land in which this right and natural and Scriptural relation between Church and State exists —separation."[143] Separation guarantees for the Missouri Synod the freedom from political interference which it holds necessary to preserve its distinctive witness. The Bible, according to the Missouri Synod, forbids neither church control of the state nor state control of the church, but God intended the two normally to stand side by side without interference.

What are the limits of political authority? The state, Hoyer says, may allow what God does not permit, but it must not command what God has forbidden. If one is commanded, for example, to murder under other conditions than war, then one should not obey, but suffer the consequences. In addition, the state cannot interfere in church affairs, or act in complete violation of morality, else Christians may have to act in opposition: "Governments have not only rights, but duties and responsibilities; when they totally fail to meet these, there may come a time when Christians may join with their fellow citizens to call the government to account and bring about reform. *When* that time comes is a question which must be considered and decided in every individual instance."[144]

Whereas the Lutheran revisionists put great stress on the involvement of the church in society, Hoyer insists that the church serves the state best by tending to its proper business, which does not include politics. As citizens, of course, Christians should fulfill the responsibilities accorded to them by the Constitution. The pastor as a citizen will take note of political issues and act according to his best conviction, but the affairs of the state do not touch his office as servant of the church. All citizens should pay taxes and vote intelligently by informing themselves of issues and the qualities of the candidates.

On some matters the church is involved. "The Church, through her ministers will enlighten the conscience of members on matters before the public as to what is right and wrong; encourage them to keep informed on what kind of laws are being considered by the legislature; if good, to support them; if not good, to oppose."[145] Such an issue would be the attempted justification by the government of Sunday closing laws on religious grounds, for the state cannot enforce God's laws, though such a measure might be defended as a day of public rest. Trying to avoid politics by distinguishing the political realm from more patently religious issues, the Missouri Synod anomalously succumbs to potential partisan involvement because all supposedly moral and religious issues tend to have political implications.

More than any other Protestant denomination, the Missouri Synod has promoted denominational schools. Unlike most Roman Catholics, however, it opposes public support of its parochial schools as a possible prelude to political interference.

The denomination is divided on the problem of Bible reading in public schools, though the Board of Parish Education favors reading without comment as the safest, but a clearly inadequate, compromise between the undesired extremes of secularization and religious instruction in the public schools.[146]

Because the Missouri Synod holds a view of education intimately associated with religion, its attitudes on church-state problems related to education differ from many other American Protestants. It upholds by inference a moderate view of separation of church and state. The Missouri Synod officially opposed the *McCollum* decision forbidding religious teaching in the public schools. The Regular Convention of the Synod said in 1950: "Unless the Church is given an opportunity to fulfill in part its commission in the context of the school, it is greatly hampered in the performance of its duty toward the children who can attend only the public schools. This is not to advocate the imposition of so-called sectarian religious instruction upon the public schools. It does advocate that the church be given an opportunity to bring religious instruction to its children in connection with the daily school program."[147]

According to Alan Jahsmann, while fear of Roman Catholic advance strongly conditions the Synod's attitude toward government support of its schools, it accepts secondary or indirect aid, while opposing direct government subsidies.[148] In many communities the problem of secondary aid becomes a Protestant-Catholic conflict, but the Missouri Synod seeks and accepts benefits such as library service, lunch and health programs, and transportation. The implication here for an understanding of Protestant church-state tactics is important, for it shows that Protestant groups like the Missouri Synod which advocate religious schools may have a policy on certain issues closer to that of Roman Catholicism than that of their fellow Protestants. The determining factor in both cases appears to be self-interest: those who oppose such welfare benefits get nothing from them, whereas those who favor them do. Both sides cloak their action under a smoke screen of statements on the nature of church-state separation without realizing their own self-involvement.

The Missouri Synod is not totally resistant to changes in Lutheran thought, and its most important theological publication, *The Concordia Theological Monthly,* has published articles by individuals quite obviously influenced by their fellow Lutherans in other branches of the confession. One, Ernest B. Koenker,[149] insists that the loss of interaction between church and state in Lutheranism, symbolized by a growth of secularism in political life, can be traced to misinterpretation of both Luther and the authoritative confessions. Citing Berggrav with approval, Koenker argues that temporal and spiritual orders are unified in their common Creator and Lord and the responsible vocation of the Christian as citizen. The confessions, he says, were designed to disentangle the church from the political concerns which corrupted it in the Middle Ages and to preserve the purity of the gospel, but at the same time they uphold the ordination of the temporal order by God and open the possibility of disobedience by affirming the existence of a law superior to the state which Christians must follow. A. M. Rehwinkel[150] insists that the Christian in a democracy has a special responsibility to form public opinion in the cause of good government, justice, and righteousness. Christians should be the conscience of the world, opposing injustice, foreign imperialism, and war.

The Missouri Synod has co-operated with other Lutheran groups in explorations of a common theological framework for church-state problems, and with the National Lutheran Council in annual seminars on "The Church and National Life," in which theologians, pastors, and public officials have probed the implications of the vocation of public life. Although one can place the various Lutheran groups on a scale ranging from the United Lutheran Church to the Missouri Synod, moving from liberalism to conservatism, the fact that individuals compose these denominations makes simplistic generalizations impossible. All Lutheran groups contain individuals who have absorbed the new directions in Lutheran thought and others who maintain traditional ways. Ultimately, one can only affirm that Lutheranism is changing, though at varying rates in its different branches.

Lutheran Contributions to a Protestant Church-State Theory

Lutheranism contributes most significantly to a Protestant church-state perspective by its attempt to interpret such problems theologically. A theological outlook has obvious dangers, for applications of the theology become so associated with the period in which they were formulated that they become irrelevant for later times; but Luther's legacy includes certain fundamental principles integral to Protestantism that are not necessarily conditioned by his own particular presentation of them. These are theocentricity, in which church and state are viewed as two expressions of God's creation and providence; the distortion of both regiments by the demonic and the need for Christians to sense and criticize this; and the response of the Christian to life in the world through love and vocation. At the time of the Reformation nearly all theologians and leaders held these concepts, but because Christians in America today do not think theologically, they have almost disappeared here.

Lacking a theological perspective in church-state problems, Protestants may approach such issues from another, perhaps a secular, context and set of presuppositions. When Protestants speak of church-state separation, their views usually stem from the rationalistic outlook of men like Jefferson and Madison or of twentieth-century secularism; on particular problems they act from anti-Catholicism or self-interest. Protestantism in the twentieth century has managed to relate Christian convictions to a variety of social, political, and economic problems, but this is not true of a different kind of political problem such as the role of religion in education and public life, or public support of religious charitable activities. Here one finds a hiatus between conviction and practice, a lack of perspective by which Protestants can rise above legal or emotional justifications.

Theocentricity would encourage Protestants to deny an absolute separation between the religious and political dimensions of life. The association between church and state would be expressed both corporately and individually, corporately because God has founded and rules through both to achieve the salvation and well-being of men, individually because the Christian is both church member and citizen.

Theocentricity rejects the humanization of church or state, which is the prevalent view among American churches. Church and state signify more than the corporate religious and political impulses of individuals. Although men on the surface do join together to form religious and political institutions, Lutheran theocentrism emphasizes a far more ultimate significance, the providential sovereignty of God, behind these actions. God acts in the state even through political instruments that do not acknowledge him.

Lutheranism offers a valuable antidote to the parochialism of American church-state analyses because of its experiences with Communism, especially in Eastern Germany, where the church has sought to see behind the ostensibly anti-Christian government the benevolence of God and to interpret Christian suffering as a punishment for the sins of the church during the Nazi period. A church-state theory that included the Iron Curtain churches and could recognize the actions of God among the godless would have been forced to probe beyond the provincialism of the American situation.

From the variety of traditional Protestant ethical perspectives, individuals would seek to ascertain the will of God and to interpret it for both state and church in their particular circumstances. American concern for social and political action, which has often proceeded from a basically humanistic understanding of Christianity and the responsibility of Christians to "do good," would gain in theological depth through emphasis on life as response to the will of God, and in realism through an awareness of the persistent and demonic tendencies toward injustice and egoism that inevitably frustrate man's hopes for society and the state. Lutheranism and contemporary Protestantism have helped each other, the former recapturing Luther's sense of responsibility for events around him, the latter envisioning its social responsibility in theological terms consistent with the Reformation.

The Lutheran emphasis on participation in corporate structures through a flexibly interpreted attitude of love would help reform the individualism and legalism of much American Protestant ethics. The theory of vocation, because it is associated with man's responsibility and has long, if distorted, roots in American Protestantism, may offer a more effective appeal to the American churches for relating their religious convictions to church-state problems than the theocentricity which lies behind vocation in Luther's outlook.

Luther's view on the differences between spiritual and temporal regiments leaves much to be desired, especially his understanding of the functions of government. His minimalist approach to government is too conditioned by traditional biblical and medieval views for ready application to the United States. On the other hand, his realistic grasp of the essential character of government as its possession of coercive power, and the necessity for citizens to obey relatively unjust laws, can well apply to adverse political situations that Christians encounter and can also serve to educate Americans who tend to understand government in rather libertarian terms.

The contemporary intellectual leadership of American Lutheranism clearly senses the need for revision of traditional Lutheran concepts of government and political responsibility. Perhaps it needs to criticize even more radically its dependence on the historically conditioned perspectives of the Bible and Luther. But a further difficulty is the generally conservative character of its membership in both religion and politics. Centered in sections of the country that are strongholds of individualism, many Lutherans oppose governmental activity for conservative political reasons, but justify it by appeal to traditional Lutheran views.

Despite the severity of Luther's estimate of the state, Lutheranism plays a significant role in Protestantism by stressing the limitations of the state in comparison with the church. The fact remains that the exercise of government requires a quite different ethic from that of the New Testament, whether one calls it compromise or an application of Christian love to problems unanticipated by Jesus and the early church. No political system can be rationalized into the kingdom of God. At the same time Lutheranism offers a consistent means by which a Christian can hold office and engage in political action without justifying himself in non-Christian categories.

Lutheranism favors a moderate separation between church and state, principally because of its theocentrism, rather than from social concern, though the latter is now beginning to play some role in Lutheran thought. Thus Lutherans join critics of organizations like P.O.A.U. whose ideology denies any significant relationship between church and state. Lutherans also sense, because of their experiences in countries with established churches, such as Germany and Scandinavia, that the American system of separation is only one of several possible solutions to the relation of church and state, and that like all systems it has strong and weak points.

The moderate attitude of many leading Lutherans toward Roman Catholicism may help produce a more creative approach to church-state problems. At the opposite extreme, however, many in the Missouri Synod hold with Luther that the pope is Antichrist, a theological judgment which cannot help but mold their perspective. Lutherans have not leapt to action whenever a church-state issue loomed, especially when Roman Catholicism was involved. This traditionally stemmed from disinterest in political problems and a feeling that the church should respond only when its own integrity is threatened by the state. But Lutherans, especially those of the Missouri Synod, have not been preoccupied with a defense of the public school against religious schools, as a great many other Protestants have.

II Christian Life
Without Political Compromise:
The Anabaptists and
Mennonites

Anabaptism

Christians of the Anabaptist-Mennonite tradition belong to one of history's most misunderstood religious groups. In the sixteenth century they suffered tragic persecution, and even today their successors continue to encounter opprobrium for their Mennonite nonresistance, Hutterite communitarianism, and inadequate Amish rural schools. Protestantism bears no stain more serious than the acquiescence and even encouragement of Luther, Zwingli, and Calvin in the persecution of these innocent fellow Christians by the "sword" of the temporal authority.

Many accounts of Reformation history have completely omitted the Anabaptists. Some may have felt that to reconstruct the views of a disparate left wing would be a wasted effort. Most historians today, however, realize that Anabaptism is "a major expression of the religious movement of the sixteenth century. It is one that is as distinctive as Lutheranism, Calvinism, and Anglicanism, and is perhaps comparably significant in the rise of modern Christianity."[1]

This study of Protestant church-state views focuses upon that segment of the sixteenth-century radicals from which the present-day American Mennonites and related denominations descended. First appearing under the leadership of Conrad Grebel in Switzerland in 1523, those usually called Evangelical Anabaptists gained their most eloquent spokesman in Menno Simons who was active in Northern Germany after 1536. They differed from three other groups among the left wing: Spiritualists or mystics such as Hans Denck and Sebastian Franck; rationalists like Michael Servetus and Faustus Socinus; and fighting eschatologists, of whom Thomas Müntzer and the Münster Communists are the best examples. The Evangelical Anabaptists upheld a central role for biblical authority, in contrast with the first two groups, and unlike the latter, did not emphasize eschatology and were nonresistant.

One can legitimately isolate the Evangelicals from the rest of their more unacceptable brethren on the left wing, inasmuch as the contemporary Mennonites stem from this group alone. A former school of thought held that the nonresistant Anabaptists developed from an original violent chiliasm. According to H. R. Niebuhr, "From violent revolution the path of development led through stubborn non-resistance and unyielding assertion by non-assertion of the principles of equality and love to an accommodating quietism."[2]

Modern Mennonite historians have effectively refuted this view by tracing the consistency and continuity of Evangelical Anabaptism from its inception in Switzerland. In 1524 Grebel admonished Thomas Müntzer, who also believed in adult baptism, to cease defending war:

> Moreover, the gospel and its adherents are not to be protected by the sword, nor are they thus to protect themselves, which, as we learn from our brother, is thy opinion and practice. True Christian believers are sheep among wolves, sheep for the slaughter; they must be baptized in anguish and affliction . . . tried with fire and must reach the fatherland of eternal rest, not by killing their bodily, but by mortifying their spiritual enemies. Neither do they use worldly sword or war, since all killing has ceased with them—unless, indeed, we should still be of the old law.[3]

The present-day Mennonites, whose scholarly examination of their tradition has made them without peers among denominational historians, correctly insist on the integrity of their tradition since the Reformation, although at times they place insufficient stress on the advocacy of adult baptism by groups whose theological views were otherwise different, but who can legitimately be called Anabaptist. The term "Evangelical Anabaptist" denotes then a particular movement which, while advocating adult baptism, was not basically rationalist, spiritualist, or eschatological.

The Secondary Significance of Baptism

Part of the problem lies in the fact that Anabaptist insistence on believers' baptism stemmed from other theological convictions; in fact, the name "Anabaptist" was applied as an epithet by their enemies, they themselves preferring to be known simply as *Brüder* (brothers).[4] Their principal objection to the term lay in its implication that one was baptized twice, whereas they held that only the baptism founded on mature confession of faith was valid, that infant baptism did not constitute a real baptism.

The problem of baptism arose from a church-state issue. Infant baptism was upheld in the sixteenth century by the *Volkskirchen*, cultural churches, which had prevailed ever since the time of the Christian triumph over the Hellenistic world. Although rationalized on biblical and theological grounds, baptism actually symbolized the common religious and political associations into which one was born, denoting participation in the state church and subjecting the citizen to religious obligations that guaranteed some degree of control over him. Church and state were so intertwined that the major Reformers were unable to follow through the implications of salvation by grace and faith by relating baptism to one's responsive personal encounter with God, rather than to birth in a particular church and state. With flimsy arguments the Reformers continued the religious sanction of citizenship which the rulers exploited, and baptism remained, as in Roman Catholicism, an occasion of objective grace. The Anabaptists, on the other hand, who also believed in salvation by personal faith and response, saw that infant baptism had no existential significance for the child. They did not, however, suffer persecution and death because of a legalistic emphasis on baptism. Their opponents in church and government, who feared and resented them for various reasons, made use of a Roman law, directed against the fifth-century heretical sect of Donatists, that rebaptizers could be killed.

Discipleship

The Anabaptists agreed with the major Reformers on nearly all theological issues. An examination of their confessions of faith does not reveal major differences, since they upheld the orthodox Apostles' Creed and the Nicene and Chalcedonian formulas. Like Luther and Calvin they interpreted the Reformation as a rediscovery of biblical authority, and at the heart of their outlook lay a vigorous insistence on justification by faith. For example, Dirck Phillips, one of the Dutch Anabaptists, said that "every Christian has sin and must confess himself a sinner, that he may humble himself under the mighty hand of God and pray the Lord for His mercy. Thus the Scripture remains true and unbroken which puts all men under condemnation and reproves them as sinners; but sin is not imputed to Christians, but has been forgiven them through the innocent death of Jesus Christ, and is covered with His everlasting love, by which He offered Himself up for us for an everlasting atonement for our sins. . . ."[5]

Although interpreters disagree on the focal tenet of Anabaptism, the most convincing evidence points to Discipleship (*Nachfolge*).[6] The Anabaptists wished to commit themselves to the example and teaching of the Lord Jesus Christ, who not only saved men from their sins but also pointed to the way of the kingdom. Although recognizing justification by faith, they felt that the New Testament also spelled out a new way of life, and that the faithful should manifest it. Luther, who emphasized salvation by grace alone (*sola gratia*) to the extent of a polemic against works, nevertheless regarded the Christian life as a loving, spontaneous response of the redeemed person, and especially in his writings on the Ten Commandments found a framework for indicating more specifically what he meant. Luther held, however, that while the Sermon on the Mount governs individual attitudes toward one's own interests, the demands of political life require a different sort of expression of love. Against this, the Anabaptists took the call to discipleship so seriously that no social or political considerations could condition the following of Jesus, and they believed that by the grace of God one could be such a disciple in the present world. The Anabaptists represented a different kind of religious experience from that of Luther: their passion was directed toward being disciples of Christ, Luther's was to achieve salvation from sin by finding a merciful God. It is on this basis that Menno Simons could criticize the major Reformers by saying: "They are not the true church of Christ who merely boast of His name. But those are the true church of Christ who are truly converted, who are born from above of God, who are of a regenerated mind and, by the operation of the Holy Spirit from the hearing of the divine word, have become children of God, who obey Him, and live unblamably in His holy commandments and according to His holy will, all their days, or after their calling."[7]

Luther probably would have agreed, for he assumed that the believer, though a sinner, would become "a Christ to his neighbor." In "On Secular Authority" he argued that piety obviates the necessity of political coercion for Christians. What seems at stake here is the nature of discipleship—the Anabaptists arguing for the unconditional response of the believer to certain key elements of the New Testament ethic. Because some of these elements were associated with political attitudes and were the very principles that Luther felt were inconsistent with the needs of corporate life in this present demonic age, the Anabaptists appeared in the eyes of their contemporaries as subverters of established modes of Christian political responsibility. But to the Anabaptists the major Reformers seemed to have hedged on the implications of the rediscovered faith: they had not gone far enough.

What did being a disciple mean? The Evangelical Anabaptists did not believe in moral perfection. Life continued to be a struggle between the impulse toward regeneration and the downward tug of the old Adam, a tension from which man could not escape. The Anabaptists denied that they boasted of sinlessness. But, in his "Reply to False Accusations," Menno Simons argued that the nominal Christian commits sin with relish, while the real Christian fears sin and fights daily against those lapses in conduct into which he inevitably falls. When a man is truly converted, he cannot avoid the claims of discipleship nor return willingly to wicked ways.[8] The Anabaptist emphasis is on fulfilling God's will, rather than one's failure to do so. The "living and quickening power of God in our hearts" molds a new creature so that he changes "from unrighteousness to righteousness, from evil to good, from carnality to spirituality, from the earthly to the heavenly, from the wicked nature of Adam to the good nature of Jesus Christ,"[9] even though he continues to sin.

The Church as the Locus of Discipleship

The Anabaptists thought of discipleship not only individually, but corporately. Their view of the church as a group of disciples committed to a distinctive—and even radical—ethic inevitably produced tension with the state, for the established churches of the sixteenth century could not realistically demand of all citizens the way of life the Anabaptists considered axiomatic for genuine Christians.

In the sixteenth century everyone in Western society, except such avowed non-Christians as the Jews, was considered a Christian. The Reformers knew that most people were not in fact Christians, so they developed a concept, implicit in Augustine, distinguishing between the visible and the invisible church, the latter embracing the real Christians among those who were formal church members. To include everyone in an ostensible church relationship, on the other hand, held obvious advantages. It gave the religious and political leaders an opportunity to inculcate the populace with a degree of divinely sanctioned morality; it enabled the ministry to present the gospel and possibly effect a genuine conversion; it took into consideration the internal character of religious faith and did not presume to judge its quality by external forms of testimony and piety.

Roman Catholicism had rejected the concept of the invisible church in favor of the visible institutional structure and a priesthood which mediated grace to the baptized. The Anabaptists, against the other Reformers, also denied the invisible church, but in contrast to Roman Catholicism, they defined the church as the community of regenerated believers.[10] The visible structure, the *Volkskirche*, accepted by both Catholics and Protestants as an essential adjunct of God's relation to man, they looked upon as no church at all.

Therefore, he who truly considered himself a Christian abjured his association with the politically sponsored *Volkskirche* and joined the community of those whose religious experiences denoted their conversion. There they formed a brotherhood in which they could practice the virtues of regeneration such as joy, love, forgiveness, and humility. In the sixteenth century as in the present, the state church lacked a sense of *koinonia*, fellowship, a defect which has often led to the formation of pietistic cells within the larger formal church. The experience of mutuality, a common sharing, which only a small group can have, marked the Anabaptist congregations from the beginning. Robert Friedmann points out that the relationship with one's brethren was as essential to Anabaptism as the relationship with God. "In fact, the belief prevails that one cannot come to God . . . except as one comes to Him together with one's brother."[11] This assumption of all Anabaptists was expressed in its most extreme form among the followers of Jacob Hutter, who insisted on communitarian living and sharing of goods as essential elements in the restoration of the church.

The integrity of the church was maintained through the ban, by which the congregation expelled unbelieving or sinful brethren.[12] The use of the ban emphasized the purity of the church, in contrast with the toleration of religious laxity by the state church.

The Separation of the Church From the State

The Anabaptists, by holding that the real church was constituted by a separated group who, upon repentance, justification, and regeneration, underwent a genuine baptism for the first time, made quite clear that they did not consider the members of the state church real Christians. Association with the state was at best sub-Christian, whereas the church represented the kingdom of God. This despised group thus became the first Protestant advocates of a separation of church and state, not on rational, pragmatic, or political grounds, but as a consequence of a theology of discipleship and the church as a community of disciples. They only wanted to keep the church apart from the state; they did not have any theory of separation. The controlling interest is the church, the consequence for the state only an afterthought. In sectarian fashion they saw the church as a voluntary, internally organized group, in which all members, equally Christian, determined the nature of Christian thought and life; and because of this understanding, they could not tolerate the intrusion of the state in the internal life of the congregation.

Reinforcing the negative evaluation of the state and its church, the Anabaptists used a two-kingdom concept like that of Luther, but with sharply different implications. The fourth article of the Schleitheim Confession of Faith (1527), sets forth the grounds for a separated church: "A separation shall be made from the evil and from the wickedness which the devil planted in the world; in this manner, simply that we shall not have fellowship with them [the wicked] and not run with them in the multitude of their abominations. . . . For truly all creatures are in but two classes, good and bad, believing and unbelieving, darkness and light, the world and those who [have come] out of the world, God's temple and idols, Christ and Belial; and none can have part with the other."[13]

All men are divided into two kingdoms, that of God, and that of the devil, in continuous conflict. The sense of dialectic characteristic of Luther, in which both church and state are the battlegrounds of God and Satan, is altered, so that the church becomes the center of God's activity, while the rest of the world is under the control of the demonic. The church is separated because the children of God's kingdom should have nothing to do with the wicked. By definition all those not in the believers' church are citizens of the kingdom of darkness, since all creatures follow either Christ or Belial. As Harold Bender has pointed out, the fact that "the church and state join in persecuting the true church is only one more bit of evidence of the wickedness of the world order."[14]

The Origins of Anabaptism

Anabaptism had its origin in these issues of church and state. Prior to 1523 Conrad Grebel was associated with Zwingli, the Reformer of Zurich. Late in that year, Zwingli concluded, despite earlier views to the contrary, that his reformation could best develop as the city council, which he regarded as a Christian body sympathetic to reform, saw fit. Grebel disagreed, feeling that Zwingli was subordinating the church to the state and inhibiting pressing reforms until the political authority, in its compromising way, decided to initiate them. Despite agreement by the spiritual leaders on the scriptural prescriptions of true religious belief and practice, they would have to be postponed, perhaps indefinitely, because the church could not act freely without political approval.

At the second disputation of Zurich in October, 1523, when Grebel insisted that they should end abuses of the Mass forthwith and Zwingli replied that the civil officials should make the decision, Simon Stumpf articulated the view that animated the forming of the first Anabaptist religious conventicle: "Master Ulrich, you do not have the right to place the decision on this matter in the hands of my lords, for the decision has already been made, the Spirit of God decides." Stumpf added that if the officials followed a course contrary to the will of God, "I will ask Christ for His Spirit, and I will preach and act against it."[15] Lack of a mandate to proceed according to the will of God within the structure of the state church logically led to the formation of a voluntary, free, separated church, where Christians could act without hindrance.

The Anabaptists set out to re-create the church of the New

Testament within such conventicles. Franklin Littell has demon-
strated that their program was one of "restitution" as well as
"reform," for they held that at some point in history, usually the
reign of Constantine, the church fell.[16] The most obvious sign of
the fallen church was its union with the state, which prevented
the church from determining its way of life according to Scripture and represented a compromise inconsistent with the days of
the martyrs. Georg Witzel illustrated this yearning to emulate the
pattern of the primitive church: "Which is the true [Church]?
The ancient, apostolic. My wish, my yearning is that the world
may go back to a true apostolic church. The *Acts* and the writings of the Great [Church] Fathers and ancient Bishops show the
way on which we must go back to it. The apostolic church flour-
ished to the time of Constantine. From then on it was perverted,
because the Bishops went over to the world."[17]

Their program for restoring the primitive church featured not
only membership for believers alone and a separation from the
world, but a pronouncedly different way of life.

The Christian Life

Anabaptist ethical principles may be divided into two categories: those internal to the church itself and those with implications
for their relationship with the state. The former are not too relevant for this study, except that by their practice the Anabaptists
and their followers marked themselves as a peculiar people and
incurred the hostility of their neighbors. They derived these
characteristics not only from the Bible, but from the view that the
kingdom of God differs from the kingdom of the world. Various
Anabaptist groups have practiced ordinances associated with the
New Testament church such as footwashing, the holy kiss,
anointing with oil, and the wearing of veils by women. In addition, many Anabaptists have consciously attempted to distinguish
themselves from the allurements and luxury of the sin-dominated
world through simple living and unadorned clothing.

The elements of the Anabaptist ethic which created the most
resentment, however, were those with political consequences, such
as their refusal to hold office, to fight, or to take an oath. The fact
that Luther willingly modified the demands of the Christian
ethic on these points indicates the seriousness with which men of
the sixteenth century upheld certain axioms of political behavior
and correspondingly feared threats to them. The Anabaptist refusal to hold office implied that those who did were not Chris-

tians, and the denial of war and the oath upset established modes of assuring external peace and internal popular loyalty. Roman Catholicism had provided an outlet in monasticism by which passionate Christians could express themselves, while order and government maintained their sanctity. Now the Anabaptists seemed to imply that being a Christian and providing for social order were incompatible.

The Sanctity of Government

It is interesting to note, however, that in spite of their assumption that the devil rules the "world," the Anabaptists held a fundamentally positive view of government. They agreed with Luther that the instrument of the non-Christian kingdom was a sign of God's providence. The author of the best study of the Anabaptist view of the state says, "All Anabaptist discussions on the nature of the state commence with the significant affirmation that the office of government is ordained by God."[18] Only one example need be cited, from the *Chronicle* of the Hutterites:

> Our will and mind are not, however, to do away with worldly government nor not to be obedient to it in goods and sanctions. For a government shall and must be in the world among men just as the daily bread and just as the schoolmaster must have the rods among the children. For because the great house of this world will not admit and let rule the Word of God, the knaves and rascals or children of this world who pursue on Christian piety must yet have a worldly and gallows-piety. . . . Therefore the magistrate is an institution of God.[19]

The Anabaptists held that the state originated from the sin of man and at times traced its inception to the time of Noah's flood. As a punishment of sin, it expresses God's wrath, but as a means of effecting necessary peace and order it reveals his love. Even a tyrannical government, then, upholds God's will to some degree.

Consequently, the Christian obeys the state. Following the injunctions of Jesus, Paul, and the author of I Peter, the Anabaptists paid their taxes, prayed for their authorities, and rendered the normal service demanded. In the words of Menno Simons, "Taxes and tolls we pay as Christ has taught and Himself practiced. We pray for the imperial majesty, kings, lords, princes, and all in authority. We honor and obey them."[20] The Anabaptists did not distinguish between good and bad governments: Government is by nature coercive in contrast with the life of the church, while obedience is a way of fulfilling God's will independent of moral evaluations of government.[21]

But the state cannot demand actions contrary to the will of God. As Simons puts it, "if they wish to rule and lord it above Christ Jesus, or contrary to Christ Jesus in our consciences . . . this we do not grant them."[22] Once again, this sounds like Luther, but the Anabaptists held a more extensive view of the divine intention than Luther did, a view which rested on the demands of the Sermon on the Mount. To reverence authority and contribute taxes provides occasion for Christian humility, but Christians may not coerce or hurt anyone.

Christians and Political Office

For this reason, even though the magistracy is ordained by God, Christians cannot hold office. The opening sentence of Article VI of the Schleitheim Confession illustrates the paradox that "the sword is ordained of God outside the perfection of Christ,"[23] for Christians follow a higher way of life than the instrument of divine judgment and blessing in the temporal order —the way of perfection. The article goes on to spell out why Christians cannot be magistrates. As if conscious of Luther's position, it questions whether one may use the sword to protect the good and punish the wicked out of love. The negative reply refers to the meekness and lowliness of Jesus, the pattern of the faithful. As Christ refused to judge between brother and brother in regard to an inheritance, so Christians should not use the sword to judge in worldly dispute. If chosen as a magistrate, one should flee, as Christ did when they tried to make him king. Despite the divine ordination of government, the Confession points to a radical dualism between the way of the world and the life of the kingdom.

> The government magistracy is according to the flesh, but the Christians' is according to the Spirit; their houses and dwelling remain in this world, but the Christians' are in heaven; their citizenship is in this world, but the Christians' citizenship is in heaven; the weapons of their conflict and war are carnal and against the flesh only, but the Christians' weapons are spiritual, against the fortification of the devil. The worldlings are armed with steel and iron, but the Christians are armed with the

armor of God, with truth, righteousness, peace, faith, salvation and the Word of God. In brief, as is the mind of Christ toward us, so shall the mind of the members of the body of Christ be through Him in all things.[24]

Different principles of biblical interpretation naturally made for differences between the Anabaptists and the other Reformers. Although Hans Hillerbrand refers to their "New Testament monism,"[25] one should be cautious about concluding that Anabaptists rejected the Old Testament. Simons insisted that "the whole Scriptures, both of the Old and New Testament, were written for our instruction, admonition and correction. . . ."[26] and he frequently cited the Old Testament. Nevertheless, in Anabaptism, the Christian lives under and finds his norms in the New Covenant. Hans Marquardt, in a sermon at St. Gall, Switzerland, in 1528, argued that "under the Old Covenant God has permitted His people the use of the sword . . . [but] the old law has been replaced by the new commandment of Christ that we should love our enemies. . . . The believer is not to be an earthly ruler, or to use violence. . . ."[27]

The Anabaptists adhered to a covenant theology, in which they accepted the validity of the Old Covenant for Israel, but assumed that the New Covenant had superseded it. Under the Old Covenant, members of the community of Israel could punish by coercion and violence, and the political officials were esteemed religious leaders; but in the New Covenant, Christ set aside coercion as a form of control and allowed only persuasion and expulsion for dealing with offenders. As one of the early Anabaptists put it, "The New Testament is more perfect than the Old. . . . Christ has taught a higher and more perfect doctrine and made with His people a new covenant."[28] Hence the Anabaptists often complained that their opponents used the prescriptions of the Bible illegitimately, for when they could not prove their point from the New Testament, they resorted to the Old.

The Anabaptist attitude reflects a radically religious commitment. The people of God take their norms for ethics entirely from the religious covenant to which they dedicate themselves. Concern for the survival of other aspects of existence plays no role; the experience of conversion demands a regenerate and different life. To the member of the kingdom of God the problems of the transient world are irrelevant. Perhaps one's actions may have consequences for the temporal order, but these are not important, for only the dedication to discipleship matters.

The early Anabaptists recognized fully the compromises in which governmental positions involved them. Even though in principle coercion served the will of God, this was an accommodation to the sin of the world that those who were called to be Christ's disciples could not follow. In a government position, many of one's acts would contravene the New Covenant ethic; a man is better able to manifest love, humility, and mercy if he lives in simplicity, far from power and coercion. The Anabaptists, although initially concentrated among craftsmen,[29] became farmers because that way of life offered better opportunities for living in peace and brotherhood.

Although the Evangelical Anabaptists generally denied the magistracy to Christians, two exceptions should be noted. One congregation, that at Nikolsburg in Moravia, founded by Balthasar Hubmaier, allowed Christians to be magistrates and to bear the sword in support of government. The local ruler, Lord Leonhard von Liechtenstein, was baptized in 1527 and became a member of the congregation without giving up his office; and in 1528 he used his authority to expel a part of the congregation that insisted on renunciation of both office and sword, most of whom became Hutterites. This congregation did not, however, last beyond 1529.[30]

The other exception is found in an interesting vacillation in the writings of Menno Simons. On the one hand he said, "We teach and acknowledge no other sword . . . in the kingdom or church of Christ than the sharp sword of the Spirit, God's Word. . . . But the civil sword we leave to those to whom it is committed."[31] In other passages, however, Simons spoke as if a magistrate could be a Christian and had corresponding responsibilities: "But him who is a Christian and wants to be one and then does not follow his Prince, Head, and Leader Christ, but covers and clothes his unrighteousness, wickedness, pomp and pride, avarice, plunder, and tyranny with the name of magistrate, I hate. For he who is a Christian must follow the Spirit, Word, and example of Christ, no matter whether he be emperor, king, or whatever he be."[32] Simons also defined for rulers "what the Word of the Lord commands them, how they should be minded, and how they should rightfully execute their office to the praise and glory of the Lord."[33] This is indeed a strange statement for one who believed that Satan dominated those outside the church and that holding office was a sin. It can be explained as an appeal to the consciences of supposedly Christian rulers who were persecuting the Anabaptists. Simons charged them to recognize that their office is not their own but a gift of God, and that they should not invade matters of faith by such measures as religious persecution.[34]

It has been argued that the question of magistracy was purely academic among the Anabaptists, because as a lower-class movement its members would not have been eligible for office. More recent research[35] indicates that at least in Switzerland such a simple generalization cannot be made and that leaders like Grebel, Manz, and Marpeck did have the education and social position to hold office. By 1529, however, Anabaptists were considered heretics in the Holy Roman Empire and ineligible even for existence, much less officeholding.

Nonresistance

The second political element rejected by the Anabaptists was bearing the sword, or nonresistance not only to violations of one's own interests but also the interests of society. The earliest testimony against war among those who later became Anabaptists seems to have been the teaching of Andreas Castelberger of the Swiss Brethren in 1523. Upon being questioned by the Zurich authorities about Castelberger's preaching, a witness replied that he "had said much about war, showing that the divine doctrine is vehemently opposed to it and that war is sin."[36] Many people in Switzerland at that time were strongly pacifist. The Swiss soldiers, noted for their superlative fighting qualities, were much sought after by pope, emperor, and kings as mercenaries. Zwingli had served as a chaplain in one of these mercenary armies and opposed the system as a sapping of national resources. At the same time Erasmus, who spent much of his life in Basel, was speculating on the pernicious effects of war on the well-being of society, and among humanists the quest for some kind of truce among the warring princes of Europe was a prime goal. The pacifism of the Anabaptists came from the Bible. Even the humanistically trained Grebel wrote Müntzer that "If thou art willing to defend war . . . or other things which thou dost not find in express words of Scripture . . . then I admonish thee . . . that thou wilt cease therefrom and from all notions of thy own. . . . Christians are as sheep in the midst of wolves. . . . They use neither the worldly sword nor engage in war, since among them taking human life has ceased entirely, for we are no longer under the Old Covenant."[37] The doctrine of the kingdoms interprets the Bible as the covenant book of the kingdom of God, whereas fighting symbolizes the way of the world.

Several aspects of the denial of the sword should be noted. One, most obviously, is the refusal to participate in war. To some extent this offered no problem for the Anabaptists, since volunteers and mercenaries did the fighting and no national military service existed at the time. The Anabaptist prohibition indicates, however, that even if called to do so, Christians cannot engage in war. On the issue of whether nations can wage war, the Anabaptist literature is silent, but wars are assumed to be characteristic of government, an institution outside the ethic of Christ. Contemporary Mennonites have emphasized that the Anabaptists expected no ultimate reconciliation between the ethic of the world and the ethic of Christ. In a brutal and warring world the church separated itself as a group from its neighbors and lived a different way of life, church and world continuing separate until the end of history.

A second dimension was the denial of the sword for compulsion in religion or for punishment of heterodoxy. Though reinforced by their own sufferings at the hands of the authorities, this principle followed from the basic impulses of the movement: the church as a community of confessed believers, the abjuration of coercion, and the imitation of Christ as an absolutely binding norm of activity. According to Simons,

> If the magistracy rightly understood Christ and His kingdom, they would in my opinion rather choose death than to meddle with their worldly power and sword in spiritual matters which are reserved not to the judgment of man but to the judgment of the great and Almighty God alone.[38]

The similarity to Luther's views in his 1523 treatise "On Secular Authority" should be noted.[39] Whether the Anabaptists would have changed if they had had political responsibility, one cannot know; for the record they consistently upheld their view that conviction determines one's religion and that conviction lies on another plane of reality from coercion. Within the kingdom of Christ the instrument of compulsion was simply to ban the erring brother from the fellowship. The major Reformers and the Anabaptists were both convinced of their positions, but the latter insisted that the preservation of purity in doctrine and practice must proceed in a manner consistent with the teachings of Christ. Since only the grace of God could lead a person to the truth, punishment of heresy by coercion could not be reconciled with the Christian covenant.

A third aspect was nonresistance in the face of persecution. The Christian should react in meekness to anyone doing him injustice. When the hostility of their theological opponents and the political authorities became intense, the Anabaptists developed a theology of martyrdom to justify themselves. "Note how that all saints, Christ Jesus Himself also, have suffered these persecutions, and how that all the pious must suffer them still. . . ."[40] The sufferings of the Anabaptists, in contrast with the prosperity of the established church, verified to them their steadfastness in maintaining the norms of the true church. The mentality of the early church and its martyrs, an eagerness to die in the name of the Lord, a joy derived from an assured commitment, the expectation of a final triumph with Christ, lived once again in the sixteenth century. Because the Anabaptists had no view of historical betterment, they looked for their redemption in the afterlife. The church by its nature is a suffering church, and though the persecutions ostensibly come from those under the domination of the devil, nevertheless, in some way they are also given by God. God often allows Satan to chastise "His elect children with His paternal rod to the end that they may hear and obey Him in his holy Word, will, and commandments, may put into practice devout instruction and piety, may fear God with sincerity of heart, may not allow themselves to conform to this world, may no longer live unto flesh and blood, and may in this way as obedient and disciplined children of God at the end be made partakers of the promised kingdom and inheritance."[41]

Nonresistance in the face of opposition sprang from the disciplined commitment of the group, but the theology of martyrdom provided a source of strength and justification when they, the patently righteous, suffered while the wicked prospered.

The Oath

A third political element the Anabaptists rejected was the oath. If nonresistance did not significantly contribute to antagonism between them and the civil officials, denial of the oath assuredly did. In the fluctuating political circumstances of the Reformation period, affirmations of loyalty to the ruling power were frequently sought. The question of loyalty was especially directed to the Anabaptists who did not accept the national religion, the symbol of religious and civic belonging, and their refusal to take an oath branded them as subverters of the political structure. The Schleitheim Confession, which devotes one-fifth of its content to the oath, indicates the importance of the issue to the early Anabaptists, although some important South German leaders like Hans Hut said that God did not forbid the oath.[42]

Scriptural authority alone sufficed to justify refusal to take an oath, for Christ forbade it to his followers, saying that man should not swear because he cannot predict or change the course of events. Although the oath continues in the world of sin, the children of the kingdom are forbidden it. Moreover, an oath would be inconsistent with the life of the Christian, who speaks only the truth and does not need to buttress his testimony by a divine affirmation.

Persecution of the Anabaptists

In their refusal to hold office, their nonresistance, and the denial of the oath, the Anabaptists placed their understanding of the demands of the Christian covenant against the political assumptions of their age. Their ideas were confused with the violent excesses of other branches of the Protestant left wing, and they suffered because aspects of their religious and social position contradicted established canons of Christianity and political thought. Most of the early Anabaptist leaders died as martyrs to their faith. In the first ten years of the movement more than five thousand of the Swiss Brethren were put to death in Switzerland and surrounding territories, and as late as the eighteenth century, Hutterites were suffering death in Transylvania and Hungary.

The relationship between religious views like those of Thomas Müntzer and the Peasants' Revolt has been noted. As early as the winter of 1521-1522, Luther had been disturbed by the activities of the Zwickau prophets, a group of spiritualist fanatics who sought to extend the reformation at Wittenberg. In the eyes of many authorities, extremism in religion went hand-in-hand with potential insurrection; Zwingli moved against the Anabaptists simply because he inferred political disloyalty from their formation of religious conventicles. Persecution of the Anabap-

tists as a group began early in 1525, when Zwingli and the Zurich
town council definitely decided to continue infant baptism and
to forbid the meetings of the Swiss Brethren. The next months
saw the beginning of widespread adult baptism among the Anabaptists, who rejected the supposition that being born into the
state church made one a Christian. In short, the association of
church and state, with its limitations on the freedom of the
church and its sponsorship of baptism without mature faith, lay
at the root of the matter.

In 1529 an imperial edict announced that "every Anabaptist
and rebaptized person, of whatever age or sex, be put to death by
sword, or fire, or otherwise. All preachers and those who abet and
conceal them, all who persist in Anabaptism, or relapse after re-
traction, must be put to death."[43] The real reason for such a
desperate measure lay in the virtually universal fear of the consequences of religious extremism and the presumption of religious
monism in society. The political leaders had no capacity to distinguish between dangerous and innocuous movements, or to see
that religious pluralism might be feasible.

The Anabaptists were tolerated in scattered areas, one of
which was Strassburg, but even here the magistrates eventually
changed to a policy of persecution. The Anabaptists were considered dividers of the church. Their views on officeholding, arms,
and the oath undermined the authority and prestige of the
magistracy. The magistrates feared possible effects of the movement on the army, government, and civic customs, and believed
it actually harbored revolutionary potential. The authorities
were annoyed by what they considered Anabaptist insolence.
There were also other charges based on incorrect information
such as disrespect for people and community of wives.[44]

Anabaptists and Religious Liberty

The Anabaptists increased the resentment of the other Reformers by their own interpretation of the persecution, for they insisted on the correctness of their views and implied that their
opponents were wrong or unchristian. Thus Simons argued that
the Anabaptists suffer "for no other reason . . . than that we do
not associate with the preachers, who by their doctrine, sacraments, and conduct oppose the Word of the Lord; that we make
the proper use of baptism and the Lord's Supper, that we avoid
all idolatry, self-righteousness, and abuses as required by the
Scriptures, and wish, as far as our weakness will allow, fervently
to fear the Lord and follow after righteousness."[45]

Strangely, the Evangelical Anabaptists, even under the burden of oppression, did not emphasize eschatology, perhaps because they wanted to avoid association with contemporary eschatological and revolutionary movements.[46] The most disastrous action of the latter groups—which led to vigorous attacks on the Anabaptists—was the attempt of the Münster radicals in 1534 to initiate the final judgment and new era in Münster, Westphalia, near the Dutch border. Surrounded by aroused and enraged Catholics and Protestants, they advocated communism, polygamy—and unfortunately, believers' baptism—before being swept away in a horrible slaughter. The beliefs of the Münster group were popularly regarded as representative of the entire Protestant left wing, although Menno Simons' first publication, called "The Blasphemy of John of Leiden," attacked the Münsterites.[47] Most of the thought of this period was somewhat eschatological, the Anabaptists' no more so than Luther's. One finds occasional eschatological references in the writings of Simons, and the Hutterite *Chronicle* speaks often of the period as "this last dangerous time," but their major emphasis lay simply on the communion of the believer with God, which would continue despite death, while their persecutors would face judgment.

In recent years, more sympathetic research into Anabaptism has recognized their contribution to religious liberty. It would be wrong, however, to relate the Anabaptists to separation of church and state on the American pattern. Their controversy with Zwingli was directed to the freedom and integrity of the church within the political and social order, and did not necessarily anticipate a formal disestablishment of religion. Nevertheless, they contributed notably to religious freedom in their rejection of the particular form of national religion of their time. Furthermore, the voluntary principle of church organization, designed to enable the Christian community to preach and practice without political restraint, lies at the heart of the present American structure of church and state. The Anabaptist insistence on Christian freedom and their capacity so to discipline members that they were able to die for the faith set a barrier against political totalitarianism.

Finally, their consistency in refusing to condone persecution of heterodoxy set a pattern for both Erastian and separationist forms of toleration. As early as 1524, for example, Hubmaier argued that the very idea of a heretic was an invention of the devil and that burning heretics violates the teaching and example of Christ. In his pamphlet, *Von Ketzern und ihren Verbrennern,*

Hubmaier used an analogy with a long tradition in the history of religious freedom, that of the wheat and the tares. "So it follows that the slayers of heretics are the worst heretics of all, in that they, contrary to Christ's teaching and practice, condemn heretics to the fire. By pulling up the harvest prematurely they destroy the wheat along with the tares."[48]

Historical Developments Among the Anabaptists

The descendants of the Anabaptists followed several directions in their relations with the state. They may be divided initially into at least three groups, although these are by no means comprehensive and cut across the numerous sects into which the Anabaptist tradition has split. One group remained in Western Europe and was especially strong in Holland; another, chiefly from Germany and Switzerland, came to America in two waves, 1707-1756 and 1815-1860; a third spent two centuries in Eastern Europe, emigrating to the United States and Canada in the late nineteenth century and after World War I from Russia.

The first group is aptly described by Troeltsch's comments on the nonresistant persecuted sects. "Based on the Protestant ethic of the 'calling,' they have all developed into groups which, in the sociological sense, must be described as 'bourgeois,' and which therefore accept existing conditions."[49] Unfortunately, Troeltsch experienced the Anabaptist tradition only in Germany and Holland. There, the Mennonites have lost many of the distinguishing characteristics of their forefathers. As early as 1570, the liberal Dutch segment, the Waterlanders, allowed their members to hold office, rather minor posts since the Calvinist Church held a privileged position. In 1795, religious restrictions were removed in Holland and the Mennonites became prominent in public affairs.[50]

The maintenance of nonresistance was not a problem for the European Mennonites, except the Swiss, before the Napoleonic Wars, but thereafter the pressures of unconditioned conscription policies destroyed their nonresistance. In 1896, for example, in Holland, a military law was passed which, though providing no exemptions for the Mennonites, was accepted by the church leaders. The Alsatian Amish and some Mennonites in Holland and Germany, on the other hand, emigrated to America.

The decline of nonresistance among Dutch Mennonites lay in

sociological pressures on the Mennonite community, which altered their status in relation to the "world." Stimulated by the sectarian characteristics described by Troeltsch, which by their very nature undermine continuation of the sectarian ideal, the Dutch Mennonites advanced in economic and social standing and encountered points of view more congenial to their new way of life. Today they are liberal in theology, aristocratic, capitalistic, and urban. They acquired many ideas from other sects tolerated in Holland during the seventeenth century, such as the Socinians, Collegiants, and Remonstrants. The traditional nonresistance became a liberal type of pacifism, which disappeared with the crisis of conscription. Second, becoming wealthy, their concern for purity and simplicity declined, and many of the wealthy married into non-Mennonite families. Third, the growth of religious toleration in Holland seems to have mitigated the uniqueness of the Mennonites, and they came to assume the expected religious characteristics of the bourgeoisie to which they belonged.[51] Since World War I, however, a minority of the European Mennonites have readopted such traditional marks of distinction as nonresistance.

This study emphasizes the church-state thinking of the Mennonites who came to America. One should recognize, initially, that they usually immigrated for reasons of church and state, because of persecution, or because of inability to maintain a free church and the traditional antipolitical symbols without interference from the state. It is not surprising, therefore, that the history of the American Mennonites evidences a vigorous insistence on the way of life upheld by their martyred ancestors.

Sociological factors also helped distinguish the Mennonites of Western and Eastern European origin. The latter, because they had considerable opportunity for self-government in the former czarist regime, do not question officeholding with as much vigor as the Western European group, which has fairly consistently avoided holding office, because of an experience among the very first Mennonite immigrants to America. In 1683, thirteen Mennonite families from Crefeld, Germany, founded Germantown, Pennsylvania, and in the next twenty-five years were joined by nearly fifty families. Together with the Quakers, they received in 1691 a charter giving them exclusive right of voting, legislation, and admission of members into the corporation, but obligating them to maintain local government. As long as the government was simple, no difficulty arose, but in time coercive instruments such as prison and whipping post appeared. In 1701, Pastorius, the civil leader of the community, complained that men willing to hold office were increasingly hard to find, several citizens having declined positions to which they had been elected. Finally, in 1707, Germantown lost its charter because it could not carry on the government that the charter required. The Mennonites and Quakers had theoretical control, but found the coercive aspects of government too contradictory to the life of Christ's kingdom to be exercised.[52]

Until the twentieth century the American Mennonites lived an isolated and unsophisticated life on the periphery of civilization. Sheltered by their rural ways and use of the German language, they clung in small congregations to the hallowed writings of their sixteenth-century forefathers, although national conflict occasionally brought them into contact with the "world." The American Constitution has never recognized the right of conscientious objection, although in wartime Congress has made special provision for the pacifist groups. In both the Revolutionary and Civil Wars the Mennonites paid a fine to avoid military service. The Mennonites of the twentieth century, however, have been compelled to search deeply into their theological background to justify themselves in a world where nationalism and social conformity do not easily accept people who deviate.[53]

A host of new problems, as well as recent research in Reformation history, have led to a level of Mennonite theological activity that compares with that of the sixteenth century. Not all Mennonites have shared in this revival; the denomination is divided into at least sixteen different branches, some of which do not associate with the others or are extremely conservative. Both the divisiveness and the lack of co-operation result from practice of the ban, the instrument of maintaining the purity of the church, which has often been exercised over trivial matters to expel brethren who simply formed a new sect. Nevertheless, the major groups such as the (Old) Mennonite Church, centered in Pennsylvania, and the General Conference, among the former Russian immigrants in the Midwest, have shared in the twofold project of historical research and theological reconstruction. The problem of church and state has claimed an exceptional amount of attention, because issues of this type cause major misunderstanding of the Mennonites.

Contemporary Developments

The Nature of the State

Mennonite thinkers have tried to distinguish more carefully the nature of the state in the light of modern political developments. They still hold the essential character of the state to be coercive and inappropriate for Christian participation. Guy F. Hershberger, probably the most influential writer on the Mennonite view toward state and society, says:

> At this point it is sufficient to say that there never has been anything like a truly Christian state on a national scale, even though there have been national states which have professed Christianity. At best we have states governing sinful societies which contain individual Christians. These Christian citizens have a wholesome influence on the society in which they live, and upon the state itself. But as long as the entire society is not Christian, the state will need to employ the coercive means which it always has used. It will continue to be primarily an organization for the maintenance of law and order, by coercive means, in a sinful society. A truly Christian society would be something quite different from anything which we know today. . . . But the coercive function would necessarily be absent; and . . . with this element removed a given society would no longer be a state.[54]

The Mennonites reject the tendency in twentieth-century liberal theology to think of the kingdom of God in political and social terms. The state as the governing instrument of a sinful society does not act from love, but from force, while the teachings of the New Testament describe the kingdom as totally nonpolitical. Thus "between the Christian and the non-Christian spheres of life there exists by definition an inevitable state of tension which can never be wholly and permanently resolved."[55]

The state is nevertheless a necessary aspect of the world that God governs. Hershberger has developed an element of Simons' thought that associates the state with the wrath of God. God will reveal his hostility to sin in a decisive way at the last judgment, but he also manifests it continuously in human society, restraining evil by means of the police power of the state, described in

Romans 13 as an institution of God "to execute his wrath on the wrongdoer." The Christian stands under authority because of its role in the divine activity, but as a member of the Christian covenant he has a limited responsibility toward it. He reverences authority as an agent of God's wrath and he may warn his contemporaries of coercion as God's answer to the violation of his divine law, but he does not really serve such an agent because he has another calling.[56] The ruler serves as God's instrument, but he is not truly righteous.

Christian Participation and Disobedience

Mennonites have had to face the fact that modern government not only coerces, but also concerns itself with human welfare, although the two functions may be intertwined. Furthermore, Mennonite writers realize that coercive and welfare aspects, once totally under the control of absolute rulers, now are exercised by free citizens. Consequently, they distinguish between political functions in which Mennonites may and may not participate. The essential criterion seems to be whether such participation requires coercion. Not only laws against stealing and murder, but also those preventing reckless driving and unaccredited people from teaching in the schools, are all directed toward the common good of society, and the Christian supports them, even though their enforcement necessitates a degree of compulsion inconsistent with the norms of the New Testament.[57] Christians may serve the public in welfare positions not requiring advocacy of war or bearing arms—teaching school, public health, or building roads—[58] but compromises of the Christian ethic—in lawmaking, the police, and the armed services—are forbidden.

When government transgresses its role as the mainstay of order and welfare, Mennonite Christians must disobey. The traditional Christian emphasis on the sovereignty of God then takes precedence. The application of divine sovereignty takes different forms in Protestantism, but among the Mennonites it becomes the justification for disobedience to the intentions of the state which threaten the Christian conscience.[59]

The defense of the priority of religious belief and practice has led to an emphasis on social and political pluralism by Mennonite thinkers like Hershberger. The tendency of the political order to control religion involves an attempt to place all of life under one authority. Totalitarian states "do not recognize the independence of religion, culture, education, and the family. They seek to impose on all citizens a uniform philosophy of life."[60] Among the Mennonites the insistence on religious integrity has often coincided with the continuation of cultural and organizational traits not appreciated by outsiders: the German language, a particular type of clothing, the communistic Hutterite system, or religious schools. Some of these have served a practical purpose in shielding the group from worldly temptations; others have been simply and uncritically reactionary. Mennonites contend that such aspects of life do not belong to the jurisdiction of the state, that welfare applies to an ordering and betterment of the given culture without altering its integrity. The state can and should enhance the welfare of its citizens through education, but it must not impose, through education or other means, a philosophy which contradicts their consciences. Thus the Mennonites stand in the lengthy Western Christian tradition, which by separating culture from government, society from the state, underlies limited government and the freedom of subsidiary groups.

The American system of church-state separation, though meeting in many ways the Anabaptist program of religious freedom, is not an ideal, for in practice it has strengths and weaknesses. The state is often able to act completely without restraints, and in national crises the church is virtually unable to testify against war. Since a man who puts conscience above government is often regarded as a disloyal citizen, the Mennonites in particular have often suffered persecution during wartime because they did not fight or contribute to war bonds. Church-state separation inhibits the freedom of the church to witness against potentially totalitarian policies by the state.[61] While recognizing that the ability to maintain their convictions under the American system is providential, the Mennonite view of the inherent sinfulness of the political order also shows them how the state violates its legitimate functions.

Contemporary Nonresistance

Witness to nonresistance and peace mark the contemporary Mennonite attitude toward war. In 1927 the Peace Problems Committee of the Mennonite Church formulated three chief aims: to strengthen the nonresistant faith of the Mennonites through publications and other means; to inform government officials of the convictions of nonresistants, to study legislation affecting the church, and to inform church members of governmental attitudes towards their faith; to interpret nonresistance to other people, especially to non-Mennonite Christians.[62]

The encounter of the Mennonites with American culture has undermined the consistency of their nonresistance. Figures are somewhat misleading because many young men in World War II were deferred for agricultural work, but according to Hershberger, of 9,809 Mennonites drafted, 46.2% served in alternate service as conscientious objectors, while 53.8% were in the armed forces. Great variation among the Mennonite branches was found, with the more isolated and conservative groups showing greater fidelity to the tradition. For example, the Old Order Mennonites and Old Order Amish were 100% and 93.5% conscientious objectors respectively.[63] Mennonites do not refuse to register for selective service, but they do not obey when called upon to support the war effort directly or indirectly through the Red Cross, the medical corps, or other adjuncts of military activity. The Mennonites throughout their history have attempted to provide for alternate service—building roads or planting forests—which they could reconcile with their conscience. Although alternate service may be unjust or a violation of religious freedom, the Christian does not resist injustice—he only resists the demand to do wrong. During World War II the government allowed the Mennonite churches to establish their own Civilian Public Service program at a cost of over three million dollars to the churches.[64] This cooperation, regarded as successful, contrasts sharply with World War I, when officials showed so little sympathy with the aims of the Mennonites that many suffered and three Hutterites actually died from mistreatment in prison.

The failure of many Mennonites to uphold the denominational position on nonresistance has led to a voluminous literature to inform young people of this aspect of Mennonite belief. One of the most complete affirmations was a 1937 statement of the Mennonite General Conference on "Peace, War and Military Service." Citing the persistence of nonresistance in their tradition, the authors argued that it "has been fully and authoritatively expressed in our confession of faith, known as 'The Eighteen Articles,' adopted in Dortrecht, Holland, in 1632 and confirmed at the first Mennonite Conference held in America in Germantown in 1725, reaffirmed in the declaration of the 1917 General Conference at Goshen, Indiana, and in the statement of faith adopted by the General Conference at Garden City, Missouri, in 1921. . . ."[65]

Despite their love for their country and their desire to work for its highest welfare, Mennonites are forbidden to fight or participate directly under the military arm of the government as combatants or noncombatants, serve in civil organizations such as Y.M.C.A. or Red Cross, which in wartime become part of the military system, purchase war bonds, manufacture weapons, participate in military training in schools and colleges, agitate or propagandize for war, or derive profit from war and wartime inflation. If by accident excess profits should result from war, they should be given to the needy or for the spread of the gospel. If their position leads to suffering or brings contempt from others, the sacrifices of their Anabaptist forefathers provide an example of the proper Christian response.

The Mennonites have dealt directly with the federal government for the protection of nonresistants. During World War II they served with Quakers and Brethren on the National Service Board for Religious Objectors, and they continue to maintain a representative of the NSBRO in Washington, who reports to the church on issues and legislation pertaining to nonresistance. Representatives designated by the executive committee of the Mennonite Central Committee testify before congressional committees on occasion. According to an analyst of religious lobbying, "the Mennonites are true to the spirit of their 'law' of nonparticipation in government, if not to the letter of the law."[66] Paradoxically, in this case the avoidance of relations between Christians and government necessitates some relations.

From time to time the Mennonites' concern for peace has led them to inadvertent political involvement, due to their support of one side of a debated public issue. In 1915 the Mennonite General Conference expressed appreciation to President Wilson for his efforts to keep the United States out of war;[67] in 1919, it protested against compulsory military training and sent a petition bearing 20,000 signatures against UMT to government officials.[68] When international situations in Nicaragua, Mexico, and China seemed acute, Mennonites drafted letters advocating peace. In 1931 the Peace Problems Committee wrote government officials encouraging efforts at disarmament in the London Naval Conference in 1930 and the planned conference for 1932;[69] and the statement on "War, Peace and Nonresistance" in 1937 commended the governments of the United States and Canada, saying that "in particular, do we desire to endorse the policy of neutrality and nonparticipation in disputes between other nations."[70]

The latter stand illustrates the dilemma of a group committed to internal nonresistance based on a distinction between an ethic of the kingdom and the ways of the world, yet eager to promote a peaceful world from concern for the welfare of humanity as a whole. Can one assume that "neutrality" and "nonparticipation" are the best policies for achieving peace in the secular world? Did not the Mennonites seek to project the Christian ethic on the secular world and thus contradict their distinction between the two kingdoms? Did they not undercut the Mennonite realism which sees that order and welfare often result from coercion and other violations of the Christian ethic? By taking such a concrete stand on a particular issue, the Mennonites adopted the same policy as isolationist and Fascist sympathizers, who were rather strong in the areas of greatest Mennonite geographical distribution and who contributed to World War II by inhibiting American support of freedom and justice against tyranny. Thus experiments in promoting peace placed many Mennonites in a dubious political role.

Nonresistance vs. Pacifism

Since World War II, a group of Mennonite theologians has distinguished more carefully the passive "nonresistance" of their tradition from the active "pacifism" of other Christians. They have been partly motivated by Reinhold Niebuhr's famous essay, "Why the Christian Church is not Pacifist,"[71] which describes the tradition of Menno Simons as "a valuable asset for the Christian faith," while denouncing other forms of pacifism as "heretical." While the "liberal" pacifist attempts to translate Christian love and nonresistance into a strategy for the solution of social and political problems without considering the contribution of coercion to justice, the genuine Mennonite position appears in Guy F. Hershberger's comments:

> Believers in Biblical nonresistance find the social gospel and the pacifism of religious liberalism inadequate, not because they do not contain some fine ideals, but because they have a wrong conception of sin, of Christianity, and of the kingdom of God. The New Testament sees a great gulf between God and the sinful world, a gulf which will continue until the final judgment, for not until then will sin be brought to an end.

The kingdom of God which the New Testament speaks of is brought into existence only through the supernatural power of God Himself. It is made up of Christians who have experienced the saving grace of God in their personal lives; who have been saved from the sinful world to a life of service to God. Such Christians are concerned for the welfare of humanity, and this influence on society may be considerable. But such changes as this influence may bring about within the sinful society of the world, however worthwhile they may be, do not constitute the kingdom of God.[72]

The decisive difference, fundamentally theological, lies in the Mennonite recognition of a persistent sin within society and government, deriving from the demonic character of the worldly kingdom that stubbornly resists transformation by love.

Harold Bender criticizes liberal pacifists for their tendency to see peace as an end in itself, whereas the New Testament regards it as a fruit of the gospel and the result of regenerate lives. He feels that they have neglected the main purpose of Christianity, salvation, and that their view of the kingdom of God as a transformed social order shows excessive optimism.[73] Instead of looking at the state as an organization to maintain order by coercion, they try to administer the state by Christian principles, forgetting that police power actually represents the wrath of God among men checking aggression by force. Although some states and leaders are better than others, the state cannot pretend, in the unregenerate social order, to express the norms of the Sermon on the Mount. For Bender, liberal pacifism is a compromise with the coercive power of the state, watering down the New Testament ethic of nonresistance, love, and the cross, to nonviolent resistance, which is, in fact, a form of resistance.[74]

The Mennonite, on the other hand, does not practice nonresistance in order to better society, but simply as a faithful follower of the way of life depicted in the New Testament. Although love may not have beneficial results, "as long as we abide in God's will as revealed in Jesus Christ we have this long-term assurance of God's blessing and benediction. And everything in God's will must have a ministry of good in the here and now."[75]

The tendency of liberal pacifism to become nonviolent resistance reveals its difference from nonresistance. Besides almost equating Gandhi with Jesus, the ethic of nonviolence calculatingly uses pacifism for particular ends such as the overthrow of

British rule in India, whereas the Mennonite does not concern himself with overthrowing a government even by nonviolent means. The Mennonite Christian renders Caesar his due by not resisting at all: ". . . [The] primary objective of nonviolence is not peace or obedience to the divine will, but rather certain desired social changes, for personal, or class, or national advantage. New Testament nonresistance is concerned first with obedience to God and the creation of loving brotherhood."[76] Whereas liberal pacifism often makes peace an ethical method, the Mennonites place peacefulness within an evangelical and theological framework.

Often accused of biblical legalism, the contemporary Mennonites have tried to establish nonresistance on a more consciously theological basis. Although some thinkers continue to defend discipleship by citing biblical verses,[77] according to both Hershberger[78] and Don Smucker[79] the heart of the Christian ethic is *agape*, self-giving love for God and neighbor. Other bases for discipleship and nonresistance are the imitation of Christ, the teaching of Jesus, and response to God's will as found in Scripture. But love receives special emphasis: "Nonresistance is applied agape. . . . [It] will always need forgiveness and justification by faith, that faith which worketh by love. It does not rest, then, on the words of the Sermon on the Mount or on this or that proof text. It rests on the central redemptive expression of God's love in the cross which climaxed a consistent life of love up to that point."[80]

Although Mennonites continue their biblical literalism, one may expect their ethics to be grounded in the future on greater appropriation of the outlook, rather than merely the words, of the Bible.

Political Responsibility

It has been noted that Eastern and Western American Mennonites differ in their attitudes toward officeholding. The Easterners continue their opposition, while allowing exceptions for positions not involving the use of force. In the Midwest, however, a number of Mennonites have engaged in politics, two even serving in the national House of Representatives. Most Mennonites throughout the country vote, although, especially in the East, opposition to voting is increasing.

The present-day American circumstances do not, however, exhaust Mennonite practical politics. In Paraguay, among five

Mennonite colonies given self-rule there, one finds an essential union of religion and government. Although the two dimensions are independent in theory, in the sense that the government is administered by civil functionaries and the church by ministers, the same people are in both. This corresponds very loosely to the system that prevailed in Russia after 1789. According to Bender, "it is true beyond the shadow of a doubt that the actual leadership of this joint life in the Mennonite colony, both in Russia and South America, has usually been largely in the hands of the elders and ministers. It is inconceivable that anything could be done in these colonies that would be basically contrary to the teachings and wishes of the church leaders. Thus in effect if not in form there is an amalgamation of church and state."[81] Unlike the situation in the old Russian colonies, government without the use of force has been possible for these completely Mennonite colonies in Paraguay. The motivation behind the Mennonites, if it be taken as consistent, is dual, both sides of which are theologically oriented: to achieve freedom for the church and to avoid coercion. In the United States abstinence from officeholding and separation of church and state are the instruments towards these ends, while in Paraguay control of government by the Mennonites and a union of church and state are the means.

The American Mennonites have wrestled with such questions as whether officeholding[82] and voting[83] result in compromises inconsistent with the Christian life. Whereas some Mennonites who have held office were not in good standing in their congregations, others have sincerely felt that the exercise of leadership did not necessarily lead to coercion. In 1956, a conference at Bethel College on "Education and Political Responsibility" concluded that Mennonites should participate more actively in government and politics, because love constrains the Christian toward social responsibility and the democratic state offers possibilities for Christian ethical expression. Because one's first loyalty is to God and the church, however, there is a point at which every Christian should withdraw his assent to political measures. A struggle over liberal theology was also evident at this conference, for despite the agreement on political concern, disagreement prevailed on the motivations. As summarized by Elmer Ediger, one view was optimistic about the possibilities of society's acceptance of the Christian way, the other pessimistic; one stressed welfare, the other the control of evil by force within society; one tended to associate democracy with the will of God, the other saw it as an enlightened part of culture, but by no means the kingdom of God. Finally, one said democracy and justice help build the kingdom, the other stressed converted Christians as a leaven within society.[84] One may discern in the latter views the traditional Mennonite emphases, while the former stem from the outlook of liberal Protestantism, which has influenced particularly the Mennonite General Conference, the most liberal group and the one most subject to non-Mennonite ideas.

The questions of officeholding and voting represent only part of a larger concern among Mennonites for political participation and social concern in line with the interests of the American Protestant churches in the twentieth century. J. Winfield Fretz[85] has voiced the views of those eager to redirect the Mennonites in politics. Emphasizing that "the arguments against Christian participation in public life in the first and sixteenth centuries are not (ipso facto) sound arguments against it today," he cites the development of democracy and the welfare function of government as modern phenomena which should stimulate reconsideration. Governmental concern with welfare has grown from popular demand, not from dictatorial decrees. Within the Mennonite tradition, the only argument against political participation has been its involvement in compromises, but why, asks Fretz, should politics be isolated as the one such area of compromise, since business also requires compromise? Furthermore, politics has higher moral implications, for it aims toward public welfare, whereas business seeks primarily financial gain. Abstinence from the political world abandons it to the evil and unprincipled; there is simply no way to avoid political responsibility. In similar fashion, Elmer Neufeld urges Mennonites, while upholding pacifism, to show their concern for humanity by influencing public policy, voting, nonviolent direct action, and holding political office.[86]

Far more typical of present-day Mennonite theologians is the view of Hershberger and Smucker. They do not deny political responsibility, but their position is stamped with a deep awareness that the Christian should act in the political order only through a Christian spirit and methods. Many political positions may be quite necessary for the successful operation of the state in a sinful world but the Christian cannot compromise by participating in them. Hershberger says that "the Christian will render society a greater service by remaining politically aloof and living a life of genuine nonresistance, than by being politically active where sooner or later he must . . . compromise this principle."[87]

The real dynamic of society does not lie in the state; state action is obviated when subordinate groups like the church effectively deal with education, health, relief, and social security. Christians should not rely too much on the state and thus become completely obligated to it. Christians can far more effectively exercise their sense of responsibility by working in other areas than politics. As Smucker puts it, "The political order will remain on the periphery of our lives, though it will be dealt with frequently. The main focus must be upon non-coercive deeds of faith and works. . . ."[88] Implied in this view is a continuing suspicion of government. The state may seem at the moment to be a welfare instrument, but government suffers throughout history from the tendency to absolutize itself. These spokesmen are conscious, for example, of occasional political restrictions on the Hutterites, the tendency of government to insinuate itself into all aspects of cultural life and to demand corresponding responses, and efforts to compel Pennsylvania Amish to participate in Social Security and to attend public schools where their children would be asked to engage in activities inimical to their consciences. The Christian may appreciate aspects of government, but as a citizen of the kingdom of God he goes his way of love, sacrifice, nonresistance, and cross-bearing. All of these, to be sure, will have political and social implications, but the ethic of the kingdom takes primacy and is not to be rejected because of its ineffectiveness in the modern world. In an era when men look to government to supply their needs, the Mennonites witness to a communitarian, interpersonal way of relating to one another. The Christian does not seek to reform the world, because he knows that by its very nature it will continue to be a mass of competing and selfish forces until the end of history; he is concerned, rather, simply to be a disciple of Christ.

The tendency of Mennonites to discuss political responsibility in terms of officeholding and voting points to the extremely individualistic way in which social ethics is conceived, in contrast with the group's own ethic, in which brotherhood and discipleship are centered on the corporate level. Mennonites have not appropriated the emphasis, widespread in Protestantism since the Social Gospel, on the church as the agent for a corporate witness to the world. Instead, discussion centers on whether individuals can be real Christians while voting or holding office. This hesitation about committing the church to a program of social action derives principally from a fear that the role of the church may be misconceived, that it will become a pressure group. Even when presenting their position on conscientious objection to government, the Mennonites do not consider themselves a lobby, but are always ready to suffer coercion rather than to coerce if government does not provide for their deferment.

Over the years, however, a reorientation on practical problems has appeared, which, though not stressing acts of the church, has turned Mennonites from protecting their individual purity by avoiding social problems, toward investigating possible solutions to social problems. In 1939 the Mennonite General Conference recognized the ambiguity of economic as well as political conflict for nonresistant Christians and appointed a Committee on Industrial Relations to make agreements with labor organizations under which Mennonite factory workers could avoid joining trade unions and thus remain neutral in industrial disputes. The church was supposed to admonish employers to avoid exploitation and unions to abjure violence: "We believe the industrial conflict to be a struggle for power with which to achieve social justice, whereas Biblical nonresistance enjoins submission even to injustice rather than to engage in conflict. . . . The Christian's first task, as we understand it, is to obey the will of God, whether the immediate consequence is justice or injustice for himself."[89] In a remarkably naive fashion the Mennonites did not realize that their efforts toward neutrality aligned them precisely on the side of the most paternalistic segment of management in the industrial conflict. Although recognizing that the activities of labor unions were directed toward social justice, they so wanted to maintain their own noncoercive position that they could interpret the movement only with respect to the piety of their own members.

In 1951, however, the same committee stated that it was "deeply concerned that the social conscience of all our people may be aroused and sharpened, so that we may sense more and more the implications of Christian love and brotherhood in the complex details of modern life."[90] The report dealt not only with nonresistance in daily life and Christian ethics in business and professions, but opposed racial segregation and discrimination, and urged Americans to raise the living standards of other countries by sharing resources with them. Although one should not overemphasize these new interests of an extremely conservative,

overwhelmingly rural Protestant group, they illustrate the awareness on the part of the Mennonite leadership that Christian love
demands a wider outreach than merely within the local community and church. In *The Way of the Cross in Human Relations,* Guy Hershberger has attempted to develop an ethic that
does justice to Mennonite principles while directing special attention to problems of race and economics. The ethic he envisions is "the way of the cross," an exploration of possible non-
coercive actions that contribute to justice. Government serves as
an instrument of God's wrath and benevolence in achieving
justice through coercion and a balance of power, but Christians
make their contribution through love and suffering. "The Christian," Hershberger says, "does not exercise vengeance in order *to
obtain justice.* He suffers, even lays down his life if need be, in
order that he might *do justice* and bring reconciliation among
men."[91] This outlook represents a distinctive approach to Christian ethics, as a way of life different from that of the rest of society rather than as a method.

The Mennonite Witness

The Mennonites are the most important representatives in
modern America of the historically significant sectarian attitude
toward the state. As such they more accurately reproduce the
views of the New Testament church than any of the other perspectives toward the state under consideration here. It should
be noted, however, that the influence of social factors on religion
prevents a complete imitation of the primitive church, especially in America where encounter with other outlooks has
altered the traditional testimonies of individuals and congregations to such an extent that many more liberal Mennonites do not
essentially differ from members of other denominations of similar
socioeconomic composition. The Mennonite denominations that
most vigorously resist the inroads of twentieth-century American
life usually do so by preserving the cultural characteristics of
past centuries. On the other hand, the more creative minds
among the Mennonites seem to have learned from people outside the denomination and are trying to relate their convictions
to modern social and political problems, while upholding important elements of the distinctive Anabaptist-Mennonite tradition.

Like the Lutherans, the Anabaptists contribute to Protestantism by grounding their position on strong theological convictions, especially the two kingdoms and Christian ethics as love and brotherhood. If the weakness of Lutheranism has been its failure to follow through on the implications of the demonic distortion of the state and the need for Christians to resist in the name of the will of God, the Mennonites have tended toward legalism and self-righteous complacency toward the rest of society. They have become legalistic because they centered their views of the state on a few absolutized principles, while neglecting to develop the more flexible and dynamic implications of their doctrine of the two kingdoms. An originally strong consciousness that they constituted the true church, confirmed by their persecution in the sixteenth century by people who purported to be Christians, has foundered on the encounter in America with individuals in other denominations who also seem to be sincere and genuine Christians. The original radical dualism of church and world held by the Anabaptists has been quietly undercut among most American Mennonites.

The Mennonites are the chief Protestant representatives of a view which demands separation of church and state on the basis of a doctrine of the church, whereas in America today separation is usually predicated on individualistic arguments. The chief Mennonite reason for advocating separation is the desire for noninterference in the life of the church. The most significant contributions to religious liberty by religious groups in history have come because the sects insisted on freedom from interference and were willing to struggle for it. The Mennonites represent an approach, at least as noble, but probably less effective: they have been willing to suffer and die for it. For this reason despite their early advocacy of religious freedom, they did not contribute to political structures for guaranteeing it and had to depend for survival on the benevolence of governments.

Because they are fundamentally interested in religious freedom, the Mennonites should be more open to a variety of possible interpretations of separation. More than most Protestant groups, they sense that church-state separation is essentially a channel for religious liberty and that separation in itself can become a source of oppression when it interferes in religious life. The denomination is committed to a strong form of political pluralism by implication, derived from its historical concern for centering such dimensions of life as education and welfare within the religious community. The desire among the more conservative Mennonites to perpetuate this tradition ranks second after nonresistance in producing misunderstanding of Mennonites by the American public. The Mennonites face the danger of confusing their religious convictions with conservative political views held by themselves and their neighbors who oppose governmental interference in corporate life for their own economic reasons.

The Mennonites have been the most effective symbols of the Christian conscience that does not yield on points of religious significance, in contrast with the tendency of most Protestants to follow uncritically the national line especially in time of war. The Mennonites remind other Protestants that the Christian ethic is essentially one of love and self-sacrifice, and that given the questionable economic and political interests of even relatively moral countries, Christians should hesitate strongly before participating in war. Unfortunately the Mennonites have obscured this testimony by absolutizing the law of nonresistance, whereas many equally sincere Christians, though rejecting war in principle, prefer to make their judgments in terms of the situations confronting them. There might be circumstances, even though exceptional, in which involvement in war would be a lesser evil. The Mennonites rectify their legalism, however, by the obvious humility with which they bear witness as *die Stillen im Lande,* the courage with which they have faced persecution, and their co-operation in registering for the draft and developing alternative programs for nonresisters.

At their best they illustrate more successfully than any other Protestant groups the unassuming suffering of Christians in the name of religious loyalties more ultimate than the state.

One may expect in the future a more varied Mennonite approach to society. Their relatively negative understanding of the state dictates Christian action principally in society rather than in the state, in keeping with the methodological possibilities open to the Christian; but it is apparent that the denomination now realizes that personal piety and purity must be supplemented by attention to the needs of individuals and groups in the world. The influence of other outlooks on the Mennonites, which have helped broaden their conception of social responsibility, endangers at the same time the distinctive and valuable witness they offer. Will the American Mennonites, as did their Dutch ancestors and as most American Protestants do, become so influenced by the norms of society that Protestantism will lack a twentieth-century equivalent of the ethic of the Sermon on the Mount, with its disinterest in the state and its attention to the kingdom of God rather than to the world? This would be a disaster to Christianity, for the Mennonites represent an essential Protestant position, and are living proof that the Christian faith does not completely mirror the impulses of culture by which history molds all religions.

III From Theocracy to Pacifism: The Quakers

The Origins

Some historians have argued that the Quakers have no coherent view of the state.[1] Not only has Quakerism undergone striking changes during its history, but it has proliferated into almost incompatible forms in present-day America. Quakers may be Eastern upper class business men, Midwest farmers and revivalists, mystics, or agitators against segregation and nuclear armaments. Common rootage in a flexible tradition enables Friends of startling diversity to co-operate under the same denominational name.

The Quaker system of congregational polity as well as the consistent stress on individual illumination undermine hope of consolidating this variety. The highest formal authority in Quakerism is the Yearly Meeting, of which there are some twenty-five in the United States, each reflecting geography as well as differing interpretations of the tradition. In America the Philadelphia Yearly Meeting has been regarded as a center of leadership, although technically it has no authority over any other yearly meeting, nor do the wider meetings such as the General Conference, the Five Years Meeting, or the Friends World Conference. Despite this relatively chaotic situation, one can ascertain some consistency of position on church and state by examining the statements of these groups and Quaker writers.

113

The impulses, methods, and goals of contemporary Quakerism typify the denomination only since the late nineteenth century and constitute an almost complete reversal of the previous
Quaker attitude. Instead of the earlier quietism, conservatism,
and withdrawal from the world, similar to the Mennonites,
modern Quakers have shown concern—at least in the yearly
meetings, larger meetings of Friends, and the American Friends
Service Committee—for social and political action directed to
such goals as peace, civil liberties, and brotherhood. The modern
direction of the Quaker outlook is usually justified on the
grounds of consistency with the first decades of Quakerism, when
men like George Fox, Edward Burrough, and William Penn
sought dynamically to apply their Christian convictions to society
and the state. Quaker spokesmen contend that quietism was an
aberration, that the original Quaker theological assumptions, if
applied to the modern world, dictate relativism of belief, the
free play of conscience, and a pre-eminently ethical interest.

An historical examination of Quakerism seeks then to determine the extent to which certain principles have prevailed or
changes occurred. Can contemporary Friends claim to represent
the "spirit" of Fox, Burrough, and Penn? If so, in what ways?
The analysis of this question produces interesting results for an
understanding of the changes and rationalizations that a religion
undergoes and of the influence of social factors in these changes.
The problem of church and state is integral to this development,
for disappointment or success in politics has led the Quakers to
react in life and thought. Several of the distinctive characteristics
of the Friends, notably their witness for peace and their refusal
to take an oath, have had political implications throughout their
history, although at various times they have been conceived
somewhat differently.

Quaker attitudes toward church and state fall into four historical periods: the formative period, the first decade from 1650
to 1660; the Pennsylvania experiment in government; the period
of withdrawal or quietism which began in England in the late
seventeenth century and in America after 1750; and the modern
period.

During the first three of these periods the Quakers did not
particularly influence other denominations, but in the twentieth
century, individuals and spokesmen across the Protestant spectrum have adopted or sympathized with the outlook of the
Friends. The Liberal or Social Gospel movement in Protestant-

ism had many common features with the Quakers. Not only did modern Quakerism build on and appropriate the intellectual and social interests of Liberalism, but the latter found the social concerns, especially pacifism, of the Friends very congenial. In the 1930's ministers in many denominations could not be distinguished in outlook from the Friends, pacifism being a predominant interest,[2] and even today Liberals in a number of denominations find the Quaker outlook on man, religion, and society more acceptable than the traditional or neo-Orthodox movements among their fellows. As this study will show, however, early Quakers did not adhere to the Liberal outlook in quite the same way that modern Friends and Liberals do.

Quakerism and Puritanism

The Society of Friends developed amid the religious confusion of the 1640's in England and represented a form of left-wing Puritanism. According to Frederick Tolles, "Quakerism as it arose in the middle of the seventeenth century cannot be understood unless it is seen as one of the variant expressions of the dominant and all-pervasive Puritanism of the age."[3] Although major Quaker historians[4] have usually argued that the Friends diverged radically from the Puritans, even to the point of representing a different kind of religious experience, it now seems clear that the Friends merely extended certain Puritan tendencies to the point that they seemed different. In the early twentieth century, furthermore, almost no historians understood or appreciated the creativity and dynamism of Puritanism, and those writing Quaker history interpreted it according to their own, more modern, liberal understanding of religion, omitting in the process elements that contradicted their preconceptions. With the influential study by Geoffrey F. Nuttall on *The Holy Spirit in Puritan Faith and Experience,*[5] and the two excellent but unfortunately unpublished doctoral dissertations by Hugh S. Barbour[6] and W. A. Cole[7] that build on Nuttall's insights, we are now in a position to make a more rounded presentation of early Quaker views of church and state.

The Inner Light

The Inner Light, which is usually regarded as the distinctive element in Quakerism and which provoked the greatest Puritan hostility, actually developed from the Puritan view of the Holy

Spirit. As Puritanism deteriorated into variant warring sects, the traditional association of the authority of Word and Spirit in Calvinism underwent significant changes. The classical Reformation used Scripture as a foil against Roman Catholicism, but it always assumed that one read Scripture according to the guidance of the Holy Spirit. Scripture was the authority, but the Spirit enabled the Christian to derive correct doctrine from it. During the 1640's, however, emphasis on the Spirit increased among the left-wing sects, as new experiences compelled them to justify themselves against traditional Anglicanism and Puritanism. The Bible clearly contains a variety of views, and the more or less unsophisticated leaders of the left wing were discovering elements other than those traditionally acceptable in English Puritanism. They emphasized fresh dimensions of the biblical view of the Spirit such as the spontaneous, charismatic, and emotional seizures of the prophets and the primitive church.

There was no sharp break between Quakerism and Puritanism; the various sects holding intermediate positions provided a transition to Quakerism. Nevertheless, various developments[8] helped to sharpen distinctions: for example, whereas Puritanism taught that the leadings of the Spirit conformed to reason, the Quakers insisted that the Spirit went beyond and might even contradict reason. Puritans were rather ambivalent on this point, hesitating to give reason an authority that would displace Scripture, but fearing at the same time the "subjective" biblical interpretations of the sectarians. Fox and the early Quakers successfully moved beyond the Scripture-reason impasse by means of the Inner Light, which they interpreted as Christ within man. Thus, the ultimate authority became neither reason nor Scripture, but Christ who communicates himself directly to the individual. Secondly, instead of testing the inclination of the Spirit by the Word, as did the Puritans, the Quakers held that the Scriptures represented the expression of the same Spirit who spoke to them personally and that the Bible should be judged by that Spirit. Consequently, in analyzing the source of his revelations, George Fox said:

> This I saw in the pure openings of the light without the help of any man, neither did I then know where to find it in the Scriptures; though afterwards, searching the Scriptures, I found it.

These things I did not see by the help of man, nor by the letter, though they are written in the letter, but I saw them in the light of the Lord Jesus Christ, and by his immediate Spirit and power, as did the holy men of God, by whom the Holy Scriptures were written.[9]

The early Friends correctly saw that the words of Scripture rested on experiences and assumed that the divine communication of their own time would not differ from that of the past. This leads to the third difference, for the Puritans held that the Bible was a final revelation, while the Friends insisted that the inspiration of the biblical writers continued in their own time. The Friends thus represented the position most intolerable to Christian biblicists in all periods, one which argues for new revelations by communication of the Spirit.

The most important distinction between Puritan and Quaker views of the Holy Spirit concerned the perfectibility of the Christian. In Christian theology, the Holy Spirit has often represented the force of God which leads believers toward holiness or sanctity.[10] Holiness to the Quaker meant infallibility in religious judgments and moral perfection. The former aspect contributed to the confidence with which the Friends argued against their opponents, while the latter set them off from the classical Reformation doctrine of the continuation of sin even among the justified (*simul justus et peccator*). Both dimensions are rooted, however, in Puritanism. History has rarely witnessed Christians as confident of the correctness of their views as the Puritans, but their assurance lay in the Scripture that spoke to them with indisputable self-evidence. The Puritans also distinguished themselves by the vigor with which they pursued sanctification and the changed life, although they always sensed the elements of evil that continued in them. Quakerism simply transferred the certainty of the Puritans from the Bible to the infallible Light within, and eliminated their reservations about moral perfectibility. Hence, the Puritan sects provided a bridge which the Quakers crossed by drawing out the implications of the radical sectarian extensions of classical Calvinist theology.

Unlike much modern Quakerism, the early Friends held a rigorous doctrine of sin, and the evangelical message they presented to their contemporaries stressed a consciousness of sin as the prerequisite of conversion. The older Quaker historians have tended to discount the doctrine of sin and to regard Robert Barclay, the first Quaker systematic theologian, as unrepresentative because of his doctrine of original sin.[11] From the time of Fox, however, Friends held that natural man was directed away from rather than toward God. But they also stressed the alternative between this old life and a new life if man would only heed the Light. There was an "ocean of darkness and death but [also] an infinite ocean of light and love, which flowed over the ocean of darkness."[12] Fox also spoke of his "two thirsts . . . the one after the creatures to have gotten help and strength there, and the other after the Lord the Creator, and His Son Jesus Christ. And I saw all the world could do me no good. If I had had a king's diet, palace, and attendance, all would have been as nothing, for nothing gave me comfort but the Lord by His power."[13] He distinguished the seed of the serpent, the state of man in sin, from the seed of the woman, Christ, the second seed becoming a synonym for the inner christological principle, the Light.[14] He thus telescoped the biblical history of redemption into two inclinations in man which had existed since the Fall of Adam, one directed toward God, the other toward the flesh and world: one evil, the other good. Following the ethical interests of Puritanism, Fox described in moral terms those who followed either inclination. Barclay, writing in 1678, differed from Fox more in sophistication rather than in outlook when he discussed the Quaker views of sin, redemption, and sanctification in the formal structure and terminology of the Calvinist theologians.

In addition to the centrality of the Spirit and the perfectibility of man, several related functions of the Spirit or Light also marked the Quaker outlook. Quakers stressed more than classical Puritanism the existential, subjective manner of discovering God —through experience or illumination rather than through the Bible. Second, the Inner Light conveys the decisive truth about God and religion. According to Barclay, "the testimony of the Spirit is that alone by which the true knowledge of God hath been, is and can be only revealed. . . ."[15] Third, following the Light constitutes the new birth or redemption by which one becomes a Christian. Through it he sees the evil of the worldly, carnal inclination, and accepts the calling of God. Because all men are potential witnesses to the Light, the Friends taught universal atonement. Fourth, the Inner Light impels the believer toward sanctification. "As many as resist not this light, but receive the same, in them is produced a holy, pure and spiritual birth; bringing forth holiness, righteousness, purity, and all those

other blessed fruits which are acceptable to God."[16] Fifth, the
Inner Light is theistic and christological, for Christ not only
lived as an historical figure, but exists within the heart of men.
The Light within becomes God within and Christ within: "To
witness God within you, the Immanuel, the Saviour, God-with-
you, is the whole salvation, there is no other to be expected than
this. To witness that God dwells in us and walks in us is to be be-
gotten by the Word of God, to be born of the Immortal Seed and
to be a New Creature."[17] Sixth, the Light was conceived of in a
corporate sense, being apprehended principally through the
small religious community, the center of worship, where all
could share in the direction of the Spirit which a particular person felt. These facets of the Inner Light validate the insight of
Cotton Mather in his complaint that the Quakers call on people
"to attend unto the *mystical dispensations* of the *light within,* as
having the whole of *religion* contained therein. . . ."[18]

The Quakers invite comparison with the Anabaptists, but the
differences should be quite clear. The Anabaptists were not
mystics, but biblicists; and they did not hold with the Quakers
that Christians are perfectible. Further consideration of Quaker
views on the state and political activity will illustrate the importance of the latter point.

Theocratic Implications for Society and the State

The Quaker attitude toward society and the state, like its view
of the Spirit, stemmed from Puritanism and featured a strong
sense of divine sovereignty expressed in apocalypticism, a close
association of religion and politics, and a theocratic concern for
social reform according to the divine will. This quotation of
Edward Burrough encompasses all of these elements:

> The very foundation of Government, and the choosing of
> Governours also hath been out of course . . . our *Kings* have
> attained to the Throne of Government *hereditarily* . . . and
> our *Parliaments* and *Rulers* . . . by . . . a way of traditional
> choice . . . after the manner of the *Heathen Nations,* and . . .
> the great and rich men have been set to rule over the poor
> . . . and the *freeborn* people hath deeply suffered cruel oppres-
> sions of *proud* and *ambitious* and *self-seeking men.*
>
> Now . . . we are in good expectations that the Lord will sud-
> denly so appear, as to free us from future oppressions in this
> respect, for we look for a *New Earth* as well as a New Heaven.

... And the Lord alone will ... be the *King and Judge* and
Law-giver over all, and will commit to giving forth and execution of Good Laws unto the power of faithful and just men
ordained of God, who will judge for him altogether and not
for man ... but will regard the Cause of the Poor, and the
Afflicted.[19]

The Puritan sects fought the English Civil War convinced that
it was a "war of the Lord." They hailed the downfall of king
and prelate, and the institution of Cromwell as head over the
Commonwealth, as the beginning of a new era in English history,
when the will of God mediated by the evangelical sects would
guide England into the millennium. Cromwell further increased
their hopes when he arranged for the selection of Parliament in
1653 by nomination of the religious congregations. Parliament in
turn quickly began to fulfill sectarian expectations by abolishing
chancery court, simplifying law and legal procedure, and secular-
izing marriage. Among the left-wing groups were the Quakers,
who shared the apocalyptic interests and hopes around them.
According to Barbour, "The intense ethical struggle and victory
which they felt in their own lives was extended into the world
as a whole. Early Friends saw the work of God in the world as
the same apocalyptic conquest as God's work in themselves; they
saw their own life work as instruments in this conquest."[20] They
thought of the coming religious era as a restitution of the pure,
apostolic church which they themselves represented. Fox spoke
of the revival of primitive Christianity: "For I was made to open
the state of the Church in the primitive times ... and the state
of the false Church that was got up since; and that now the everlasting Gospel was preached again over the head of the beast,
whore, and false prophets ... which had got up since the
apostles' days."[21]

The prime concern of the sects was religious toleration, which
was established by Cromwell. The early Quaker emphasis on religious liberty did not stem from religious relativism or the
integrity of the individual conscience, but from the absolute
authority of God, whose communication to man through the
Spirit demanded religious freedom. Friends spoke at times of
conscience, but they understood this as a point of contact with
God.[22] Government, they felt, should acknowledge that the
same Spirit which guided the individual also guided the state,
and should guarantee free access by all men to that Spirit. The

attempt of the previous political order to control religious thought represented its worst failure in fulfilling God's will. Because the Holy Spirit could speak to any man, the Quakers advocated religious liberty for all—as Fox put it, for "Jew, or papist, or Turk, or heathen, or Protestant."[23]

Although religious freedom was a good beginning, the theocratic impulses of the Quakers impelled them to urge appropriate means for actualizing the millennium in England and the world. The accession of Cromwell and the acts of the Nominated Parliament, especially the institution of toleration, seemed to satisfy many of the sectarians, but the Quakers represented a minority who insisted on a revolution that would make the Christian and Puritan outlook the law of the land. To achieve this they were willing to follow whatever methods seemed indicated, though their hopes centered on a peaceful transformation through appeal to the people, Cromwell, and the Army in continuing the "good old cause."

The Friends directed themselves principally against a symbol of the old religious oppression—the collection of tithes for the support of an established clergy. They did not act from opposition to taxes or from a legal concept of separation of church and state, but because they felt that churches and ministers supported by public funds were idolatrous and lacking the Spirit.[24] In so doing the Friends conformed in an extreme way to the classical sectarian view that God communicates to men charismatically and not institutionally. Their prophetic zeal to perfect a theocracy in England led the Friends to emphasize what amounted to a separation of all religion from any type of relationship with the state, whereas most of the sectarians seemed content with an established church and noninterference in dissent. The Quakers found intolerable the continuation of an established church in an England destined for the millennium, and they not only refused to pay tithes but made themselves obnoxious by denouncing and disrupting religious meetings in "steeplehouses" by "hireling ministers."

Cromwell's concern for toleration conflicted at this point with the theocratic interests of the Quakers. Though sympathetic with them and eager to allow them religious freedom, he would not countenance their violations of the religious freedom of others; and in order to protect other religious groups, he permitted the oppression and imprisonment of Quakers by local authorities.[25] Thus the ironic situation developed in which Cromwell, who was committed to tolerance, in the name of public order acted intolerantly toward the Quakers, who also believed in tolerance, but whose theocratic views would not countenance an established religion. Early Quakerism created a bad impression in the eye of the public, which seemed relatively satisfied to halt English religious development where it was. Upholding the Puritan principles that government should do what was unconditionally right, the Friends argued for civil disobedience in the name of the will of God. Whereas the Puritans and Scottish theorists of political resistance like Knox and Buchanan had based their positions on the Bible or natural law, the Quakers resisted on the basis of what the Spirit told them should be the next direction of society.[26]

The Quaker expectations for society represented in one respect the sober ethical aims of Puritanism. They opposed such things as excessive drinking, entertainment on holidays, cheating, frivolity, and baubles like ribbons and jewelry, and like the Puritans they expected government to aid in the suppression of these vices. The government should help illuminate obviously corrupted consciences, especially in a godly England. Barbour senses the similarity of Puritan and Quaker outlooks on this point: "One suspects that Friends and Puritans alike shared such an intense hatred of everything which they considered vicious, and had warred so actively against vice in themselves, that they took it for granted that it redounded to the Glory of God to suppress vice outwardly wherever they found it."[27] The Quaker adoption of simplicity in clothing, their refusal to do "hat-honor," and their use of "thee" and "thou" reflect the same outlook, for they apparently assumed that society would adopt the equalitarianism that they themselves held on religious grounds.

Fox and his followers, however, also attacked injustices in society. One of the major complaints of the lower-class Leveller Party within the Army had been directed against the severity and inequality of treatment before the law. Fox continued to criticize this, as well as signs of prosperity among the few, such as their use of gold and finery while the poor went hungry. Injustices in economics and society marked the unfinished character of the English revolution, a situation that the saints should point out and rectify. Many of Fox's shorter writings sound like the polemics of Old Testament prophets, as he condemned the failure of the magistrates to deal with the poor, hungry, and widows.[28] In

"A Warning to all the Merchants in London and Such as Buy and Sell," he criticized the economic avarice and dishonesty of his time[29]; and in an appeal "To Both Houses of Parliament" he called on the rulers of the land to act in peace and righteousness, to allow the righteous and meek (like the Quakers) to hold office, and to abolish capital punishment for theft, and punishment for refusal to swear, fight, do hat-honor, or for speaking against the evils of the time and calling people to repent.[30] Fox did not act from rational concepts of justice, but spoke charismatically from an outlook that sensed the inconsistency of brutality and injustice with a millennial vision of society.

The early Quakers were not nonresistants, nor did they hold doctrinaire convictions against coercion in government. Historians have long been puzzled by the fact that early Quakers, even Fox, had an ambiguous attitude toward fighting. The Friends often spoke of war as rooted in lust, from which Christians had been converted, and they opposed certain military ventures; but at the same time they did not forbid Quakers to serve in the Army, and occasionally they urged Cromwell to fight for particular causes. In a careful, step-by-step analysis of the events of the 1650's, W. A. Cole[31] has proposed an explanation for this ambivalence, namely, that the Friends conditioned violence upon whether it advanced their theocratic and millenarian interests or not. Their attitude toward the sword "depended largely on the use to which it was put."[32] Just as they disrupted by violence church meetings that they considered idolatrous, so they willingly sanctioned war and coercion to advance the cause of the Lord. Cole has shown how the Quakers' expectations from Cromwell and the Army as warriors of God deteriorated into bitter disappointment, eventuating in a decision to seek their aims by purely peaceable means.

The early Quakers were neither "political antinomians" nor doctrinaire pacifists. They were men who believed that their inflexible devotion to the principles of civil and religious liberty was inspired by the Spirit of God, and who were confronted by a widespread retreat from those principles by their former comrades in arms. And if they did not deny the justice of the revolutionary cause in the civil wars, they could neither cooperate with the men who were betraying it nor share in the plots of some of their contemporaries.[33]

The Quakers found themselves in a dilemma, for they were eager to continue the reformation of English political and religious life begun in the Civil War, but they suspected the intentions of the people in authority and those who sought authority. One such group was the Fifth Monarchy Men, who advocated a violent seizure of power by the religious left wing and sought to enlist the support of the Quakers.

Early Quakers and Officeholding

Whereas the Anabaptists denied the religious relevance of government and abjured officeholding, the Quakers interpreted government as a potential agency for effecting the will of God. This is reflected in their activity in the 1650's toward two aspects of officeholding: admonishing Protector and Parliament of divine responsibilities, and their willingness to hold office themselves if the time seemed appropriate. As for the first, Fox and his associates took it upon themselves to advise Cromwell face-to-face, and in writing, on public policy.[34] Cromwell apparently wanted the support of the Quakers and even regarded them as religiously significant, but his political realism and sense of compromise in achieving the common good prevented him from fulfilling all of their demands, especially the abolition of tithes. As long as Cromwell lived and the Commonwealth Army continued, the Quakers did not give up hope that government might heed them. Unlike the Anabaptists they felt that political office had a direct relation to the will of God and could be perfected if authorities seriously obeyed God. Isaac Penington gave expression to this Puritan-Quaker concept: "As Government came from God, so the righteous execution of it depends upon God. . . . Every man needs God's help daily, else he may err in his course, and governments and governors need God's help much more, in the many intricacies and perplexities which they often meet with. And God is nigh to them in their difficult cases, who wait upon him for counsel and direction."[35]

The Quakers also defended their right to hold office when they were expelled from it, and on at least two occasions felt that they should take office themselves since they were the saints, and all Puritans held that the saints should help direct society. In 1654, when Cromwell asked for an oath of allegiance from all soldiers and others employed by the government, many Quakers were removed from military and civic responsibility. A number of Quakers protested against this disenfranchisement of the nation's most important citizens, and in 1656, at one of the earliest yearly meetings in Balby, Quakers were urged to resume office if possible.

> That if any be called to serve the Commonwealth in any public service, which is for the public wealth and good, that with cheerfulness it be undertaken, and in faithfulness discharged with God, that therein patterns and examples in the thing that is righteous ye may be to those that are without.[36]

In 1659 restrictions on the Quakers were lifted, and a number of them submitted a declaration indicating their right to hold civil and military office. Claiming that they had been expelled from office simply because of being Quakers and not because of unfitness, they argued that "we are not thereby made incapable to serve our country and country-men in the lowest employments and places that are any ways tending to the thing that is just, and to the suppression of that which is evil, or to the procuring good unto our Countrey."[37] Several Friends were appointed commissioners of the militia, and the government seemed ready to turn at last to them for significant leadership. The French ambassador wrote that the government was relying on the Quakers, that "the Spirit of God, by which they are ruled, now permits them to take part in the affairs of this world, and the Parliament seems inclined to make use of them."[38] Fox, however, saw this moment as a time of "plots and bustling and the arm of the flesh,"[39] rather than the culmination of the kingdom of God, and warned his followers against siding with any movement.

Early Quakers and Coercion

Because of their millennial outlook, the Quakers assumed that the coercion characteristic of government would in time be replaced by peace. They regarded the eschatological vision of the beating of swords into ploughshares as an imminent, historical reality in England. The necessity to use the sword indicated to them the unfinished task, which in time would be replaced by the peaceable co-existence of all men. According to Penington, "I speak not this against any magistrates' or people's defending themselves against foreign invasions, or making use of the sword to suppress the violent and evildoers within their borders (for this the present state of things may and doth require, and a great blessing will attend the sword where it is borne uprightly to that end, and its use will be honourable); . . . but yet there is a better state, which the Lord hath already brought some into, and which nations are to expect and travel towards."[40] The Quaker hope of the millennium made corporate the peace that contact with the Inner Light brought to the individual. The vision of peace on earth was foreshadowed in the frequent association by Quakers of lust with war and the recognition that the peace of religious experience symbolized a solution to the problem of war.

Fox, for example, while in prison in 1651, was offered a position as an officer during a Royalist plot, but he replied, "I lived in the virtue of that life and power that took away the occasion of all wars, and I knew from whence all wars did rise, from the lust. . . . But I told them I was come into the covenant of peace which was before wars and strifes were."[41] The early Quakers cut through the dissociation of individual and public morality that nearly all Protestantism had held, not because of an optimistic view of man in society, but because they felt that God would establish in a corporate form the religious restoration that small conventicles of Quakers were already experiencing. Just as God overcame the carnal principle in man through his Spirit, so the lust (or self-centeredness) that produced strife would disappear in the imminent eschaton. This expectation of the Friends has continued in a noneschatological and nontheocentric form on the assumption that social morality and perfection are extensions of the same phenomena in individuals and that radical betterment of society can be achieved within history. The Anabaptists also had theocentric and millennial hopes, but their fulfillment lay beyond history; the Quakers differed principally because of the influence of the Puritan theocentric and eschatological motifs in their formative years.

The same presuppositions that formed their attitude toward government governed Quaker participation in the Army. Early in the 1650's the refusal of the Friends to swear an oath and to respect military distinctions led to their expulsion from the Army. Not only did they tend to subvert military discipline, but refusal to take an oath symbolized disloyalty during a turbulent time of plots and counterplots, when all subjects were expected to affirm political loyalty. Apparently the Quakers did not at first realize the contradiction between their religious beliefs and continued presence in the Army; but when their superiors dismissed them, they faced the question whether they could be soldiers or not. The very fact that Quakers were discharged in-dicated to them that the Army was cutting itself off from the prophetic voice, and such leaders as Fox, Howgill, and Bur-rough protested against the dismissals.

Those who assumed that the Army was the agent of God never doubted the validity of bearing arms, but during the 1650's the refusal of the government to follow Quaker advice produced doubt among the Quaker leaders that the Army was continuing the work of the Lord. Individual Friends began to refuse to fight in Cromwell's army, not because they opposed war, but because the purposes seemed egoistic. Thus George Fox, the Younger, who left the Army when he became a Quaker, warned against wars for the self-interest of the Army, saying that "much of the wars which hath lately been entered into hath not been for the peace, safety and well-being of these Nations."[42] The failure of the Army to fulfill the Lord's intent was cited by George Fox in an address "To the Councill of Officers": "Oh! How are men fallen from that which they were at first, when thousands of us went in the front of you, and were with you in the greatest heat, who looked not for the spoil, but for the good of the na-tions. . . ."[43] The Friends probably would have supported Crom-well in any military venture, if he had shown his intent to be a divine instrument. Fox wrote to Cromwell: "O Oliver, hadst thou been faithful and thundered down the deceit, the Hollander had been thy subject and tributary, Germany had given up to have done thy will, and the Spaniard had quivered like a dry leaf wanting the virtue of God, the King of France should have bowed his neck under thee, the Pope should have withered as in winter, the Turk in all his fatness should have smoked, thou shouldst not have stood trifling about small things, but minded the work of the Lord as he began with thee at first."[44]

The Quakers were fairly certain of the direction Cromwell should take because they saw the events of their time in religious terms. The overthrow of Charles I and Anglicanism were pre-liminaries to the destruction of the chief centers of wickedness—the Catholic powers and the papacy. Like all Puritans, the Quak-ers were fiercely anti-Catholic and looked on the pope as the Antichrist. England represented the firmest bulwark against the papacy, especially if it fulfilled its promised destiny. Because Eng-lish patriotism was a religious attitude, and the fall of Rome the consummation of the war of the Lord, the Quaker admonitions to war become understandable. The Friends supported Cromwell in

his subjection of the Irish rebels, and Burrough wrote him giving
advice on the conduct of his Spanish war, urging him not to make
pacts with idolators but to seek his own honor in battle. The
Army, he said, might have to avenge "the blood of the guiltless
through all the Dominions of the *Pope*."[45] In his charge "To the
Councill of Officers," Fox said, "To them that do well, the sword
is a praise. . . . And if ever you Souldiers and true Officers come
again into the power of God which hath been lost, never set up
your standart until you come to *Rome,* and it be atop of *Rome*
then there let your standart stand. . . ."[46]

The Adoption of Peace as a Principle

The Commonwealth failed to heed the words of the prophets
and saints, and Friends were imprisoned. To Cromwell such acts
were essential for public order and religious toleration, but to the
Quakers they represented a failure to fulfill his godly mission.

When Cromwell died, confusion ensued in England until the
restoration of Charles II in May, 1660. Fox felt that even those
who purported to be carrying on the cause of the Lord actually
were seeking their own ends, the most notable being the Fifth
Monarchy Men, who tried to inaugurate the fifth, eschatological
kingdom in January, 1661. In 1659, Fox sent a letter to his followers which already indicates the reconciliation of the theocratic and peaceable motifs in his thought. When the temptation came to participate through force, the Friends rejected it,
turning instead to the peaceful kingdom within. With the dissolution of the Army, all militant aspirations disappeared. According to Cole, "the Quaker leaders, including Fox, did not
adopt a pacifist position until it became clear that the cause of
liberty could no longer be advanced by political means, and that
the attempt to do so would only harm the Quaker movement."[47]
Force having been found ineffective in practice, it now became
rationalized as wrong in principle. The restoration of Charles II
changed the Quaker attitude from the high hopes of the 1650's to
a deep pessimism, but the eschatological element remained in the
expectation that God would eventually establish his kingdom in
society, the Quakers witnessing to it meanwhile by peacefully
waiting.

At the beginning of 1661, when the Fifth Monarchy Men acted
and Quakers fell under suspicion, they sent to the new king "A
Declaration from the harmless and innocent people of God,
called Quakers, against all plotters and fighters in the world,"

containing the position that has remained normative among Quakers ever since. Arguing that God had redeemed them from the lusts of men which produced wars, the authors of the declaration continued:

> All bloody principles and practices, we . . . do utterly deny, with all outward wars and strife and fightings with outward weapons, for any end or under any pretence whatsoever.
>
> . . . .
>
> And as for the kingdoms of this world, we cannot covet them, much less can we fight for them, but we do earnestly desire and wait, that by the Word of God's power and its effectual operation in the hearts of men, the kingdoms of this world may become the kingdoms of the Lord, and of his Christ, that he may rule and reign in men by his spirit and truth, that thereby all people, out of all different judgements and professions may be brought into love and unity with God, and one with another. . . .[48]

Fox believed that the deterioration of the political situation represented the just judgment of God on England's leaders for betraying "the good old cause" and ignoring the prophets of God in the Quaker Society.

The Period of Persecution

The adoption of peaceful measures marks the end of the first period of Quakerism. Under the later Stuarts, the Quakers suffered persecution that far exceeded anything they experienced under Cromwell. Initially suspect because of their refusal to take an oath of loyalty to the new regime, they endured in addition the Restoration policy of making religious dissent as difficult as possible. The Quaker Act, passed in 1662, provided penalties against their opinion on oaths and their public assemblies. A further source of punishment lay in their refusal to pay tithes. Although they believed that they should obey government and be loyal to rulers, they would not co-operate on this matter and usually were penalized by distraint of property. From 1660 to 1675 the Quaker relation to the state was marked by suffering.

Beginning around 1675, however, they renewed their political interests, directing them toward achieving relief from their disabilities. They began the "Meeting for Sufferings," a centralized gathering for reporting the condition of Friends and seeking relief by insisting on "the fundamental laws of England" and instructing Friends on their rights before judges and other officials. By publishing accounts of the Quaker sufferings, they prompted popular support for religious toleration.[49]

Turning their attention to the men who formulated policy, the Friends, led by William Penn, lobbied in Parliament and before the king, the Meeting for Sufferings urging support of men who "are against persecution and Popery, and that deport themselves tenderly towards our Friends."[50] The Yearly Meeting even rented a room in a coffee house near Parliament, which led an historian shortly thereafter to write that "it was indeed somewhat scandalous, to see, when any Bill or Petition was defending, wherein the Quakers had their Account or Design, what crowding, what solliciting, what treating and trading there was by that sly and artificial set of men. . . ."[51] Penn sympathized with the attempts of James II, who was secretly a Roman Catholic, to lift restrictions against dissenters, because he saw the potential benefits to Friends as well. And though the Quakers aided in the over-all effort that produced the Act of Toleration in 1688, Penn's association with James placed the Quakers in a bad public light for years afterwards because he was suspected of Jacobite leanings.

The Beginning of Quietism

Once toleration was a reality in England, the Quakers there ceased political activity and began the period of quietism, which spread to America after the governmental experiment in Pennsylvania. Quietism, or withdrawal from political activity, followed logically for Friends from the fact that they could not hold office because of their aversion to the oath of office. Nor could they sue for their debts, carry out customs and excise transactions, defend their titles, give evidence, take part in corporations, or answer prosecutions by ecclesiastical courts for refusing to pay tithes. Their difficulties were symbolized in 1698, when John Archdale was elected to Parliament but forbidden to take his seat because of the problem of the oath.[52]

Meanwhile the Friends formulated their attitude toward a political authority that they did not share, whose methods of coercion they did not like, but toward which they wanted to show their loyalty and counteract suspicion of subversion. William Penn summed up the Friends' concept of government along traditional Christian lines: "Nor ought they [the Quakers] for this to be obnoxious to civil government, since if they cannot fight for it, neither can they fight against it; which is no mean security to any state. . . . But though they were not for fighting, they were for submitting to government; and that, not only for fear, but for conscience-sake, where government doth not interfere with conscience; believing it to be an ordinance of God, and where it is justly administered, a great benefit to mankind."[53] A major theme of Quaker political thought in this period was that Quakers make the best citizens, because they obey from love and conscience, not from fear or utility.

Quakers continued to contrast their vision of a higher ethic with the existent political order, as in Barclay's evaluation of magistrates as imperfect Christians: "And therefore, while they [magistrates] are in that condition, we shall not say that war undertaken upon a just occasion, is altogether unlawful to them. . . . The present confessors of the Christian name, who are yet in the mixture, and not in the patient suffering spirit, are not yet fitted for this form of Christianity, and therefore cannot be undefending themselves until they attain that perfection."[54]

The Quakers thus envisioned a continuum of religion and morality rather than the radical dualism of the Anabaptists, who considered those who coerced in a different kingdom from the members of the church. In Quaker thought, men ranged from subjection to carnality and evil, to spirituality and perfection, and their place in the spectrum was indicated by their way of life.

The Friends now began to feel that peace and love offered methods by which evil and coercion in society could be overcome. Throughout their history, when patriotism blinded their contemporaries, Quakers have addressed themselves to rulers of the enemy, as well as their own rulers, in order to promote peace. This universal evangelical and peaceable appeal began with George Fox, who wrote letters to the rulers of Turkey, Malta, Austria, France, Spain, China, and the Pope, among others. After 1660, with a deep concern especially for toleration throughout the world, and committed to peaceful appeal as a method, prominent Quakers called on men everywhere to listen to the Light within. They tried especially to influence rulers, because they felt that they could best ameliorate social conditions by changing the hearts of men who held political responsibility. Quaker universalism, which contrasted with the nationalism and parochialism of most Protestants, grew out of an altered millenarianism. The original Quakers hoped that Cromwell's Army would inaugurate the world-wide kingdom of God, but after 1660 they changed the method to persuasion, while retaining an international vision.

One of the foremost expressions of Quaker internationalism was William Penn's "An Essay Towards the Present and Future Peace of Europe" (1693), in which he proposed a European parliament. Confronted with the problem of enforcement of decisions, Penn rather ambiguously indicated that if any particular states should refuse to obey the decisions of the parliament, "all the other sovereignties, united as one strength, shall compel the submission and performance of the sentence. . . ."[55] Although one critic thinks Penn was so idealistic that he did not see the contradiction between his plan and the Quaker testimony for peace,[56] it can more readily be explained by the Quaker recognition that the religious commitment of most people was quite limited.

Governmental Experiments in America

The theocratic impulses of Quakerism gained a final expression in the American colonies before the Society settled as a whole into political and theological quietism. Without opportunities for politics in England, the Friends turned their attention to economic activity with a vigor that made them extremely prosperous and politically indifferent. Penn could write to his children in 1699: "Meddle not with government; never speak of it, let others say or do as they please; . . . I have said little to you about distributing justice, or being just in power or government, for I should desire that you should never be concerned therein."[57]

In America, on the other hand, the hopes of the millennium reappeared, not only in Pennsylvania, but also in Rhode Island and the Carolinas. Whereas in England the Quaker leadership frowned on involvement in political parties and especially on officeholding, the Quakers in America did not hesitate to apply their principles to public life. Although animated by a vision of what peaceful methods might accomplish, unfortunately the demands of office so compromised Quaker principles that eventually they either had to abandon their principles or withdraw from politics.

The Rhode Island Quakers, who rendered decades of public

service, including the governorship for a number of terms before the Revolutionary War, chose the first alternative.[58] They not only accepted responsibility for using coercion to maintain internal order, but committed the colony to war. In general they tried to avoid war, but once it seemed necessary, they compromised. The Rhode Island Friends even contributed one of the outstanding military leaders of the Revolutionary War in Nathanael Greene, but he was disowned by his Meeting. The Quaker leadership in Rhode Island did not absolutize the principle of pacifism, but saw in public office an opportunity for Christian vocation and felt that some dimensions of political life by their very nature required coercion.

The Quakers in Pennsylvania, on the other hand, sought to carry on government while committed to nonviolent methods, and for this reason their compromises and final abdication from political office seem more tragic. The restrictions on Quaker political life in England turned Penn's attention to America, where he combined a staunch English patriotism with the Quaker concern for a godly society: "For my country, I eyed the Lord in the obtaining of it [Pennsylvania]; and more was I drawn inward to look to Him and to owe it to His Hand and power than to any other way. I have so obtained it, and desire that I may not be unworthy of His love, but do that which may answer His kind providence, and serve His truth and people, that an example may be set up to the nations; there may be room there, though not here, for such an Holy Experiment."[59]

A Holy Experiment! These words indicate the relation of religion and politics that Penn had in mind in establishing Pennsylvania. The new colony reflected the Quaker views on noncoercion and freedom of conscience along with the older Puritan views of society. The first legislation in Pennsylvania in 1683 provided for no religious test except belief in God, permitted officeholding to all who professed to believe in Jesus Christ, extended suffrage and freedom of conscience, but at the same time passed laws against swearing, dueling, cockfighting, stage plays, lotteries, and drunkenness.[60]

More interesting, however, for understanding Quaker political thought are some of Penn's comments in his preface to the Frame of Government. The king, aware of the dangers to the new colony from Spaniard and savage, authorized Penn "to levy, muster and traine all sorts of men . . . to make warr and pursue the enemies and Robbers . . . and by God's assistance to vanquish and take them, and being taken, to put them to death by the law of Warr. . . ."[61] But Penn had a different understanding of government. For one thing, he did not provide for coercive power, but thought his colony would be like the government of Adam when man ruled the world as God's deputy and "there was no need of coercive or compulsive means." Anticipating the welfare functions of modern government, he said: "They weakly err, that think there is no other use of government than correction, which is the coarsest part of it; daily experience tells us, that the care and regulation of many other affairs more soft and daily necessary, make up much the greatest part of government; and which must have followed the peopling of the world, had Adam never fell, and will continue among men under the highest attainment they may arrive at, by the coming of the second blessed Adam, the Lord from heaven."[62]

Government he held to be "a part of religion itself, a thing sacred in its institutions and end," because it represses evil and thus emanates from the divine power, though "the one [divine power] is more free and mutual, the other more corporal and compulsive in its operations: but that is only to evil-doers; government itself being otherwise as capable of kindness, goodness and charity, as a more private society."[63] There was a correlation of political and individual potential: ". . . there is hardly one form of government in the world so ill designed by its first founders, that in good hands would not do well enough. . . . Governments, like clocks, go from the motion men give them, and as governments are made and moved by men, so by them are they ruined too. Wherefore governments rather depend upon men, than men upon governments."[64]

The Quaker leaders of Pennsylvania tried valiantly to implement this notion of the essential goodness and noncoerciveness of government in a society populated by men of good will. Extremely small groups that share a common philosophical or religious outlook have occasionally avoided coercion and authority, but the expanding colony of William Penn encountered problems for which his original vision had no solution. Interestingly, one of the most penetrating criticisms of the Quaker government in Pennsylvania comes from Guy Hershberger, the Mennonite, who judges it to have been a failure because of its unrealistic view of man and its utopian view of government, deficiencies he feels could have been corrected by Mennonite presuppositions.[65]

The Quakers initially solved a problem of conscience by accept-

ing the use of coercion for violations of domestic law, while rejecting external conflicts, wars, for any reason whatever. In this way
they could maintain domestic stability, punishing wrongdoers to
the extent of the death sentence for murder; and although a
number of Quakers had qualms even about this, they solved the
problem to their satisfaction by leaving its administration to non-
Quakers. The periodic wars of the late seventeenth and early
eighteenth centuries, however, produced the most serious crises
for the Quaker-dominated legislature. The first such occasion
came in 1692, with King William's War, when the crown took the
government completely out of Penn's hands because it failed to
support the war. When he received it back again in two years
and was admonished to "provide for the safety and security
thereof," he agreed to refer to the council and assembly all royal
orders for defense. Nevertheless, he hoped for better things, indicating to his followers that the "circumstances we are under will
not permit another method at this time. . . . We must creep
where we cannot go, and it is necessary for us, in the things of life,
to be wise as to be innocent."[66] In 1710 and 1741, the Pennsylvania Assembly was again asked to respond to military situations
and after much struggle it voted money "for the king's use,"
though the members knew that it would go for militia and armaments. Although this represented a compromise, they felt that
they were preserving unstained their pacifist scruples.[67]

The one really consistent person in the Pennsylvania experiment was James Logan, Penn's secretary, who did not distinguish
between a defensive war and civil police force. When he arrived
in Pennsylvania and learned that the Quakers there opposed
defensive warfare, he disagreed so much that he never became
active in the Meeting. He recognized that civil government as
well as defensive warfare is based on force, and consistency
demanded abjuration or acceptance of both. In 1741 he urged
the Quaker members of the Assembly to go the way of the English Quakers, paying taxes and living peaceably, but staying out
of public office, for by denying self-defense they could not decide
in a manner consistent with the common good and the requirements of the English crown.[68]

After 1741, pressure upon the legislators to resign came both
from American Friends, who felt that Quaker principles were
incompatible with political obligations, and from the London
Yearly Meeting, which sent Samuel Fothergill as agent to bring
the American Quakers into line. The American Meetings after

1741 emphasized the problem by stressing strict pacifism and the inner life. In 1756, when the governor and council of Pennsylvania declared war on the Delaware and Shawnee Indians, six of the Quaker legislators resigned, admitting that officeholding was now equivalent to military service. The remaining Friends in the legislature, by delaying to vote military measures that the government wanted, provoked a movement to require an oath of all officeholders. Because this would have led to their complete political disablement, most of the remaining Quaker legislators resigned or refused renomination.[69] The Philadelphia Yearly Meeting climaxed this series of events by passing a minute requiring all members to separate from government or face disownment. Hershberger sees this date, 1758, as a turning point in Quaker history, because for the first time officeholding was forbidden to members. The Society had now come full circle, from theocracy to denial of officeholding.[70]

No one can solve the problem of the success or failure of the Quaker holy experiment. Quakers tend to see its good points, its innovations in criminal punishment and religious freedom, and its exemplary treatment of the Indians.[71] Political realists, on the other hand, emphasize the ambiguous moral position into which the Friends were driven. They replaced a responsibility for the welfare of society with a legalistic adherence to pacifist purity; and when confronted with having to take an oath, they withdrew all means of continuing the humane laws they had instituted. Furthermore, while personally avoiding war, their security was maintained by others willing to fight. Insulated from the problems of non-Quakers in America and subject to the legalistic and perfectionist admonitions of the London Yearly Meeting, they did not wrestle with the peculiar problems of government in an American context.[72]

The Pennsylvania experiment has been emphasized because it reveals important elements of the Quaker attitude toward politics after the first eschatological decade, elements that continue to find expression in modern Quaker policy. First, the theocentric and eschatological element remained, but was no longer so central. To be sure, Penn's expectations for his colony rested ultimately on a strong sense of God's guiding grace, but he and his followers lacked the sense of *kairos,* of being instruments of a fresh expression of God's historical action. Rather, one finds a commitment to a method, peaceableness, by which *man* will institute a society according to God's will, whereas the first Quakers were open to the strange and sometimes morally ambiguous ways in which God acts in man. The disruption of God into historical process was replaced by growth if men will love and act without coercion. Second, in the early years of Quakerism it was assumed that a conversion underlay an individual's living a changed life, whereas in Pennsylvania it was believed that men have a natural inclination or capacity to conduct themselves in the way of the kingdom. The early Quaker sense of a natural tendency toward sin, from which man must be awakened in order that by attending to the Spirit within he might follow the way of perfection, was replaced by the view that natural man is essentially good, and that the witness of peace and noncoercion will lead him to live according to that goodness. Third, the original eschatological element changed from a kingdom oriented to the will of God and guided by God's prophets to an essentially ethical realm of brotherhood, peace, and love.

Barbour has also noted a fourth change, concerning the justification for religious freedom. In the early period the Quakers appealed for freedom for the Quaker conscience enlightened by the infallible Spirit, which all men could appropriate. After 1660 they emphasized the rights of conscience with a special appeal to the consciences of the readers of their literature.[73] The Friends substituted a rationalistic emphasis on the dignity and integrity of the conscience of all men for the charismatic and religiously centered insistence on freedom as the only way that the Spirit can freely speak to and move man. All of these changes, evident in the American colonial period, underlie contemporary Quaker attitudes and justify an interpretation of present-day Quaker social attitudes as closer to the mood of the holy experiment than to the founders of Quakerism.

Quietist Characteristics

As quietism enveloped the American as well as the English Friends, like the classical sect they looked on the state with indifference and emphasized the abstinence of religiously committed persons from the temptations of civil power. In fact, their views on church and state parallel startlingly those of the Anabaptists and Mennonites. A perusal of the minutes of the London Yearly Meeting after 1689, on oaths, civil government, war, and militia, reveals the chief Quaker interests to be the promotion of piety according to the spirit of Christ and "giving no offence or occasions to those in outward government, nor way to any controversies, heats, and distractions of this world, about the kingdoms of it; but to pray for the good of all, and submit all to that divine power and wisdom, which rules over the kingdom of men."[74] The antipolitical motif became intensified as time went by, so that in 1780 Samuel Scott, commenting on the parliamentary elections, could say that "the devil cometh forth, and hell from beneath";[75] and in 1820 Thomas Shillitoe urged Quakers not to vote, a step that even Scott had not envisioned. Quakerism thus developed a dualism along the Mennonite pattern, by which the world is associated with the devil and the kingdom of God with a withdrawn, sectarian, and peculiar people. As Scott put it, "Israel is to dwell alone, and not to be mixed with the people," and Shillitoe urged Friends to "keep that ear closed which will be itching to hear the views of the day. Avoid reading political publications and as much as possible newspapers."[76]

The Spirit lost its prophetic power as a link between religious experience and the rest of the world, as a source of judgment and creativity toward the state. The Inner Light illuminated the individual and the worshiping community and produced its impact through personal piety, purity, and suffering reflected to those who cared to see. Rather than being a stimulus to combat and political change, the Spirit became a religious experience *sui generis*, in contrast with other modes of activity in the world about. Religiously, Quakerism became even more mystical. The Spirit in Christian history has been either charismatic, an ecstatic seizure driving men to action, or passively mystical, causing men to see communion with the divine as a more significant relationship than association with finite things. Early Quakerism illustrates the former, quietism the latter. Rufus Jones has emphasized the doctrine of sin as the touchstone of quietism:[77] the estrangement of natural man contrasted with the guidance that God gives through his spiritual moving. Religion for the Quaker became a means of annihilating his own inclinations, concentrating on the subjection of self so that God might break into the emptiness and fill it with his plenitude.

The sense of separation was fortified by an absolutizing within the sect of the Puritan ways that the Friends had once tried to promote in all of society. While cultivating abstinence from music, dancing, the theater, and other inventions of the devil to which the world had succumbed, they further undercut the conversionist and experiential motif of the founders by adopting in 1737 birthright membership and disowning members who married non-Quakers. Daniel Boorstin describes the legalistic quality of Quaker ethics in this period as follows:

> The very ways which earlier Quakers had used to show contempt for rank and custom gradually became themselves customs as rigid as those they were meant to displace. The Quaker's refusal to remove his hat became as arrogant and purposeless as the non-Quaker's insistence on hat-honor. The drab costume of the Quaker, meant at first to express indifference to outward garments, became a uniform to which the Quaker attached more importance than his neighbors did to their gayer garments. Silence became a "form" of worship, and even the spontaneity of Quaker sermons became compulsory. The same paradox existed in nearly every distinguishing feature of Quaker life, from their use of "thee" and "thou" to their ways of marriage and burial.[78]

Having been frustrated in their attempts to relate their convictions to the state because of restrictions against them and by the contradictions in their own theory, Friends made themselves a religious elite in a fallen world.

Strangely, however, the quietist period produced some of the greatest Quaker social meliorists. John Woolman is a case in point. A profound mystic who felt that Quakers should resign all public office, Woolman nevertheless exerted a definitive influence in committing the Society of Friends to an antislavery attitude. His convictions proceeded from simple compassion, but also from the sense of religious equality cultivated in the Meetings, while his method was "friendly persuasion." One should note that Woolman particularly directed his efforts towards Quakers, urging them to free their slaves, though he was willing to present his case to anyone who cared to listen. He adhered vehemently to moral appeal rather than to political action.

Anthony Benezet, another Friend, exerted strong antislavery influence outside the Society, principally through persuasion and writing. Quakers felt they could relate their moral convictions to non-Quakers through a stress on moral reason and conscience that corresponded to the rationalism of the late seventeenth and eighteenth centuries. Barbour has pointed to this tendency, which continues in the present day, to associate the Spirit with

the moral impetus of Quakers which they receive in worship,
while hoping for similar action among non-Quakers through
stimulation of consciences.[79] During the quietist period most
Quakers were so withdrawn that they did not concern themselves
with any social dimension, especially outside the Society; but a
few distinguished individuals so absorbed rationalist thought that
they saw the possibilities for further extension of their ethical
interests by getting the assistance of others, even though the
latter did not ostensibly draw from the same spiritual resources
that a Quaker could. Conscience and reason played very little role
in the essentially charismatic outlook of early Quakerism, but at
the time of quietism they became the foundation of Quaker co-
operation with men of "good will."

Through focus on problems like slavery, the welfare of the
Indians, and the condition of the insane, another politically important change appeared. Whereas early Quakerism directed itself
in Puritan fashion to the whole of society and expected a radical
readjustment of public policy in all dimensions of life, the reformers of the quietist period sought an outlet for their compassion in particular areas where they could operate without compromising their absolute restrictions against oath-taking and
fighting. Thus one might call them reformist, directed toward
particular problems rather than toward society and government
as a whole. Such an approach, to be sure, has obvious merit, and
much social betterment has been achieved through the private
activity of individuals and groups who ignored government. It
might even be argued that this approach fundamentally underlies
the American system of government, inasmuch as government
ordinarily intervenes only when private resources fail to solve
public problems. Its real difference from classical Protestantism
lies in the decline of the theocratic impulse, because the demands
of a peaceful way of life, understood very legalistically, remove
government from the implementation of God's will. The Friends
replaced theocracy with a religiously-motivated compassion directed to social reform, but because most Protestantism in the
eighteenth and nineteenth centuries had also lost its theocratic
outlook, or saw it in moralistic or uncritically national terms, the
Friends became luminaries of social sensitivity in an age of
neglect.

The struggle with political responsibility in Pennsylvania
cemented the Quaker position on war. In the Revolutionary War
the Yearly Meeting disowned without hesitation combatants who

were members, and Quakers throughout the colonies suffered derision and distraint of property, as well as misunderstanding from both Tory and Colonial sides, because of their failure to contribute to the conflict in any way. A small group of Friends, whose patriotic inclinations led them to fight for the American cause, formed a schismatic but short-lived group called "Free Quakers," who adhered to Quaker worship and living habits, but allowed freedom of judgment on matters of political and public life.[80] In the Civil War the Quaker conscience was caught in a dilemma between two objectives, to free the slaves and to maintain the witness against war. Some regarded the conflict as a holy war to end slavery and fought on the Union side, but the Yearly Meetings officially took an opposite policy, even disowning members who gained deferment by paying three hundred dollars.[81] The Quakers were able to maintain their integrity on war in this period because the Society was essentially legalistic in its ethical outlook and, as a group, disowned without hesitation any who did not conform to their peculiarities. Like all legalist, sectarian bodies Quakers had come to adopt certain signs which distinguished them from less perfected Christians, and refusal to adhere to them led to automatic expulsion.

The Decline of Quietism

Even though philanthropic and reformist activities originally represented attempts within a quietist framework to express social concern, they became in both England and America the means by which quietism was undercut. Theological influences also contributed, for many of the Friends fell under the impact of the Evangelical movement, which intensified their interest in social problems, especially slavery. One should not assume that during the quietist period Quakers were immune from contact with other religious groups. Rationalism and Evangelicalism contributed to the schisms of the nineteenth century, giving special emphases to the various branches of the Friends; but the common avoidance of war and politics transcended the divisions. Interest in issues like slavery promoted an activism among a minority of Quakers which eventuated in the resumption of political office by a few individuals. When Friends cared enough about issues, they compromised, if necessary, to achieve solutions to them. Two helpful studies, by Erica Martineau[82] and Leroy C. Ferguson,[83] show how in England and America, respectively, quietism was abandoned, though slowly and under criticism, because of the social interests of a minority.

Martineau argues that in England the antislavery movement was the main force leading to the breakdown of quietism, for it involved the whole Society and brought it into co-operation with other denominations and social radicals. Having solved this problem, Friends turned their attention to further issues such as the struggle against the Corn Laws. Repeal of the Corn Laws being possible only through Parliament, Friends became active in promoting parliamentary reform as a means to bring about social reforms.[84] This represented a pronounced change from the previous attitude of the London Yearly Meeting, which had cautioned Friends in 1784 not to leave the country for the city because rural existence maintained quietness and Quaker integrity more successfully,[85] and had objected to the removal in 1828 of Quaker political disabilities for fear of "creaturely activity."[86] The leader of the nineteenth-century Quaker politicians was John Bright who, as one of the great reformers of his day, led the struggle in Parliament against the Corn Laws, for the enfranchisement of the nonpropertied classes, for Irish reform, and against uncritical British involvement in wars. The Quakers were concentrated so heavily among the industrial and commercial classes, however, and so committed to philanthropy as the expression of Christian concern, that even Bright did not criticize the prevailing laissez-faire views of the day.[87] Although Bright was an exception among nineteenth-century Quakers, throughout the century men who were interested in social and political problems pried the Society from its preoccupation with separation. They felt that the cause of social reform was inhibited by energy misdirected internally and that Quakers should accept unequivocally those responsibilities by which concern for other people could best be actualized.

In America, similarly, Quakers engaged actively in the antislavery cause to the extent of violating laws against assisting fugitive slaves. The Yearly Meetings in the quietist period had always expressed reservations about submission to laws violating conscience, but this had come to refer pre-eminently to fighting. Antislavery Friends like Charles Osborne, editor of various antislavery publications, and Levi Coffin and Isaac T. Hopper, leaders of the underground railroad, were so convinced of the immorality of slavery that they engaged in illegal and secret

activities, both against the government and against the admonitions of their Quaker Meetings. The Quaker opposition to
slavery had led by the end of the eighteenth century to the
manumission of slaves by members of the Society; but the
majority of Friends apparently disapproved of the radical measures advocated by the New England abolitionists and opposed
participation of Friends in politically oriented antislavery societies. In 1841, the Indiana Yearly Meeting announced its opposition to Quaker participation in "mixed associations" and use
of meeting houses for antislavery lectures and meetings. When
Coffin and Osborne refused to obey, they were removed from the
Meeting for Sufferings and eventually led in organizing the
Indiana Yearly Meeting of Anti-Slavery Friends, which embraced
about a twelfth of the total Indiana group and lasted until
1857.[88] This incident typified the struggle within Quakerism in
this period and was reflected in a number of schisms throughout
the country.

Quakerism, especially in the Midwest, was strongly influenced
by revivalism and its zeal for temperance; but here as with
slavery the opposition to involvement with government deteriorated when faced with righteous conviction. In 1885, responding
to charges that its activities were leading to political partisanship,
the Temperance Committee of the Indiana Yearly Meeting said:

> True, indeed, it is not the mission or business of the Church
> of Christ to take part in politics, as the term is generally un-
> derstood.
> Nevertheless, when great principles are at stake, when moral
> questions come before the people for decision, whenever such
> an issue as the preservation of national peace, or dispensing
> justice to Indians, the maintenance of the Sabbath, or the
> suppression of the drink traffic, comes up for settlement, and
> one political party champions the right while others defend the
> wrong, Christians would be recreant to their duty, disloyal to
> their Lord, and cowardly in the face of their enemies if their
> voices were not heard clearly and boldly vindicating the
> truth.[89]

Much earlier, in the mid-nineteenth century, Quakers throughout
the Midwest had petitioned the legislatures of their states for
laws to prevent importation and sale of intoxicants. Nearly all
of the issues with which they were concerned had a political

dimension in that their suggestions required altering of laws or policies, or their position corresponded or disagreed with that of certain political parties. The later quietist period was thus torn by tension between the desire to remain aloof and the sense of responsibility for social wrong.

This is the dilemma of any sect which develops ethical interests beyond the individual and small community. The conservatives in the denomination sense the compromises involved and seek to counter them by a radical dualism between the church and world and by a purely sectarian ethic. But Quakerism had a far broader history, encompassing theocracy, governmental experiment, and social reform. The world for them was not a realm of darkness but was composed of individuals like themselves with consciences that could be persuaded, and they had caught the vision of a perfected American society that attracted Evangelical Protestantism in the nineteenth century.

This renewed interest in social issues coincided with the appropriation of Liberal theology by Quakers in both England and the United States. Groups like the Mennonites and rural Friends remained relatively isolated from the biblical, historical, and scientific studies underlying Liberalism, but those upper-middle class Quakers who lived in the cities and attended the universities, imbibed the new currents of thought. By the end of the nineteenth century the Society embraced strange contrasts of fundamentalist, traditionally passive rural Friends, and urbane, educated liberals, strong among the Hicksites in America. Under Rufus M. Jones, Isaac Sharpless, and other men associated with the Quaker colleges, the latter group gradually assumed the leadership of the Society, with the result that on the public level Liberalism in thought and social interest today characterizes the Society.

Contemporary Quaker Interests in the State

The contemporary Quaker view of the relationship of church and state reflects both traditional and distinctively modern elements. It differs from the Lutherans and Mennonites in its lack of system, and shows relative disinterest in the usual church-state problems such as religious instruction in public schools, government aid to religious schools, and the attitude toward Roman Catholicism, that vex both transformationist and separationist outlooks. The major reason lies in the concentration of Quaker attention on the specific areas to which it feels especially committed. Some Quakers, however, sympathize with Protestants and Other Americans United for Separation of Church and State. The executive secretary of the Friends Committee on National Legislation, E. Raymond Wilson, was one of its founders, but his more recent relationship has been minimal. The *Friends Journal* has also printed an article by a high official of P.O.A.U., which was promotional in intent;[90] but this type of issue has not claimed extensive Quaker attention. What there is derives from the historical Quaker interest in the preservation of religious liberty, but present official Quakerdom finds threats to religious liberty in other areas than P.O.A.U. does.

In a statement on "Religious Liberty and Political Action," Wilmer A. Cooper, former administrative secretary of the Friends Committee on National Legislation, sees religious liberty and church-state separation fundamentally in terms of a structure by which Christians, individually and collectively, can influence political decisions. While accepting the legal structure of church-state separation, the brunt of his argument is directed toward avoidance of the supposition that religious and moral convictions play no role in political decisions: "It was certainly not the intention of our founding fathers, who made provisions for the separation of church and state in our Constitution, to divorce religion from politics. What they were concerned about was that there should be no particular 'establishment of religion,' or preferential treatment of one religion as opposed to another, but this is not to say that religion should have no influence upon government and political decisions."[91] The Quakers have not been greatly concerned over the usual church-state problems and lack a formal church-state theory because ethical interests control their outlook.

The Nature of the State

Between the mid-nineteenth century and 1911 the tenor of official Quaker views of the state radically changed. Whereas Friends had previously been urged to be meek and quiet, submissive to all laws not in conflict with religious faith, and to regard government as a necessary institution to which they should be faithful, in 1911, the London Yearly Meeting declared:

> The free institutions under which we live give many of our members a direct share in the responsibilities of government

and in forming the healthy public opinion that will lead to purity of administration and righteousness of policy. This responsibility belongs to them by virtue of their citizenship, and our members can no more rightly remain indifferent to it, than to the duties which they owe to their parents and near relatives. Men and women of alertness, intelligence, and high principle are needed today, to combat the indifference, ignorance, and self-interest which are continually impeding the wise solution of great national questions.[92]

The concentration of Quakers under "free institutions" in the Anglo-Saxon world has helped mold their understanding of the state. All of their statements in the twentieth century presuppose the right and obligation of popular participation in the formation of public policy. One finds no sign of an alternative understanding of Quaker responsibilities under a totalitarian state. This association with democracy is made explicit in the report on "The Individual and the State" at the Friends World Conference in 1937.[93] To the question what form of government seemed best according to Quaker ideals, the report pointed to Penn's dictum that "a government is free to the people under it, whatever be the frame, where the laws rule and the people are a party to those laws."[94] The report said further that only a democracy provides the freedom of expression and the opportunity for peaceable change which are essential to Quakerism, though a democracy does not per se guarantee religious liberty.

The Friends have chosen, then, a position between a divine sanction for any kind of government, and a positivistic view of government as a given institution vested in whoever holds it. For them government is an extension of the wills of the members of society, who create it to do things that they cannot do alone. "The root principle of the State must be found in the divine order of the universe which gives men capacity to organize for constructive purposes."[95] The focus here rests on the divine intention that men organize, not the divine will that there be a government. This is of great importance for a Protestant political theory, for it directs attention to the nature of man in his corporate expressions for an explanation of the state rather than to the sovereignty of God, in contrast with both Reformation Protestantism and classical Quakerism. Thus Quakers have freed themselves more or less from traditional categories and are able to make a fresh analysis of the state.

According to the Book of Discipline of the Philadelphia Yearly Meeting, the state has two aspects: coercion and welfare. As a source of coercion it does not conform to Christian principles as the Friends interpret them, though Friends do not oppose all forms of coercion. Police protection is "necessary and helpful," but war is "contrary to the will of God."[96] Continuing the tradition of the Pennsylvania experiment, Friends have seen that society would degenerate into chaos without internal police protection. The police preserve an order defined by the citizens themselves, while the use of physical force is an incidental, not an essential, part of their function. Despite this provisional acceptance, however, many Quakers, like the Mennonites, will not serve as police.[97]

The Philadelphia Discipline goes on to say that Friends have always obeyed the state, though subject to the religious principle that prime allegiance belongs to God. If the commands of the state seem to violate God's law, Friends should prayerfully try to reach a Christian decision. If conscience compels them to refuse obedience to the laws of the state, and if the decision "involves legal penalties, Friends generally have suffered willingly and fearlessly for the sake of their convictions."[98]

Political Meliorism

The problem of resistance to laws is merely a part of a larger topic, the Quaker expectations of the state, or as the 1911 statement puts it, "purity of administration and righteousness of policy." In the 1930's, when individuals throughout Protestantism were captured by the vision of an earthly kingdom of God, Quakerism reflected this hope to an extraordinary degree. The traditional schism in Protestantism between Christian and political life was minimized in a statement like the following: "As our life here and now is bounded by the state, we should feel the importance of its approximating as far as possible to Christianity. . . . We must desire the complete Christianizing of the state; otherwise the Christian cannot have the freedom for spiritual development which he holds to be the meaning of life."[99]

What do the Quakers understand to be the marks of a Christian society? The modern view differs strongly from that of the first Friends in being essentially humanistic in its valuation. This humanism is based, nevertheless, on the theological notion of the presence of the Inner Light in every man, or in a more modern form, the dignity and worth of every man. According to an analyst of Quaker views on foreign policy, "The function of government, for Friends, is thus fundamentally spiritual. It is to aid in the spiritual development of individuals, to eliminate from Society those things which pervert, stunt, and retard the spiritual growth of individuals, and to aid and encourage its citizens to express and live according to the most profound insights they can attain. Governments, therefore, have both a negative and a positive function, police powers and welfare powers."[100] The sequence of thought moves from a recognition of the spiritual nature of man, to an emphasis on the value of the person in whom God appears, to an abhorrence of forces that violate his integrity. The latter is reflected in particular Quaker ethical emphases such as dislike of violence, respect for individual rights, tolerance of other views and actions, the equality of all men, democracy as a political method, and concern for human needs. The biblical justification for some of the quietist actions has been abandoned for this essentially anthropocentric stress on the spiritual integrity of man.

The hope of Christianizing the state has impelled Friends to engage in both domestic and international activity. This required the formation of continuing organizations by which policy could be developed, rather than merely addressing the state when Quaker interests were threatened. In America the two chief agencies have been the American Friends Service Committee, founded in 1917, and the Friends Committee on National Legislation, in 1943. The former agency has served principally as a center of information and action on a variety of problems involving peace and relief of people suffering from military and social injustice. The F.C.N.L., however, is the spearhead of present-day Quaker association with the state.

The F.C.N.L. grew out of the difficulties of the Quakers in providing for governmental consideration of conscientious objectors. In the early 1940's the Friends, along with the Mennonites and Brethren, had lobbied against selective service. Although unsuccessful, they had succeeded in obtaining relatively liberal provisions for conscientious objectors. The Friends War Problems Committee, a temporary group, was the Quaker agency for this endeavor, and it continued to observe legislation of interest in Washington, not only concerning conscientious objection, but also peace and the problems of postwar rehabilitation.

Aware of the need for a permanent agency, a widely representative group of Quaker bodies met in Richmond, Indiana, in

1943, and formed the F.C.N.L. From the very beginning it was more than a peace lobby and sought to translate "Quaker principles" into all forms of political action. In a policy statement issued in 1944, the hope for "Christianizing the state" was tempered to the concern that "governments shall act wisely and justly in furtherance of the well-being of the people. Mankind's biggest job now is to eliminate the institution of war, to prevent the militarization of the human mind, and to create a true world community."[101] Denying to itself the traditional pressure methods of legislative lobbying, the F.C.N.L. has tried to work in the spirit of the Friends, presenting their point of view with courtesy to members of Congress and the administration, "exploring with them the problems to be solved; endeavoring to win the assent of reasonable minds and enlist sympathies with the objectives sought."[102] Recently the emphasis on exchange of views has been strengthened by a redirection of many of the resources of the American Friends Service Committee to discussions, both in the United States and in other countries, in which prominent political leaders meet with philosophers and religious thinkers. This unstructured discussion differs from the friendly but organized persuasion for stated policies carried on by the F.C.N.L., though both methods are regarded as true to Quaker principles.

Although the F.C.N.L. is chiefly interested in peace and its related problems of reorienting American foreign policy, promoting disarmament, and supporting and improving the United Nations, its statement of policy for 1960-1961 indicates positions on relief, distribution of surplus food, the Peace Corps, free trade, civil liberties, civil rights, capital punishment, problems of the American Indians, alcohol and narcotics addiction, obscenity, and many other problems.[103] The F.C.N.L. attempts to fulfill two objectives by this division of interest. Its principal attention to peace reflects a concern that in times of intermittent cold and hot conflict between the United States and other nations, Americans tend to forget the implications of American policy because of nationalistic semi-hysteria; at such times, Quakers are among the few with courage to emphasize the horror of war and the necessity of ultimate solutions through disarmament. On the other hand, the extension of the F.C.N.L. to other areas broadens the scope of involvement, so that Quakers cannot be accused of being peace fanatics.

The twin agencies, F.C.N.L. and A.F.S.C., have brought Quakers a startling amount of attention and, especially among other Protestants, a great deal of respect. Although conservatives often tend to consider them subversive because their positions do not correspond to the current trends of national policy, the consistency of their idealism has earned widespread appreciation, even by those who do not fully agree with them. Liberal Protestantism tends to evaluate idealism very highly, and most reflective Protestants sense that their own actions represent forms of compromise. One finds the most positive response to relief activities when Quakers ignore the conflicts of political powers and address themselves to the needs, usually of the innocent, who suffer in these conflicts.

Contemporary Friends are examining critically their methods for social and political action on two levels, the responsibilities of officeholders and of citizens.

Officeholding

Since the modern awakening of Quakerism the minutes of the various Meetings have been full of encouragement for Quakers to hold office. This has resulted, especially in England, in public responsibility far in excess of the numerical percentage of Quakers among the population. In the United States the Quakers have furnished a president, Herbert Hoover, and a vice-president, Richard Nixon, as well as other public officials. These actions reflect a Quaker tradition since the seventeenth century, that Christian and moral individuals can shape the character of the body politic. The Quaker dilemma arises from the fact that nearly every member of the Society who has exerted a significant influence on the political life of his day did not adhere absolutely to Quaker norms. With a new perspective and a new sense of realism, high officeholders have felt responsible to the needs of their constituents in such a way that their actions violated strict pacifism, or they acquiesced in one injustice in order to prevent another. Thus, the Pennsylvania situation has been repeated, and Quaker officeholders seeking in an ambiguous way to promote the common good suffer from the sniping of disappointed perfectionists on the sidelines.

The issues among the Quakers revolve around the degree of toleration of the compromisers by the perfectionists, and the sensitivity that Friends have for the reasons why responsibility usually leads to compromise. The absolutist contribution to political life cannot be accurately measured, for it results essentially in witness and changed attitudes. In his thoughtful little pamphlet, "Quakerism and Politics," Frederick B. Tolles expresses a broad outlook toward this dilemma:

Let me call the two positions the relativist and the absolutist. And let me suggest that perhaps each one needs the other. The relativist needs the absolutist to keep alive and clear the vision of the City of God while he struggles in some measure to realize it in the City of Earth. And conversely, the absolutist needs the relativist, lest the vision remain the possession of a few only, untranslated into any degree of reality. Which position an individual Friend will take will depend, I suppose, on his temperament.[104]

Tolles feels, however, that the method of "friendly persuasion" represents the distinctive Quaker contribution to Protestantism and political life. This method rests, moreover, on two philosophical principles held by modern Friends, which many liberals in other denominations share: that man is not fundamentally and irrevocably ruled by self-interest and will respond to appeals to his better nature; and that moral individuals significantly influence national policy. As a matter of fact, these principles are implied in both Quaker methods, though the absolutists often tend to stress the possibility of extreme change in man and society more than the relativists do.

Love and Political Change

This kind of struggle within Quakerism presupposes that Christians must act in politics, as in all things, with love. Love plays in Quakerism a threefold role, as do other Quaker principles, in attitude, goal, and method. The centrality of love is a phenomenon of the twentieth century; it has always been a motif within the Society, but it has existed concurrently with emphasis on other moral principles and on human personality. Friends have often emphasized love as an attitude of sensitivity to others' needs and feelings, in contrast with the hatred and egoism from which many in the world act. Brotherhood and world peace, correlates of love, would best describe their goal. But love is also a method, and here Quakers probably differ from most other Protestants in the rigor with which they use it. As a recent statement of the A.F.S.C. puts it, "Love endures and overcomes . . . hatred destroys; . . . what is obtained by love is retained, but what is obtained by hatred proves a burden."[105] A moral order in

the universe, or perhaps in the will of God, guarantees the ultimate failure of actions of violence and the final success of actions
of love. The active character of love is implied in a statement in
1912 by the London Yearly Meeting:

> The universal Peace that we set before us as our ideal is not
> a passive condition, in which the virile energies of mankind
> will atrophy from want of exercise; it is an active movement
> toward the oneness of all humanity and the realization of the
> Kingdom of God on earth; it involves participation in a cam-
> paign of the most strenuous character against organized forces
> of evil; and as such it offers unbounded scope for the most
> consecrated zeal and courage of the most devoted followers
> of Christ.[106]

In their quest for loving methods, the Friends have come to
emphasize, since the 1930's, the Gandhian technique of nonviolence, *satyagraha*. An early expression of this was Richard
Gregg's *The Power of Non-Violence*,[107] and it underlies the
present Quaker proposals for international peace in the pamphlet, "Speak Truth to Power." The latter document combines
the nonviolent way with a sophisticated analysis of the modern
world situation which attempts to show that the present milita-
rism fails in motive and method, and a psychological consideration of the positive impact of love upon individuals. Although
the authors of "Speak Truth to Power" purport to recognize "the
existence of evil" and "inevitable conflict," they uphold at the
same time the traditional Quaker view that one must "trust all
the way and unreservedly in man's capacity for goodness."[108]
Friends were much impressed with the success of nonviolence in
attaining Indian independence and more recently in mitigating
racial discrimination in the southern United States. So were other
Protestants, but the Quakers differ in the sense of commitment
to this as a policy.

An interesting feature is the transformation of original Quaker
concepts by *satyagraha*, to the extent that some statements sound
more Hindu than Christian. To be sure, Quakers have traditionally spoken truth quite fearlessly, truth defined as justice and
peace, motivated by love. But *satyagraha* is something else, *satya*
(truth) and *agraha* (grasping), manifested principally through
ahimsa (nonviolence), based on the Hindu view that such fulfillment of the *dharma* (law) becomes a source of power to effect

noble ends. As Reinhold Niebuhr has pointed out,[109] nonviolence as a method for political objectives is not the same as the nonresistance of Jesus' teaching, which is neither a method nor directed toward social goals. In this respect the Mennonites stand closer to the outlook of the Sermon on the Mount than do the Quakers, and one might also question the extent to which nonviolence really corresponds to the outlook of any other period in Quaker history. In the early part of the twentieth century the emphasis seems to have been on the implementation of moral principles in government and society rather than the Hindu view that nonviolence paradoxically overcomes evil because of a cosmic principle of truth. Quakers who emphasize nonviolence in this form are often those most removed from the Christian tradition, for whom religion is a generalized and nondogmatic mysticism and who find the Hindu outlook more congenial than most of Protestantism. The seriousness with which modern Friends are committed to *satyagraha* sometimes indicates a reduction of the Christian faith to a new legalism, that of nonviolence, which is inviolable. In practical terms *satyagraha* would be reflected in a reorientation of foreign policy toward disarmament and economic aid given selflessly. It assumes that such a method would finally yield more in peace and preservation of humanity than the present use of military means.

Nonviolence, though fundamentally a method of general Christian influence on society, at its most striking is associated with civil disobedience, for example, to laws requiring segregation or policies of building nuclear submarines. The implications of such an approach are vast, for they raise the possibility of disobedience on moral grounds to any laws or policies contradicting Quaker principles. These implications have not been fully explored either in India or in America. The use of nonviolence against segregation was supported by public opinion in many parts of the country, as well as by the authority of federal law against state laws. The protests by a few pacifists, including some Quakers, against the launching of nuclear submarines was by such a small group that they did not significantly affect official policy. Although public opinion sympathizes more with nonviolent than violent disobedience, one can conceive how a widespread use of the method might lead to social chaos, for no set of laws completely fulfills the exacting norms of justice and morality. Toleration of relative injustice and imperfection is essential for the continuation of society. The Quakers have traditionally had a limitation, however, on absolute conscience through the admonition of others in the Society.[110]

The major contribution of the Quakers is their loyalty to a Protestant motif, that in the name of the freedom of the church, or the will of God, or justice, one may serve both God and the state best by disobedience and even resistance in some form. Such an attitude on the part of subordinate groups is tolerated to some extent within the limits of the common good by the American system of government. The Philadelphia Yearly Meeting pointed out in 1943 that "disobedience may be the best means to call a state to its obligations."[111] The abiding peril of nonpacifist Christianity is loss of self-criticism and failure to understand the interests of the nation's enemies. American Quaker pacifism, especially in the modern period, has been accompanied by a cogent puncturing of American pretensions and a sensitivity to the historical factors that produce hostility to America in other countries. The danger of the Quakers, on the other hand, is a relativism which damns all combatants and equates the evil of a Nazi slaughter of the Jews or Communist slave camps with American racial discrimination and other injustices.

The Quaker attitude toward the state has in practice centered on the implications of state authority for the traditional pacifist position. Peace has been the major objective of social action; the defense of conscientious objection has been the chief concern in wartime; the right of pacifism has been the prime example of disobedience to political authority. The Quaker tendency toward absolutism on peace and nonviolence, as well as their assumptions about the goodness of man and the capacities of society and the state, have been critically examined by some modern Quaker thinkers. Friends have not participated in recent Protestant theological movements, probably because these have led to a widespread renunciation of the liberal Protestant acceptance of pacifism. The contemporary world of thought and action among Quakers stands strangely apart from present trends in English and American Protestantism; it holds to a rationalistic world view tinctured by mysticism and concerned with peace in a warring world.

Quaker Revisionism

This schism has disturbed a few Quaker thinkers. One area of reassessment, in response to Reinhold Niebuhr's criticisms of pacifism, has been to recognize the radically evil tendencies in man and society, and to urge more realism about the nature of man and of historical progress.[112] Mulford Q. Sibley, for example, argues that Quakerism does take evil seriously, that it sees a demonic element in human nature, especially in the tendency to glorify force and seek power as an end in itself. The Friends' use of peaceful means is therefore designed to make certain that the destructive forces in society will not increase.

> An adequate social and political philosophy . . . would see with pacifism the dangers lurking in centralization of power and would question the possibility, given the raw human stuff upon which political and economic structures must repose, of any lasting resolution of the problem of power becoming violence. It would maintain, again with pacifism, that the imminence of violence will confront any future society; but that it is possible through the development of training for non-violent resistance to keep the tendency to violence within much narrower limits than in the past.[113]

Sibley's ethic is motivated by commitment to pacifism, however, rather than an open-ended quest for a successful approach to political and social problems. Thus he wants to examine the implications of pacifism, rather than to formulate a broad Christian ethic. Despite his acceptance of the omnipresence of evil, he hopes for a revolution in modern political life through the employment of nonviolence: "Christ's atonement is seen to be, not some magic propitiation of an angry God, but rather a demonstration of the means which His followers are to utilize in reconstructing human life. His ideal is a Kingdom of God to be established politically here on earth as the result of a technique which constitutes the heart of His doctrine."[114] Sibley feels, nevertheless, that pacifism needs self-criticism, because of its deficiencies in understanding the distinction between violence and nonviolence, the nature of power, the irrelevance of some pacifist actions for effecting policy, its tendency to oversimplify economic and political problems, and nineteenth-century views of inevitable progress.[115]

Perhaps the most creative Quaker thinker today, one whose writings reflect a strong interest in the problem of the state, is Richard K. Ullman, an English Friend, whose *Between God and History*[116] is a significant theologically-grounded presentation of Christian ethics. More than any other Quaker today he has read and appropriated the new currents of Protestant thought, and he sees the chief need of the Quaker ethic and its attitude toward the state as a rediscovery of the theocentrism and sense of sin of earlier Friends. Alone among Quakers he seems to feel that the state is more than merely an extension of man's will and reason. For him, the state is an order of human existence ordained by God, not a social contract. Quakers have a continuing responsibility for political life in all its dimensions, both good and evil. In other words, the Christian seeks a way in which concern for social well-being can be expressed within particular contexts, rather than committing himself to pacifism in an absolute way.

Ullman, interestingly, reflects the influence of Dietrich Bonhoeffer, the Lutheran, though Lutheran thought is virtually anathema for most Quakers. For Ullman, the Christian lives in an unavoidable tension between good and evil, seeking to be relevant, but not so relevant that his methods become grossly immoral. Rejecting the Quaker emphasis on pure principles, Ullman argues that one simply explores two avenues: seeking action that is likely to produce good results, and seeing if the action is moral.[117]

Quakers, he feels, must be more aware of the ambiguity of their pacifism. They must see that war, though abhorrent to Friends, is the chosen means by which the state, which renders many services throughout the lifetime of its citizens, chooses to continue that beneficence. In wartime, government protects the conscience of the Quaker.

> But I know nevertheless that my choice lies between being a corporate sinner with the others, or a parasite on other people's sin. Choosing the refusal of war-service as the lesser evil, I still feel that there is great impurity in this very act of trying to become purer: while I refuse to soil my own hands, I participate willy-nilly in all the benefits provided and protected by those who may be less scrupulous. . . . They may wish to be as loyal to Christ as any of us, but they find the sacrifice of their own integrity less reprehensible than the refusal of self-sacrifice in solidarity. Though I do not think that I would decide as they do, I feel much closer to them than to such absolutists as take their stand without qualms.[118]

This type of outlook contrasts sharply with the tendency of most Quakers to draw a line between principled and utilitarian, good and evil, methods, mainly because Ullman accepts the inevitabil-

ity of sin in all ethical action, whereas most Quakers act non-
violently because they want to avoid sin. For Ullman this obscures the reality of grace, "the God-given capacity to discern sin
and overcome it, at least momentarily; and to accept the existence of evil that in all its mysteriousness can yet never annihilate
our ultimate hope."[119]

The ultimate hope is the kingdom of God, but this does not
come from man's activity. Like the Quakers of the first decade,
Ullman believes that the Christian faith is an experience of the
presence of the kingdom and an expectation that God will extend
it. "If we presume to try and work for the Kingdom that is to
come, we do not work for the Kingdom but for utopia."[120] Like
the early Quakers he also insists that peace was a witness by the
Quakers to the kingdom, that it will not become a political reality until Christ establishes it. Modern Friends have humanized
the notion of the kingdom and of peace by thinking of the world
as an international political society, formed by a constitution and
characterized by peace, without recognizing the spiritual pre-
conditions necessary. Pacifism in Ullman's thought is theocentric
rather than legalistic, the witness of a Christian to a changed life
which his religious experience has produced, but also to a God
who acts in history and by his mysterious grace will transform
society so that the life the Christian now knows will become
universal.

Ullman has contributed the most significant criticisms one
could make of the Quaker view of the state. He sees that a once
theocentric outlook has become secularized to such an extent that
the religious characteristics of the Society become secondary and
the Christian origins of Quakerism obscured. The failure of the
Society to appropriate the new Protestant interest in the Reformation, of which Quakerism was originally a part, is especially
serious. Rather than ignoring the new currents of thought, a
more valid program for Quakerism would be to emphasize the
elements it shares with Protestantism in the seventeenth century
and today, along with distinctive Quaker contributions such as
the transformation of men's lives through encounter with God
and the abhorrence of war. Quakers need theological depth in
their outlook to remedy the absence of a really consistent theory
of church and state.

It should be noted that Ullman's revisions develop from his
appropriation of a view of the two kingdoms similar to that of
other Protestant groups, but once a part of the early Quaker

tradition. Theocratic impulses among Fox and his associates sprang from a consciousness that God ruled society and the state as well as the church. Because they believed in God's dynamic action in history, the Quakers like other Puritans envisioned the state not merely as an expression of God's creation and judgment but also of his redemption. To stress the potentiality and capacity of government may be the major contribution of Quakers to a Protestant church-state theory, in opposition to Lutherans and Mennonites, who emphasize the inescapable limitations of the political order under a theological framework of creation and judgment. Such a Quaker contribution would be strengthened if they saw the transformation of the state as an act of God working within man, rather than as an expression of man's goodness.

Most sophisticated Protestant thought holds that society and the state cannot be permanently bettered. The title of Reinhold Niebuhr's early book, *Moral Man and Immoral Society,* contrasts the morality that individuals exhibit with the unethical character of society and the state. The Quakers, on the other hand, by insisting that one cannot limit the capacity for justice on the part of the state, may provoke Protestants to question the supposed immorality of the state. Although government seeks its own interests, these interests may well be peace rather than war, justice rather than injustice, noninterference with other nations' sovereignty rather than imperialism, or development of international law and organization rather than selfish nationalism.

Although these aims ought to be pursued by appropriate means, which could include armaments and perhaps war, the fact remains that some governments seek beneficial goals while others do not. Religious groups might well consider their responsibility to promote a national purpose consistent with Christian ethics, the fostering of positive attitudes toward it among the citizenry, and the strengthening of structures for maintaining it. One could cite many examples of the "morality" of government, for example, when it resists popular impulses to drop nuclear bombs or to declare war, or when it carries through policies of social welfare or justice against vigorous opposition. Naturally, all such actions are partially impelled by political pressure and often by a broad perspective on the consequences of certain actions, but not completely. Thus the Quakers may contribute to the debate in Protestantism about the nature and moral possibilities of political power. But they will draw a more attentive ear if they can avoid humanistic, nineteenth-century views of inevitable progress, and appropriate instead the early Quaker view of the evil impulses and imperfect character of unconverted men and nations. They might learn from the experiences of Quaker political leaders in colonial Rhode Island rather than idealizing the Pennsylvania experiment.

Such a program would not necessarily jeopardize the Quaker interest in remaining pacifist. Christians with a variety of perspectives toward the state, even Lutheran, might well conclude that given the present potentially disastrous consequences of war, Christians simply cannot fight, or that the ambivalence of all modern nations in their foreign policy does not justify Christian participation in combat. The chief problems of Quaker pacifism have been its unwillingness to recognize the integrity of Christian nonpacifists and its questionable grounds for pacifism, such as secular views of human virtue or historical progress rather than more consciously Christian assumptions. For this reason, Protestants like Reinhold Niebuhr have considered the Mennonite witness a genuine, admirable expression of Christianity, while castigating Quakerism for "heresy"; and H. R. Niebuhr has placed Quakers in the category of culture-Christians in his classification of Christian social attitudes.

The Quakers are indubitably correct in emphasizing war as the most serious problem in the world today. Its effects on human attitudes and its destruction of life should lead Christians to promote peace and often to oppose aspects of national policy. Quakers can promote a more widespread Protestant voice in dealing with problems of peace and war and also argue for the virtue of peaceful methods if they evaluate them from their Protestant heritage rather than depending on a program of *satyagraha* as the only solution to international issues. Like the Mennonites, the Quakers can play an important role in Protestantism by constantly emphasizing the contradiction between Christian ethics and the values of a political society, that Christians can only reconcile them with great difficulty and perhaps not at all, and that they have a responsibility to protest against national policies that run counter to the common good of the nation or of mankind. Too often Christians fear or neglect to make this kind of witness.

The passionate interest of the Quakers in peace and social justice represents a form of judgment upon Protestantism, but the Friends need to develop their thought on other types of church-state problems, to wrestle with the relation of religion to public life, and of public authority to religion. Their ethical interests prevent them from succumbing to a schism between church and state, but no American Quaker writers show that they have been interested in or analyzed the implications of their convictions for the American system of church-state independence. Their ethical interests must be placed within a larger context, one which moves beyond the responsibility of the individual for politics and of the state as simply a type of human organization.

IV Separationism:
Defenders of the Wall

Most of American Protestantism has been divided since the late 1940's into two different positions on church-state issues. Before 1945, twentieth-century Protestants had not formed specific permanent organizations and study commissions to work on church-state problems, although many had taken positions on such issues as the appointment of an ambassador to the Vatican City or public financial support of religious schools, and had opposed or defended Alfred E. Smith, the first Roman Catholic candidate for the presidency.

The Development of Modern Separationism

In the late 1940's, two closely related events turned Protestant attention to church-state issues and led to a crystallization of thought in an area that previously had not been systematically examined. One was the formation of Protestants and Other Americans United for Separation of Church and State in 1948; the other was the publication of *American Freedom and Catholic Power* by the lawyer and journalist, Paul Blanshard, in 1949.[1] Mr. Blanshard's book sounded a call to Americans to preserve separation of church and state and to defend the integrity of the public schools against threats by the hierarchy of the Roman Catholic Church.

Whereas Mr. Blanshard's book was a one-man effort, P.O.A.U. included leaders from a variety of religious groups, some of which do not ordinarily co-operate with other denominations. In addi-

161

tion to such nationally known leaders as Bishop G. Bromley
Oxnam of the Methodist Church, Edwin McNeill Poteat, president of Colgate-Rochester Divinity School, and John Mackay,
president of Princeton Theological Seminary, the early promoters
included Louis D. Newton, president of the Southern Baptist
Convention, Clyde Taylor of the National Association of Evangelicals, and Frank Yost of the Seventh Day Adventists.

In its "Manifesto" P.O.A.U. combined a defense of church-state
separation with some specific aims clearly reflecting a concern
with Roman Catholicism. Announcing that they wanted to "enlighten and mobilize public opinion in support of religious
liberty as . . . embodied and implemented in the Constitution by
the separation of church and state," the authors pledged to resist
every attempt by law "to widen the breach in the wall of separation of church and state." More precisely they opposed the ambassadorship to the Vatican, federal and state laws granting
financial aid to church schools, and public transportation and
textbooks for parochial school students. They also offered to
assist citizens or communities seeking aid "to protect their public
schools from sectarian domination, or resisting any other assault
upon the principle of separation of church and state." Denying
that they were "motivated by anti-Catholic animus" this distinguished group of churchmen staked out as their battleground,
defense of the principle of church-state separation.[2]

Some Problems in Church-State Separation

In the past fifteen years there have been several Supreme Court
decisions that either clarified or obscured the separation of
church and state in America. Two of the cases concerned the
teaching of religion in the public schools. In *McCollum* v. *Board
of Education* (1948)[3] the Supreme Court invalidated a system of
"released-time" instruction in Champaign, Illinois. Protestant,
Roman Catholic, and Jewish leaders in that community had
worked out with school authorities a system by which pupils
went once a week to special classes within the school building
for sectarian instruction by teachers from the churches and synagogues. Public schoolteachers co-operated by keeping attendance
and escorting the pupils to the special classes. Pupils whose parents objected sat instead in a study hall. The "rationalist" mother
of one of the pupils took the case to the courts, and by an 8-1
decision the United States Supreme Court argued that the use of
public facilities and inferential compulsion violated the es-

tablishment of religion clause of the Constitution. In 1952, however, in *Zorach* v. *Clauson*[4] the system of "released-time" in New
York was upheld by 6 to 3. The chief differences from the Champaign plan lay in the absence of implementation by public
officials and teachers, and in the fact that the classes were held
not in the school but in nearby churches and synagogues. Students
whose parents so requested were released from school an hour
early once a week to attend religious classes. The distinction between these cases seemed a bit subtle for the average American
and might be expected to lead to divergent reactions from Protestants; moreover, the dicta in the two cases implied two different interpretations of church-state separation. In *McCollum*,
Justice Black, speaking for the Court, described separation in
the metaphor of a wall:

> Neither a state nor the Federal Government can set up a
> church. Neither can pass laws which aid one religion, aid all
> religions, or prefer one religion over another. Neither can
> force nor influence a person to go to or to remain away from
> church against his will or force him to profess a belief or dis-
> belief in religion. . . . No tax in any amount, large or small, can
> be levied to support any religious activities or institutions. . . .
> In the words of Jefferson, the clause against establishment of
> religion was intended to erect "a wall of separation between
> Church and State."[5]

In the *Zorach* case, however, Justice Douglas modified this extreme division between religion and government.

> The First Amendment . . . does not say that in every and
> all respects there shall be separation of Church and State.
> Rather, it studiously defines the manner, the specific ways, in
> which there shall be no concert or union or dependency one
> on the other. That is the common sense of the matter. Other-
> wise, the state and religion would be aliens to each other—
> hostile, suspicious, and even unfriendly. . . . We are a religious
> people whose institutions presuppose a Supreme Being. . . .[6]

An even more disconcerting case for Protestants was *Everson*
v. *Board of Education* (1947),[7] in which, by a 5-4 decision, the
Supreme Court upheld state policies of extending welfare services to pupils in religious as well as in public schools. In this

instance, New Jersey had permitted communities to provide transportation for pupils attending nonprofit private schools, which in this instance meant Roman Catholic Schools. The problem of a Protestant attitude toward Roman Catholicism plays an important role in distinguishing the various Protestant church-state theories, and it is worth noting that the "pupil benefit" theory tended to benefit Roman Catholic, not Protestant, students, and indirectly, many Protestants charged, the Catholic Church itself. Perhaps more than any other church-state issue, the referenda throughout the country after the *Everson* decision to provide bus transportation for parochial school students tended to become conflicts between Protestants and Catholics. The *Everson* decision was also undoubtedly the chief spark that led to the formation of P.O.A.U.

Two other church-state issues became sources of controversy about the same time. One was President Truman's nomination of Mark Clark to be ambassador to the Vatican City. Just before World War II, in 1939, President Roosevelt had appointed Myron C. Taylor as his personal representative there. At that time a number of Protestant groups protested because of alleged favoritism in the assignment of a representative to a religious as well as a political leader, but accepted the president's political judgment that this appointment would benefit the United States in a time of crisis. In 1951 Mr. Truman proposed to strengthen this precedent by officially recognizing the appointed representative as an ambassador. The reaction of Protestants was vigorous and virtually unanimous, with all the major denominations protesting what they considered a dangerous innovation and a violation of church-state separation.

The other issue concerned public aid for parochial schools. Although Catholic students had benefited indirectly from welfare funds validated in the *Everson* case, the Federal and state governments have not in modern times contributed directly to the program of religiously controlled schools in the form of buildings or salaries. In 1949 Representative Graham A. Barden introduced in Congress a bill to provide federal aid for "public elementary and secondary education." Francis Cardinal Spellman of New York proposed that Roman Catholic schools share in these funds. Mrs. Franklin D. Roosevelt, however, in several eminently fair articles, sought to show why aid should go to public schools alone. Cardinal Spellman then sent a violently critical letter accusing her of a "record of anti-Catholicism." According to Stokes, "No religious issue in recent years has brought a more immediate re-action."[8] The final outcome of the controversy between Mrs. Roosevelt and Cardinal Spellman was public reconciliation and a statement by the Cardinal that Catholics sought only the second-ary benefits guaranteed by *Everson,* but Protestant-Catholic ten-sions had entered once again into an issue involving the relation of church to state.

This series of church-state problems has combined with Blan-shard's criticism of Catholic power and the formation of P.O.A.U. to inaugurate an era of new interest among Protestants in the type of issues raised. Each year since has witnessed new problems and, usually, forthright Protestant responses: nuns teaching in public schools; Sunday closing laws; public support of parochial schools in certain communities; censorship of movies and books by religious groups; Bible reading in the public schools; refer-enda on laws forbidding contraception; and many others. In 1960 the campaign of the Roman Catholic John F. Kennedy for the presidency of the United States climaxed the postwar preoccupa-tion with church-state problems, and Protestantism divided in its response to the first successful Catholic aspirant to the nation's highest office. Hardly had the new administration begun when the problem of aid to religious schools arose again, the Catholic hierarchy opposing Mr. Kennedy's program for federal assistance to the states for improving public schools.

Two clearly definable Protestant approaches have appeared. One, here called separationism and represented by P.O.A.U., in-terprets separation in strict terms, as an absolute wall between church and state. It has cited with approval the dictum of *McCollum* (originally in *Everson*) and has spoken of preventing incursions upon, or breaches in the barrier between, ecclesiasti-cal and political organizations. This position has also been marked by a sense of conflict and opposition with Roman Ca-tholicism, which it interprets as the chief threat to church-state separation because of its presumed desire to promote an ultimate union of church and state while gaining at present special privi-leges, especially financial benefits, for itself.

The Origins of Separationism

These staunch defenders of church-state separation can trace their origins to certain English Puritan sects, especially the Baptists, of the late sixteenth and early seventeenth centuries.[9] The Anabaptists, to be sure, first advocated a break between religion and the state, but their tenuous status kept them from contributing significantly to the political movements that produced American separation of church and state. However, their stress on believers' baptism and refusal to regard the state establishment as a true church set the pattern for the English separatists. The Anabaptists and Mennonites spent most of their history in Central and Eastern European countries where religious freedom came not from sectarian pressure, but from the benevolence of government. In the Anglo-Saxon world, on the other hand, while religious freedom owes much to the prudence of government, hardly any other course would have been possible because of the demand by the sects for toleration and eventually separation of religion from the state. The Anabaptists lived quietly and hoped for the best, but the separatists of the Anglo-Saxon tradition seized the initiative and struggled for what they regarded as their religious and political rights.

There seems little doubt that the difference lay principally in the Calvinist outlook of the English group. Although on certain theological points the early Baptists and other sectarians consciously opposed Calvinism, at the same time they shared the Calvinist sense of God's dynamic will applied to all dimensions of life and felt the sense of certitude proper to the elect.[10] While the Anabaptists had no significant expectations for secular society and willingly perished rather than act violently, the Calvinist sects, feeling that nonresistance did not contribute to the glory of God and the prosperity of the elect, struggled to preserve themselves with the religious intensity that marked all forms of Calvinism.

During the latter half of the sixteenth century individuals of Anabaptist persuasion were active in England, but no evidence remains of their influence on the formative figures from which sectarians and Baptists arose.[11] John Smyth, who is usually regarded as the founder of the Baptist Church, encountered the Waterlander Mennonites in Holland and eventually joined them in 1610, but the part of his congregation important for subsequent Baptist history remained loyal to their English Calvinist tradition. The fact that the small group of English sectarians who eventually became Baptists had contact with Dutch Mennonites at a time of evolution in their thought and practices, undoubtedly confirmed them in their consciousness of being similar to and yet different from the courageous survivors of the original left wing of the Reformation, but the real character of Anglo-Saxon separationism, particularly its political and church-state views, comes from its Calvinist-Puritan associations.

Robert Browne

The first significant separationist leader in England was Robert Browne,[12] who founded a congregational church at Norwich around 1580, but fled to Holland in 1582, where in three published tracts he presented his views. His controlling interest was the doctrine of the church, which he felt was composed of the godly elect alone. To alter the structure of the church to a presbyterian form represented the prime concern of the Puritans. Their insistence stemmed from the conviction that the primitive church of the New Testament had functioned according to the presbyterian system, and biblicists that they were, they insisted that church government as well as theology should conform to the scriptural pattern. Browne was the first of what became an expanding wing of Puritanism which doubted the self-evidence of presbyterianism in the New Testament. In fact, he discerned clear signs of congregationalism—the independence and voluntary nature of each individual congregation, directing its own life and ascertaining the divine intention unsullied by the interference of any higher entity, whether bishop or presbytery. Rejecting the parish system in favor of gathered conventicles of the elect, he argued that the "Kingdom off God Was not to be begun by vvhole parishes, but rather by the vvorthiest, Were thei never so feuve."[13] The church was ". . . a companie or number of beleeuers, which by a willing couenaunt made with their God, are vnder the gouernement of God and Christ, and keepe his Lawes in one holie communion: Because they are redeemed by Christe vnto holines and happines for ever from whiche they were fallen by the sinne of Adam."[14]

This understanding of the church grew not simply from a scrutiny of the New Testament, but followed rather reasonably from the Protestant emphasis on individual experience in justification and the Calvinist doctrines of election and sanctification. Calvin and his Puritan followers, accepting these experiential tenets along with the desirability of an established church, were somewhat inconsistent; they subjected both genuine and nominal Christians to the godly discipline of church and state but allowed only those who were Christians by experience to participate in the Lord's Supper. The Calvinist view of the elect, which intensified the distinction between the visible and the invisible church, guaranteed that sooner or later some form of sectarianism would develop within that branch of the Reformation, just as consciousness of religious experience and sanctification produced the same result among the Anabaptists within a Lutheran and Zwinglian matrix.

Browne's emphasis on election led to both voluntary and separated churches. This differentiated him from Henry Jacob and the Puritan founders of Massachusetts Bay who called the Anglican Church "our dear mother," and insisted that they had "sucked . . . from her breasts" the knowledge of salvation.[15] Although Jacob and the nonseparatist congregationalists would not tolerate the interference of the magistrate in the interior religious life of the congregations, they advocated and established a system in America by which the government formally adopted and promoted congregationalism as the official religion of the realm. Browne, on the other hand, promoted a "Reformation without tarying for anie," which meant not to tarry within the national church, but to form immediately separate conventicles divorced from Anglicanism. Lacking the confidence of the majority of Puritans that in time the national church would evolve in a presbyterian or congregational direction, he felt that the purity of the elect should be preserved from the idolatry of the established church. Most Puritans were satisfied with the freedom to preach within the structure of the church, but Browne held even this to be inconsistent with the will of God, a distortion of the free activity by which God spoke his pure word to the elect. He thus opposed the conscious Erastianism of the Anglicans and the unconscious Erastianism of the Puritans who looked for government to adopt the Reformed faith as set forth at Geneva.

Browne denied to the civil authorities the right to promote religion in any way. He envisioned a development of the faith in which the pious elect would form groups independent and separate from parishes or formal structures, but once these were organized, the government would paternally protect them. His complaint against the Elizabethan settlement lay not in the Queen's lack of tolerance, but in her misapprehension of the will of God in supporting Anglicanism rather than congregationalism.

Yet may they [magistrates] doo nothing concerning the Church, but onelie ciuilie, and as ciuile Magistrates, that is,

they haue not that authoritie ouer the church, as to be Proph-
etes or Priestes, or spiritual Kings, as they are Magistrates
ouer the same: but onelie to rule the common wealth in all
outwarde Iustice, to maintaine the right, welfare, and honor
thereof, with outward power, bodily punishment, & ciuil forc-
ing of me[n]. And therfore also because the church is in a
commonwealth, it is of their charge: that is concerning the outward prouision & outward iustice, they are to looke to it; but to
co[m]pell religion, to plant churches by power, and to force a
submission to Ecclesiastical gouernement by lawes & penalties
belongeth not to them. . . .[16]

Nor was this all. The magistrates were obligated to "suppress
and root out by their authoritie all false ministeries, voluntarie
Religions and counterfeyt worship of God. . . . And on the other
hand to establish & mayntein by their lawes every part of Gods
word his pure Relligion and true ministerie to cherish and
protect all such as are carefull to worship God according to his
word . . . yea to enforce al their Subiects . . . to do their dutyes
to God and men. . . ."[17]

Such was the confidence of the elect that the government would
immediately perceive the truth of religion once-formed and
stamp out all contradictory interpretations. An abnegation of
governmental patronization apparently represented too startling
a step for Browne, as it did for other early separationists. In forming separatist groups, nevertheless, they acted with great courage,
for by defying the comprehensive policy espoused by Elizabeth
they subjected themselves to harassment, exile, and even death.
Their views provide an important transition away from the
Anglican and Puritan assumption that reformation should proceed through the national church. Their lack of a fully developed
and consistent position on the relation of church and state may
be ascribed to their pre-eminent theological concerns. They were
not interested in defining their relation to government, but in
challenging the view that the establishment represented the
elect saints. In defining magistral responsibility, they mouthed
inherited Calvinism rather than examining the implications for
church and state of their view that the elect form the church
voluntarily, separate from the unsaved and sinful who obscure
the nature of Christianity by frequenting a church organized
by government. They were not interested in toleration, except
for themselves, and consequently followed without question the

Calvinist tradition that government patronize the true religion, even when they felt the true religion had no relation with the state. Their certainty of being the elect dictated both their separation from the national church and their demand that government protect them.

The Rise of the Baptists

The next stage for separationism took place in Holland, where refugees from the persecution of Elizabeth and James found a haven. Although initially intolerant, a few creative spirits, impelled by their principles and experiences of persecution, came to dissociate Christian faith from political coercion. The key figure was John Smyth, a Cambridge graduate who moved from Puritanism to separatism and in Holland founded what became the Baptist Church. The exact role of the Mennonites in Smyth's career is hard to determine.[18] Although he knew of the Mennonites, there seem to have been no extensive relations between them and his small congregation. In 1609, however, apparently through examination of the Bible and undoubtedly aware of the Mennonite position, he concluded that infant baptism had no validity and baptized himself and his followers. It is noteworthy that he did not initially go to the Mennonites for baptism, because he did not regard baptismal succession as important, but rather that one indicate his state of belief and symbolize it by baptism. On this point the Baptists set themselves off from the other Calvinist separationists, who continued to utilize the church covenant as the determinant of church membership. Given the absence of direct references to infant baptism in the New Testament, Smyth might well have reached his position without any influence from the Mennonites, but the adoption of this distinguishing characteristic brought him into closer association with them.

In 1610, when Smyth petitioned to join the Mennonites, a minority of his congregation under the leadership of Thomas Helwys did not follow him but continued to uphold Calvinist views that made adoption of the complete Mennonite outlook impossible. Nevertheless, like the Mennonites they rejected predestination in favor of unlimited atonement. This undercut their original sectarian emphasis on election, but enabled them to continue their view of the church as a group set apart by belief, conversion, and regeneration. They thus moved an additional step beyond the original English sectarian position, holding the church to be the voluntarily converted rather than the elect gathered in a covenant, and emphasizing believer's baptism as a symbol of this difference.

In late 1611 or early 1612, Helwys' group returned to England and, as the first genuine Baptist congregation in England, began to worship surreptitiously outside London. Helwys wrote a series of books in which he pointed out the differences between Baptists and both Puritans and Mennonites. Holding to separatism, baptism, and general atonement, in distinction from the Puritans, the Baptists also rejected the political features that produced public suspicion of the Mennonites: refusal to take an oath, hold office, or fight. Despite their willingness to conform to governmental expectations on these matters, Baptists were persecuted in England simply because their separatism contravened the national religious policy. For this reason the Baptists did not thrive in early seventeenth-century England, and only the unstable political and religious conditions of the 1640's enabled them to expand, gain a significant voice, and function openly.

Nevertheless, from these obscure beginnings sprang the first serious non-Erastian proposals in England for toleration of all religious groups. In article 12 of a Baptist Confession of 1611 published in Holland it was argued "that as one congregation hath Christ, so hath all. And that the word of God cometh not out from any one, neither to any one congregation in particular, but unto every particular church, as it doth unto all the world. And therefore no church ought to challenge any prerogative over any other."[19] This article springs from the theological assumption that God communicates to congregations and opposes church authoritarianism, especially as found in Anglicanism. But a corollary is the denial of political control over the separationist religious conventicles, or any congregation, for that matter. Coercion in religion violated the Baptist understanding of how man apprehended God, and they found no more convincing proof than the governmental suppression of the free word of God under the Anglican policy. Their outlook was essentially theocentric, rather than individualistic, and though not absolutely committed to congregationalism, they regarded voluntary congregations as the best means by which the word of God might be mediated in an unfettered way. In this respect they did not differ from the main body of Puritans, who also gathered in groups within the Anglican Church for preaching services; but the Baptists came to espouse toleration because they were willing to risk theological error in order to counteract the tendency of men to set themselves up as arbiters of God's word.

The Confession of 1611, and the writings of Smyth, Helwys, Leonard Busher, and John Murton expand the implications of the Baptist views. In his important work, *A Short Declaration of the Mistery of Iniquity,* Helwys attempted to distinguish the political sphere, in which the magistrate acted, from religion, where God ruled. Following his distinction to its logical outcome, Helwys argued that even Roman Catholics and Jews, though heretical, had the right to relate to God as they deemed appropriate "for mens religion to God, is betwixt God and themselves; the king shall not answere for it, neither may the king be iugd [sic] betwene God and man. Let them be heretikes, Turcks, Jewes, or whatsoever it apperteynes not to the earthly power to punish them in the least measure."[20] It was only natural that, given this emphasis on the experiential dimension of religion, the Baptist spokesmen should argue against religious coercion.[21] Moreover, they insisted that unlike the Anabaptists they held no implicitly subversive political doctrines. The title of Murton's book reveals this: *Objections Answered . . . That no man ought to be persecuted for his religion, so he testify his allegiance by the Oath, appointed by Law.*

Several writers have emphasized the significance of Arminianism, as held by the early Baptists, in promoting views of religious liberty.[22] While adherents of a strong doctrine of election tended to consign all outside the church to perdition and corresponding temporal penalties, Arminianism stressed the capacity of all individuals to respond to God's decree, holding that whoever heard and believed would be saved while those who did not would be lost. The Baptists, consequently, insisted that any man, no matter how steeped in error at the moment, might be persuaded in the future; and to coerce and destroy him would frustrate the will of God that all be saved. The main body of those who adhered to the Calvinist doctrine of predestination and election tended to demand toleration only for themselves, but the Baptists sought toleration even for those with whom they disagreed. Again, their motive was evangelistic, the communication of God's word, combined with an awareness of God's sovereignty over the religious life, rather than a defense of the human conscience. During this period the Baptists did not advocate what could be called separation of church and state, but they did oppose coerced uniformity of the national religion as it affected religious freedom.

The Baptists were not the only separationists at this time who advocated toleration on the basis of religious conviction. John Robinson, the teacher of the Scrooby congregation that immigrated to America as the Pilgrims, traveled the same intellectual road as Smyth from governmental protection of the true religion to general tolerance. In his early period, when he came from England to Holland, Robinson lamented the willingness of the Dutch to receive his group, for he regarded the exile as a stage before they would return to England and dictate religious policy. Criticizing the Baptists for exempting the magistrate from religious responsibility, he said that the Scriptures direct the ruler to "alter, devise, or establish nothing in religion otherwise than Christ hath appoynted, but proves not that he may not use his lawfull power lawfully for the furtherance of Christ's Kingdom and Lawes."[23] Later in life, however, Robinson utilized a doctrine of election to justify religious freedom for all. Because God had chosen the redeemed, who would persevere under any conditions, it did not matter whether the unregenerate conformed to a set of religious practices, since no human power could save men. Nor was God "pleased with unwilling worshippers, nor Christian societies bettered, nor the persons themselves neither, but the plain contrary in all three."[24] Thus both strict Calvinism and Arminianism contained the seeds for a policy of toleration.

Separationism in the English Civil War

Until 1643, however, the future of religion and toleration in England rested in the hands of the Anglicans and Puritans, for the separationists lacked the social position and strength of numbers to press their cause. The development of the Puritan Army and the unmuzzling of the forum and printing press found the Baptists one of a variety of groups pressing for separation and religious freedom. The feature that seems to have bound these groups together was their conformity to the sectarian characteristics described by Troeltsch and their determination to guarantee religious freedom by destroying all plans to establish and publicly support a religion. Otherwise, they ranged from relativists and mystics to religious communists, but all can be considered left-wing Puritans.[25]

The Baptists were representative, especially since many congregations called Particular Baptists were being founded on a

platform of predestination and election in distinction from the
General Baptists who stood in the tradition of Smyth and Helwys.
The Baptist leaders of the 1640's such as Hanserd Knollys and
Henry Denne participated in the chief left-wing activities of the
time: printing of pamphlets, combating the king, and preaching
to the Army. Richard Overton, a leader of the Levellers, was
also a Baptist. The Baptists were set apart from the others by
their rejection of infant baptism. The examination of separationism in this period, then, is concerned not merely with the Baptists, but with the other groups, some short-lived, which contributed to democracy and religious liberty. Individual sects did
not play distinct roles, although sectarianism as a whole did.

Separationism and Anglo-Saxon Democracy

Reinhold Niebuhr has pointed out that the Protestant contribution to the limitation of political absolutism and the formulation of a pluralistic, tolerant society stems from these sects.[26]
According to William Haller, "If plutocracy may be said to have
first reared its head among the orthodox Calvinists, democracy
may equally as well be said to have stolen up behind the orthodox in the guise of the heretics, the mystics and enthusiasts of
all sorts whom the preachers summoned to bear part under the
banners of Christ in the war of the spirit on wickedness in high
places."[27] This observation may be corroborated by comparing
some major features of democracy, especially in its English and
American form, with parallels in sectarian thought of the
1640's. One could cite, for example, the sovereignty of the people,
government by elected representatives, the limitation of power
because of its corrupting tendencies, inviolable popular rights,
and the free functioning of corporate groups as major features
of democracy. Although the political convictions of the left-wing
Puritans appear in a number of documents and are reflected
in the Army debates, the brief remonstrance of the Levellers,
"An Agreement of the People" (1647),[28] will be used as chief
illustration.

The sovereignty of the people underlies the demand for the
selection and limitation of parliament. The Levellers, who purported to speak for the people, argued that "the power of this,
and all future Representatives of this nation is inferior only to
theirs who choose them,"[29] indicating that the authority of the
governing representatives derives from a more fundamental
source within the nation, the people, who bestow upon them

their position and power. The election of representatives was the key issue in the Leveller program. At this time the right of suffrage in England was limited to people of propertied, social, or intellectual status, but the Levellers advanced the suggestion that they who had fought in the Army to preserve the integrity of England should also be able to participate in elections. In fact, the "Agreement" implies a complete reassessment of the role of government as an instrument of the people rather than of vested interests. John Wildman in the Putney Debates insisted, "Every person in England hath as clear a right to elect his representative as the greatest person in England," because it is questionable "whether any person can justly be bound by law, who doth not give his consent that such persons shall make laws for him."[30] Colonel Ireton, speaking for the propertied class against the Levellers, agreed that the origin of determining law lay in the people, but he defined the people as those who "are possessed of the permanent interest in the land."[31]

The interest in popular sovereignty and suffrage grew out of the religious situation. Through the religious congregations and discussions in the Army, the lower classes finally gained a degree of expression after centuries of silence. Although their program reflected the interests of the lower classes, the form of their religious life intensified a democratic view of government. The left wing was thoroughly congregational, and in their conventicles, election of leaders and ministers took place with each Christian having an equal voice. The equality of the religious man promoted views of political equality, and the form of democratic and elective church government was translated into the political sphere, because to the left wing the two spheres of existence were not sharply separated. In fact, many envisioned an England transformed by the religious congregations into the kingdom of God.

To counter corrupting tendencies of unchecked power, "An Agreement of the People" provided for selection of parliaments every two years.[32] Furthermore, the manifesto specified in considerable detail the responsibilities and limitations of Parliament. For example, it could make and alter laws; abolish and establish offices, courts, and magistrates, conduct war and deal with foreign states; but it could not interfere in religious life, impress men into military service, or discriminate in the establishment or application of laws, for "no tenure, estate, character, degree, birth, or place, do confer any exemption from the ordinary course of legal

proceedings."[33] The Levellers called these limitations on government "our native rights."[34] The principles of regular elections
and a bill of rights are clearly foreshadowed in these proposals.

The "Agreement" also included a significant statement that
defined, not only the social priority and independence of religious groups, but their freedom to express their convictions on
society and public policy. Anglo-Saxon democracy distinguishes
itself most sharply from totalitarian democracy in this respect,
that the religious group typifies any peaceable social group, with
which government ordinarily cannot interfere but which nevertheless can influence government. According to the "Agreement"
"matters of religion, and the ways of God's worship, are not at
all entrusted by us to any human power, because therein we
cannot remit or exceed a tittle of what our consciences dictate
to be the mind of God, without wilful sin; nevertheless the
public way of instructing the nation (so it be not compulsive)
is referred to their discretion."[35]

The Significance of Seventeenth-Century Separationism

Some of these characteristics have a longer history than does
Protestantism. The assent of the people to their rulers, the limitation of political officials by natural law and traditional rights,
and the independence of the religious and cultural spheres of
life are principally products of the medieval period. But when
one focuses on historical influence in England, America, and
other nations affected by the Anglo-Saxon theory of government,
the significance of the left-wing separationists looms large. Frustrated in England in the seventeenth century, many of them
emigrated to America, and constituted a ready reservoir of support for advancing democracy in the eighteenth century. The
American separationist leaders in the early years of the American
republic actively supported measures increasing political suffrage,
because, like the Levellers, they represented the lower classes
who stood to benefit from it, but also because these features of
democratic theory had always marked their outlook on politics.
In England the views of the Levellers lay dormant, but did not
die. A recent historian of early nineteenth-century political reform traces the humanitarianism of the Anglican Evangelicals
and the Dissenting Churches through Wesley "to the revolutionary Protestantism of the seventeenth century. The religious faith
of the Independents in Cromwell's Army is the source of the
ideas and the aspiration that produced the liberal reforms of the

early nineteenth century."[36] The contribution of this group of Protestants to Anglo-Saxon democracy has made it difficult for them to understand and deal successfully with other types of political and church-state systems. Perhaps more than any other Protestant segment they tend to associate American political characteristics that resulted in part from their religious fervor with the definitive Christian position.

The "Agreement" indicates in extraordinarily lucid fashion the left-wing insistence that religious matters lie in the province of God and not of political power. And though government cannot interfere in religion, nevertheless the religious, who are the saints, have the right of "instructing the nation." The basically Puritan character of the left wing becomes most apparent here, for the word of God held central place both in guiding the congregations as the Holy Spirit directed, and in admonishing and reforming society. A situation in which Christians could not have criticized society would have been intolerable to such men. They did not hold to separation of church and state in abstract or rationalistic terms, but they followed through the implications of their conviction that God's will be communicated to the church and direct the course of society as a whole. As one of them said, "Christ reigns among us in the commonwealth as well as in the church, and hath his glorious interest involved and wrapt up in the good of both societies respectively."[37]

The emergence of the sects from a persecuted and obscure group into a powerful national voice also produced the first important statement in English life of what one might call separation of church and state. The first separationists, preeminently interested in the free activity of God's word and seeking religious freedom for themselves, quickly developed a view of general toleration; but such a program was envisioned within a society that seemed irrevocably committed to a state establishment, and the most the sects could hope for was toleration of their dissent. The overthrow of Anglicanism and the failure of Puritanism to seize control of the situation led certain of the sectarians to question the wisdom of an established church at all. The voluntary congregation that chose and supported its own minister was the system which they, the religious voice of the nation, employed, and they saw no reason why the state should support either priest or Puritan minister. Doubting that a man who owed his position to the state could discern the word of God that might at times condemn the state, they felt that one

could best ascertain the will of God through spontaneous inspiration of the Holy Spirit, discussion of the Bible, or similar measures within the small group. The abolition of tithes, which
would have ended the establishment, consequently became an
established feature of the Leveller program. The following provisions from "An Appeal to Parliament" (March, 1647) are
typical:

> And also tithes and other enforced maintenance are still
> continued, though there be no ground for either under the
> Gospel, and although the same have occasioned multitudes
> of suits, quarrels, and debates both in former and latter times.
>
> [That] . . . tithes and all other enforced maintenances . . .
> be for ever abolished, and nothing in place thereof imposed,
> but that all ministers may be paid only by those who voluntar-
> ily choose them, and contract with them for their labours.[38]

The Sectarian Views of Church and State

During this period the sects seem to have held at least three
views on the relation of church and state, all of which opposed
the official establishment of religion.[39]

One was millenarian and is usually associated with the Fifth
Monarchy Men, who included Baptists like Thomas Collier.[40]
They anticipated that in their own lifetimes God would establish
his kingdom through laws and officers appointed by Christ. They
argued that the millennium would advance when the Spirit
gathered together families, churches, and corporations to rule
the world until the personal appearance of Christ. The present
responsibility of the saints was to "associate together into several
church-societies and corporations (according to the Congregational way), till being increased and multiplied, they may combine into general assemblies or church-parliaments (according
to the Presbyterian way); and then shall God give them authority
and rule over the nations and kingdoms of the world."[41]Although
this view envisioned a future period when the saints would
rule the earth, the spontaneous, charismatic manner of its development points to its advocates' conviction that God's action,
rather than a formal church-state union, would be the means of
its furtherance. Just as the sects co-operated in the Army, so they
would work together, imbued by the Spirit, to make national
decisions according to the will of God. Hanserd Knollys, the chief

Baptist leader, without describing in detail the actualization of the kingdom, represented an eschatological outlook in his *A Glimpse of Sion's Glory* (1641), where he argued that God had given the kingdom to the common people, who experience it now in their congregations, and that in the near future he would universalize it through the return of Christ himself.[42]

The second view of separation was held by Roger Williams, who is usually claimed as a Baptist, but more properly belongs to the broad stream of seventeenth-century Puritan sectarianism. He ended his life as a Seeker, one for whom none of the existent sects represented the true church. Perry Miller has conclusively shown the theocentric, Puritan character of Williams' outlook, and indicated that he did not directly contribute to the theory of American church-state separation;[43] but Williams was an influential figure in England in the 1640's, appearing there twice for extended periods to influence his contemporaries.

Williams' understanding of church and state sprang from a disagreement with the Massachusetts theocrats that they represented the new Israel. He regarded this as a misunderstanding of Scripture and a travesty of the nature of the church, which he held to be invisible, the unknown elect chosen by God's inscrutable will from among all nations and religions, and marked by a holiness that contrasted with the sordid and fallen character of the rest of society. Williams advocated separation of church and state because the true church could not be equated with any visible body. For men to claim they represented the church was "to subject this holy nation, this heavenly Jerusalem, the wife and spouse of Jesus, the pillar and ground of truth, to the vain, uncertain, and changeable mutations of this present evil world."[44] The pattern of the Old Testament theocracy he held inapplicable under the New Covenant; rather the religious purity of Israel maintained by the sword foreshadowed the purity of the church maintained by its spiritual integrity alone. He differed from the millenarians, furthermore, by denying that Christian congregations would eventually become universal and inherit the kingdom. Rather he saw a sharp schism between church and world, almost in Mennonite fashion.[45]

The magistrate is concerned with justice, peace, and morality, not with religious matters. Williams compared the commonwealth to a ship whose passengers include Jews, Turks, and Roman Catholics, as well as a variety of Protestants, none of whom are compelled to attend a particular service of worship

nor restrained from their own form of devotion. The captain
of the ship is responsible for following the course and administering rules and order.[46] In other words, Williams held that society
could maintain civil peace even with many religious groups,
that it could punish them if they violated the secular laws, but
not if they attended to their peaceable worship. He thus advanced
beyond the view of earlier Erastian figures on toleration by so
separating the civil and political functions that even support
of one or several religions did not fall under the purview of the
magistrate, any more than did the activities of a commercial
company. He argued that the continuation of even a grossly
false religion would not injure the true church any more than
"poison hurt[s] the body when it is not touched or taken,"[47]
just as it would not injure the state so long as worshipers did
not violate a civil law. The only concern of the state is that civil
peace be maintained and laws obeyed.

Williams was chiefly interested in religious persecution, especially as he found it in New England, and did not elaborate a
political theory except in relation to the church. He did not
prescribe norms for government in detail, as the Levellers did,
except to point out that the people determined their form of
government. He spoke of the powers of government, like a good
Puritan, in a biblical context, "to publish and apply such civil
laws in a state as either are expressed in the word of God in
Moses' judicials . . . so far as they are of general and moral equity
. . . ."[48] Usually referring to the latter six commandments of the
Decalogue as a set of principles for guiding government, Williams with his biblical perspective differed from the third theory
of church-state separation held by many Levellers. As a good
Puritan he expected any society in Christendom to enforce the
same moral laws that Massachusetts did, although he willingly
admitted that one could not expect the high moral tone in
modern society that ancient Israel had upheld.

The Levellers, on the other hand, tended to replace the biblical framework of Puritanism with a natural, almost secular
ethic. Whether they derived their concept of a primal social
contract from the Scottish theorists, Rutherford and Buchanan,
or from the role of the covenant in congregational policy, they
agreed that at some time in the past, people held certain fundamental rights and founded governments to guarantee them.
However, intervening governments had denied the implicitly

democratic origins of society by violating these rights, a situation which the Levellers sought to rectify.

In the Putney debates, Wildman and Colonel Thomas Rainborowe illustrated the Leveller rationale of government by referring either to natural rights or traditional customs prevalent before the inception of tyranny. Whereas the Puritans held a highly dynamic sense of the will of God, based on the outlook of the Old Testament, Wildman depersonalized the divine will and implied that one apprehended it through a reasonable interpretation of justice.

> [The case is] is yet [more difficult] in civil matters; [for] we cannot find anything in the word of God [of] what is fit to be done in civil matters. But I conceive that only is of God that does appear to be like unto God—justice and mercy, to be meek and peaceable. I should desire therefore that we might proceed only in that way . . . to consider what is justice and what is mercy, and what is good, and I cannot but conclude that that is of God. Otherwise I cannot think that any one doth speak from God when he says what he speaks is of God.[49]

This statement reflects a radical shift of emphasis in the Puritan left and actually meant the death of what can be called the Puritan outlook. Wildman was quite justified in insisting that the supposedly charismatic, but actually cacaphonous, definitions of God's will demanded new criteria for determining social and political norms.

The Secularization of Separationism

The theocratic outlook of Calvinism had tended to undercut the medieval separation between nature and grace, and as Woodhouse shows,[50] the Levellers now proposed once again to separate grace from nature, leaving the civil order to the realm of nature. For Wildman such a procedure did not mean abrogating the will of God, for he, like all Christian advocates of natural law, assumed that justice and goodness represented God's intentions. But inasmuch as man's reason apprehended natural law and ascribed it to God, anthropocentrism crept in and initiated that rapid development in English life toward a rationalism that put God in the heavens and left men to decide what constituted natural rights and obligations. Even in the Putney debates a

dispute over the meaning of the natural arose, because the
Levellers and Independents had different conceptions of what
reason dictated as norms for society.

The millenarians represented the most Puritan of these positions, because they attempted to carry through in apocalyptic
terms the social vision that the Puritans had guarded during
their decades of waiting. Williams wavered between the Puritan
and the secular view in defining different norms for church and
state, although he continued to think of the moral obligations
of society in scriptural, Puritan terms. Even the natural law he
cited in the form of the Decalogue. The Levellers completed
the theory initiated by Williams, providing for the new secular
state a natural ethic which in time would be secularized, while
leaving the religious congregations free to monopolize the dynamic expression of Protestantism through religious experience
alone. The Levellers, to be sure, did not make their suggestions
in a secular, but rather a religious spirit. Their attempt to develop a justification for their position paved the way, however,
for a separation in English religion between the sacred and the
secular. The development of spirituality in the congregations
was accompanied by a secularization of the political order on
norms discovered by natural reason.

At this point the ambivalence appeared that characterizes
much of modern separationist history. On the one hand, the
failure of both millenarian and Leveller programs and the restoration of monarchy in 1660 led them to accept the independence
of the political order as long as the spiritual life of their congregations was guaranteed. Thus, most of the left wing gave up the
fight for abolition of tithes under Cromwell. In America, where
sectarian dissenters gained great strength, religious liberty and
separation of church and state became the major social concerns
of Baptists and similar groups. On the other hand, sectarianism,
especially in America, could not shake off its Puritan past and
felt compelled to exercise to some extent its moral concerns in
society. But it has been unable to determine a theory for its efforts and has wavered between continuation of the older Puritan
social norms and an ethic of reason or natural principles underlying the civil order. It has developed tensions or contradictions
between a principle like separation of church and state and the
Puritan program for society, between commitment to a religious
ethic and the association of the political order with other norms
like democracy or constitutionally guaranteed human rights.

This is why the separationists in the twentieth century blissfully, but inconsistently, advocate a wall of separation between church and state, while virtually controlling the moral and religious life of areas in which they predominate, or why they vigorously call their followers to adhere to religious rather than secular values, while sanctifying principles of government that were obviously promoted by rationalists in the eighteenth century.

While the next century and a half witnessed the political triumph of the middle classes and their religion of established respectability, the lower-class churches, which continued to hold separationist views, declined in significance. One searches in vain for evidences of a popular surge to religion like that of the 1640's; Protestantism in fact declined in the whole Anglo-Saxon world, and even in a religious stronghold like New England active church members were an educated and prosperous minority. The poorer people, scattered in rural areas of New England, lapsed into religious indifference as much from failure to conform to the social as to the religious demands of the churches. The Anglican colonies had never had strong churches, the isolation of the settlers and the shortage of ministers contributing to the general deterioration of Anglicanism in this period.

Revivalism and Separationism

The revitalization of Protestantism in America through the Great Awakenings of the eighteenth century significantly strengthened those groups holding separationist sentiments. The New England phase of the revival is usually associated with the Congregationalist Jonathan Edwards, who was anything but a separationist, but the social fruits of the revival were more important than Edwards' rationalization of it. The Baptists benefited most strikingly in numbers and organizational strength, in the process becoming the backbone of one of the two major forces that supported the American system of church-state separation. Until the Great Awakenings the Baptists were one of the smaller religious bodies. They were considered in New England extreme religious radicals who threatened political and religious unity; they were tolerated in Virginia, but were required to function at specified meeting places.

Although the revivals began under the auspices of men from the transformationist tradition, they introduced a note into

American religion that strengthened the separationists more than the transformationists.[51] The emotionalism, for example, corresponded more to the excesses of Civil War sectarianism than to any other Protestant outlook. Secondly, the revivals seem to have attracted the lower classes, who did not respond readily to the now staid and autocratic official Congregationalism. Thirdly, revivalism raised the issue of lay versus ordained, of charismatic versus educated, clergy; and where it had the most vigor, it simply ignored the parish system which the establishment had carefully maintained.

But more significant than any of these factors, the revivals emphasized the spirit of conversion, of adult encounter with the Christian faith as a vital experience, which conflicted with the formal system of institutional membership fostered by both Congregationalists and Anglicans. Religion as belief and regeneration flamed again. The revivalist party in Congregationalism began to question the credentials of the parish clergy who opposed the revival, doubting they were either genuine or converted Christians. When the establishment rebuffed the revivalists' insistence on a converted ministry, many revivalists left and formed separate Congregational and Baptist churches, a number of the former eventually associating with the latter. According to Wesley M. Gewehr, the Great Awakenings revived the same outlook among many people which had produced views of democracy and church-state separation in the 1640's.

> The evangelical doctrines, when brought to bear upon the great mass of the population, produced a democratic feeling, developed a degree of self-respect, and inculcated ideas of self-government. The very essence of these teachings was to place all men on a plane of exact equality in the Christian Church. . . . The Great Awakening gave rise to popular forms of church government and thus accustomed people to self-government in their religious habits. The alliance of Church and State, the identification of religious with civil institutions, was found to be detrimental to the cause of religion.[52]

Wherever revivalism spread, especially in Virginia, Baptists increased, colliding with the moribund establishments that feebly relied on political support for their defense. In Virginia, for example, the activities of itinerant preachers who refused to list their meeting houses led between 1768 and 1776 to the imprisonment of nearly fifty for "disturbing the peace" or refusing to give bond to keep the peace in the future.[53]

The Baptist-pietist-revivalist party now began to press for church-state separation in earnest. Its leaders were Isaac Backus[54] and John Leland,[55] both of whom came from the New England revivalist, separatist congregational tradition before finding their spiritual home among the Baptists. Backus was the agent of the Warren Association, a confederation of Baptist congregations formed especially to advance the cause of religious freedom. Between 1756 and 1767, he preached innumerable sermons,[56] especially on religious freedom. He also appeared before the courts and legislatures of Connecticut and Massachusetts, as well as the delegates of all the colonies both before and after the Revolution.

The Revivalist-Rationalist Alliance
for Church-State Separation

American church-state separation stems not only from the revivalists, but also from the thought and activities of the rationalists.[57] Rationalism developed great strength in both England and America in reaction to the dogmatic and divisive fanaticism of seventeenth-century religion. As early as the first years of the eighteenth century in America, rationalism in conjunction with separationist views was found in the thought of John Wise, Congregational minister at Chebacco, Massachusetts. On the surface, Wise seemed merely a defender of the extreme congregationalism of the New England Way against tendencies to form associations with authority over individual congregations; but his books, written in 1713 and 1717, betray appropriation of a rationalist tradition that led him to defend himself solely by appeal to reason and natural law, the heart of his position being an emphasis on "an original liberty instamp upon his [man's] rational nature."[58] Although Wise did not discuss church-state theory, he became an important theorist of democracy by translating his predilection for congregational polity into the political order, while his stringent defense of human integrity and the independence of religious congregations militated by implication against any form of religious coercion from above. The Enlightenment developed major inroads into that center of Puritanism, Boston, and by the mid-eighteenth century its leaders like Charles Chauncy (1705-1787) and Jonathan Mayhew (1720-1766) were among the most important intellectuals of New England. On the question of disestablishment in New England, the men of an Enlightenment outlook favored separation of church and state, while the more conservative Calvinists opposed it. Chauncy stated his convictions straightforwardly in the following words: "We are, in principle, against all civil establishments in religion. . . . It does not appear to us that God has entrusted the State with the right to make religious establishments."[59]

The New England rationalists tried to combine the Enlightenment with Calvinism, but in other colonies the intellectual and political leadership fell upon a more urbane, less passionately religious group—men like Washington, Franklin, Jefferson, Madison, George Mason of Virginia, and Ethan Allen of Vermont. Nourished on the philosophy of John Locke and the French rationalists, they approached problems from a perspective of reason, tolerance, and harmony. They looked with horror on the religious zealots of the seventeenth century, and regarded the Toleration Act of 1689 as a triumph of sound judgment. They had a passion for a democratic republic and religious freedom, although they understood democracy to mean the rule of the middle class and the protection of their economic interests from interference by the English monarch or the capricious inclinations of the masses. Both transformationists and separationists joined them in the revolt against England and the establishment of a republic, but against state churches in the various colonies and for the provision for church-state separation in the Federal Constitution they had only the support of the dissenting and revivalist religious groups.

Whereas the revivalists tended to favor church-state separation because they feared the intrusion of the state into religious life, and their religious convictions forbade their supporting a religion with which they did not agree,[60] the rationalists acted out of an opposite concern, fear of religious intrusion into political and economic life. Their outlook was essentially Erastian, but they tried to solve the problem, not by subjecting religion to state control, but by removing religion from state control. The God they worshiped was a creator who established rational and harmonious laws to guide the universe, laws consistent with their interests such as the formation of government by social contract, and the noninterference of government in economic affairs. The moral values they upheld coincided with the outlook of prosperous and intelligent men confident in the rectitude of their way of life and aware of their responsibility for promoting prosperity and caring for the handicapped through paternalism: reasonableness, sympathy, benevolence, honesty, friendship, and respectability.[61] More than anything else they abhorred the active and angry God of Calvin and Puritanism, before whom even man's benevolence stood shattered, and who allowed no dimension of life to escape from his will.

One could hardly imagine a more unlikely coalition than revivalists and rationalists, and the extent of their common interest should not be exaggerated; but they agreed in opposing Anglican or Congregationalist attempts to determine what views the individual believer should support. To the revivalist, this did not represent true and experienced faith; to the rationalist it meant the coercion of a conscience which should discover truth for itself. As Sidney Mead has pointed out, this essentially unstable alliance lasted only long enough to achieve immediate aims and then fell apart, although there were some common convictions, such as the appreciation of the moral aspects of religion, the emphasis on religion as a matter between God and man without need of institutional mediation, and the understanding of the church as a voluntary organization of like-minded believers.[62] Against the older orthodoxy and ecclesiastical tradition they relied on simple appeal to the Scriptures, although the revivalists stressed the gospel of the primitive church while the rationalists equated the teachings of Jesus with the self-evident natural moral law. Two minority groups thus combined to press for church-state separation even when the nation was occupied with problems of war. Minorities they were, but both had great influence beyond their numbers: the rationalists with their political, economic, and social power; the revivalists with the most dynamic religious force of the day, the irrepressible energy that religious experience stimulates.

Disestablishment in Virginia

The most significant battleground against state establishment, Virginia, one which had important consequences for the structure of federal separation, illustrates this alliance excellently. In the two decades prior to the Revolution, the most important dissenting groups vastly increased in the South as a result of revivalism. The Separate Baptists, a product of the New England revivals, quickly became the spokesmen for other Baptists and in

1772 submitted the first of many petitions to the Assembly for
"Liberty of Conscience." Unlike the previous Baptist groups that
had settled in Virginia, they were unwilling to accept mere toleration, but demanded an end to all the privileges of the Anglicans, persisting in this effort until the adoption of the Bill for
Establishing Religious Freedom in 1785. They directed themselves not simply against the Anglicans, but against any financial
association of the state with the church, defeating the attempt of
many distinguished Virginians, including Washington, to provide
for assessment of each citizen and allocation to the church of his
choice. The Baptists argued instead that "the holy Author of our
religion needs no such compulsive measures for the promotion of
his cause; that the gospel wants not the feeble arm of man for its
support; that it has made, and will again, through divine power,
make its way against all opposition; and that should the Legislature assume the right of taxing the people for the support of the
gospel, it will be destructive to religious liberty."[63]

The other religious group that stood out in the development of
religious liberty in Virginia was one usually associated with re-
strictive Calvinist orthodoxy—Presbyterianism. These Presbyterians were different. Principally Scotch-Irish, they had been a dissenting group to a privileged establishment in both Ireland and
Virginia and had become advocates of religious freedom. More
significantly for the point under consideration, they were revivalist in outlook. The Hanover Presbytery, formed in 1755, to which
they belonged, was virtually the personal product of Samuel
Davies, a graduate of the Log College, a school for training revivalist ministers in the middle colonies, and a member of the
New Side, the revivalist wing of the Presbyterian Church. Davies
originally had to struggle for inclusion of his group within the
Virginia system of toleration, since the antirevivalist Presbyterians, who were regarded by the colonial government as the real
Presbyterians, opposed the interlopers from the North because
of their revivalist heterodoxy and refusal to hold fixed parishes.
The Hanover Presbytery, beginning in 1776, joined the Baptists
in memorializing the General Assembly in favor of separation. In
1784 they opposed the general assessment plan for all denominations in these congregation-centered words: "We hope that no attempt will be made to point out articles of faith, or to settle
modes of worship, or to interfere in the internal government of
religious communities, or to render the ministers of religion independent of the will of the people whom they serve."[64]

Along with these revivalist religious groups, three Episcopalian laymen, Mason, Jefferson, and Madison, played the most significant role in Virginia disestablishment and subsequently in the nation as a whole. Madison had studied at Princeton where the New Side Presbyterians held sway, but like the other two men, he represented the tolerant, rationalistic latitudinarianism that marked Anglican intellectuals in the eighteenth century. The two most important documents in the theory of Virginia separation, Madison's "Memorial and Remonstrance" (1784) and Jefferson's "Act for Establishing Religious Freedom," reflect in a striking way the rationalistic outlook. The latter, for example, in a preface struck out by the legislature, points to "the evidence proposed to their minds" as the source of the opinions and beliefs of men, and contains references to freedom of the mind, natural rights, and discussion as the chief ways to truth.[65] Despite the cooperation of revivalist and rationalist in the actual struggle for separation of religion from the state, the former group did not contribute significantly to the theory of separation in Virginia and the United States, which is based on a patently rationalist philosophy.[66]

The Rationalist Influence on Separationism

The coalition of revivalist and rationalist has continued as the chief Protestant force upholding the separationist view, although they split in the early nineteenth century. Revivalism should perhaps be broadened to include, after the revivals of the nineteenth century and the assimilation of their converts into more settled churches, the large wing of conservative and evangelical Protestantism. Rationalism has gained chief expression through Unitarianism; but especially in the twentieth century many liberals who do not differ strikingly from the thinkers of the Enlightenment have been important spokesmen for their denominations on church-state matters. For all of these, separation of church and state is virtually an article in a religious creed.

The coalition fell apart for the first time over the issue of rationalist sympathy for the French Revolution, although social and theological differences made their alliance unstable from the beginning. The American rationalists had never been what are usually called "deists," who combined a religion of reason with a strong opposition to revealed and organized religion. Jefferson and Madison stressed the general agreement of all religions, attended church, and expressed appreciation for the co-operation of the revivalists, but deists like Thomas Paine openly advocated infidelity and supported the anticlerical measures of the French Revolution. In the late eighteenth century American Protestantism feared that the rational and democratic ideas espoused by Jefferson would eventually undermine religion and social order, as they were doing in France. The New England theocrats or transformationists had no doubt that they would and aligned themselves with the Federalist Party against the supporters of Jefferson. Many of the separationists, on the other hand, remained with the rationalists until disestablishment in Connecticut and Massachusetts, but were already co-operating with the transformationists on measures with which rationalists did not sympathize, such as the conversion of the frontier and foreign missions. The result was that infidelity and rationalism, which seemed on the verge of triumphing in 1790, were turned back in the great surge of revivalist religion in the nineteenth century. The significant figures of American religion became the ministers, both transformationists and separationists, who set the moral tone and influenced public policy. Traditional Puritanism and theological orthodoxy perished under the sweep of the reconstructed transformationists and separationists, who worked together through much of the nineteenth century in the great project of making America a Christian land through the indirect means offered by the American system of separation.

The association of the revivalist separationists with rationalism left its mark, however, by intensifying the tendency already observable among the Levellers to justify themselves by natural rather than theological reasons. Individualism, clearly adopted from Jeffersonianism, now became a trademark of Baptists and other revivalists; freedom of religion took second place to upholding separation of church and state; the justification for action on church-state problems was based on constitutional rather than religious grounds; the free conscience rather than the conscience to which God speaks gained in value. Consequently, on church-state matters the revivalists have had little difficulty continuing to co-operate from time to time with liberals on the opposite end of the theological spectrum. Professor Mead has pointed out the anomalous character of this tendency and partly illuminated the source of anti-Catholicism among the separationists:

Hence when Protestantism vigorously rejected eighteenth century rationalism . . . it cut itself off from the theoretical justification for the religious freedom it ardently espoused in practice. And it has never been made clear that the practice can be given theoretical justification on the premises of traditional orthodoxy which the bulk of the denominations have professed to accept. Hence at present the strange inclination of Protestant guardians of separation of church and state against real or imagined Roman Catholic "threats" to accept as their own the purely "secular" defenses being promulgated, and in a way that implies the equation of Protestantism with secularism. There seems to be too little realization that identification with secular defenses of this "good" cause could be as disastrous for Protestantism as for Roman Catholicism.[67]

Separationism in the Nineteenth Century

The difference between transformationists and separationists in the nineteenth century is very difficult to define with precision, because of their co-operation on many issues. The nineteenth century can well be considered the greatest in the history of evangelical Protestantism. Although theological differences and denominational schisms continued, this was also the time when denominational differences lost their meaning in the mind of the average American and a simple revivalist theology captured most of the major churches, unquestioned until modern science and biblical criticism led to a new type of liberal-conservative split at the end of the century. The pressing need to win the settlers of the West to Protestantism, of manifesting American destiny in religious form by combating the heathen faiths of Asia and Africa, and of electing religious men to office and upholding a relatively Christian standard of morality in public life and policy brought Protestants of many denominations together in a common enterprise. Nearly all, except Old Calvinists and Unitarians, agreed on the value of revivalism, missions, and social and political activity, and some Unitarians even co-operated on matters like abolition of slavery from different presuppositions. No matter what segment of Protestantism one observes, the same vigorous social concern appears. Bodo's study of the transformationist theocrats,[68] Cole's[69] of the early nineteenth-century northern evangelists, Smith's[70] of the pre-Civil War revivalists (especially those with perfectionist tendencies), and Hudson's[71] of the Protestant movement as a whole—all emphasize a coalescence of transformationist and separationist motifs, from the former taking the impetus toward activity in society and from the latter the understanding of churches as voluntary, nonestablished institutions.

Nevertheless, certain differences of later significance can be recognized between the two positions. Bodo's study has attempted to distinguish between theocrats and what he calls "anti-theocrats" within what appears to be a homogeneous movement. The anti-theocrats include the separationists, both revivalist and rationalist, whose presuppositions and policies on church and state constitute a traceable continuation of separationism. Although the anti-theocrats included political leaders who resented the transformationist intrusions into their affairs, as well as Unitarians who disliked their theological conservatism and revivalism, the revivalist, evangelical wing is best represented by the Baptist, John Leland, and perhaps by the Methodist, Peter Cartwright.

Bodo has shown that several assumptions bound the anti-theocrats together, some of which clearly reflect the influence of the Jeffersonian and Jacksonian stream of American politics. The transformationists tended to support the Federalists and Whigs, who championed a restricted electorate and the defense of New England traditions; but Leland and Cartwright staunchly supported Jefferson and Jackson, and that political outlook influences their church-state views. In 1802 a commentator on church life in Boston detected the anti-Federalist inclinations of the Baptists.

> The Baptists, by attaching themselves to the present administration, have gained great success in the United States, and greater in New England than any sect since the settlement, even beyond comparison. This seems to be a warning to the churches of the older denominations. . . . The Congregationalists begin to be alarmed at the great progress of the Anabaptists [Baptists], but the progress is not from their opinions, but from their political situation to oppose the busy clergymen [the transformationists] who are tools of the anti-Jefferson party.[72]

According to Bodo, the chief feature of the separationists was their individualism.[73] Leland, for example, was a key figure in the transition of the Baptists from a congregation-centered to an individual-centered denomination, building on the rationalistic arguments used by Backus in furthering religious freedom. In a memorial to the Continental Congress in 1774 Backus argued that "religion is a concern between God and the soul with which no human authority can intermeddle; consistently with the principles of Christianity, and according to the dictates of Protestantism, we claim and expect the liberty of worshipping God according to our consciences, not being obliged to support a ministry we cannot attend. . . ."[74]

Backus and Leland developed an individualistic concept of freedom of conscience, not only because of their interest in conversion but also from their association with the individualism of the Enlightenment. One can see already in Backus' quotation an understanding of religion as an engagement of the soul in a coordinate relation with God. The right of the individual who has the capacity to relate to God became the chief argument for religious freedom, unlike the seventeenth-century Baptists who sought religious freedom to enhance God's sovereignty over the religious life of individuals and congregations.[75] The form, nature, and significance of the church receded behind a preoccupation with the conversion of single souls, and the church represented no more than a voluntary compact of individuals. Leland claimed to baptize "the penitent INTO Christ—the church receives them into *fellowship*."[76] Such individualism, expressed in various ways, has continued to mark Baptist arguments on the relation of church and state.

Individualism led, furthermore, to rejection of the organized pattern of political morality which Calvinism and Puritanism had advocated. Evangelicals like Leland held that if left alone without external helps, man could adequately develop his religious life. Like Jefferson, they wanted as little government as possible. Leland became, for example, the leading clerical opponent of congressional chaplaincies, Peace Societies, temperance associations, and the movement against Sunday delivery of the mail, not because he favored infidelity, war, drunkenness, or violation of the Sabbath, but because he opposed making moral principles into laws violating the rights of the individual.[77] Leland suspected correctly that the transformationists of his day were trying to achieve through moral influence the closest possible approximation, under conditions of church-state independence, of the New England tradition. Consequently, as Bodo says, he was "a perfect counterfoil for the theocrats. . . . Whatever they advocated, he opposed."[78] Representing an extreme form of emphasis on voluntary expression of moral behavior, he opposed laws dealing with morality as an infringement on the individual right to act according to his inclinations.

This outlook also manifested a high degree of optimism. The

separationists did not think legal coercion necessary because they assumed that the common man, especially if converted, could maintain order and promote welfare by himself. Leland had a boundless confidence in the capacities of the frontier American and of the nation as a whole, if only they could express their natural moral sense unfettered by governmental policy. Leland said that "individuals often break over the bounds of moral honesty to injure their neighbors," but "this is not more frequent than it is for legislative bodies to overleap their legitimate domain."[79] In contrast with the theocrats, whose view of original sin tempered their optimism and led to doubt of the political capacities of the unsophisticated multitudes, Leland followed Jackson in supporting the widest possible extension of suffrage. Leland's optimism even extended to his interpretation of the Catholic question. He believed that American institutions would resist or convert the Catholics, but he argued at the same time that if they became the majority then they should have the right to determine policy, because under the American system the majority rules and is presumably right.[80]

The separationists, whether Baptist or Unitarian, stressed the primacy of the New over the Old Testament. Leland argued that if the New Testament were not sufficient to determine the mode of Christian life, then "either the wisdom or the goodness of Christ is deficient."[81] But cut off from the Old Testament, the separationist minimized the sense of social responsibility, divine judgment, and historical involvement—all notably lacking in the New Testament.

Thus individualism, optimism, and New Testament monism came to characterize the once Calvinist Baptists and denominations like the Methodists whose Arminian theology was even more congenial to these concepts. Whereas the contemporaneous transformationists had great interest in and hope for American society because church-state separation gave them the opportunity to mold it, the separationists rejoiced in American separation because it gave them liberty to direct themselves and others to God. They valued political liberty because it made man free to come to God in his own way, though they tended to confuse political with Christian liberty.

It was at this time that the Baptists substituted for what had been a complex theological tradition a few basic principles centered on individual conversion, congregational church government, baptism by immersion, and, usually, separation of church and state. The similarity between these minimal elements and the reduction of Christianity to a few tenets in the Enlightenment is not coincidental. Like Jefferson, Baptist leaders such as Leland were principally interested in practical matters, ignoring and writing little on traditional theological subjects. They stressed concrete results in numbers of baptisms and moral changes resulting from the revivals. Both Backus and Leland centered their writings on politics, religious freedom, and problems of the local church, while on the fundamental principles of a revival theology, they saw no grounds for disagreement with others engaged in the great work.

Where Methodist and Baptist revivalism spread, it nevertheless significantly altered society and culture, not so much through law as through cultural influence. In the early history of the nation, the distant frontiers and rural areas were the least christianized and, according to accounts, the least affected even by minimal standards of morality. Both aspects seem to have spurred the concern of the pious in the traditional churches to extend the gospel and moral renovation to the West. So effectively did revivalism capture the rural areas of the country that today the reverse is true; the church people in the small towns of the South and Midwest lament the low church attendance and deteriorating morality of the big cities. Although the factor of mobility plays an important part in undermining traditional norms in both periods, the point should be clear that a revivalist, conservative, moralistic theology marks the less densely populated areas of America. There traditional moral norms hold sway, ministers exercise more influence in the community, religious participation is greater, and Protestant religious symbols and activities have widespread public acceptance. This last feature is especially important because it conflicts with the major social principle of the separationists, separation of church and state.

Methodists and Baptists started late in the educational field, as did the states where they made their greatest conquests. There, even more than in a transformationist area like Massachusetts, public schools reflected the community consensus in such customs as reading the Bible, reciting the Lord's Prayer, devotional exercises, and occasional exhortations by local ministers. These practices were usually not instituted by law, but passed as accepted procedures; beginning in the mid-nineteenth century, however, in more urban, Eastern areas, the public school with Protestant symbols encountered Roman Catholic and then Jewish and secular

criticism. Consequently Methodists and Baptists were the chief
Protestant denominations, outside Congregationalism, that did
not institute religious schools when public schools gained the
ascendance in the nineteenth century.[82] This is not mere happen-
stance, for in the areas where they had great strength, the ideas of
Protestant evangelicalism were indirectly transmitted to pupils.
Their attitude was not, to be sure, unambiguous, and especially
on religious features that involved law, such as Bible reading in
the public schools, Baptists often were found opposing them.
Through cultural influence, however, more than through legal
institutions revivalism made rural America Christian, in a manner described by Philip Schaff as the "free expression of personal
conviction and of the national character" with an "even greater
power over the mind, than when enjoined by civil laws."[83]

Separationism and the Social Gospel

The separationists became the chief heirs of the revivalist tradition when the transformationists abandoned it for the Social
Gospel and its aftermath. It is often hard today to realize that
Jonathan Edwards, the greatest theologian America produced,
Timothy Dwight, president of Yale, many other college presi-
dents, and the major seminaries of the East, with the exception
of Harvard, participated in the movement that is associated today
with Billy Graham and Oral Roberts. Revivalism, furthermore,
which is often aligned today with political and social conservatism, was a dynamic force for social change up through the Civil
War.[84] The Social Gospel was an extension of this reforming impulse in American religion, continuous with the past. The slavery
issue having been solved, religious leaders turned to the neglected
consequences of economic injustice, bringing to bear a more sophisticated analysis of the problems borrowed from the newly developing social sciences. The Social Gospel arose, however, in the
urban, more educated circles of Protestantism at the very same
time that biblical criticism and biological and anthropological
science were also influencing the formulation of unorthodox interpretations of the Christian faith. These latter aspects of Liberalism were more intolerable to revivalism, even in its Baptist and
Methodist forms, than was the quest for social justice. Many laymen, to be sure, would have resisted the infringements on *laissez-
faire* that economic reconstruction implied, but so did laymen

and ministers on a large scale among the denominations that accepted the Social Gospel.

One could conjecture whether the liberal-conservative (fundamentalist) schism would have occurred over the issue of social reform. The "Fundamentals," the fundamentalist platform of 1912, dealt solely with theological matters. The antagonism of the conservatives to social reform grew from their feeling that it had become a new gospel; in the revivalist tradition conversion and religious conviction always preceded moral interest. By 1920, at any rate, a realignment of American Protestantism had occurred; on one side stood defenders of the inerrancy of the Bible and orthodox tenets like belief in the Virgin Birth and the substitutionary atonement, while on the other were advocates of a reconciliation between Protestantism and modern science. The former upheld the mode of social influence developed from revivalism, a concern for individual morality such as alcohol, sexual sins, divorce, and the frivolities of modern culture like cosmetics, movies, and dancing. They felt that the election of religious and moral men to office offered the best means of achieving moral expression in public life, while they worked within social groups to enhance Christian morality. At times, the power of this wing came to center on one particular issue of legislative import such as prohibition, the enactment of which represented their greatest social victory.

A foray into the public forum, like the prohibition experiment, contradicted the church-state theory of the evangelical wing of Protestantism, for now, more than any others, evangelicals upheld the separationist viewpoint. Such inconsistency, however, is not startling when one surveys the actions of religious groups in society which often act from self-interest while holding an ideology principally to combat their opponents. The enemies of the revivalist wing are Roman Catholicism and transformationism; because both hold theological views implying some relationship between church and state, the revivalists have tended to emphasize the tradition of Backus and Leland for their own purpose.

The same association of self-interest with advocacy of church-state separation can be found among some liberals adhering to the separationist point of view. They fear not only Roman Catholicism and its proposals for changes in American life, but also excessive influence on society by evangelical Protestants. They recognize the problem described by Daniel D. Williams: "I remember the remark of an American political leader, not un-

friendly to the Baptists, that in one state of the Union the political scene was the most completely church-dominated of any in
America; and the church in this case was Baptist. Such is the fate
of a church which is so completely interwoven with the life of the
community that ecclesiastical power and prestige at some points
become inseparable from political power."[85]

The liberals who are also separationists oppose the attempt to
regulate moral and religious conduct by any group, although they
usually think that religious groups can and should take positions
on broader questions of public policy. As Protestants, they tend
to see the major threat to freedom from Roman Catholicism;
hence they are willing to ally with evangelical Protestantism to
protect religious freedom and church-state separation from the
"intrusions" of Catholics. The irony of liberalism in its repeated
emphasis on absolute church-state separation while engaging in
political activities is illustrated by Paul Blanshard's association
with P.O.A.U. as a special counsel, while his wife, Mary Blanshard, is a registered lobbyist for the American Unitarian Association. If there were a wall of separation as Mr. Blanshard says,
Mrs. Blanshard could not continue her activities.

The Baptists as Separationists

Describing the major characteristics of contemporary separationism is difficult because the position cuts across Protestant
opinions and denominations so completely. Its chief strength lies
in the present-day revivalist and rationalist wings of Protestantism, and its chief organizational expression is P.O.A.U.[86] Because
much of its effort is directed against Roman Catholic activities, it
may attract anti-Catholic fanatics who embarrass the bulk of the
membership, while at the same time it may interest scholarly
specialists in constitutional law who feel that American church-
state relations are moving for practical reasons toward a greater
separation and want to strengthen that trend. Others may feel in
all sincerity that one major problem jeopardizes a healthy church-
state relation—the tendency of Roman Catholics to gain financial
support for certain projects.

This study is primarily interested in *theological* perspectives
toward church-state relations. Many people act for nontheologi-
cal reasons, such as defense of what they consider an essential
principle of American democracy, but the vigorous Baptist sup-

port of P.O.A.U. and church-state separation, both now and in the past, points to one relatively consistent, religiously motivated oulook. Baptists feel that their tradition supports them on this stand, that church-state separation marked their origins, that they fought for its inclusion in federal and state constitutions, and that they represent today its chief defenders. This chapter has thus far indicated the impulses of the Baptists and similar religious groups since the seventeenth century, for in all periods the Baptists have been part of a broader movement, whether sectarian, dissenting, or revivalist. Today, for example, the National Association of Evangelicals, a group dedicated to conservative theology, revivalism, and missions has resembled the Baptists in church-state perspective.[87] The extreme difficulty of examining Protestant views by denominations is illustrated in the N.A.E., which includes in its membership four small Mennonite bodies and three Quaker yearly meetings. All of these represent, however, the wings of their traditions influenced by nineteenth-century revivalism and are thus close to the practical outlook of the Baptists and N.A.E.

Separationist writers of this point of view are extremely disinclined to relate theological convictions to their position on church and state in any significant way. A few, principally Baptists, have done so and will be used for illustration. The most important is Joseph M. Dawson,[88] a founder and vice-president emeritus of P.O.A.U., and former secretary of the Baptist Joint Committee on Public Affairs. Because the Baptists are not really monolithic on church-state issues, attention will also be given to criticism within the Baptist Church of some expressions of the Baptist position.

Religious Individualism

Although Baptists of the younger generation read the theological writings of non-Baptists, both the American and Southern Baptist Conventions are strongly influenced by a theology centered on the religious significance of the individual. Perhaps the most influential exponent of this outlook was E. Y. Mullins (1860-1928),[89] president of the seminary in Louisville and for decades the leading Baptist theologian in America. Reflecting the association of the Baptists with nineteenth-century revivalism, this individualism has been conversion-oriented and is usually called "soul-competency." A speaker at the Baptist World Alliance Meeting in 1955 described it as follows:

Baptists are agreed upon the fundamental doctrine of the competency of the individual soul to deal directly with God without the intervention of parent, priest or sacrament. . . . From this doctrine of the competency of the individual soul comes our belief in the autonomy of the Church and the democracy of believers within the church. . . . Inherent in the same basic doctrine is our belief in the right of the individual to interpret the Scriptures for himself under the guidance of the Holy Spirit.[90]

The Baptists thus carried to its final conclusion an aspect of Luther's thought which he himself did not emphasize but which was perhaps implicit in his religious experience. Luther insisted on the necessity of individual encounter with God, though he subjected this experience to the authority of the gospel as found in the Bible. Furthermore, because he was principally interested in the sovereignty of God, he directed his attention to the manner in which God acted, which led him in turn to discuss the church, the mediator of the gospel to the individual. Luther principally stressed individualism through the experience of justification by faith as over against the *ex opere operato* character of the Roman Catholic sacraments. The Baptists, on the other hand, begin theological discussion with the individual soul as a candidate for conversion. The competent soul in the Baptist tradition is not a mystically-oriented entity, but a soul that can believe.

It has already been noted that this doctrine stems from the nineteenth century and that the early Baptists, who were chiefly interested in the freedom of God, defended free consciences and congregations as part of an understanding of divine sovereignty. When equated with the dignity and integrity of the individual, the origins of soul competency especially reveal themselves. Individualism as an intellectual phenomenon is associated with the Enlightenment and found fertile soil for expansion in America, where frontier conditions and unlimited opportunities tended to accentuate it. An eighteenth-century rationalist could almost have written this Baptist statement: "Let it be understood now and always that the basic doctrine of Baptists is the dignity, sanctity, and competency of the individual believer. I do not mean to say that we put the doctrine ahead of our belief in the sovereignty of God . . . or of justification by faith . . . or of the necessity of religious experience . . . but it is this belief in the dignity, sanctity, and competency of the individual which Baptists through the years have felt compelled to emphasize."[91]

In a preface to a pronouncement on religious liberty adopted by the American, Southern and National Baptist Conventions in 1939, one finds that the first of the principles that "animate the activities of the Baptists . . . which they hold clearly to be taught in the New Testament" is "the worth of the individual." This concept of "the dignity of the individual" is based, the statement says, on "the conviction that every soul possesses the capacity and the inalienable right to deal with God for himself. . . ."[92] The use of the term "inalienable right" further associates the contemporary Baptist outlook with the leaders of the American Revolution rather than with its prior ancestry, the Puritan wing of the Reformation.

The Baptist-rationalist alliance in the development of American institutions has thus left its imprint, not simply on Baptist church-state theory, but in the very heart of their theology—despite the contention of Baptist writers that they base their views on the Bible. According to Joseph M. Dawson, Jesus preached a message of liberation centered on the dignity and worth of the individual, who can choose between new life, and sin and death.[93] Baptists, especially the more conservative segments, claim so strongly to represent the New Testament church that they lack a sense of the history of Christianity in the intervening period. If anything, this is a heritage of nineteenth-century revivalism, which telescoped the gospel into a few simple principles while turning its back on the discussion of historical controversies that filled traditional theological writings.

When, on the other hand, Baptists have moved beyond the simple equation of the New Testament church with the contemporary denomination, they have developed a critical sense, discerning the confusion of American culture with the Baptist perspective. The journal of the Baptist Historical Association, *Foundations*, serves as a source of vigorous intradenominational criticism. The highly respected historian at Colgate-Rochester Theological Seminary, Winthrop S. Hudson, traces "the great tradition of the American churches" to Puritanism and discerns its original concern with doctrines of the church: its independence of any power other than that of God, its voluntary membership, and the limited authority of the visible church because of men's tendency to substitute their own views for those of God.[94]

The Individual and the State

The Baptists' emphasis on individualism causes them to see the nature of church and state in terms of the individual and the state. Thus, in contemporary separationist thought one finds little or no recognition of the significant pluralistic social philosophy by which the rights of corporate groups are guaranteed, and which many interpreters regard as one of the chief characteristics of Anglo-Saxon democracy.[95] Ironically, the Baptists in the seventeenth and eighteenth centuries helped shape pluralism by insisting on independence of thought and functioning for their religious groups against the attempts of various governments to establish a monolithic religious policy. While many Protestants see the churches as prior institutions which the state cannot violate, with distinct functions in the implementation of God's will in the world, separationist theory differentiates between the political and religious expressions of the individual man. This is well illustrated in the previously cited Baptist pronouncement of 1939:

> We acknowledge ourselves to be citizens of two commonwealths, one earthly, the United States, the other heavenly, the Kingdom of God, and we claim the right to be good citizens of both. We recognize the sovereignty of the State and we give allegiance to the State, but we cannot give to the State the control of our consciences. We must obey God rather than men.
>
> The business of the government is to make good laws; our business is to make good citizens who continue to demand the enactment of better laws, embodying higher and still higher ethical standards. The end of governmental administration is equal justice under law. The end of our endeavor is the establishment of the will of God in the hearts and institutions of men. If one of us accepts an office in the government, he recognizes it not only as a public trust, but also as a divine entrustment; for the powers that be are ordained of God. In a democracy like ours, it is possible to be a loyal American and a devoted Christian. This is true because religious liberty is an essential part of our fundamental law.[96]

In this statement one sees the individual participating in two voluntary societies, in each of which he has certain inherent rights, his personality being molded and directed in two fashions by two institutions into the American-Christian.

The influence of American individualism on this statement is highlighted when one examines an exposition of the Council of the Baptist Union of Great Britain and Ireland in 1948. The British Baptist experience has been a struggle for the integrity of their congregations within a tolerant established church system upheld for traditional and cultural as much as religious reasons, and unlike the Americans they did not help create a new society predicated on Enlightenment concepts. Thus "Christ's Lordship over His Church" leads them to insist "that churches formed by His will must be free from all other rule in matters relating to their spiritual life," including the right of self-government and the privilege of applying Christian convictions to the problems of contemporary life.[97] Like the Puritan-Baptist movement of the seventeenth century, the British theory centers on the divine sovereignty over the universal church, of which individual churches are expressions. The grounds for religious freedom depend, not on the integrity of the individual, but rather of God, whose will to guide men in local congregations the political order cannot defy. The British statement is also interesting because of a reference to "the growth of the omnicompetent state" which threatens the freedom for which Baptists have fought. No more lucid argument for political pluralism could be found within a religious context. Furthermore, it reflects a fear of political power as the essential threat to religious liberty rather than religious power, which preoccupies Baptists in America.

Religious Liberty

Baptist church-state theory moves from soul-competence, or the integrity of the individual, to the most sacred right of the human person, religious liberty.

> Our chief concern is religious freedom. The origin of this freedom is in the nature of man as the creature of God. As the climax of all His creation, God made man in His own spiritual image, the only creature in the universe capable of fellowship with Him, capable of thinking His thoughts after Him. . . . In order that this responsibility should be real and genuine, it was necessary that man should be endowed with freedom of choice. . . . Religious freedom is not a gift or privilege granted by the state. . . . It is an inherent inalienable right which civil governments should recognize and respect, but which was bestowed upon man when he was created in the spiritual image of God.[98]

Baptists in America usually understand religious freedom in conjunction with separation of church and state, as an outgrowth of their very early refusal to accept mere toleration, and their battle against privileges accorded to any denomination. Religious freedom through separation of church and state was the greatest contribution of the Baptists, along with other groups, to the theory and practice of politics.

Baptists in America, however, tend to absolutize church-state separation and lack insight into the variety of methods for achieving religious liberty. Moreover, they often do not understand critics who discover imperfections or problems in the American system of separation. The Italian Jewish jurist, Francesco Ruffini, argued, for example, that jurisdictionalism, or control by the state, offered an even better way of guaranteeing religious freedom. European experiences, he felt, proved that political control or Erastianism had been the chief and most effective means of providing for minority religious rights and curbing the impulse toward power and oppression by established churches. The impulse of the state in these instances was not religious but politically prudential. Separation of church and state he found to be a mixed blessing, for under the anticlerical regimes of France and Italy, it became a means of restricting the churches from many activities in which they had once felt free to act. An absolute separation of church and state, for example, would deny the right of religious groups to promote particular policies and lead to secularization of government, marriage, and the armed services, the denial of draft exemption for clergy, and other measures. Ruffini further felt that separation of church and state, through social and cultural pressure, restricted independent, nonconventional religious thought, because religious associations oppose "any form of rival organisation . . . especially if the latter takes the form of disbelief."[99]

If Ruffini's evaluation mirrors the perspective of one immersed in a struggle between the Catholic Church which opposed the new Italian state, and a political order of distinct anticlerical tendencies, the Baptists in America likewise are guilty of parochialism in associating religious freedom irrevocably with separation of church and state. The position of Baptists in other countries on issues of religious liberty reveals that separation does not follow automatically from Baptist principles but from the historical experiences of Baptists as part of the Leveller movement and in the struggle for freedom in America. In England and

Sweden, for example, the guarantee of religious freedom for Baptists within an established church system has led to a different perspective for dealing with church-state problems.

English Baptists tend to accept both an established church and free churches, because they hold a more universal view of the church than do many American Baptists, particularly Southern Baptists, and regard Anglicanism as one expression of it and Baptists as another. One leading English Baptist scholar, H. Wheeler Robinson, regarded the religious establishment as an anomaly in the present pluralistic religious situation of England, but said that Baptists are "probably less disposed today to promote political action for its removal and prefer to leave this, in the interest of religion, to the more or less inevitable course of events. . . ."[100]

The most important foreign critic of the Baptists in America, however, has been Gunnar Westin, professor of church history in the University of Uppsala in Sweden.[101] According to Westin, the Baptist view of religious liberty developed originally as a form of defense against persecution and was designed to prevent the state from meddling in religious affairs. Referring to this as the "old-time Baptist view" and "an uncomplicated negative idea of religious liberty," Westin argues that it has value as a principle of defense when religious or political totalitarianism threatens; but in modern democratic countries (apparently including Sweden, with its established church, as well as America), where religious persecution no longer prevails, a new view is needed, which seeks co-operation between Christians and the state for the good of society. Westin insists that "There is no use of an eternal opposition and a reiterated protest, as if nothing had happened in our western state life since the days of Roger Williams and John Bunyan. . . . There is no use to take an attitude of suspicion and hostility, when we are called upon to cooperate in a Christian manner to build the community where we share with others various freedoms."[102]

Baptists from America might agree, because Westin's position, apart from acceptance of the state church, corresponds to the practical actions and concerns of the separationists. But in discussing further issues, Westin implies the inadequacy of the ideology of separation of church and state, especially the insistence on "absolute separation." Citing the support of Scandinavian Baptists for religious teaching and hymn singing in the public schools, Westin justifies it as a natural and valuable procedure in promoting Christian ideals of morality and civil order, and one which does not violate religious freedom since non-Lutherans may have their own religious teachers. "It would be fatal, if the public education should be totally devoid of religion."[103] Like many English Baptists he feels that symbolic religious gestures point to the Christian culture and traditions of the nation and that the alternative is a misleading understanding of national history in nonreligious terms.

Applying his theory to the United States, Westin recognizes that conflicting principles are involved and insists that solutions are compromises, not simple answers based on a wall of separation doctrine. Noting breaches in the American "wall," Westin says that the problems here are much more complicated because of "the far wider engagement of the denominations, but also because of the competing and expanding large church organizations with a strict confession and discipline, especially the Roman Catholic church."[104] The point is clear that Westin is admonishing his American colleagues to combine their principles with some sense of the relativities of history by dealing with church-state problems in less dogmatic, less negative ways.

Separationists and Separation

The Baptist interest in church-state separation has led them to enter P.O.A.U. in large numbers and furnish it with much of its leadership. Probably no other denomination has so unquestioningly supported its program. Since P.O.A.U. does not represent denominations, the four major Baptist conventions in America founded in 1941 the Baptist Joint Committee on Public Affairs to act in Washington as their representative, and its three executive directors, Rufus W. Weaver, Joseph M. Dawson, and C. Emanuel Carlson, have been leaders on church-state matters. Although independent, the Baptist Joint Committee acts on the basis of principles and policies held by Baptists, as enunciated by the co-operating conventions. Until recently it worked closely with P.O.A.U., and the leadership of the Committee even claimed to have proposed and organized P.O.A.U. A recent study of the Baptist Joint Committee shows that church-state relations, more specifically defense of separation, occupy the Committee overwhelmingly.[105] Thus it seems that when Baptists think of "public affairs," they refer to church-state issues.

What do Baptist separationists mean by separation? The *locus classicus* comes from a letter of January 1, 1802, by Thomas Jefferson to the Baptists of Danbury, Connecticut:

> Believing with you that religion is a matter which lies solely between man and his God, that he owes account to none other for his faith or his worship, that the legislative powers of government reach actions only, and not opinions, I contemplate with sovereign reverence that act of the whole American people which declared that their legislature should "make no law respecting an establishment of religion, or prohibiting the free exercise thereof," thus building a wall of separation between church and state.[106]

The metaphor of the "wall" has served the separationists well, though the extent to which Jefferson understood this literally is hard to determine. The separationists, to clarify their position, have appropriated the *Everson* dictum of 1947, which defined for them not only the constitutional view, but their own aspirations.[107] The most important clauses were those forbidding state and federal governments to pass laws "which aid one religion, aid all religions or prefer one religion over another," to force a person to go to church or profess beliefs or disbeliefs, to levy a tax "to support any religious activities or institutions" or "openly or secretly participate in the affairs of any religious organizations or groups and *vice versa*." They have generally ignored the modification of this dictum in *Zorach* v. *Clauson* and have strangely opposed the transportation of parochial school pupils which *Everson* validated.

The separationists, with the possible exception of the rationalist wing, have not consistently upheld either the Jeffersonian or Eversonian definitions of the constitutional clauses. At times they have opposed features associating government and religion such as Bible reading and religious classes in the public schools; but in practice they have acted against features benefiting other churches, especially Roman Catholicism, while withholding criticism of those that benefited themselves. If the rationalists are more consistent than the revivalists and Baptists today, the difference lies in their reasons for upholding church-state separation, because they not only oppose state support of religion, but also the interference of the churches in public life. Because the separationist churches want not only to convert individuals, but to create through them a new religious and moral tone in the nation, the left wing looks with suspicion on too much religious influence in society, fearing social compulsion in the form of religion. An illustration is the recent book by Paul Blanshard, *God and Man in Washington*, which excoriates the religious façade among public figures and in politics, but the Baptists and evangelicals, who also purport to be separationists, extol these same features. The evangelicals and Baptists, in effect, utilize the rationalist ideology for defining church-state separation, while they act in the fashion of the nineteenth-century revivalists, or more simply in their own interest. Actions by their opponents call forth the ideology of the "wall," though they do not apply the same criterion to themselves.

The separationists thus represent one side of a continuing debate in American life and constitutional law on the nature of church-state separation. One's position depends greatly on the authorities he uses, whether on the one hand, the views of Jefferson, and especially Madison, the *Everson* dictum, the developing tendencies in the Supreme Court, the conviction that religion and politics do not mix, or on the other hand, the traditional association between the churches and government, the *Zorach* dictum, or the feeling that religion and politics cannot be separated. The support of the separationists for church-state separation thus extends to a particular interpretation of separation, for while the transformationists tend toward pragmatism and relativism, the separationists operate at least in ideology with an "absolute principle" of separation.

One should emphasize the unsolved nature of this problem because of the tendency of the separationists, especially those in P.O.A.U., to regard supporters of other interpretations as subverters of the constitution and dividers of Protestantism. A comment by Dawson illustrates this: "The Constitution may not easily be changed by legislation; it might be by means of interpretation. There are those who, like termites, work in subtle ways to undermine it; who try to subvert it by seeking to make it mean something less than complete church-state separation. They diligently seek to set aside the traditional, historical acceptance of the Constitution as judicially interpreted, and to substitute instead an outmoded European concept."[108] Having pledged his support to the judicial interpretations of the Constitution in this statement, Dawson goes on to oppose the *Everson* decision for "having breached the wall of separation."[109]

Dawson compounds his inability to determine whether to stand

on the judicial interpretations or the wall of separation by undercutting his statements on absolute separation through advocacy of
a relation between religion and society which corresponds to the
self-interest of evangelical Protestantism. Thus he argues that
when a principal or teacher calls on an *individual* to pray, read
the Bible, or give a religious talk in the public schools, or when
the legislature or armed services hires an *individual* to act as
chaplain, this does not breach the wall of separation. On the
other hand, he charges that religious classes like those invalidated
by *McCollum* do violate it and worst of all "in the end . . .
would result in delivering the public schools into the hands of
the dominant religious group of a given locality. . . ."[110] One
wonders whether this distinction does not stem from an uncritical attitude toward the way in which the Southern Baptist
Church, to which Dawson belongs, promotes evangelical Protestantism in the South. There it has a religious hegemony, and
services even by individuals so express its outlook that many
public schools, without benefit of legal arrangements, through
cultural influence and individual actions, reflect the values of
Southern Protestantism.

Dawson also speaks warmly of the traditional religious symbols
and actions of public officials, because through religious magistrates "every religious group . . . contributes to the nourishment
of religious ideals among the people, and to the conviction that
the laws of God are to govern the laws of man. . . ."[111]

Several assumptions seem to underlie Dawson's outlook. One is
suspicion of legal arrangements with government, if the moral
influence of Protestantism can have the same effects through individuals imbued with Protestant values. Another is the conservative Protestant rejection of the Social Gospel and the outlook of
analysts such as Reinhold Niebuhr who replaced moral influence
and good men in government with a stress on group action and
analysis of power conflicts in society. Still another is the individualism and simple gospel of revivalism, as it has continued
among the Baptists.

The curious contradiction between a theoretical separation of
religion and politics along with active involvement in politics is
revealed in the following statement by a leader of the National
Association of Evangelicals. Under the heading, "Evangelicals do
not want the church in politics," James D. Murch proposes instead that the churches inculcate a responsibility for politics
among their members and that "lay groups" promote political

action: "These groups also supply evangelicals with information about candidates for office in ample time before city, county, state, and national elections so that they know the record, standing, and qualifications of each candidate regardless of party. Such groups expose corrupt political machines by giving the facts about the candidates who are machine controlled."[112] For groups of church members to imply which candidates to support on the basis of their association with "political machines" goes far beyond groups like the National Council of Churches in specificity. Nearly all other religious groups confine themselves to issues, whereas the N.A.E. in this instance deals with candidates.

The point is that the separationists have not thought through the relationship between their interests and activities and the ideology to which they are committed. Activity in society and politics has a long and honorable history within Anglo-Saxon Protestantism, as well as in the democratic and church-state structures which it has helped erect. If a religious group for various reasons thinks that a wall of separation between church and state is a desirable objective, then the least one can ask is that it be consistent and apply the same norm to itself. Unfortunately, the quest for a wall by a religious group denies the existence of a wall, because the group must abrogate certain measures now relating church and state by crossing the wall to work against them. To petition government to shore up breaches in the wall involves an influence upon government that could not take place if there were such an impregnable wall. In actuality the separationists are not consistent, and the metaphor of the wall serves principally as a fortress to oppose Catholics and others whose church-state activities do not correspond with those of the separationists. Thus Dawson also speaks of "a true cooperative relation between church and state"[113] in the same book in which he reiterates the absolute character of church-state separation; and the National Association of Evangelicals has taken such politically loaded positions as opposition to federal aid to schools, support of Bible reading and distribution in public schools, released-time religious instruction, legislation restricting the advertising, sale, and use of intoxicants, and laws to protect the United States from Communism.[114]

The Consequences of Separation as a Principle

The tendency of separationists to apply a strict separation especially to Catholics and to exempt themselves from its provisions results in part from a supposition that since church-state separation has resulted from the influence of evangelical Protestantism on culture and is a Protestant belief, Roman Catholicism is somehow incompatible with church-state separation. Because the separationists so often represent a congregational polity, they interpret the constitutional clauses in a way validating their particular understanding of religion and church organization. Conrad H. Moehlman, for example, in *The Wall of Separation Between Church and State,* associates the American constitutional system with such theological and philosophical views as the fundamental responsibility of the state for marriage, that "only reason and conviction . . . should direct religion," "the taxing of the people for religious purposes will destroy religion," and allegiance to "foreign states . . . ecclesiastical as well as civil" must be given up by American citizens.[115] The issue, as the Catholic theologian John Courtney Murray indicates, lies in whether the clauses of the Constitution are a "theology" or "articles of peace."[116] In a perceptive critique Murray has argued that in American Protestantism at least three groups: the "free churches," the separationist left wing who are the heirs of eighteenth-century rationalism, and culture-Protestants, seem to equate separation with their own religious point of view. Murray's analysis would apply to any group which argued that the separation of church and state implied anything about the nature of religion (as an individual experience or a matter of the private conscience) or church organization (voluntary, congregational, or without reference to an authority living in another country). That separationists ground the First Amendment in certain Protestant tenets is revealed in the comments of Moehlman above and in the contention of Dawson that the Constitution largely grew out of a Protestant culture based on the Bible and modern science, while the Catholic culture, which "opposes" it, is based on the formulations of the hierarchy and an outmoded science.[117]

The ideological commitment of Protestant separationists to absolute separation leads them to base their position on legal rather than on theological arguments; it results in a sharp separation between the religious and the secular, between the framework in which one conducts his spiritual life and the framework for social and political activity. This schism has a long history in separationism, going back to the Leveller program and the breakdown of Puritanism, strengthened by the adoption of a rationalist justification for church-state separation during the struggle for

disestablishment. The loss of the theological motives that underlay the passionate quest of Baptists and other sectarians for
religious liberty especially in the seventeenth century leaves the
contemporary separationist with no other alternative than to base
his case on constitutional grounds, which he presumes to be a
Protestant ethical expression and hence inconsistent with Roman
Catholic assumptions.

The Separationist View of Roman Catholicism

Having simplified church-state separation into an absolute
principle, and lacking historical awareness and self-criticism,
separationists use the complex realm of church-state relations as a
forum for a dubious attack on the integrity of American Roman
Catholicism. Most of them, of course, simply do not see the contradictions into which a doctrine of the "wall" drives them. Poor
education and a limited historical perspective among Protestant
evangelicals on the expressions that both Protestantism and
Roman Catholicism take toward society and the state also contribute to the emotionally loaded atmosphere. The replacement
of a Protestant society by one heavily Catholic in areas like New
England, and a series of public symbols of Catholic activity like
the Vatican ambassadorship, the quest for support of parochial
schools, and the successful candidacy of a Catholic President—all
have fed long-dormant Protestant fears.

Why does anti-Catholicism exist at all in Protestantism? The
answer lies partly in the historical struggle between Protestants
and Catholics for the religious hegemony of Europe during and
after the Reformation. Americans have combined these inherited
religious emotions with political loyalties from the sixteenth to
the eighteenth centuries, when England found itself opposed by
an array of Catholic powers during its emergence into a great
nation. Throughout the seventeenth century in both England
and America, Protestants regarded Catholics as threats to both
religious and national unity, potential agents for nations hostile
to England. Even in the most tolerant American colonies Catholics suffered limitations because of this politico-religious conflict.
The fact that the overwhelming majority of the first citizens of
the United States came from Protestant countries nourished the
sense of destiny which many of them felt about America as a
Protestant haven.

When Roman Catholics increased through immigration in the
early nineteenth century, anti-Catholic violence broke out, pred-

icated on the Catholic threat to the Protestant culture and free institutions of America.[118] American Protestants had already associated themselves with separation of church and state in a way that left Protestantism free to extend its influence to social and political institutions, while Catholicism was associated in their mind with the backward regimes and state establishments of southern Europe and Latin America. Furthermore, the Catholic Church was engaged in a savage conflict with revolutionary movements in Western Europe, many of which advocated separation of church and state from anticlerical motives. Protestant Americans, except for the transformationists perhaps, did not distinguish between the conservative democracy and moderate separation produced in America and the egalitarianism and antireligious separation of the traditionally Catholic countries. Periodic outbursts of anti-Catholicism in America, especially at times when other issues did not occupy the nation's attention, attest to an historically based undercurrent of hostility among Protestants.

Catholicism also represents features intolerable especially to sectarian Protestantism. It refuses to abrogate the establishments which it maintains in many countries, where Protestants sometimes suffer restrictions or forms of intolerance. Conscious of the variety of ways in which church-state relations can be handled, Catholicism does not idealize separation but accepts whatever form guarantees its independence and activities. Its liturgy and symbolism represent features repugnant to sectarian Protestantism with its Calvinist and Puritan background; and in its objective sacramentalism it mediates a religious experience of a different order than that of evangelical Protestantism. Its hierarchical church structure is one, especially in Anglican dress, against which the separationists have often battled, and the very opposite of the "voluntary principle" which many Protestants see enshrined in the Constitution.

More than anything else, however, Roman Catholicism has a different understanding of church-state separation than the separationists. Catholic spokesmen throughout American history have expressed a high regard for the American constitutional arrangements,[119] but their high evaluation derives from an understanding of separation in a form rather close to that of the transformationists. Catholics with their long experience in Europe realize that separation can mean more than one thing and that Catholics have benefited from the American system because of the implicitly positive evaluation of religion by government, the freedom to organize and educate as they wish, and the opportunity to influence society by taking public positions on moral issues. Catholic writers on church-state problems stress the flexibility of American separation, and the Catholic Church has sought its own interests within that framework. Its activities have represented, to be sure, "breaches" in the wall of separation, if there were a wall; but the overwhelming majority of the issues on which it has acted, whether matters with legal implications or simply social pressures, have been consistent with the relation between religion and society in America.

The recent issue of federal aid for parochial schools is a case in point. Although Mr. Kennedy and the secretary of Health, Education, and Welfare indicated that in their opinion across-the-board loans were unconstitutional, this did not make the Catholic Church subversive in pressing for benefits which it felt it deserved in a legally undetermined area. To non-Catholics, and especially to separationists, such actions represent an intolerable form of political pressure by a religious group, but Catholics would regard them merely as actions of any religious group which is free to take a position on a matter it considers just.

The most noteworthy characteristic of the separationist outlook is a perspective, varying in degree among its representatives, which governs responses to Catholic actions. Whereas they see Protestant activities in society as sincere, Catholic actions are potentially subversive, threats to the Constitution, or displays of "Catholic power," whether they are a growth in membership, a parade or carnival, or a statement of the hierarchy on a current issue. The Catholics, to be sure, have not helped themselves by their distinction between a "thesis" and a "hypothesis," the differentiation by nineteenth-century theologians between the "ideal" union of church and state and the acceptable separation of the two,[120] which led many Protestants to think that Catholics were steadily working toward a transformation of the First Amendment into an eventual establishment of their faith. The best minds in European and American Catholicism have now questioned this way of dealing with the matter, though more traditional Catholic spokesmen always insisted that the thesis did not obligate Catholics to work for a church-state union. But many non-Catholics felt that Catholic actions were preliminary skirmishes in the ultimate goal of undermining church-state separation.

Separationists have often seen themselves as crusaders defending true Christianity and a providential separation of church and state against a superstition which sought to enslave Americans and stamp out Protestantism. However, public disfavor toward open intolerance has led separationists to disguise their essentially anti-Catholic attitude under a noble rationalization, the defense of church-state separation, a principle whose ambiguity has enabled them to promote their own interests while opposing those of Roman Catholicism. Open opposition to the papacy, once a Protestant axiom, is not acceptable in a pluralistic America, but support of a popular secular value serves the same purpose. Paul Blanshard illuminatingly correlates opposition to Catholicism with church-state separation when he says that P.O.A.U. "has specialized in defending the wall of separation between church and state against Catholic encroachments."[121] Frequently the more overt anti-Catholic animus appears when defenders of church-state separation make contemptuous comments about Catholic religious beliefs and practices such as the hierarchical system of authority, the practice of celibacy, or engagement in social issues.

This delineation of shortcomings in the separationist view of Roman Catholicism should not obscure the real differences between Protestants and Catholics on religious and social issues. The relationship between Roman Catholicism and Protestantism is ultimately theological, but one should be able to state theological similarities and differences without hatred and distortion. If the social and political implications of both faiths were objectively examined, with a sensitivity for the variety of interpretations and actual historical associations with government that they have taken, one would discover that both Protestantism and Catholicism have promoted a variety of governmental forms, and that both have supported political and religious freedom as well as oppression. Real issues could then be dealt with openly and fairly, with awareness of theological and social differences, and of the limitations and flexibility of American church-state separation. As it is now, separationists seem to evaluate church-state problems by a secular norm of separation and receive their dynamic from ill-informed and questionable prejudices.

This is especially unfortunate because separationism has shaped profoundly the democratic form of government and church-state separation, and it could contribute significantly to a future Protestant church-state theory. In fact, Protestantism cannot ignore the heritage of separationism: its passionate stress on the integrity of individual religious conviction, its awareness of the danger to religion from too intimate an association with political leaders and structures, and of the political motivation of infant baptism, its emphasis on the charismatic and spontaneous manner of God's activity, the necessity for some degree of religious freedom for the complete activity of the church, and the value of church-state separation in guaranteeing religious freedom. But many thoughtful persons within Protestantism are turning away from the separationist tradition because of its intolerance, divisiveness, and inclination to create church-state problems where none exist. Strangely, these are the very charges that P.O.A.U. often makes against Roman Catholics.

Separationist Revisionism

Many Baptists do not share the vigor of their colleagues in P.O.A.U., and the more sophisticated Baptist journals reflect this discontent. Probably the most significant figure in reassessing the Baptist stand has been the present executive director of the Baptist Joint Committee on Public Affairs, C. Emanuel Carlson. Dr. Carlson's role as critic and innovator may seem startling, because he has served on the board of trustees of P.O.A.U. and directs an organization founded to preserve church-state separation in separationist terms and as such responds to the often ill-considered resolutions of Baptist bodies throughout the country. Carlson's writings, however, reveal him to be a creative thinker on church-state matters within the context of his Baptist affiliation, seeking to temper Baptist self-righteousness, raising critical questions about the simplistic way in which Baptists have dealt with these issues, and influencing them toward a more responsible confrontation with Roman Catholicism and governmental policy.

Carlson argues that Baptists, in exploiting the vocabulary of church-state separation for their own purposes, have implied a discontinuity between the two orders that they do not really intend. Taking a theocentric perspective he says that "God never intended church and state to be separated in history. The two institutions must exist and work out their programs in the same chronology, the same localities, with more or less the same people, and experiencing the impact of the same current events."[122] Rejecting both absolute separation and co-operation,

Carlson insists that an area of interaction lies between the two where "some coordination, correlation, and adjustment of plans and programs may take place,"[123] and that Baptists should see separation as an agent for preserving the freedom of the individual religious believer and the activity of the church. The necessary elements of separation for the latter interests are as follows: organization and administrations, constituencies, sources of income, powers and methods, educational programs, and purposes and justification.[124] Carlson feels that history has revealed American separation to be the most effective means for guaranteeing religious and ecclesiastical freedom, and more than most Baptist spokesmen he sees church-state issues as problems rather than self-evident conclusions.

Carlson has proceeded somewhat more cautiously in tempering Baptist views of Roman Catholicism. The Baptist Joint Committee, unlike P.O.A.U., did not demand answers to a set of questions on church and state from Catholic candidates in the 1960 presidential campaign. More significantly, however, Carlson has challenged what he calls the Protestant policy of "containment" of Catholicism. Not only does he think that it strengthens the other group and promotes public sympathy for it, but it tends to transform Protestantism into a negative anti-Catholicism.

A containment strategy would tend to set us in opposition to everything that Roman Catholics stand for. Where they act, we would react. They would take the initiative, we would take the negative. They would favor Christian education, we would oppose it. Where they build hospitals, we would refuse to build hospitals. Where they urge morality and social standards, we would criticize them for it. Whatever our disagreements may be with Roman Catholicism, nonetheless there is enough of Christian residue in concept and program so that we cannot afford to let our movement be shaped on the basis of negative response to their expressions and efforts.[125]

Finally, Carlson has experimented with more adequate theological bases for the Baptist church-state position, which should "come closer to the zenith of our loyalties." Because the Christian gives ultimate loyalty to Christ and his methods, historically Baptists have refused to use political power to advance the kingdom of God. Freedom of conscience is a correlate of the commitment to Christ as Lord and finds further foundation in God as

creator of man, the redemption and Christ's claim on man, the
ministry of the Holy Spirit in his life, and the authority of the
Bible as the guide to his life and faith.[126] Carlson is implying here
something more than the integrity and competence of the soul.
Human integrity for the Christian finds meaning only in the context of the activities of the Trinity, and political coercion prevents man and the church from responding to ultimate loyalties.
The difference may seem a bit subtle, but Carlson apparently
sees that individualistic anthropocentrism has replaced the original Baptist theocentrism, that the usual Baptist justification of
religious freedom and church-state separation stems from its long
association with American rationalism, and that the prime Christian affirmation of faith points not to something about man, but
to the manner in which God has acted. Theological reconstruction
is thus related to a more adequate view both of separation and
of Roman Catholicism.

A somewhat different form of separationism which emphasizes
the recovery of a more adequate doctrine of the church as the key
to a consistent approach to church-state problems has emerged
in the writings of the Baptist, Winthrop S. Hudson,[127] and two
Methodists, Franklin H. Littell[128] and Dean M. Kelley.[129] At the
heart of their position lies a contrast between the Anabaptist and
left-wing Puritan "free church" tradition, which struggled to
separate the church from support or control by the state, and the
"faith in faith" or faith in the "American way of life" that per-
vades modern American society. They argue that Protestants, by
looking to the state for sanction and support, have persistently
neglected the responsibilities of Christian stewardship and de-
luded themselves into thinking that society was Christian.

As a result of stimuli from Baptists, left-wing Puritans, and
the circumstances at the time of the American Revolution, the
churches through disestablishment were provided with their
most creative situation since Constantine. Because only committed persons became Christians, the churches could demand an
exemplary discipline and activity from their members. The vitality bestowed on the churches by the legal status of disestablishment and the religious commitment to voluntarism expressed
itself in the evangelical and social fervor of the nineteenth century, making it the "great century" of Christianity. But there
was a fateful flaw in this development. For the churches looked
back to the fleshpots of Egypt, their established status, and acted
on the assumption that this was a Protestant nation by symboliz-

ing their religious commitment in political form and by impos-
ing Protestant moral norms on the nation as a whole. Not only
did the churches try to recover the privileges eliminated by the
First Amendment, but government as well sought a religious
sanction for its ambivalent enterprises by promoting public religion.

While almost no contemporary American wants a formal state
church, the contemporary acceptance of Protestant, Catholic, and
Jewish identification holds a seductive temptation, for, as writers
like Will Herberg[130] and Peter Berger[131] have pointed out, society has sponsored a common-denominator faith that is not
true to any of the American religious traditions. The acquiescence of the churches in this patent idolatry represents a loss of
vitality and integrity, so that, according to Hudson, "the pressure to call upon the state for help becomes almost irresistible—
the more so because it is no longer possible to distinguish clearly
between the gods of society and the God of the church."[132] The
frantic concern of Protestants to maintain traditional relationships with a government that today must be responsible for a
pluralistic society has coincided with a deterioration of the spirit
of nineteenth-century Protestantism.

These spokesmen voice great concern about unfair manipula-
tion of the "wall of separation" doctrine. Littell, for example,
diagnoses the separationist anti-Catholicism as an intransigent
resistance to pluralism in the name of a Protestant culture that
never was. The "wall of separation" concept is criticized as a
slogan to advance the self-interest of the Protestant churches, a
slogan that is inadequate because the American tradition allows
the churches to influence society and the state in a manner consistent with pluralism.

Hudson, Littell, and Kelley represent a genuine attempt to
recapture the church-centered perspective of seventeenth-century
separationism and to apply it consistently to the problems of
today. On the surface they hold many of the more conventional
separationist positions, but for a different reason—the integrity
of the church. Thus they oppose religious symbols in public
schools and buildings, not because of anti-Catholicism or defense
of the wall of separation, but because history indicates that the
vigor of the churches varies in inverse proportion to their reli-
ance on government. This viewpoint thus accentuates a persistent
though diversely interpreted motif of Protestantism: the sharp
difference in form and function of church and state. They would

emphasize the total reservation of religious symbols and activities to the churches, while maintaining the right of the churches to influence society and the state.

Instead of the anti-Catholicism so prevalent among separationists, they would stress Protestant-Catholic-Jewish dialogue in a genuinely neutral society. Anti-Catholicism would diminish because Protestants would no longer assume the existence of a Protestant society, while dialogue in full integrity could take place without competition from a political religion that does justice to none of the traditions.

Hudson, Littell, and Kelley regard the recent religious revival as a threat more than a blessing. The growth of Protestant membership since the nineteenth century has diluted a once clear-cut faith and diminished the discipline and vitality that rely on God and not the state. With a virtual Anabaptist emphasis, they urge the church to draw back from the world to recover its integrity, pruning from its membership those who confuse the Christian faith with the norms of society and who are unwilling to make Christ central in their lives.

This position has a great deal of promise, though it is clearly in an embryonic stage. It has self-criticism and consistency, while standing in closer touch with the theocentrism of the seventeenth century than the rational anthropocentrism of much of the Protestant evangelical wing. Still unsettled are a number of questions, such as the nature of the Christian faith which so differs from the American faith, or the relation between the First Amendment and the traditional practices accepted under it which these spokesmen regard as inconsistent with true voluntarism, or the relationship between this rather sectarian view and the ecumenical movement. But this is a new and clearly sophisticated form of separationism, which has much time to grow.

The Significance of Separationism

Separationism is historically the most significant of the Protestant positions considered in this book, but paradoxically in its contemporary form it is probably the most questionable. It illustrates the fact that often the most creative forces become the most atrophied when circumstances change and new problems make old answers irrelevant. Protestantism has often shirked its responsibilities for social change; having given up the independ-

ent religious voice that Roman Catholicism has maintained, it
has tended to follow the inclinations of the government under
which it found itself, and to sanction social changes already accomplished by other groups in society. Separationists, however,
helped mold two great and creative political forms, Anglo-
Saxon democracy and church-state separation. Their actions
were at least partly based on self-interest, for they represented
the lower classes and the dissenting congregations, but they
effectively related their self-interest to an affirmation of the
divine sovereignty over all of society, the free-functioning of
religious conversion and activity by congregations and individuals, and the inconsistency of persecution in the name of Christianity. Like the Mennonites, separationism helps refute simplistic theories that interpret religion as a mere reflection of culture.

But the passage of time has made these emphases secular dogmas with little relation to the religious spirit underlying separationism. Within the context of an established church behind
which one particular interpretation of Christianity prostituted
itself by using political power to maintain its privileges, separationism was an expression of dissenting groups consistent with
the best ethical outlook of Christianity. It represented a judgment upon the confusion of the dominant church and an affirmation by the sects that man should not hinder God's free actions by
political structures. The flexible system of separation enunciated
by the American Constitution prevented special privileges while
preserving the givenness of religious life free from governmental
interference. In this form it corresponded to genuine religious impulses, but the contemporary defense of absolute separation bears
little relation to the Protestant spirit. Under certain circumstances a wall of separation might be necessary to protect religion
from political or ecclesiastical totalitarianism, but one finds no
evidence that Protestantism needs to take such a position today.
Rather, the mainstream of current separationism is engaged in
a crusade with secular forces to defend a legal concept that is
not consistent with American tradition and probably does not
represent the best means to further Protestant concerns.

The tendency of separationists to adopt the ideological principle of absolute separation while functioning in a manner which
assumes a moderate separation, can be traced to the source of
separationist, and probably most Protestant, involvement in
church-state matters—anti-Catholicism. In the sixteenth and
seventeenth centuries opposition to Roman Catholicism was prob-

ably a life-and-death matter for Protestants. Without the intense fear and hatred of the revived papacy promoted by religious and political leaders, the distinctive interpretations of Christianity fostered by Protestantism might have perished. But this historical contingency has passed.

A responsible and fair understanding of the differences between Protestantism and Catholicism, and a defense of Protestant interests when they may be threatened by Catholics, is quite distinct from a distorted, almost paranoid anti-Catholicism. This issues in false assumptions such as the Protestant character of America, distorted use of Catholic writings through misquotation and removal from context or assuming that the most disagreeable Catholic writers are the voice of the church, and refusal to condone even the most minimal Catholic actions in society, actions presupposed by every other religious or social group in the nation. The reprehensible nature of much separationism, especially that of P.O.A.U. and more extreme groups, is revealed by the utter dishonesty with which its representatives use Catholic materials to paint the Roman Church as an ever-present threat to American institutions. It is not surprising that many Protestants, originally interested in church-state issues and attracted by P.O.A.U., are now seeking other organizational expressions of their concern. This explains the extensive discussion of church-state problems in many denominational circles. The leadership senses that something is wrong with the conventional Protestant views, that further study is needed on the nature of separation and especially of Roman Catholicism.

Because the evangelical wing of Protestantism represented by separationism possesses extraordinary vitality, and the American church-state solution so strongly stems from separationist influence, a reformation of contemporary Protestant church-state views requires separationism, but one with a sense of historical perspective and self-criticism. Fortunately some Protestant thinkers and leaders, as we have seen, are wrestling with the problems in a promising way.

V   Moderation and
Pragmatism:
The Transformationists

Transformationism has developed into self-awareness during the past fifteen years in response to the separationist approach to church-state problems. Its chief differences are its moderate interpretations of American church-state separation and its restrained attitude toward Roman Catholicism. These characteristics are illustrated in two articles from the periodical most consistently representing the transformationist position, *Christianity and Crisis.* Many Protestants hailed the *McCollum* decision as a landmark in preserving religious liberty;[1] but on July 5, 1948, twenty-seven churchmen and theologians led by John C. Bennett showed that Protestantism was not monolithic by arguing that the decision seemed "unwarranted by the language of the first amendment" and resulted in a situation "in which forms of co-operation between Church and State that have been taken for granted by the American people will be endangered."[2] The second example comes from an article by the managing editor of the journal, Wayne H. Cowan, who, on June 26, 1961, called on the leaders of Protestants and Other Americans "to cease and desist from their blatant anti-Catholicism and to move beyond . . . the holy war from which they impugn the patriotism of their adversaries. . . ."[3]

These two characteristics are closely related and spring from the transformationist or theocratic tradition associated with Calvin and transmitted to American culture, especially through the New England Puritans. One could not accurately call the twentieth-century representatives of this position Calvinists or theocrats. In fact, many more obviously Calvinist Protestants deal with church-state relations in the opposed separationist manner.

But both the moderate attitude toward church-state separation and the general hesitation to oppose Catholic positions stem from conscious recognition that Christianity has a responsibility for society and the state. A radical separation of church and state would inhibit the channeling of Christian influence on government. The relative absence of anti-Catholicism can be explained by the fact that the transformationists conceive the role of the church very much as Roman Catholicism does. Although the Roman Catholic Church during its long history has acted toward various states in a manner inconsistent with American church-state relations, the heart of Catholic theory has always been that the ecclesiastical institution has a *moral* authority over the government. This has never been interpreted as a right of the church to make political decisions, with the possible exception of the abnormal period from Innocent III (1198-1216) to Boniface VIII (1294-1303), but to define moral standards such as the natural law which the state should observe in its legislation and policy.[4] The transformationist representatives have been self-critical enough to see that opposition to certain Catholic interests meant undercutting similar positions essential to Protestants as well.

Where the issue has been the nature of church-state separation, transformationists have sided with Roman Catholics in defending a situation within American life by which a positive relation between church and state could continue, where each could communicate with the other and by working together advance the common good of society. This has not necessarily meant cooperation, which would seem ruled out by the legal precedents, but that the churches could advise the state on policies of common interest, and the state was not barred from assisting religious groups when pursuit of public welfare required it, such as in education and health.

Although this typifies the present transformationist position, past expressions of Calvinist and Puritan theocracy were exceedingly anti-Catholic. Theocracy, however, in Reformation Europe and subsequently in America, worked in a different context, one which sought to institutionalize its religious and moral convictions in an overwhelmingly Protestant society, with very little understanding of or encounter with Catholicism and still hopeful of consummating the Reformation through an ultimate conquest of the papacy. Contemporary transformationists, on the other hand, recognize the inescapability of religious pluralism in America and the advantages of church-state independence, while American life has brought them into engagement with Roman Catholics and fostered a new evaluation of what it once considered the Antichrist.

The Calvinist Origins of Transformationism

The similarity between transformationists and Roman Catholics in upholding the right and responsibility of the church to express its ethical concerns in the political order is not surprising. The theocratic impulses of John Calvin were merely one aspect of the medievalism which the Reformation reflected. Luther's understanding of reality in theocentric terms, and the continuation in Protestantism of the fundamental Christian political concepts of dualism, the created and fallen character of the political order, and the Christian evaluation of political life have already revealed the Protestant assocation with medieval Catholicism. Whereas Luther, however, tried to free the political order from interference by the church and conceived of its capacities in the minimal terms of natural justice, Calvin adopted the sacramental vision of the Middle Ages, which saw all of reality as a mirror of God and his purposes for mankind, a *corpus Christianum*. The state, like all natural phenomena, though maintaining its integrity within the temporal order, was a steppingstone by which man was aided in living the Christian life. Calvin altered this pattern chiefly by eliminating the distinction of the natural from the supernatural order and by intensifying the theological or Christian significance of the state. Wilhelm Niesel has noted that Calvin's discussion of the state follows his treatment of the Church, the Word, and the sacraments, implying that the state "exists for the good of those who in this perishable world belong to Christ and his eternal kingdom. . . . Christ as the Head of His Church is also precisely the Lord of this world."[5]

Here lies the fundamental difference between the church-state theologies of Calvinism, Lutheranism, and Anabaptism. Luther saw the state as an expression of God's creation, but accorded to the church alone historical responsibility for man's redemption: the state was to the church as law to gospel, essentially of a differ-

ent order. The Anabaptists were even more severe in their limitation of the state, which at best expressed the wrathful benevolence of God, while Christ ruled in the conventicles of Christians
separated from political life. Calvin, to be sure, separated the
function of church and state, but unlike Luther and the Anabaptists he felt that the state could and should exercise a godly,
christological, salvific purpose. In this respect he was more
medieval in his social philosophy than either of the other two.
The eminent Roman Catholic historian, Christopher Dawson,
has recognized this.

> For on the one hand the Catholic political tradition in the
> narrower sense, i.e., the historic type of the Catholic state,
> agrees with the Lutheran-Continental tradition in its author-
> itarianism, its conservative traditionalism, and its acceptance
> of a strict corporative order of society. On the other hand, it
> stands far closer to the Western-Calvinist tradition in its view
> of the relation of the Church to the state, in the primacy of the
> spiritual power, above all in its conception of Natural Law.

> In this respect it [Calvinism] carries on the traditions of
> medieval Catholicism and of the Gregorian movement of re-
> form to an even greater degree than did the Catholicism of the
> Counter-Reformation itself.[6]

The Calvinist tradition has contributed to Protestantism a
distinctive outlook toward the state, though in sixteenth-century
Geneva Calvin was better able to implement it than were his
successors. In fact, only a few almost unconscious motifs remain
today from the vision of a Protestant *corpus Christianum* that
Calvin upheld, and these have been modified by new political
conditions that Calvinism promoted and to which it reacted.
The practical consequence of Calvin's theocratic views was to
maintain the authority and independence of the church against
the Erastianism into which Germany and England fell. Wherever
Calvinism spread, it found means for combating the political absolutism that was enveloping Europe. Roman Catholicism and
forms of Calvinism became the most effective forces blunting the
edge of political totalitarianism because both not only insisted on
the integrity of religious life, but sought to guide society as well.
Lutheranism had as vigorous a sense of the independence of religion from political influence as did Calvinism, but it looked to

the state to guarantee the church. Calvinism, on the other hand, assumed that the church should help direct society, but by developing instruments for exerting pressure on the state, it succeeded principally in guaranteeing its own integrity.

Calvin did not seek rapport between the church and the state through a control of the state by the church. He held rather that the church should determine freely, without interference from the political order, the dimensions of life directly concerned with religion. The civil government, on the other hand, should act in terms of the will of God, seeking in God's Word how best the political order could contribute to the salvation of its citizens, as well as providing an orderly and beneficial temporal setting for their daily life.

His insistence on the authority of the ecclesiastical officials in religious matters led to a struggle between Calvin and the political authorities that lasted throughout his lifetime. In 1536, after the city council of Geneva had adopted the Reformation, Calvin was invited to help establish and define the new faith. Given the correlation of citizenship with church membership, Calvin and William Farel, his associate, assumed that they could require of the citizens conformity to a common set of beliefs and practices. The church would tolerate no interference from the civil government in matters of belief, religious discipline, and ecclesiastical punishment; but it expected the state to help it carry out its mission. The people had decided for the Reformed faith, and Calvin expected them to pursue it with a minimum of resistance. But the city council was also under the influence of Erastianism, as mediated by its neighbor, Bern; and when it attempted to institute certain Bernese religious practices without Calvin's approval, Calvin insisted that an ecclesiastical synod should decide. When his complaints went unheeded, he became an exile in Strassburg from 1538 to 1541.

The subsequent history of the Genevan church reveals a high degree of compromise between Calvin and the city authorities rather than a complete reservation of ecclesiastical decisions to the church. On a variety of religious issues such as the election of elders, the appointment of ministers, and the administration of church finances, the political authorities held decisive power.[7] The most effective weapon Calvin managed to retain for the church was the right of excommunication, although many prominent citizens sharply questioned his use of it.

Calvin's Views on Government and Resistance to Tyranny

Calvin set forth the duties of the state in his *Institutes*. Against religious utopianism he argued that "the spiritual kingdom of Christ and civil government are things very different and remote from each other,"[8] and he called the Anabaptist view of government "a polluted thing, which has nothing to do with Christian men."[9] The political order in seeking the welfare of its citizens assumes a responsibility for promoting their religious life, though Calvin saw this also as a glorification of God through the political as well as the religious authority. The civil order should suppress idolatry, blasphemy, and sacrilege, because "this civil government is designed, as long as we live in this world, to cherish and support the external worship of God, to preserve the pure doctrine of religion, to defend the constitution of the Church. . . . But if it is the will of God, that while we are aspiring towards our true country, we be pilgrims on the earth, and if such aids are necessary to our pilgrimage, they who take them from man deprive him of his human nature."[10]

Calvin frequently cited the Old Testament to justify governmental support of religion. Although he dissociated himself from the correspondence of religious and political authorities characteristic of ancient Israel, he tended even more than Luther to use the Old Testament where it suited his purposes. His pre-eminent theological concern was to be true to Scripture, which included for him both Testaments. The Calvinist tradition has continued to distinguish itself by its use of the Old Testament, especially in its understanding of governmental responsibility and the meaning of history.

Calvin held, furthermore, that the pagan writers all stressed the religious responsibilities of government, that "no government can be happily constituted, unless its first object be the promotion of piety, and that all laws are preposterous which neglect the claims of God, and merely provide for the interests of men."[11]

The theological responsibilities of the magistrate enabled Calvin, even more than Luther, to justify political office as a vocation.

Calvin's discussion of government in the *Institutes* stresses the independence of its activity from determination by the officials of the church. Like medieval Catholicism, his theory of church and state assumed two independent authorities, directed toward the temporal and spiritual weal of the realm, co-operating because essentially they have different functions. But just as confusion of spheres of activity led to the great institutional conflicts of the Middle Ages, so the application of Calvin's theory in Geneva obscured the spheres in which church and state acted.

The core of the controversy lay in the consistory, the agency of the church by which Calvin tried to enforce discipline in society as a whole. Discipline as a theological category applied to all citizens because virtually all purported to be Reformed Christians. "It may be said that Calvin's supreme aim was to produce a Church that deserved the name of holy. Religion to him was an essentially moral thing, vindicating its claim to authority . . . only by its ethical effects."[12] Whereas Luther felt that the Christian could console himself as a sinner in a wicked society through trust in God, Calvin insisted that by initiative and effort Christians should live a life witnessing to their conversion and glorifying God.

At a time when Roman Catholicism was fighting back, not only by arms, but by theological reconstruction and piety, Calvin insisted that Protestant centers should shine as cities set on a hill, worthy symbols of the truth they confessed. The consistory was Calvin's instrument for assuring this. Composed of ministers and laymen, it undertook to deal with whatever Scripture or godly-good taste defined as inconsistent with a Christian society. This pointed inevitably to the variety of crimes and misdemeanors usually dealt with by civil authority, so that its investigatory powers drastically overlapped those of the magistrate. Although the consistory used punishments consistent with ecclesiastical authority such as reprimand and excommunication, the expected co-operation between church and state produced numerous instances in which offenders were discovered by the consistory and then referred to the political power for temporal punishment. The criminal (or sinner) in Geneva found himself subject both to spiritual and temporal penalties. Because civil government protected society from heretical contamination, and because the church could use only spiritual sanctions, the state bore official responsibility for the death of religious deviates like Servetus, having been given this dubious and onerous task by the church officials. The extension of the consistory into all dimensions of moral life undercut in practice Calvin's careful distinction between church and state and led to the simplistic judgment that Calvin established a church-state union in Geneva. But in this context it also illustrates the way in which a moral concern helps undermine theological niceties.

Calvin agreed with Luther against the Anabaptists on most of the disputed aspects of political life such as the sanctity of the magistracy, the right of the magistrate as Christian to coerce in executing the judgments of law, the legitimacy of defensive war, the responsibility of Christians to take an oath, and the necessity of fighting to protect the common good of a society.

On the surface his view of responsibility to authority resembles that of Luther. Distinguishing the office from the person occupying it, he contended that Christians should esteem officials because of the office they fill, even if they happen to be ignorant or cruel.[13] Because the political authority fulfills tasks prescribed by God's historical and salvific intentions, one cannot "resist the magistrate without, at the same time, resisting God himself; . . ."[14] Drawing from Old Testament examples, Calvin argued that virtuous and just rulers mirror God's benevolence, while unjust and tyrannical authorities punish the sins of the people, who should blame themselves instead of revolting against a sovereign set up by God. If one suffers, he should reflect on his sins, which God punishes by the cruel ruler.

Like his contemporaries Calvin feared popular insurrection, and he directed these words to the ordinary citizen; but his aristocratic inclinations led him to a reservation in his counsel of complete submission, of great importance in the later development of Calvinism.

For though the correction of tyrannical domination is the vengeance of God, we are not, therefore, to conclude that it is committed to us, who have received no other command than to obey and suffer. This observation I always apply to private persons. For if there be, in the present day, any magistrates appointed for the protection of the people and the moderation of the power of kings, such as were, in ancient times, the Ephori, who were a check upon the kings among the Lacedaemonians, or the popular tribunes upon the consuls among the Romans, or the Demarchi upon the senate among the Athenians; or with power such as perhaps is now possessed by the three estates in every kingdom when they are assembled; I am so far from prohibiting them, in the discharge of their duty, to oppose the violence or cruelty of kings, that I affirm, that if they connive at kings in their oppression of their people, such forbearance involves the most nefarious perfidy, because they fraudulently betray the liberty of the people, of which they know that they have been appointed protectors by the ordination of God.[15]

Two pages after this striking statement Calvin concludes his *Institutes*. His view was unique among the Reformers, though it had some antecedents in the Western Christian political tradition, such as John of Salisbury's sanction of tyrannicide. But its significance lies in its historical development; later Calvinists exploited it to rationalize a Protestant resistance to the excesses of monarchical absolutism. Calvin himself continued to be an extreme conservative and did not follow through the implications of this passage by advising any of his numerous correspondents to use it, even though some lived in countries where Calvinists suffered oppression from established Roman Catholicism. In the fierce political struggles of the next century, however, which significantly shaped the character of present-day political thought, structure, and church-state relations, good Calvinists found themselves like the Ephori and Demarchi, sometimes as nobles, more often as members of parliaments, opposing their monarchs and promoting limitations on royal absolutism.

Calvin held that the "violence," "cruelty," and "oppression" of kings do not conform to God's expectations, but he fell into the same sort of ambivalence between the divine and the demonic as Luther, taxing the Christian with the problem of deciding whether he should self-critically accept travail as a form of God's punishment, or oppose it as a travesty of God's intentions. The Calvinists eventually called on their sense of religious certitude for an answer, settling on "idolatry" as the touchstone of an illegitimate regime, which applied in practice to Roman Catholicism or tendencies in that direction. This corresponded to that feature in Calvin's thought which saw the value of government in its execution of godly responsibilities, but sensed the proclivity of government to regard itself as divine, no longer subject to the will and Word of God. Though this tendency could assume a variety of forms, the most serious one, which even the ordinary subject should refuse, was the command to disobey God: "The Lord, therefore, is the King of Kings. . . . If they command anything against him, it ought not to have the least attention; nor, in this case, ought we to pay any regard to all that dignity attached to magistrates, to which no injury is done when it is subjected to the unrivaled and supreme power of God."[16] This characteristic of Calvin's political theory does not essentially differ from other

Protestant outlooks, which counsel disobedience to decrees requiring sacrilege or immorality. One finds no more consistent motif of Protestant thought than the recognition of a final point where the civil order violates its responsibilities.

Calvin's predilection for an aristocratic form of government led him, however, to place fundamental responsibility for the rights of the people on the lesser magistrates. This did not stem simply from dislike of absolute monarchy, but from his pronounced doctrine of original sin. Although he felt that forms of government depend on circumstances, he contended that "either aristocracy, or a mixture of aristocracy and democracy, far excels all others," because kings do not have the self-restraint to uphold justice or the prudence to ascertain by themselves the common good. "The vice or imperfection of men . . . renders it safer and more tolerable for the government to be in the hands of many," for mutual assistance, but also to restrain the arrogation of excessive power by any single individual.[17]

A strong view of original sin can move in either of two directions: toward restraint of the masses because of their destructive tendencies, or toward restraint of unlimited authorities because of the temptations of the power they hold. Calvinism has followed both directions, though rarely has it recognized similar problems of destructive egoism on the part of the nobles or economic leaders who constitute the aristocracy. Calvin's attempt to avoid the pitfalls of both democracy and monarchy, drastically qualified though it was, associated Calvinism with the form of government usually called representative, under which a select group of men exercises the highest political power. Their numbers counter the potential absolutism of one single ruler, but being select they possess the virtue and wisdom to determine the common good better than the masses. The latter assumption was bolstered by the Calvinist views of election and sanctification, which recognized degrees of Christian grace despite the inevitability of sin, and looked for a government of godly men, the rule of the saints, who because of their religious status could better resist temptation and ascertain the will of God for society.

Calvinist Political Development in France and Scotland

In countries like France and Scotland, where Calvinists found themselves initially countered by a strong and dominant Catholic state, Calvin's high estimate of the aristocracy combined with his limited right of resistance to contribute significantly to democratic theory. The French Huguenots, led by Admiral Coligny, attempted first to persuade the monarchy to adopt Protestantism, but this policy perished with the massacre of St. Bartholomew in 1572, when the regent, Catherine of Medici, agreed to the slaughter of seventy thousand Protestants and confirmed the official Catholicism of the realm. During the next few years, however, the Huguenots wrote a series of documents which, in the words of Ernest Barker, "should never be forgotten by any who confess the cause of liberty, civil and religious."[18]

The most significant of these documents of French Calvinism was the *Vindiciae contra Tyrannos* (1579), attributed to Philippe du Plessis Mornay, which sums up and expands earlier Huguenot tendencies.[19] The heart of the argument lies in the third query, on resistance to the oppression and ruin of a state by a prince, where a sophisticated and potentially democratic social contract theory appears. The monarchy, it holds, was originally instituted by the people, who transferred to the king power to guarantee their well-being and can withdraw it if the king does not administer it according to justice and the common good. God holds rulers responsible to the original source of their authority, the people, and the lower officials of the nation and neighboring princes must rescue the rights of a people oppressed by a tyrant. The extreme traditionalism of the document is reflected in its denial of the monarch's right to make new laws, and its charge to him to defend the laws previously assented to by the people. The *Vindiciae* features a three-way relationship, among God, ruler, and people, unlike traditional Christian political theory, which held a ruler responsible only to God, whose will was defined by justice and the natural law. But the Huguenots argued that God guaranteed a contract between king and people, that government was instituted not merely as an element in God's sovereignty, but to guarantee the fundamental rights of the populace.

Similar political views among the Scottish Calvinists paralleled the French developments. John Knox, who had lived in England and fled the persecutions of Mary Tudor, had his opinion on "the monstrous Regiment of Women" further soured by his encounters with Mary Stuart in Scotland. As G.P. Gooch has shown, Knox's views developed gradually, but by 1557 he had concluded that "it is not less than blasphemy to say God commanded kings to be obeyed when they command impiety."[20] In his *History of the Reformation in Scotland* Knox recounted a number of conversations with Mary in which he utilized his role as mediator of the will of God to justify resistance. The following is typical:

> Think ye (quod she), that subjects having power may resist their princes.
> If their princes exceed their bounds (quod he), Madam, and do against that wherefore they should be obeyed, it is no doubt that they may be resisted, even by power. . . . God forbid . . . that ever I take upon me to command any to obey me, or yet to set subjects at liberty to do what pleaseth them. But my travail is that both princes and subjects obey God.[21]

Two other Scottish thinkers of significance elaborated views of popular sovereignty, George Buchanan in his *De Jure Regni apud Scotos* (1579)[22] and Samuel Rutherford in *Lex, Rex* (1644),[23] both of which became textbooks for revolution-minded Calvinists in other countries as well. Both emphasized the relativity of government as an instrument of popular intentions and the primal transmission of authority to rulers selected by the people. Questioning the sanctity of hereditary monarchy, they held that the people in establishing their civil societies prescribed through nature and law the limitations of the king. In case of violations, the contract was annulled and the people, through their leaders, had the right to replace the unfaithful regime by one more cognizant of its incorporating responsibilities. According to Rutherford, the people "measure out, by ounce weights, so much royal power, and no more and no less . . . [and] take again to themselves what they give out upon condition if the conditions be violated."[24] In Scotland the chaotic political situation enabled the Calvinist church to speak with authority; in fact the Kirk became the source of order and national unity, and only in Scotland did Calvinists achieve the degree of authority in guiding the destiny of the society that they had in Geneva. In most other European countries the momentum of the age lay instead with the extension of royal authority.

Puritan Beginnings

In England the Calvinists were called Puritans, for strategy indicated they become a purifying party within the Anglican Church. The political situation there differed from that of Scotland, France, and Holland, especially after the accession of Elizabeth. Under the Catholic monarch, Mary (1553-1558), Calvinists like Knox and Bishop Ponet justified resistance and deposition because of Mary's presumed violation of her agreement to seek the welfare of the people. But Elizabeth was not Roman Catholic, and though not a pure Calvinist she abstained from persecuting Protestants. Although Elizabeth did not accede to the Puritan proposals but carried through a policy of political determination of religion along the lines of a Catholic-Protestant compromise, her actions did not justify active resistance, and the possibility always remained that in time the Puritans could gain control of the church.

The Puritan reforms are usually associated with the elimination of symbols and vestments, the centrality of preaching rather than liturgy in the service, and severity in ethical behavior. All of these are true, but the core of the Puritan program represented an element of political thought drawn from Calvin's original scheme in Geneva. Elizabeth, who typified the movement toward political sovereignty in early modernity, was impatient with the interference of the church in what she conceived to be the national interest. The English Reformation, despite the presence of theologians like Thomas Cranmer, was the most dubious of all the reform movements from a religious point of view, for the Tudors broke off relations with the papacy, not from driving religious convictions, but because they wanted religion and morality to follow rather than contradict national purposes. Elizabeth, wishing to avoid the religious persecution that occurred under Henry VIII and Mary, promoted a tolerant and comprehensive church. Under her Erastian policy she persecuted only those religious views that seemed to threaten national unity, and avoided religious disputes by basing conformity on participation in a common liturgy. As one historian has assessed Elizabeth's religious policy, she anticipated that "the common bond of her people would in future be not their religion but their nationality. . . ."[25] The two extremes against which she moved were radical Catholics who plotted to kill her and return England to Rome, and radical Protestants who rejected the association of true religion with a national church and withdrew into separate conventicles. But in addition to comprehension the Elizabethan settlement maintained the traditional form of church government, the hierarchy of bishops, with Elizabeth herself assuming the position of "Supreme Governor" over the church. She did not act merely out of reverence for the traditional form of polity, but clearly saw that she could exercise closer authority over the church through a system by which she appointed the bishops, and they, in turn, controlled clergy and laity.

Elizabeth's Erastianism contradicted at key points the Calvinist-Puritan understanding of church and state, although they agreed with her that religion and public life were inextricably intertwined. Drawing their inspiration clearly from Geneva, the Puritan party led by Thomas Cartwright sought a revision by which the church could direct civil society according to the will of God rather than the church's being directed by the will of the monarch. Representatives should be chosen by parish members in good standing, and these representatives in turn would choose members of a series of larger bodies to govern the church. The system was not democratic, but aristocratic, for once the parishioner indicated his choice, he had to obey in religious and moral matters his ecclesiastical superiors.[26]

The most obvious result of these proposals would have been the independence of the church from political control, but its advocates envisioned an England like Geneva, under the guardianship of consistories, supervising morals and advising political officials of their responsibilities in advancing the kingdom of God. It is not surprising that, given Elizabeth's political orientation, she paid no attention to the arguments of the Puritans that they could prove their position from Scripture, or that the great hope of the Puritans, James I, who had experienced firsthand the Calvinist system in Scotland, said at the Hampton Court Conference in 1604, "If you aim at a Scottish presbytery, it agreeth as well with monarchy as God with the Devil." The late sixteenth and first half of the seventeenth century in England suffered the consequences of the fundamental church-state conflict of the time, whether national absolutism could compel religious institutions to do its will, or whether the medieval and Calvinist understanding of the independence of the church and its right to speak against the state and exert influence on society would continue.

James quite correctly saw that the Puritan position diametrically opposed the extension of his own royal interests, and though the Puritan party exercised great strength, especially in the growing commercial and professional classes, the crown probably had the bulk of popular support. The Tudors had led England into significance, defeated Spain in 1588, and provided a unity through the crown that feudal Scotland had to achieve through the influence of Knox and the Kirk. It took nearly three decades before the Stuarts dissipated the good will and popularity developed by Elizabeth.

Frustrated in their efforts with Elizabeth and James to extend the Reformation in England further along Calvinist lines, the Puritans set to work consolidating their strength where they could. Politically, this meant the House of Commons, while religiously, they formed conventicles within the church, where they spread their views through preaching, often on Sabbath afternoons after the regular Anglican service. Large segments of the English changed from the frivolity and confidence of the Elizabethan age to one of the most seriously religious populaces in Western history.

> No greater moral change ever passed over a nation than passed over England during the years which parted the middle of the reign of Elizabeth from the meeting of the Long Parliament. England became the people of a book, and that book was the Bible. . . . Elizabeth might silence or tune the pulpits; but it was impossible for her to silence or tune the great preachers . . . who spoke from the book which she had again opened for her people. . . . The whole temper of the nation felt the change. A new conception of life and of man superseded the old. A new moral and religious impulse spread through every class. . . . The whole nation became, in fact, a church. The great problems of life and death, whose questionings found no answer in the higher minds of Shakspere's day, pressed for an answer not only from noble and scholar but from farmer and shopkeeper in the age that followed him.[27]

These small groups fostered among the Puritans a form of church life centered on the local congregation, where the participants chose their "teacher," and mutual interest rather than parish residence bound them together. It is not surprising, therefore, that when the Puritans finally had an opportunity to reform the national ecclesiastical structure along presbyterian lines, it conflicted with and foundered on congregational tendencies that had been nurtured within the parish churches for decades. The English Puritans never actualized their dream of a united Christendom along the Genevan pattern, because as William Haller puts it:

. . . the movement they had promoted had already brought into being a mode of religious organization, elastic, protean in its adaptability to changing folk experience, and in the event quite ineradicable. That condition . . . which permitted every Englishman, as one to whom liberty was natural, to go his own road to heaven at his own risk, had its beginning in those more or less unrecognized, unacknowledged, and sometimes disallowed groups of like-minded godly souls who, from about 1570 on, fell into the habit of joining together, for the most part within the church, in order that they might engage whom they would to expound the Word of God to them.[28]

The interaction between the Puritans who refused to be silent and the policy of a prudent government led to toleration. The Puritans, intolerant themselves, indirectly contributed to tolerance by testing, as a minority group, the comprehensiveness of the governmental policy. The historian of English toleration, W. K. Jordan, has argued that the Puritans, by upholding the integrity of the human conscience in religious matters against political authority and insisting that the soul of man is bound only to God, countered the attempt of the government to reduce the English populace to one religious mold.[29] The most important determinant of toleration lay in the royal recognition that the national interest could advance despite the religious diversity, since the Puritans chose to remain within the church and their persecution would only divide the nation.[30] As a minority group Calvinism helped promote tolerance with the vigor and self-confidence with which Calvinists believed and acted. The same religious certainty led them to repress dissident views when they could and to insist on their rights against dominant religious groups.

Puritan Theocracy vs. Anglican Erastianism

The Puritans held a positive view toward the government as long as it did not persecute them. Elizabeth, and to a lesser extent, James, had the prudence to realize that the quietly growing strength of the Puritans was too strong to exorcise without cutting off many of the more significant elements of the populace. Especially strong among the merchants and lawyers, the Puritans held also the tacit support of a number of the nobility. Cambridge was their intellectual stronghold where, indoctrinated by an exceptional group of teachers, a whole generation of Puritan preachers went out to show their contemporaries how England properly should consummate the Reformation. Despite official rejection of their views, the Puritans bided their time until a related series of political and religious events widened the schism between the royal authority and themselves and led to the upheavals of the 1640's.

It is rather hard today to understand the degree of hostility to Roman Catholicism that prevailed in England in the seventeenth century. Nationalism and religious conviction acted together in the thinking of the average Englishman, involving hatred and fear of Spain, England's chief rival; hostility to the papacy and commitment to the English church as the major reasonable alternative; and the memory of Bloody Mary's persecutions and marriage to Philip II of Spain. The policies most intolerable to the nation, and especially to the Puritans, who regarded Roman Catholicism as idolatry, were those directed toward rapprochement with Roman Catholicism in religious or political form. Englishmen felt that their future lay in support of Protestant nations like Holland and dissident groups like the Huguenots, and they thrilled to the military exploits of the Protestant monarch, Gustavus Adolphus of Sweden. In the latter part of the reign of James, and increasingly under Charles I, the crown and church drew steadily closer to the Catholics.[31] This appeared politically in the negotiations for a Spanish or French wife for Charles, but also in the failure of the crown to support Protestant countries, the toleration of Catholics at court, and the decision of Charles in 1629 to rule the country without Parliament, where Puritans had their political voice.

The Anglican Church, which had been a genuinely middle-of-the-road institution under Elizabeth, now began to lean more toward Rome. The preference for papacy over Puritanism was especially evident in William Laud, the dedicated ecclesiastic who began to harry the Puritans while bishop of London after 1628 and extended this policy throughout the entire nation when he became archbishop of Canterbury in 1633. During the 1630's many Puritans departed for America to make an unfettered attempt at a Calvinist commonwealth; others went to Holland; while those at home lived without political representation and were harassed with greater intensity as the decade developed.

Laud began his campaign in a way cleverly designed to undermine the public forum of the Puritans, in an area, however, that inflamed their underlying self-righteousness about communicating the Word of God: he tried to suppress the preaching and pamphlets that represented the Puritan apologia. In 1629 he acquired from Charles a decree limiting church lecturers and private chaplains, and in 1633 he ended the activities of a wealthy group of Puritans who had been buying up benefices in order to establish Puritan ministers in them. Laud exercised extreme savagery against Puritan pamphleteers, turning them over to the Star Chamber for imprisonment and often mutilation. These measures, combined with a strong emphasis on the liturgical and symbolic aspects of Anglicanism that the Puritans detested, could not help but intensify the ire and desperation of the intensely religious and self-righteous Puritans. Church and crown combined, furthermore, in advancing the divine right of kings, a political theory that struck at the heart of the Calvinist understanding of the relationship of God and the state. This view, propounded by James I against Jesuit advocates of the papal right of monarchical deposition, now became a chief element in the rationale of Laud and his associates, who as a minority looked to the crown for support.[32] The dissolution of Parliament had been preceded by lectures from Laud and others on the necessity of submission to royal demands for revenue that Parliament considered unjust and unwarranted in common law. According to Laud, "The King's power is God's glory; and the honour of the subject is obedience to both."[33] The beginning of the end for this policy came, however, when Laud decided to force the Church of Scotland to adopt the Book of Common Prayer, a move which that doughty group felt violated the independence of the Kirk. When the Scots covenanted to resist and in fact defeated the royal army, Charles had to call Parliament back into session.

Parliament immediately began to change the religious system of England. Although parliamentarianism developed throughout the 1640's, stimulated by ideas from the Scottish theorists that eventually enabled Parliament to justify its execution of the king, the principal interest of the representatives around 1640 was religious. Amid a barrage of sermons and pamphlets comparing the times with selected periods in the history of Israel, the Puritan Parliament beheaded Laud, abolished the independent courts from which they had suffered, established monthly fast days, and assembled the leading divines of the nation at Westminster to lay down a theological program for a godly commonwealth.[34]

The Division of Puritanism

The consummation of the presbyterian system, however, never succeeded, because English religious opinion split into a variety of irreconcilable groups. In addition to presbyterians, led by the Scot, Robert Baillie, and the episcopalians, who followed the king in his conflicts with Parliament, a group appeared in Parliament called Independents who, under the leadership of Thomas Goodwin, emphasized the freedom of the local congregation to organize and teach what it wished and opposed the establishment of a presbytery or higher group that would choose ministers and exercise discipline. The Independents, who reflected the congregational experiences of Puritans under the Anglican system, were the parliamentary voice of what apparently constituted a much larger group, especially among the lower classes, which included Baptists, Quakers, Diggers, Levellers, and other nameless sectaries. The single established church, by which Protestantism had presented a façade of unity against resurgent Roman Catholicism and behind which a small group of theologians had claimed to represent the religious convictions of the nation, now fell apart when the political confusion allowed nonconformist literature to circulate. The radical subjectivism and denominationalism inherent within Protestantism broke loose, and since the direction could not be reversed, religious variety compelled a readjustment of church-state relations in the Anglo-Saxon world. By the end of the Civil War presbyterianism had declined, and when Cromwell assumed authority, his commonwealth was predicated on toleration of all orderly religious congregations, and both conservative and left-wing Puritanism held a doctrine of regicide in the name of God.

It should be emphasized that during the 1640's, the Protestant tendencies examined in this chapter and the previous one on separationism overlap. Left-wing Puritanism committed itself to religious toleration; its grounds were neither legal nor rationalistic, but grew out of a concern for the freedom and independence of religious functions from control either by an established church or by the state. The Independents shared this concern for the expression of God's Word. In Massachusetts, where congregationalism was the view of the overwhelming majority of the authorities, it became an established system; but in England the Independents, discerning that they could never institute their outlook throughout the entire nation, argued instead against a presbytery that would limit their freedom, while accepting toleration for obnoxious sects in order that they themselves might be tolerated.

The real problem for English Puritanism was to reconcile its theocratic perspective with the toleration of other religious out-

looks. The solution came in two stages. During the latter part of
the Civil War, all except the more conservative Puritans, who returned to the side of the king, dedicated themselves to the cause
of the Army and saw in its triumphs the hand of God. Independents and left-wing Puritans brought into the center of their thinking an apocalyptic outlook, the expectation of the future divine
kingdom that lurks in the biblical view of history. England would
become for them not merely the place where the Reformation
would finally triumph, but their own actions were inaugurating
the eschaton. During the 1640's they could agree on the general
direction despite their disagreements: it lay with the extirpation
of both Anglicanism and the tyrannical king who opposed the
saints. The Army, the real power in the nation, became a forum
for religious congregations, where preachers of many interpretations exhorted their listeners that God stood by their side.

Thus congregationalism as a form of religious organization was
reconciled with the theocratic outlook which nearly all of these
groups held because the issues on which they agreed took precedence over those on which they disagreed. Hovering under the surface, however, were irreconcilable expectations. The Levellers, for
example, expected with the downfall of the king serious changes
in the legal and electoral structure, including the shocking proposal of universal suffrage. The Diggers, on the other hand,
hoped for a redistribution of land and abrogation of the inequality between rich and poor. A number of the left wing had moved
beyond mere toleration of their congregations to destruction of
the formal relationship between church and state through the
termination of tithes. These millenarian assumptions contradicted the essentially conservative outlook of Cromwell and the
Independents, who thought that Parliament should represent
the educated and propertied classes and envisioned theocracy in
the form of an established, though tolerant, church.

The conflict came to a head in a series of debates in 1647-1649
within the Army on God's intentions for national policy. Cromwell, who had no intention of yielding his position, moved
against the Leveller leaders and replaced the monarchy with a
program on Independent principles. In this second stage the millenarian hopes of most of the people relaxed, seemingly satisfied
by the Cromwellian regime. Cromwell continued to support the
parish system with tithes and allowed freedom for nonconformists
to function. Thus the independence of the religious congregations persisted, and Cromwell instituted within society a number

of Puritan principles on which there was greatest unanimity. Only a few groups like the Quakers and Fifth Monarchy Men sought to disinter the "good old cause" and urge even more severe Christian requirements on the nation.

The height of the theocratic inclinations in English Puritanism came then in the 1640's and was bolstered by an appropriation of millenarianism. The frustration of these hopes, however, stimulated the development of their opposite, separationism. Religious groups centered on the inner life of the congregation rather than on the advancement of a godly society. The momentary flaming of theocratic passion in England was replaced by a deepened spirituality of nonconformist congregational religious life and an increased secularism and religious indifference by the state. The Latitudinarians who succeeded the Puritans advocated toleration on grounds of public order, reduced religious impulses to a minimum, and disallowed God's will as a consideration in their political and economic activities.

Transformationist Theocracy in Massachusetts Bay

The emigration of a distinguished group of Puritans to New England in 1630 led to the most effective implementation of theocratic principles in the English-speaking world. The influence of the Puritans in American life conveyed an unavoidable expectation of a Christian transformation of society to American religion. The departure of the group coincided with their repression under Laud; though consistent with their adherence to the English church, they did not consider themselves separatists. As they sailed past Land's End, Francis Higginson is said to have cried, "We do not go to New-England as separatists from the Church of England; though we cannot but separate from the corruptions in it: but we go to practise the positive part of Church reformation, and propagate the gospel in America."[35]

Perry Miller has revived an interpretive insight of Champlin Burrage, that the New England group represented a distinctive segment of the Puritan party, the nonseparatist congregationalists.[36] Although incredibly inconsistent in upholding these two contradictory motifs, their biblical and theocratic outlook explains them. In the early seventeenth century men like Henry Jacob began to doubt that the New Testament clearly taught the presbyterian system that Calvin found so self-evident; instead they concluded that adherence to Scripture demanded that each congregation be self-determining. But their theocratic outlook dictated that the congregations constitute a state church. In fact, they envisioned a system by which the government would require religion to be organized according to separate congregations. This pattern, in effect, was established in Massachusetts Bay, much to the horror of the presbyterian Puritans in England. The Independents, who emerged in England during the Civil War and whose leaders had been in exile in Holland, were of the same outlook on church polity.

In New England the Puritans labored to create a theocratic society, but they lacked organizational structures above the congregations by which the will of God could be mediated. They partly solved this difficulty by limiting officeholding and suffrage to those who were clearly Christians, intensifying a tendency in Calvin which distinguished nominal Christians from those who by their understanding of doctrine, experience of conversion, and good fruits had encountered Christianity in the deeply existential way that Puritanism valued. Although everyone had to attend church, only the real Christians participated in the "church covenant" or played a role in the politics of the colony.[37] Immigrants came to Massachusetts for a variety of reasons, but by limiting political participation to the religiously oriented minority, theocratic motivations continued to direct the over-all policy of the colony.

The leaders of Massachusetts had no pattern for forming a government, since the Reformation had related itself to already existing political structures. Not surprisingly, they developed a flexible system amenable to the admonitions of the ministers, in which the "General Court" selected by the active church members became in effect the legislature, and it in turn chose the higher officials such as the governor. John Cotton revealed the origin of this system in commenting that it "is better that the commonwealth be fashioned to the setting forth of Gods house, which is his church: than to accommodate the church frame to the civil state."[38] The chief political concern of the leaders of the colony was to provide a structure separate from the church, conscious of its religious responsibilities, while at the same time not acquiring sufficient power to act beyond its prescribed ends. Like all Calvinists they suspected the self-seeking inclination of institutions that had power to oppress.

In a statement on "Limitation of Government"[39] Cotton set forth some of the chief elements of the transformationist view of government up to that time. Government he regarded as an institution ordained since Adam's Fall to restrain man's anarchic impulses. Men enter such a compact voluntarily (just as the New England Puritans also saw the organization of the church in covenantal terms), but each covenant community governs itself according to particular circumstances. Government is a natural expression of man's inclinations since the Fall, though its form may vary:

> It is . . . most wholesome for magistrates and officers in church and commonwealth never to affect more liberty and authority than will do them good, and the people good: for whatever transcendent power is given will certainly overrun those that give it and those that receive it. There is a strain in a man's heart that will sometime or other run out to excess, unless the Lord restrains it; but it is not good to venture it. . . . It is necessary, therefore, that all power that is on earth be limited, church-power or other.[40]

The Massachusetts Puritans consequently insisted on a separation of political and religious offices, so that the same person could not hold an important office in both church and state.

Godly magistrates who realized their responsibilities and frequently consulted with the ministers determined the divine will for the colony. A nineteenth-century apologist for Puritan society described the role of the preachers as follows:

> As a body of enlightened patriots, whose opinion it was important to obtain, they were consulted by the political authorities in every hour of difficulty; and although cases might be found in which the leading men among them, at least, did not advise their fellow-citizens wisely, it was much otherwise in the great majority of instances. Such was the state of things throughout the whole colonial age; and to this day [1844] in no other country is the legitimate influence of the clergy in public affairs—an influence derived from their intelligence, united with religion, virtue, and public spirit—more manifest, or more salutary, than in New England. . . . The influence of Winthrop, and Haynes, and Bradford, and Eaton, was not greater or happier than that of their compeers and coadjutors, the Rev. Messrs. Cotton, and Hooker, and Brewster, and Davenport.[41]

Unlike England, where the Puritans directed their efforts toward obtaining independence for their religious life and limitations on monarchical power, New England was regarded as an ideal society, "a city set on a hill," comparable to Geneva in perfection.

William W. Sweet[42] has argued that the Massachusetts government was more Erastian than theocratic, for while the clergy had no direct control over the government, the governor and his assistants settled disputes among the congregations, determined the fitness and appointments of newly arrived ministers, and called synods such as that which formulated the Cambridge Platform. The failure to maintain separation of spheres naturally broke down from both sides because of the theocratic intentions of the leaders; intrusions by political leaders into religious matters and the extensive influence of the minister on public life sprang from convictions about God's will in society, mediated by saints who ruled in both church and state. In the event of failure by one of the two authorities directing society, the other could fulfill a role of admonition and action. As the Cambridge Platform pointed out, "The power and authority of magistrates is not for the restraining of churches . . . but for helping in and furthering thereof. . . ."[43] And such patently religious dimensions as "idolatry, blasphemy, heresy, venting corrupt and pernicious opinions, that destroy the foundation, open contempt of the word preached, profanation of the Lord's day . . . and the like . . ." were "restrained and punished by civil authority."[44] The definition of these obligations resulted from a specific plea to the churches to determine how far the magistrates might intervene to maintain the religious unity and peace which was their most important responsibility.

The determination of the colonists to maintain their theocracy made them extremely stubborn toward the home government, even when the latter was under Puritan control. During the 1640's and 1650's, as England changed its policy under pressure from the variety of religious sects, Massachusetts refused to yield its conservative pattern of theocracy, especially on the issue of toleration. The New Englanders looked on themselves as Puritanism triumphant, while their English brethren were at best Puritanism militant. The New England Articles of Confederation state that the Puritans came to America "to advance the kingdome of our Lord Jesus Christ, and to injoye the liberties of the Gospell in puritie with peace. . . ,"[45] but they harbored no doubt about the form of the kingdom and the nature of true liberty as submission to an already determined truth. With the confidence that only religious certitude gives, Thomas Shepard pointed out that Massachusetts did not banish "any for their consciences, but for sinning against conscience . . . or some other wickednesse which they had no conscience to plead for."[46] The Puritans thus refused to distinguish between the obligation of conscience to do God's will and the allowances of civil authority for the frailties of the human conscience, but in so doing they mirrored the views of the bulk of mid-seventeenth-century Protestantism. Only the more radical sects advocated another course, although many governments extended toleration for practical reasons.

The issue of tolerance did not arise seriously until Roger Williams and Anne Hutchinson moved from presumed orthodoxy into heresy, although the founders had anticipated their policy toward such dissidents before they left England. As in Geneva, the magistrate enforced the divine intention. According to the Cambridge Platform, "If any church, one or more, shall grow schismatical, rending itself from the communion of other churches, or shall walk incorrigibly or obstinately in any corrupt way of their own, contrary to the rule of the word; in such case the magistrate is to put forth his coercive power, as the matter shall require."[47] Although the Baptists also suffered, the chief targets of New England intolerance became the Quakers, for obvious reasons: their greater departure from orthodoxy, their apparent threat to civil order, and their stubbornness in returning to the colony even after banishment. Only intervention by the crown in England (and before that, by Cromwell's officials), along with a decline in religious zeal within the colony, guaranteed toleration, although Quaker persecution did not end until 1677.

It is not necessary to trace the deterioration of the New England theocracy. The seeds were already planted shortly after its inception in the departure of such distinguished figures as Thomas Hooker and Roger Williams to start colonies where the more repellent features of the Puritan utopia would be absent. The outstanding zeal of the founders did not last more than one generation, although a few later figures like Cotton Mather and Jonathan Edwards typified their forebears in ages when they stood almost solitary among those who had replaced religious passion with reason, freedom, or economic activity. As time went by, one could no longer say that colonies like Massachusetts looked to God for guidance. Rather, vestiges of the theocratic form without the spirit remained, such as the worst features of the religious establishment, which the Baptists, led by Isaac Backus, progressively whittled down. When final disestablishment came to Connecticut in 1818 and Massachusetts in 1833, that epoch in the Calvinist, theocratic, transformationist outlook ended which assumed a formal co-operation between church and state in effecting a godly society. Especially in the United States had this become unrealizable. The original nonestablishment clause of the Constitution applied to the Federal government and not to the states, but the downfall of the establishment in Massachusetts signaled the fact that religious multiplicity within individual states forbade establishment of any particular religion, even in a state like Massachusetts with its Puritan heritage.

The Revival of Transformationism in the Nineteenth Century

One cannot, however, understand contemporary transformationism without some attention to a transitional stage that reached its apogee in the early nineteenth century. Several excellent studies have explored how the defenders of theocracy reacted to disestablishment and the adoption of the voluntary principle by all of the American churches.[48] New England Calvinism underwent a renaissance in the late eighteenth and early nineteenth centuries, inspired intellectually by Edwards and the Americanized and modernized interpretations of his views called Hopkinsianism and the New Haven theology, stimulated by revivalism in New England with hopes for an even more fruitful field of expansion in the West, and intrigued by the new interest in foreign missions promoted by a small group of Hopkinsian students at Andover Seminary. Although the transformationists abandoned the formal religious establishment, they did not give up their sense of responsibility for society and the state. They felt their political responsibility so strongly, in fact, that historians do not hesitate to call them "theocrats." Heirs of the Puritans, they admired the now defunct society of John Cotton and tried to defend the remnants, but they did not resist intransigently because they discerned new fields for transformationist activity.[49]

The key figure in the transition was Lyman Beecher, leader of Connecticut Congregationalism. Depressed by disestablishment and calling it "as dark a day as ever I saw," Beecher came to acknowledge it "the best thing that ever happened in the State of Connecticut."[50] He and others saw that the will of God could mold society just as effectively without legal associations, through the prestige and exertion of the churches. There were two sides to the program by which Beecher anticipated a new christianization of America: action by religious groups and the election of religious men. The first appears in his comment during an election sermon in 1826, "The application of religious and moral influence is . . . the great duty to which as a nation we are called."[51] The second is revealed in this summary of the obligations of civil rulers: ". . . [they] owe to God and their country now, the same illustrious piety, the same estimation of God's word, the same attendance upon the ordinances of the gospel and cooperation for their support, and the same strict and pure morality, which rendered the civil fathers of our land so illustrious in their character."[52]

The similarity of these features to the original Puritan impulses should be noted. The principal reason for the establishment of religion in Geneva and elsewhere had been to mediate the divine intention to society, while a secondary reason, to protect the religious life of the populace was fulfilled through Christian magistrates. The election of Christians to office guaranteed that government would heed Christian admonitions, would continue and strengthen the churches, and in some instances could even implement the Puritan hope that "saints" should hold political power. God's glory and rule could be expressed through symbols and public acts. Although no formal relation existed between Christianity and the state, religious values and individuals exerted extraordinary influence in nineteenth-century America; according to Daniel Webster, "Christianity—general tolerant Christianity—Christianity independent of sects and parties—that Christianity to which the sword and the fagot are unknown . . . is the law of the land."[53]

The religious mood of the early nineteenth century quickened the theocratic hopes for a new version of the Puritan utopia. The striking results of the revivals, the sense of carrying Christianity to the ancient cultures of Asia and Africa, the increased church membership after the lull and agnosticism of 1790, the growth and expansion of America internally and in world importance, kindled both historical and eschatological expectations. The

theocrats extended their vision to the nation as a whole and fore-
saw a mixed religious and national destiny for America. During
the establishment, on the contrary, they had preferred to leave
the rest of the nation to others and cultivate the tattered remains
of Puritanism which they called the "standing order."

The continuation of the Puritan vision of a political order
under God helps explain the distinctive character of American
church-state separation. The theocrats saw religious liberty and
church-state separation as opportunities instead of threats. Their
originally negative reaction partly lay in the association of rationalistic advocates of liberty and separation with the antireligious
spirit and disorder of the French Revolution, behind which the
French government moved to extirpate the influence of religion
from social and political life. The religious revivals of the early
nineteenth century in America and public disfavor toward the
skepticism of men like Paine in part prevented American church-
state separation from following the French pattern. Beecher and
his colleagues realized that the church, to be effective, had to
formulate new strategies to fit the new situation. This meant not
only the extension of evangelical Christianity and co-operation
among the denominations, but a vigorous preservation of the
traditional symbols that denoted the Christian and even Protestant, though not especially sectarian, character of America.

The most creative enterprise was the development of societies
by which men like Beecher sought to channel the religious energy
from the revivals in ethical directions that would make society
more Christian and indirectly influence national policy. In 1813
Beecher founded the Connecticut Moral Society, which he described as "an influence . . . distinct from that of government,
independent of popular suffrage, superior in potency to individual efforts, and competent to enlist and preserve the public
opinion on the side of law and order."[54] Such corporate groups
with religious backing and moral interests came to highlight
American life. They focused on such diverse concerns as Bible
distribution, Sabbath observance, peace, education, and such
evils as slavery, cruelty to prisoners, alcohol, and prostitution.
Although not as effective as in Puritan Massachusetts, where a
word from the ministers almost automatically meant public sanction for a particular moral position, the reform societies became
the influential voices of the church in the nineteenth century.
The co-operation of the various denominations in these enterprises so influenced society that Winthrop Hudson in speaking

of the voluntary societies could call the nineteenth "the great century" of Christianity.[55]

Although the transformationist impulses stemmed from a small and educated group of New England Congregational clergymen who consciously were attempting to adapt the theocentric motivations of their Puritan ancestors to American church-state separation, their outlook quickly caught fire among Christians in many denominations. Nevertheless, they did not lack opposition in American Protestantism. At least two features distinguished them from their opponents. First, they clearly emphasized the theocratic motif which they inherited from traditional Calvinism against rationalism, Americanism, individualism, or humanism. Although they often succumbed to views that associated God's will with American expansion and destiny, they sought at the same time to hold themselves and society under the direction of God. In an era when men spoke much of natural rights, the theocrats found their pattern in the Bible:

> This, then, was the underlying structure of the theocratic pattern: Biblical legalism, drawn largely from the Old Testament, whence it derived the assurance of God's concern with nations as nations; the belief in the election of the United States as God's new Israel; and the resulting sense of duty to make the United States conform to God's law and to her own God-given destiny. It followed as a matter of course that the clergy considered themselves divinely commissioned to cast the United States in the theocratic mould and . . . to regulate the morality of the nation.[56]

Closely related was the second theocratic feature, a pessimistic view of man which, in an age when Americans began thinking seriously in perfectionist terms, led them to emphasize instead the need for proper direction and restraint of the populace. In their opinion the French Revolution proved decisively the pernicious outcome of too great an emphasis on human capacities, and they tried to mold American society differently. Whereas the French Revolution conceived of freedom in an absolute, unlimited way, the theocrats saw it rather in its classical Christian sense, as the responsibility to learn the true and do the good. American society could not, therefore, yield to caprice, but through moral societies, revivals, and home missions religious men like the theocrats would enable people to use their freedom in the proper manner.

The theocratic emphasis on original sin had political implications also, for the theocrats tended to support the party of order, tradition, and aristocracy, the Federalists and later the Whigs. The opposition Democrats were tainted by association with the radicalism of Jefferson and the French Revolution, and the consequences of Jacksonian democracy such as the low level of political controversy, disorders at the polls, and the frantic scramble for offices. All of these, they felt, sprang from the undisciplined inclinations of the masses. Their distrust of the masses issued in another element often associated with a strong view of original sin—aristocratic inclinations; the theocrats preferred to limit suffrage and officeholding to the moral and intellectual elite in society.

John Bodo, in a study of the social views of the theocrats, feels that their view of original sin, in contrast with the exuberant optimism of early American nationhood, gave them a degree of social criticism, stressing God's judgment as well as his sovereignty over the country.[57] They applied it naively, unaware that their evaluations often represented their own political, regional, and class interests. Nevertheless, a strong doctrine of original sin as a source of social criticism has continued to mark transformationism.

The theocratic approach to Roman Catholicism is illuminating.[58] This was the period of nativism, when many evangelical Protestants, torn by fear and prejudice, engaged in reprehensible persecutions of Catholics. Although nearly all Protestants held anti-Catholic views, they acted from different motivations. The theocrats based their position on theological rather than nativist grounds; they regarded the influx of Catholic immigrants as a form of religious competition from a church with dubious political associations (since the theocrats felt that democracy and freedom were Protestant products). Consequently they worked for the conversion of the Catholics, while disputing their religious views and actions and watching suspiciously their political ones. Unitarians like Channing, on the other hand, thought that as a superstition Roman Catholicism would disappear, while John Leland, the Jeffersonian Baptist, with heady enthusiasm for American institutions, felt that Catholics could not achieve any destructive aims because the American structure would resist them. The theocrats avoided Nativist extremes like

The Awful Disclosures of Maria Monk and the American Protestant Association, while attempting to keep attention directed to the problem as a theological rather than a political one. Far more successfully than other Protestants they avoided evaluating the issue in terms of American or political values and then opposing Catholicism on the grounds of its incompatibility with American institutions—an important point for the continuing transformationist outlook.

The theocratic outlook competed throughout the nineteenth century and into the present day with two other religious or semireligious approaches to reality and social problems in American life. One is that of sectarian or separationist Protestantism, which at times has closely co-operated with and seemed virtually akin to the revivalist wing of the theocrats. Figures like Charles G. Finney, the Presbyterian revivalist, who moved from Hopkinsianism to a more simplistic revival theology and supported Jackson and abolition, seem to straddle both transformationism and separationism. The other approach has been liberal and humanistic, appreciative of values such as individualism and the rights of man, optimistic and progressive. Its greatest religious exponents were the Unitarians, but they were supported by many of the nonreligious educated. Both separationists and Unitarians opposed theocracy and vigorously advocated separation of church and state. Against both, the theocrats, having once accepted church-state independence, fought for the greatest possible christianization of society consistent with religious freedom. Religious symbols and holidays, exemption of churches from taxation, military and legislative chaplains, and the appreciation of religion by government represent the theocratic legacy.

The conflict among these various outlooks explains in part the hesitation of many theocrats to adopt slavery as an issue. The espousal of abolitionism by many Unitarians led the theocrats to explore alternative solutions such as colonization of the slaves in Liberia. By 1850, however, many theocrats who had originally preferred to exert themselves on less divisive reforms had taken public stands against the slavery system in the South.

Nineteenth-Century Transformationism and Education

During this period the inclusion of religious teaching in the public schools was one of the most important church-state issues. The middle of the nineteenth century, under the leadership of

Massachusetts and the creative secretary of its board of education, Horace Mann, witnessed the transition from private to public control of education and the elimination of sectarian influences upon the public schools. Although Mann is usually regarded as the founder of secular education in America, he actually represented the spirit of theocracy in applying broad, evangelical Christianity to education through the teachings of the Bible. In his final report, in 1848, he pointed out that the elimination of sectarianism (Congregationalism) from education in no way meant the end of religious instruction.

> I believed then as now, that religious instruction in our schools, to the extent which the Constitution and the laws of the State allowed and prescribed, was indispensable to their highest welfare, and essential to the vitality of moral education.

> Our system earnestly inculcates all Christian morals; it founds its morals on the basis of religion; it welcomes the religion of the Bible; and in receiving the Bible, it allows it to do what it is allowed to do in no other system, to speak for itself.[59]

The supposedly objective character of this type of religious instruction reveals itself on more careful scrutiny to be an expression of biblical, evangelical Protestantism. Nineteenth-century Protestants assumed that anyone who read the Bible with an open mind would automatically embrace Protestantism; Roman Catholics at the time were suspected of antibiblicism because they opposed reading of the King James version and the obviously Protestant biases in the moral teaching and text-books used in the public schools, such as the McGuffey readers.

Despite pretensions of objectivity, the public schools of the nineteenth century were indisputably Protestant, a situation which naturally led Roman Catholics to intensify development of their own parochial school system. Outside of the Lutherans, for whom religious schools became preservers of German culture as much as transmitters of religious doctrine, the chief Protestant advocates of private schools were the Old School Presbyterians and the Episcopalians, both of whom had doctrinal peculiarities that inhibited their participation in the evangelical theology and activities of the theocrats. The decline of Protestant religious schools came not only from practical factors like financial difficulties and the shortage of teachers, but from the association in the popular mind of Roman Catholicism with parochial schools and of Protestantism with public schools. The Old School Presbyterians, for example, suffered from ambivalence toward private schools, many of their members preferring to go along with the broad Protestantism offered in the public schools.[60] The Episcopal journal, *The Churchman*, initially a prominent advocate of Episcopal schools, changed in the 1870's to a strong stand for public schools because of fear of Roman Catholic "threats" to the public schools.[61] The attitude of the Congregationalists is particularly interesting. When the movement for universal education developed, they accepted full state control, criticizing both Protestant and Catholic attempts to form parochial schools. The role of religion in the public schools represented in the field of education what the theocrats were advocating in society as a whole, a middle-ground between establishment and neutrality.

The relationship of the theocratic motif to education has been emphasized because of the widely held assumption that Protestants produced the secular or neutral public school in the nineteenth century. It is suggested here that such a school would have been anathema to the segment of American Protestantism that included its most significant leaders, the theocrats; that they did in fact help develop the public school, but in a disguised Protestant form; and that the "neutral" school is actually a product of forces and social developments in the twentieth century. The transformationists continue in the twentieth century to experiment with the inclusion of religion in public education while frowning on the secular school.

Transformationism and the Social Gospel

A straight line leads from the theocrats to many advocates of the Social Gospel, although one finds more typical heirs among subsequent critics of the Liberal theology that underlay the Social Gospel. The most important contemporary journal representing transformationism, *Christianity and Crisis,* was founded to represent the point of view of those who had "gone beyond" Liberalism via the neo-Orthodox or neo-Reformationist position. The central emphases of this group have been theological elements traditionally associated with theocracy from Calvin to the nineteenth century, namely, evaluation of society in terms of the will of God rather than of human or social capacities, appreciation of the Old Testament prophetic concern for society as well as the New Testament focus on salvation, and the criticism of self and social structures which follows from a recognition of the innate human corruption called sin. But the original Social Gospel also reflected the highly developed reformist motif that has helped shape the nature of American religion, though in its more uncritical forms it appropriated the optimism and progressivism of American culture and nineteenth-century idealistic philosophy. The Social Gospel represents an important advance in Protestant ethical theory, however, by undercutting the two major blind spots in theocracy as held in the early nineteenth century, namely, its uncritical attitude toward American economic theory and structure, and its tendency to equate political and national interests with the will of God. By questioning the identification of Christian economic ethics with capitalism and often by replacing a vision of American greatness with pacifism, the Social Gospel broadened the sense of criticism that the theocrats had held. Moreover, the Social Gospel approached society, not as did the reformers of the nineteenth century who focused on particular and obvious evils and needs, but with an awareness of radical defects in the very presuppositions and foundations of society. To transform capitalism to some form of socialism and to replace war with peace represented a far more serious transformation than their predecessors had foreseen.

The transformationism of the Social Gospel is shown in a revealing incident that occurred in 1924. A group of churches wrote to Congressman Tinkham of Massachusetts about some pending immigration legislation. The legislator replied:

It is one of the fundamental principles of the American Government . . . that there shall be in the United States complete separation of the Church and the State as religious and political entities, and that there shall be no interference one with the other. The action of certain Churches, of certain denominations . . . in passing resolutions in relation to legislation of a secular character . . . is indefensible. It is my settled opinion that some of the great lawlessness and actual crime in this country to-day is directly caused by the loss of respect for the Church and its teachings on the part of the people, because Churches abandoning spiritual affairs and direction have become quasi-political institutions.[62]

The religious groups retorted that the "Federal Council does not consider any question involving principles of right and justice as being secular." This story is significant because of the argument of Mr. Tinkham that American separation of church and state relegated the churches to religious affairs alone, while the spokesmen for the churches argued that in Christianity politics is not separate from religion, that God has an intention for society as well as the church which the churches must mediate and make effective.

Modern Transformationism and Church-State "Separation"

The transformationist view has emerged since World War II as an application of the social and political ethic developed since the Social Gospel to such neglected problems as religion in public education and governmental policy toward religion. It is not surprising, therefore, that the fundamental axiom of transformationism is the refusal to interpret the American system of separation in an absolute sense, as a "wall" between the churches and the state. Its spokesmen prefer, for example, "independence" of church and state as a more accurate description of the American tradition embodied in the First Amendment. However, their point of view proceeds not simply from an acceptance of the constitutional and judicial clauses, but from the recognition that they could not express their ethical interests without some relation between the religious and political orders. An early example of this viewpoint may be found in the following discussion by Luther A. Weigle, former dean of the Yale Divinity School:

> The separation of church and state is a sound principle, but one that is much misunderstood. It means that church and state are mutually free, and that neither may rightfully control the other. It does not mean that church and state, being mutually free, may not cooperate with one another. And it does not mean that the state acknowledges no God, or that the state is exempt from the moral law wherewith God sets the bounds of justice for nations as well as individuals.
>
> The separation of church and state does not require the

separation of civic duty and religious faith. A state degenerates into tyranny if its citizens abandon conscience when they approach the polls, and forget God when they are in public office. And no man has true religion who . . . fails to use it as a resource for daily living and for public service.[63]

The similarity between Weigle's statements and those of a Roman Catholic like John Courtney Murray is pronounced. Both argue for the right to interpret separation because the principle is not self-evident, that church and state are independent but co-operating entities, that the state should acknowledge God through some symbolic action and legislate according to the moral law, and that the citizen has a responsibility and right to bridge the gap between church and state by relating his Christian convictions to matters of public policy.

As the transformationist position has developed throughout the 1950's, its representatives have shown little interest in retaining the religious symbols originally imbedded in American culture by the theocrats, because their chief ethical interest has centered on the significant economic, political, and international aspects of public policy. But at the same time they cite these vestiges of the originally Protestant culture of America as witnesses to the Christian convictions of many of the people who helped found the nation, as well as to a degree of mutual influence and co-operation between church and state in American tradition. John C. Bennett points to an "officially recognized theism"[64] in the Declaration of Independence, many state constitutions, and the prayers and pious comments of political leaders and legislatures which verifies the statement of Justice Douglas in *Zorach v. Clauson:* "We are a religious people and our institutions presuppose a Supreme Being."[65] Bennett and other transformationists take the present religiously pluralistic character of American society seriously and prefer to accentuate a generally religious rather than a specifically Christian or Protestant character in American institutions.

The transformationists also point to the co-operation between religion and government on common problems such as the religious welfare of the armed services, religious instruction in education, and the health and welfare of all citizens as expressions of the friendly, appreciative view of religion held by the American government. One could not expect otherwise with the relative absence of anticlericalism in American history; the religious convictions, however conventional, of most men who held high public office; and the widespread acceptance of the transformationist motif in American religion, that religion can influence government through the voting of citizens, the actions in office of pious men, and the statements and actions of the churches. While describing many of these aspects as forms of co-operation, the transformationists have generally tried to avoid the word "cooperation" as a substitute for "separation" of church and state, because co-operation has not been the norm or purpose of American church-state relations.[66] Rather, the norm has been independence, but co-operative acts have occurred when the interests of church and state overlapped in a particular area.

Why do the transformationists refuse to espouse the concept of separation when so many of their fellow Protestants struggled in the past to separate church from state and continue to uphold this as a major principle? In addition to their conviction that an absolute separation is not consistent with the intentions of the writers of the Constitution, nor reconcilable with the ethical interests of Protestantism, the transformationists feel that secularism offers a threat to the aspirations of the churches within American society. Their attitude toward secularism is not unambiguous, for they share with men of a secular philosophy such ethical interests as the promotion of social justice and civil liberties, and they have often worked with them in achieving these goals. In fact, the more thoughtful transformationists have refrained from the wholesale indictments of secularism that the pious in America often make, nor have they insisted with particular vigor on maintaining religious symbols and programs that would violate the freedom of non-Christians or the nonreligious. But on some issues they think there is a choice to be made between a religious or a nonreligious philosophy, and in such instances the benefit should go to religion, as long as the nonestablishment clause and religious freedom are not violated.

The Problem of Education and Religion

The chief field of conflict has been education, where public schools in recent years reflect an outlook that, according to Bennett, rejects the religious traditions "as authoritarian and inimical to the democratic educational process."[67] It has been noted that the nineteenth-century transformationists gave the public school warm support because of its generally religious and even

Protestant character, but in the twentieth century individuals and organizations motivated by the outlook described by Bennett have greatly diminished the religious dimensions of public education.

The transformationists distinguish between discriminatory and nondiscriminatory religious aspects of education. They have opposed required religious classes or practices contrary to belief, such as saluting the flag by a Jehovah's Witness, while supporting nondivisive, co-operative arrangements between churches and public schools by which pupils receive religious training in their own traditions. Furthermore, where community consensus has accepted such features as Bible reading, they have advocated their retention. Transformationists were deeply disappointed over the *McCollum* decision which declared unconstitutional an enterprise by which Protestants, Roman Catholics, and Jews had co-operated with the public schools of Champaign, Illinois, to provide voluntary classes in their respective traditions. They felt that in protecting the sensitivities of one nonreligious pupil, the Court had replaced a provision for nondiscriminatory instruction, consistent with American tradition, with a dangerous secularism or neutralism.

The critical outlook of the transformationists toward the neutral school is one of the most difficult elements for the average American Protestant to understand. Most Protestants assume that the American church-state arrangement delegates religious instruction to family and church, while the public school shuns "divisive" religious dogmas and teaches only secular subjects. The transformationist rebuttal has two points.[68] First, it denies that the public school has traditionally avoided religious matters and insists that the secular school is an innovation. Second, it argues that neutralism is not really neutral, but implicitly involves a philosophy with antireligious connotations. Transformationists insist that education, along with other cultural spheres, must find its center in religion. In the nineteenth century, for the first time in Western history, a segment of Christianity, part of American Protestantism, gave up its responsibility for education. Until then both Protestants and Catholics held that the church, not the state, determined the content of education. The reason for religious determination of education lay in the traditional Christian conviction that the decisive truths of reality and salvation were expressed in the Christian revelation and that if these were true, all other truths were in some way related. Thus they associated natural science with the doctrine of creation and interpreted history within a Christian framework, the center of which was the revelation in Jesus Christ. Truth was a unified system, and religion could not be compartmentalized as one subject alongside others which contradicted it.

Given this philosophy of education, the transformationists have criticized the secularization of the public school in the twentieth century. Being pragmatic in orientation, they have recognized that in some instances traditional religious instruction could not continue in classes composed of a variety of religious groups, but they have proposed at the same time nondiscriminatory ways in which religion could relate to education so that pupils would not assume that religion had no significance for the disciplines studied in the public school. Religion is bound up with church and home, to be sure, but it must also focus on all aspects of life. The transformationists in effect hold a view of education similar to that of the Roman Catholics, but they have tried to further it within the public school structure rather than through denominational schools, because the public school is almost the only educational agency that most Protestants can presently conceive. The seriousness with which they view educational secularism, however, has led some spokesmen in major Protestant denominations to suggest that Protestants may join the Catholics in the private school movement. One generally transformationist Protestant group which has long promoted its own schools is the Protestant Episcopal Church, though their small numbers and high costs have tended to limit them to a minority within the denomination.

A moderate view of church-state separation, based on the conviction that Christian ethics requires it, and a struggle to include religion within an increasingly secular curriculum mark the transformationist outlook. It tends to distinguish between religious freedom as a principle and separation as a policy.[69] American separation is seen as a sociological necessity because of the religious heterogeneity at the time of the founding of the nation: it guaranteed religious worship and expression against dominance by either church or state. To accept the American system of church-state independence is to recognize its practicality, not to affirm it as a religious principle.

The chief problem for transformationists in advancing their view of education lies in the complacency with which most Protestants accept the public school as an essentially secular agency, especially in the urban areas of the country. Where, for example, as in small towns, religious symbols continue to have vitality in education, they are presupposed and unopposed by the predominantly Protestant populations; but where they have been eliminated in the more pluralistic cities, most Protestants do not consider the reconciliation of religion with other disciplines through symbols and instruction worth fighting for.

One of the most secularized Protestant denominations, the Congregational-Christians (now part of the United Church of Christ), has also been the most consistently transformationist. In the late 1940's a group of Congregational-Christian leaders, led by Thomas B. Keehn, carefully worked out a transformationist approach to church-state problems, including a positive approach to the role of religion in education:

> By their opposition to the use of public funds for the support of private and parochial schools as such, Protestants are not to be understood as favoring a secularized system of public education. While it is the responsibility of each religious group to provide what it considers to be an adequate religious training for the members of its own group, it is the responsibility of public education to provide for all an understanding of and loyalty to those religious beliefs and practices which have so largely determined the character and tradition of our democracy. In this seeking to influence the nature of public education, we must unite with other faiths in agreement on the character and importance of these great religious principles.[70]

Although this statement typifies transformationism, one hesitates to judge how influential it was on the rank and file of the denomination. One often finds transformationism strong among theologians and denominational leaders, but lacking influence in local congregations.

Transformationism and Roman Catholicism

The attitude of Protestant individuals and groups toward Roman Catholicism is a prime factor in determining church-state attitudes. Since World War II denominational statements under the rubric "church and state" have tended to be criticisms of Roman Catholic "intrusions" on the benevolence of the state, and the major Protestant groups have substituted opposition to Catholic actions for a systematic presentation of the suppositions with which they approached church-state problems. Unlike the separationists and P.O.A.U., most transformationists do not interpret Roman Catholic social and political actions as part of a larger threat to American democracy and church-state independence.

The transformationists could not in consistency oppose the social and political activity of American Roman Catholicism, because Catholic concerns closely resemble their own. It might be argued that Catholicism seeks to a greater degree measures that correspond to its own institutional self-interest in the form of financial aid to parochial schools and the Vatican ambassadorship; but transformationism has similar interests in its concern for Bible reading and religious instruction in the public schools, continued maintenance of religious symbols, and tax exemption for churches. The types of issues on which churches act often follow self-interest, among both Protestants and Catholics, but both have also supported policies justified by the wider good of society: international, economic, and social. The transformationists are inclined to think of Roman Catholics as potential allies in preserving what both understand to be the traditional relationship of church and state against the views of separationists and secularists. They sense that most of the usual criticisms of Roman Catholicism on closer examination are no greater violations of separation than comparable Protestant actions.

Consequently, contemporary transformationists emphasize "Protestant-Catholic relations" and "dialogue." One of the most significant products of this interest is a "Study Guide" by the Massachusetts Council of Churches on "Relations between Church and State and Inter-Faith Relations as They Bear on Church and State."[71] Although the authors represent churches from all over the United States, the study appeared in a state where Roman Catholicism in recent years has greatly increased not only in numbers, but in political and social influence. The authors make the following suggestions for enhancing interfaith relations. The first is self-examination when preparing to criticize policies by other groups, for "the history of Roman Catholics, Orthodox, and Protestants in regard to church-state relations is not in any case pure and perfect."[72] Here the sense of relativism and historical perspective questions the uncritical association of Protestantism with religious freedom and Roman Catholicism

with oppression. The readers are urged to respect the rights
both of minorities and of majorities in advocating measures.
The fourth suggestion points to the need of continuing dialogue:
"Try patiently and persistently to achieve a continuing dialogue
between persons in your own and other churches regarding the
issues of church and state on which there appear to be differences
in view. Such a dialogue may reveal that some supposed differences do not exist, and it will help to clarify and even to resolve
others."[73] When problems do occur, Protestants are urged to go
privately to responsible persons in the other group rather than
explode the issue publicly, to learn to "discriminate between
molehills,"[74] to be conservative and courteous about public
statements, and to apply the Golden Rule to interfaith as well as
to personal relations. The co-ordination of interfaith relations
with church-state relations in the same pamphlet marks the
transformationist perspective.

To focus on dialogue does not mean for transformationists
an abdication of Protestant responsibilities to protect themselves
and the things they value from being undermined by Roman
Catholic interests and values. But they sense that the issues are
more complicated than merely a Protestant defense of church-
state separation and a Catholic attack upon it. The Protestant
stance should not merely be one of reaction to Catholic actions,
for in many instances Protestants might find themselves agreeing
with Catholics. Since transformationists agree with Roman Catholics on moderate separation of church and state, ethical expression in society, the integration of religion with education, and
the deleterious consequences of secularism for the traditional
American relation of church and state, a correspondence of views
would be expected on more specific issues. Thus, in the study
guide of the Massachusetts Council of Churches, the authors
examine a number of tension-filled issues such as financial support for parochial schools and hospitals, released-time classes,
and the chaplaincy, presenting a fair, careful analysis of the
arguments on both sides, attempting especially to understand the
position of the Catholic Church and leaving the final decision
to the reader.

The transformationists have also taken very seriously the efforts
of Roman Catholic theologians like John Courtney Murray to
show how Roman Catholic social theory is consistent with the
American system of church-state independence.[75] The theoretical
dimension is very important, because it helps determine the

perspective with which one views Catholicism, whether as a group attempting to promote a privileged or even established position for itself, or as a supporter of the Constitution. John C. Bennett has been an important figure in transmitting to Protestants the results of contemporary Roman Catholic speculations on church and state. In his chapter, "A Protestant View of Roman Catholic Power,"[76] Professor Bennett wisely indicates that the "attitudes of Americans toward Church-State relations depends [sic] in considerable measure on their attitude toward Roman Catholicism."[77] While recognizing the implicit problems in the Catholic acceptance of dogmatic intolerance (outside the church there is no salvation) and the authoritarian structure of the hierarchy, Bennett says that theoretically and practically these do not necessarily lead to civil intolerance or rejection of democratic political authority. Citing a number of areas of Catholic action that cause justifiable irritation and resentment among Protestants, Bennett argues nevertheless that "it is a mistake to project them in indefinitely extended form upon the future and to allow all of our thinking about Roman Catholicism and most of our thinking about Church-State relations to be controlled by them. . . ."[78]

Instead, Protestants should recognize characteristics of Roman Catholicism that contribute to a more positive image of its activities. For one thing, Roman Catholicism varies so greatly in different cultures and countries that the "difference between French Catholicism and Spanish Catholicism almost belongs to the study of comparative religion."[79] Bennett sees American Catholicism as a more effectively organized and pastoral institution than its Latin American counterpart, but lacking in the rich cultural and intellectual outlook of the French church. Two elements in the American environment, strong competition from non-Catholic sources and the presence of a liberal democratic political tradition, can and should contribute to a more creative Roman church in America. Second, Bennett points to the immigrant background of American Catholicism which has struggled to overcome economic and social disadvantages, and whose aggressiveness and resentment are sociologically conditioned and reasonably understandable. Third, he notes and emphasizes the division of Roman Catholicism on the theory of religious liberty and interprets the new currents as a significant, consistent social philosophy which has gained considerable support among both clergy and laity in America. Finally, he tries to counteract the tendency of Protestants to regard the most obnoxious Catholic positions and actions as the official view of the church by showing that on most public issues Catholics are divided; for the church, while defining morality, cannot specify the form or necessity of its application in civil law. These four features, Bennett feels, cannot shape decisively the future directions of American Catholicism, but "they may help to release us from the exaggerated fears that are based upon past experience in this country alone."[80] Protestants, he holds, should lay more stress on these positive features of Catholicism and join with Catholics in greater co-operation on moral and political issues.

As far back as 1950, the Congregational-Christian Church defined Protestant-Catholic relations in an equally appreciative and self-critical way.[81] Like their forebears, the theocrats, they set the discussion on theological grounds, arguing that the fundamental difference between them lay in the doctrine of the church, and that Catholic exclusive claims had at times denied religious freedom to other religious groups. Although problems of church-state relations and religion in education grew in both Protestant and Catholic cases from differing theological views, the emphasis of the Congregational-Christian statement was "that in an unfriendly world *all* Christians must witness unitedly to their faith."[82]

While opposing in moderate fashion the Catholic quest for financial aid for parochial schools and suggesting instead agreements on religious instruction within the public schools, the Congregationalists set forth a program for Protestant-Catholic relations predicated on the need for self-examination, study, and co-operation. Pointing perhaps to the most embarrassing fact about Protestant activity on issues of church and state, they indicated the need for clarification of their own position on religious freedom and church-state relations. "We cannot compromise on essential principles, but we must know what these principles are."[83] This revealing comment was paired with an insistence that Protestants needed to involve themselves in thoughtful study and research on Catholic policies and theory. Secondly, the statement urged Protestants to co-operate with Catholics where there was agreement on specific objectives, while controversial issues should provoke mutual study and contacts. Finally, they should seek with Catholics to translate the ethical implications of their faith into the social, economic, and political order, while giving "respectful consideration" to Catholics when the latter could not co-operate with Protestants because of conscientious differences of opinion.

The past five years have witnessed a slowly but gradually changing attitude toward Roman Catholicism among Protestant spokesmen and denominational officials, the result of transformationist influence. Dialogue and co-operation, as well as an objective evaluation of church-state issues, have come to dominate the outlook of the National Council of Churches and some denominations, and Protestant churchmen have lined up either in this camp or in P.O.A.U. The major denominations of Protestantism thus show signs of moving beyond dealing with church-state problems by an uninformed opposition to Roman Catholic actions.

Problems of Pluralism

Contemporary transformationism recognizes that its presuppositions imply a particular political philosophy best illustrated by the development of Roman Catholicism and Judaism into major American religious groups. This philosophy is pluralism. The major characteristics of transformationism that have been noted reflect pluralism as a political outlook: the understanding of separation which provides for the influence of religious perspectives on public policy, the theistic rather than secular view of American culture, the appreciation of religious as well as secular education, and efforts toward co-operation on common problems with Roman Catholics and Jews. Will Herberg's analysis of American religion, *Protestant-Catholic-Jew*, reminded Protestants of something they should have realized over a hundred years ago, that one cannot think of American religious composition solely in Protestant terms, but that factually then, and in the public psychology now, three religious identifications prevail in American society. The psychological dimensions are the most important, because in the past the dominant economic and social standing of the Protestants enabled them to look down upon Catholics and Jews, but the rapid social ascent of immigrants has overturned this way of thinking.

The chief problem with which pluralism wrestles is to reconcile acceptance of many religious groups with the right of each to influence society as its religious convictions indicate. A related problem is the avoidance for the sake of the common good of a tyrannical domination by the convictions of one or several of the groups. The transformationists have tried to solve these by pointing to the consensus represented in American tradition and among the religious groups today.

Even though much modern neo-Reformation theology, which has strongly influenced the transformationists, stresses the discontinuity between Christianity and the generalized religious and moral principles that Protestants held during the earlier part of the twentieth century, transformationists in America have also tried to spotlight their agreement with Roman Catholics and Jews. In examining the possible areas for co-operation, the transformationists have almost turned their backs on such ethical interests of traditional evangelical Protestantism as prohibition of alcoholic beverages and Sunday closing laws. Rather they have sought agreement on theistic symbols and social action justified by the common good of society.

The advance of this enterprise has been threatened, most transformationists hold, by the fact that the religious revival of the 1950's has promoted a common religion based on public symbols of piety and the participation of high officials in religious activities, which is not true to the Judaeo-Christian tradition, but represents an exploitation of religion to sanctify aspects of the American way of life and provide a sense of security and self-esteem in a time of international crisis and competition with Communism. Such a folk-religion does not reflect a genuine expression of pluralism, but rather the opposite; it is the creation of an insecure society and does not spring from the religious roots of the nation's constituent religious groups. According to John Bennett, "When the word 'God' is used it should mean to the citizens not some common-denominator idea of deity but what they learn about God from their religious traditions."[84] The chief element of the Protestant-Catholic-Jewish heritage that is missing is the outlook of the prophets, who directed their criticism in the name of God's judgment against the tendency to sanctify society or nation. In short, the contemporary culture-religion lacks the strong sense of sin as corporate pride that has marked transformationism throughout Protestant history.

Recognition of the tendency for men and groups to use religion for dubious purposes has thus replaced the eagerness with which the theocrats of the early nineteenth century sought to elect "religious" or "good" men to office. Instead the continuity with the transformationist past lies in the insistence that the religious groups of the nation be allowed to challenge the tendencies toward idolatry in government as well as to bring religious convictions to bear on policy. The transformationists have come a long way since the time when certain Protestant assumptions were so widely shared that pious men in office would guarantee their implementation, to the present when they look suspiciously on public religious affirmations that are not grounded on a strong sense of humility, confession, and divine judgment. The common front of the Judaeo-Christian tradition as a foundation of American society is thus directed not simply against forms of nonreligion, but also against an American culture religion that is essentially a dissipated and secularized reflection of the self-interest of the populace. The separationist view, on the other hand, continues the mode of Christian influence on government developed in the early nineteenth century, advocating a wall of separation between religion and government, but moving through it by electing pious men to office and promoting a form of morality within law that is evangelical Protestant in outlook.

Relations With Secularists

While on certain issues the transformationists stress the religious tradition of America against the secularists, on most issues they take seriously the presence of secularism as a "fourth religion" with interests upon which Protestants can agree. In general, transformationists do not engage in denunciations of secularism, except on issues where secularism tends to "deny to most of the people opportunities for positive religious expression in the context of their national life."[85] Far more significant, however, is the desire of transformationists to advance religious influence on public policy by using the moral consensus which includes even the nonreligious. Transformationists have responded to the ethical sensitivity of people and groups which purport to be secularist, as well as to their frequently penetrating criticisms of traditional religion. One of the most important chapters of John C. Bennett's *Christians and the State* is on "Christian Ethics and the Moral Consensus," where he points out that the moral standards of the West stem from a Christian and classical heritage, and that Christians can agree with non-Christians of good will on equal human rights, justice, spiritual and cultural freedom, order, peace, commercial honesty, personal discipline, compassion, and other norms: "This conception of the overlapping of the moral awareness and convictions of Christians and non-Christians allows the Christian ethics to have its own grounding in revelation, its own motivation in response to the love of God, its own refinement and expansion through the sensitivity that is the fruit of Christian love. It allows for parallel contexts of faith which support the ethical awareness and convictions of non-Christians."[86]

The commitment of the transformationists to the social betterment of their environment, but also to a serious recognition of the plural loyalties of Americans, has produced a significant reassessment of the traditional concern for the state, one which has come a long way from the monolithic society of Massachusetts Bay to an effective yet tolerant application of Christian ethics to the problems of mid-twentieth-century America.

The Quest for a Perspective

Quite recently, transformationist writers and representatives in the denominational and ecumenical bodies have tried to ground their views on a more systematic theology of church-state relations. Their perspective could best be interpreted in its initial stages as a reaction to inadequate attitudes on church-state separation and Roman Catholicism by fellow Protestants in terms of a few minimal convictions rather than a consciously theological countermovement. Their effort has not been as easy as that of the Lutherans and Mennonites, because transformationism embraces individuals in a wide variety of denominations, with no common theological position except descent from a long-forgotten Calvinist doctrine of sin and a passion to bring society under the will of God. The tendency of Protestants to respond to church-state issues without examining their assumptions now seems to be changing among transformationists. They generally feel that Protestants, unlike Roman Catholics, lack carefully defined bases or theological principles for dealing with church-state problems, with the result that Protestants usually justify themselves by legal norms rather than Christian convictions.

In 1959, for example, the General Assembly of the United Presbyterian Church, the most direct heir of Calvinism and a church which has traditionally taken outspoken positions on church-state issues, especially those involving Roman Catholics, sensing vacuity in its church-state attitudes, authorized the Moderator:

> . . . to appoint a special committee, working in co-operation with the Department of Social Education and Action and in consultation with other groups, to interpret the meaning of the

doctrine of separation of church and state *in the light of the Reformed tradition,* so as to clarify the rights and responsibilities of religious groups in our pluralistic society [and] to apply its findings to the most salient issues of church-state relations. . . .[87]

This committee symbolizes the discontent among denominational leaders about the traditional Protestant approaches to church-state problems, but one should not be overly sanguine about widespread revisions among the denominations at large. One of the best short study guides on church-state problems was authorized by the Board of Social and Economic Relations of the Methodist Church,[88] but when that denomination met in its quadrennial meeting, it affirmed a rather uncritical support for separation of church and state and P.O.A.U.

The chief development to note, however, is an awakened interest in church-state theory among nearly all of the major denominations, and in most cases the development of thought either from no consistent theory or separationism toward transformationism. Spearheading this enterprise is a study of the whole area co-ordinated by the Department of Religious Liberty of the National Council of Churches, with a National Study Conference on Church and State due in 1964. Some indication of the questions which the transformationists are trying to answer may be found in the N.C.C. research proposals. It urges the development of "Christian insights" on church and state so that "1) If Protestant principles are in jeopardy, they may be safeguarded by co-ordinated and consistent action; 2) Christian principles may be agreed upon, rather than individual Protestant groups following the dictates of expediency, or uncritically accepting legal or sociological definitions that do not harmonize with Biblical concepts."[89] Besides probing the relationship of Christianity to religious liberty and church-state separation, implying that they might be secular rather than Christian concepts, the proposals emphasize for examination the doctrine of the church as it relates to the state: its role in legislation, the limitations of church influence on the state, the assumption of religious functions by the state, and the right of resistance to civil authority.[90] It is presumed in these proposals that a proper solution to more practical issues hinges for Protestants on a prior definition of a perspective for dealing with them.

One should emphasize that transformationism holds no consistent theological position on church and state, but is groping toward one with several approaches prominent. So far, the most thorough approaches presented have been those of Merrimon Cuninggim in *Freedom's Holy Light* and John C. Bennett in *Christians and the State*.

Dr. Cuninggim, former dean of the Perkins School of Theology, Southern Methodist University, and now executive director of the Danforth Foundation, draws his theological elements from an analysis of religious freedom as it has developed in the American Constitution and legal tradition. His association with transformationism comes from his strong ethical interests, from his contention that American religious freedom involves "independence and interdependence"[91] rather than separation, and from his rejection of P.O.A.U. as a confusing threat to religious freedom and a contradiction of essential Protestant objectives. Cuninggim is less sympathetic to Roman Catholicism than most transformationists and tends to place them in the same dangerous bracket with P.O.A.U. because they are "wedded to some theory of establishment."[92] Because he evaluates Protestant, Catholic, and secular positions in terms of whether their theories and actions really accord with religious freedom and moderate separation, he can class the presumed quest for self-interest and special benefits by the Catholic hierarchy with militant secularism, while putting Catholic apologists like Wilfred Parsons and James O'Neill with P.O.A.U. as more subtle forms of the same tendencies.

Cuninggim does not hold to religious liberty as a secular principle, but regards it in the American tradition as a product of the Judaeo-Christian outlook, which provides its most satisfactory theoretical support today. It is based on the following biblical principles: 1) The brotherhood or relatedness of all men, founded on their common status as children of one God called to love one another. 2) The equality of men, not in capacity, but in essence, similarly derived from the biblical doctrine of creation. 3) Belief in a God who is creator and father of men, his creatures. This sets the tone for the positive rather than hostile view of religion characteristic of American religious freedom, giving a preference to religion over nonreligion. 4) Man as a morally dualistic creature, inclined to creativity, which liberty helps channel, but also to sin, which causes him to abuse liberty. 5) Freedom of the will in religious and moral matters, which religious coercion violates.[93]

Cuninggim concludes that a particular interpretation of religious liberty and separation of church and state is grounded historically on Christian convictions and can be regarded as a legitimate expression of the Christian ethic today. The major problem with which he wrestles is the conflict between the religious conscience and the purposes of the state. He feels that the constitutional solution conforms to Judaeo-Christian values in American society. For example, the courts did not support the Mormons when they insisted on polygamy as a religious belief, although in *Girouard* v. *U.S.*[94] they accepted the pacifist convictions of a Seventh Day Adventist, because pacifism could be defended in terms of the biblical ethic, while polygamy could not. Cuninggim's attempt to reconcile Protestantism with American church-state relations thus takes the distinctive direction of showing that the latter really depends on the former.

Bennett deals with the problem of the state from a more independent presentation of the Christian perspective. Differing from Lutherans and Mennonites in his theological method, he bases his propositions not on the Bible, but on an application of general elements in the broad Christian tradition to the contemporary political and social situation to test their relevancy. Bennett takes very seriously the eschatological perspective of the New Testament, reflected in indifference toward the state and social institutions, as well as the development of political institutions unknown to the New Testament writers. Consequently, one cannot absolutize the New Testament outlook on the state; in fact, only two elements really have much relevance for today, the God-given character of government, and its tendency to act beyond its bounds, to which Christians should respond with acceptance and rejection respectively: "The most that we can learn from the New Testament is that there must be political authority, that the Christian should take a positive attitude toward the order-creating functions of civil government because in and through them the providence of God is at work in preserving essential conditions for human life, and that the state should be kept in bounds and not be allowed to usurp the place of God."[95]

Bennett feels, furthermore, that the Christian view of man has implications for the state, especially its emphasis on sin, although government also results from man's creativity. The state serves first as an institution to restrain the sinfulness of men by promoting social order. This feature most typified Reformation Protestantism; and Lutheranism and other highly confessional theologies continue to emphasize it. For Bennett, government has a concern for order more fundamental than its provision for freedom. Secondly, government embodies or symbolizes sin. The twentieth century seems to validate this contention through the expansion of a totalitarianism which has violated human rights and become imperialistic in the name of a nationalistic or pseudo-idealist ideology. Bennett thus demythologizes that feature of Lutheran and Mennonite thought which saw the state as the arena of diabolic action into an emphasis on the special temptation that political power offers to men who hold it. Thirdly, Bennett argues that the creativity of all government is limited by the corporate egoism and irresponsibility of the groups it embodies, a phenomenon which qualifies the virtue of even relatively good governments.[96]

Protestantism has often justified conservatism toward the political order through these aspects of corporate sin, and to Bennett they should provide a deep realism about Christian estimates of government; but he also appropriates the liberal appreciation of government as a creative source of value and justice. Governmental coercion not only helps achieve order, but also promotes freedom, peace, and justice. "It seeks an order that is just and humane and when it restrains evil, it seeks not only to protect or rescue innocent victims, but also to reclaim the offenders.[97] The successes of the modern welfare state verify the ethical potentialities of government as a resource for human betterment even against strong opposition. The shift in emphasis from retribution to rehabilitation in the treatment of criminals also indicates that government can move beyond strict justice to consideration and sensitivity for the particular needs of human beings. Bennett thus feels that the emphasis on original sin in Reformation thought has one-sided consequences for the political order in failing to sense the ethical dimensions of political institutions. His position thus represents a reformationized liberalism or liberalized reformationism, retaining the stress on sin which transformationism has traditionally held as a means of making more realistic the social vigor and expectations of Protestant liberalism.

In his discussion of three more specific problems—resistance to political authority, the role of law, and the meaning of democracy —Bennett relates Christian principles to contemporary theory and problems in these areas.

He feels that the question of resistance to political authority is not an either-or proposition, although following Calvinist tradition he does consider it an option. The Christian concern for human welfare, however, limits resistance to extraordinary situations, inasmuch as almost any government is better than anarchy. The sovereignty of God over Christians enables them to justify political resistance when the actions of men violate the will of God, but their view of sin leads them to sense the ever-present disorder, promoted by human egoism, underlying all social order. Bennett would regard resistance as illegitimate unless there were reasonable likelihood of establishing a new order. Civil disobedience to particular laws serves Christian purposes well, although in democratic countries other methods ordinarily are more effective for making changes.[98]

Acknowledging that "the whole modern period has been a period of the loosening of the relationship between the law of the state and the law of God," Bennett describes Protestant thinking about this relationship as "confused or non-existent."[99] Although Protestants assume a difference between just and unjust laws and regard the state as under divine judgment, they have not elaborated a philosophy of law as the Catholics have in the form of natural law. Nevertheless they seem willing to utilize law for ethical purposes when they are in positions to legislate and to interpret the law, and many Christian groups have influenced legislation by throwing their support to one side or the other. As vital segments of public opinion with the capacity to influence decisions, Christians, Bennett thinks, cannot cease criticizing and evaluating the law in the light of the norms they consider valid. From the biblical tradition Protestants learn that God's will stands over the state and supports elemental human rights. In his small volume, *Christian Ethics and Social Policy*,[100] Bennett proposes a Protestant counterpart to natural law, "middle axioms," which are general principles of social policy more specific than the love motive of Christian ethics, yet general enough to leave their application to the faith and wisdom of the individual in his own context.

In evaluating democracy,[101] Bennett points to the hesitancy of Christians to equate their faith with any particular political system, while noting at the same time the elements of Christian faith that contributed to democracy. The doctrine of original sin and the transhistorical character of the kingdom of God militate against giving any historical entity complete credit for conformity to God's will, for all systems are subject to corruption and remain unconsummated within the present era. Interpreting democracy as a system of consent and participation in government by the populace, and freedom of expression by all individuals and groups, Bennett rejects the optimistic theory of democracy based on the innate virtue and perfectibility of human beings. Democracy is grounded, rather, on the sovereignty of God which limits all human authorities; the love of God that seeks the material and spiritual well-being of all men and does not consider their social and political standing; and most distinctively, the doctrine of sin which illuminates the tendency toward oppression and corruption that tempts any unchecked authority, no matter how benevolent. Reinhold Niebuhr's famous aphorism vividly describes Bennett's point, "Man's capacity for justice makes democracy possible; but man's inclination to injustice makes democracy necessary."[102]

An Evaluation of Transformationism

Both of these attempts at a theology of church and state contribute to the transformationist outlook, while their unfinished character offers hope for a relatively united attitude by the major Protestant denominations. Significant leadership by the National Council of Churches in promoting a consistent position faces problems, because the National Council includes not only diverse transformationist views, but representatives of outlooks considered in other chapters. It can, however, stimulate denominational rethinking on church-state matters, because without developing a detailed alternative, it is the chief agency other than P.O.A.U., embracing a variety of denominations and dealing with such problems.

The extension of the transformationist perspective throughout the denominations encounters the stubborn tendency of Protestantism to adopt cultural or nonreligious elements into its thought, so that Protestants more willingly base their church-state position on defense of Protestant institutional interests, resistance to Roman Catholicism, or a sloganlike interpretation of the American Constitution than on a view of the sovereignty of God which involves self-criticism, appreciation of views different from one's own, and the espousal of ethical concerns that often clash with the popular consensus.

The chief contribution of transformationism to Protestant

church-state theory lies in its attempt to relate to problems of the twentieth century a motif that underlay the Reformation and has asserted itself unevenly throughout Protestant history: the prophetic principle. Correlating the sovereignty of God, a vigorous social ethic, and a strong view of sin, the prophetic principle represents a re-creation within Protestantism of the dynamic spirit with which the prophets denounced the sins of Israel. The principal failure of Protestant prophetism has lain in the refusal to apply the theocentric principle of criticism to itself, even though Protestantism's major significance in the Judaeo-Christian tradition may be its rediscovery of this element of biblical faith. Luther, however, did not criticize effectively either his own theological dogmatism which prevented him from understanding the Anabaptists or the gross injustices of the political authorities upon whom he depended for support. While Calvinism and Puritanism applied the sense of criticism to political institutions, the doctrines of election and sanctification, originally intended to safeguard the sovereignty of God in effecting man's salvation, stimulated a self-righteousness and fanatical certitude among them.

The transformationist tradition has so consciously stressed the omnipresent activity of God that it would not allow society and the state to evade his will and judgment, but the almost inevitable proclivity of even transformationists to absolutize some facet of their finite world tended to obscure the objectivity with which they interpreted God's will. Too often their proposals for government represented their own political and economic interests mixed in with elements of a more dispassionate, theocentric judgment. It is doubtful, given the human tendency toward self-adulation, whether one can make a totally disinterested judgment, but prophetism distinguishes itself by constantly attempting to separate the divine from the idolatrous.

Transformationism reflects a high degree of maturity in criticizing the Protestant misrepresentations of Roman Catholicism and avoiding the temptation to use Catholicism as a scapegoat. It is doubtful, however, whether the mistreatment of Catholic immigrants by the dominant Protestant groups in the early history of this country has yet been squarely faced. Nor is it easy for transformationists to admit their failure to take the Catholic positions on issues as seriously as they take their own, or to concede that probably as many religious tensions in American society result from Protestant ignorance and tactlessness as from

Catholicism. In short, one sees an attempt at rapport with Catholicism and a vigorous rereading of Catholic writers, taking them as sincere rather than "jesuitical," though with little willingness to recognize that a changed Protestant attitude invalidates numerous previous charges against Catholicism.

One wonders also whether the self-interest of Protestantism does not dictate the change of stance represented by transformationism. Even if moderate separation conforms to the American legal and social tradition more closely than extreme separation, one can easily show a decline of religious symbols and co-operative arrangements between religion and public authority as American society has become more pluralistic. The exigencies of American pluralism may in time require a total separation of church and state, except perhaps on the most minimal level of individual influence. Could transformationism be a last-ditch, rather reactionary effort by the Protestant leadership to preserve the battered remains of an earlier Protestant culture, doomed to final extinction in the future? And could the quest for dialogue with Catholicism be merely a pragmatic and long overdue recognition of the Roman Church as an ineradicable element in American life, with which Protestants can and should co-operate to advance their mutual self-interest? Moreover, just as social and political factors contributed to the development of Protestantism out of Roman Catholicism and to the multiplicity of Protestant denominations, sociologists now recognize the impact of social and political forces upon church unity, reflected in the many co-operative and unitive actions among Protestant denominations. Could the overtures to Roman Catholicism stem essentially from the pressure toward unity in all of American life rather than from religious convictions? In short, contemporary transformationism might simply reflect the present state of American religion, pluralistic, marked by a high degree of denominational co-operation along with a leveling of religious differences, conscious of its opportunity to influence public authority.

A mature transformationism must ask these questions, applying the prophetic principle to itself. One of the startling things about transformationism is its confused state. Certain leaders have sensed that something was wrong with Protestant church-state actions, as have many outside the church who have observed self-interest dictating church-state positions. The Protestant opposition to a Vatican ambassador was an attempt to make into a church-state issue a matter of foreign policy judgment, while

Protestants have often provoked religious tensions by their positions against extending governmental welfare benefits to Catholic institutions and citizens. Perhaps transformationism represents a delayed recognition of the bankruptcy and lack of realism in their church-state policies by Protestant leaders who now see what has been obvious for a long time, but who lack theological resources to develop new directions. The most minimal objective studies now taking place in the denominations reveal the obvious, that Protestants have functioned in this key area through misinformed anti-Catholicism and legal rather than religious norms.

To some extent transformationism corresponds to this unflattering picture, but the predominance of the most self-critical and socially concerned minds in Protestantism within that camp rescues it from merely mirroring the tugs of modern American life. A small group of men in the late 1940's, such as Reinhold Niebuhr, John C. Bennett, F. Ernest Johnson, and Thomas Keehn, who were suspicious of the motives of P.O.A.U. from the very beginning and have never hesitated to give credit to Roman Catholicism where they felt it was due, and who opposed the *McCollum* decision because of their transformationist convictions, have been the most consistent and thoughtful representatives of the position. They have sought to maintain the integrity of Protestantism in its social expressions and in its image of itself and of other religious groups. They have unhesitatingly criticized the assumptions upon which they and other Protestants acted, while not being critical to the point of ineffectiveness. The abandonment of a self-righteous approach to church-state problems and the development of transformationism has been an application of a prophetic sense of divine sovereignty and criticism which these figures have emphasized in other spheres as well.

Transformationism represents the most promising contemporary Protestant approach to church-state problems if for no other reason than its espousal by the more acute, self-critical theologians and denominational leaders, so that the mainstream of Protestantism seems to be moving with it. If kept to a minimum of principles such as moderate views of church-state independence, accuracy in treatment of Roman Catholicism, a realistic assessment of contemporary American pluralism, and continuing self-criticism, it can be used by denominations with more self-conscious traditions, as well as becoming an integrated position in itself. The chief problem of transformationism is that it really is not a form of church-state theology; it reflects the divided character of the denominations and individuals who represent it. Consequently, transformationism usually becomes a practical, more critical and objective approach to church-state issues.

One finds a variety of literature analyzing particular church-state problems, proposing solutions in the spirit of transformationism, but with little or no attention to the religious perspective with which one approaches such problems. The Lutherans and Mennonites present the most telling criticism of transformationism. They would simply insist that before one can evaluate particular problems, Christians, because they are Christians, must have some very clear ideas about God and his role in history, the nature of the church and the "world," of which government is a part. Transformationists may exhibit noble virtues like realism, fairness, and tolerance, but they do not really have a conscious, articulate, clearly Christian perspective. The major belief associated with transformationism, a God whose creation is good, but corrupted by men, who seeks to transform his world, is, however, a good beginning.

Conclusion

The most difficult obstacle to a common Protestant viewpoint on church and state lies in a diversity of positions, five of which have been considered, which can all claim to be Protestant. They not only diverge in assumptions about theology and Christian social responsibility, but particular issues so preoccupy some traditions that they mold their conceptions of the state. Among the Lutherans, Mennonites, and Quakers, moreover, these are not the issues usually associated in the public mind with church-state problems. How does Quaker pacifism relate to the separationist concern for church-state separation? Or how can one reconcile the transformationist quest for social change with that of the Mennonites for purity of the church? Interdenominational statements on church and state have often achieved some agreement by neglecting particularly uncongenial views, usually those of the Mennonites and Quakers, but they have tended to founder on the rocky differences between the separationists and transformationists. Or they have ignored the problem of perspective by attempting to solve the more concrete issues facing the churches in the American forum, disregarding the absence of any principles by which to deal with these issues.

The Relevance of Protestant Diversity

One might argue in a rather oversimplified way that the chief political emphases of the five traditions are as follows: 1. For the Lutherans church and state must maintain their proper functions as ordained by God, separate in function, though united in God's sovereignty and man's response. 2. The Mennonites insist that the state must not violate the attempt of the Christian community to

281

respond to the demands of the Christian life in an uncompromis-
ing way. 3. The state for the Quakers must actualize as far as
possible the Christian norms, especially by upholding peaceful
aims and means in foreign policy, while respecting the integrity
and equality of all citizens in its domestic actions. 4. The
separationist affirms the beneficial results of absolute church-state
separation for both church and state. 5. The transformationist
maintains that Christians and the church must have the right to
help shape society and the state according to the will of God.

These differences should not produce despair among Protestants, if each tradition is willing to learn from the others. It is
more important for Protestants to recognize that God works
through Protestantism than that they define once and for all and
in detail a doctrine of church and state. An examination of the
history of Protestantism reveals that each perspective, when
upheld by men whose religious convictions outweighed their
other loyalties, contributed to Christian integrity. Nevertheless,
each position, despite its significance, contained elements of corruption that impelled the development of new perspectives.

By defending the independence of the political order, Luther
attracted the support of the Northern European rulers and preserved the feeble flame of Protestant faith against Counter-
Reformation efforts to extinguish it. When he and other Reformers succumbed to the temptation of guaranteeing the welfare
of their newly founded churches by uncritical support of political
authority and religious unity, the Anabaptists sprang into prominence by defending congregational freedom to interpret differently the meaning of the Christian faith. The tendency of both
to abdicate the traditional responsibility of the church for
society stimulated the transformationist outlook, but when the
latter began to interpret the will of God for English society in
terms of its own political, economic, and religious self-interest, it
produced a swarm of dissenting sects that insisted on the distinction between religious and political life. When the sects accepted
too readily the secular aims and means of the state, the Quakers
argued that Christianity presumed a changed way of life for the
individual which extended to government as well.

To outline these developments does not imply a "dialectical,"
structured view of history, but assumes that God has been ac-
complishing something through Protestantism, and recognizes
that Protestant faith and autonomy have survived political,
social, and internal threats. It assumes that God acts in history

through a variety of human perspectives and actions, that truth about church and state is not propositional, but can be provisionally discerned if one looks at history with a critical openness to what God has tried to do. It is not presumptuous to compare such a theory of revelation with that of the biblical writers, who were not defining doctrines, but seeking from events in the life of Israel or of Jesus clues to what God intended. Theology avoids pretension when it tells how God seems to have acted rather than by defining in concepts or propositions the nature of God, church, or state.

The truth of Protestant church-state perspectives may be said to lie in the contributions that each has made and can make when God uses them as instruments to achieve his will. This might mean that truth lies in a variety of perspectives held in tension which would provide the resources for appropriation by Protestants in different periods and societies. It would probably be unhealthy if Protestantism lost any of its traditions, for one can envision how each in some way brings out a contribution neglected by the others. The "answer" to the relationship of church and state today may rest in only one of the perspectives considered, or in several, or perhaps in some yet unformulated view. Only history can tell.

But what can the contemporary Protestant do? He can critically but sympathetically examine his denominational or theological tradition to see what it says about God's will for church and state, but more significantly he can perceive the limitations of his tradition, when he notices that other Protestants have interpreted Protestantism and its relation to the state differently. He can learn from Roman Catholicism which shares with Protestantism and Eastern Orthodoxy a loyalty to the larger Christian tradition. By assuming with the Old Testament prophets that God also works through the state, even hostile states, the contemporary Protestant would still further enlarge his perspective. He might emerge more self-critical, more willing to learn from others, more open to the mysterious ways by which God communicates with man.

The variety of Protestantism drives an observer who wants to conclude something about Protestant views to such a "relativism." A relativism does not deny the common bonds of convictions, but takes seriously the high degree of disagreement on most issues. To look at church-state perspectives as a Protestant, rather than as a Lutheran, Quaker, or transformationist, is to see several important truths. 1. God achieves his purposes through and in spite of the variety of Protestant positions. Variety is not necessarily wrong, for God has used the proliferating tendency of Protestant church-state views to accomplish discernible purposes. 2. Protestants in each of these groups can learn from the others and should be attentive to a voice of judgment that other groups have to offer. 3. Protestants would sense the partiality of all views on church and state. This partiality springs from man's sin and lack of self-criticism, but also from the finitude which stamps his existence. Recognizing the value of their own traditions, they would nevertheless hesitate to absolutize them, but would be open to insights from Protestant and other groups whose views differ from their own. This sense of relativism and self-criticism inherent within Protestantism may well be the most important Protestant contribution to church-state theory.

Sources of Protestant Diversity

Before considering other elements of a Protestant perspective, let us examine the reasons for the partiality of Protestant views, some of which were suggested in the "Introduction." Clearly the forces that have developed alongside Protestantism in the modern world have tended to shape Protestant church-state views.

Those traditions that accepted the patronage of absolutist states have not escaped unscathed. German Lutheranism continues to bear the unfortunate consequences of its long association with Prussian absolutism, and the contemporary discussion within American Lutheranism represents an attempt to shake off this heritage by rediscovering Luther and dealing more critically with the Lutheran tradition. The widespread estrangement from Christianity of the masses in Protestant Europe results from the association of the churches with conservative and ruling classes when the nineteenth-century social revolutions undercut their power.

Secularism represents a constant threat to church-state theories that were once indisputably theocentric. Secularism, which may often aid religion by pointing out its shortcomings, also expresses itself by replacing religious values with the autonomous ones of modern culture. Wherever churches have become willing purveyors of such political norms as freedom, democracy, patriotism, or security from Communism or radicalism, they have consciously or unconsciously equated political with religious norms rather than remaining in tension with them and criticizing them. Even in a tradition like the Lutheran, where service in the magistracy and the defense forces was a highly regarded Christian vocation, such activities in theory could not be undertaken uncritically, but were subject to Christian judgment. In an outlook like that of the Mennonites, where the tension between Christian ethics and the values of the world was felt more severely, to be a magistrate or a soldier was too compromising for a Christian.

Americanism is only a special category of secularism, which has molded American church-state theories with a provincial perspective. In its simplest form this is represented in an inability on the part of American Christians to appreciate other church-state forms than their own and a tendency to associate their own church-state situation with the Christian faith. In its more simplistic propaganda, the separationist perspective often equates American separation with the teaching of the New Testament, while Quakerism may be somewhat uncritical in its idealization of democracy and church-state separation. Perhaps the most pernicious example today of American influence on Christian political views is the unquestioned assumption by many Christians that God is on the American side in the cold war against Communism.

A reflective Protestant church-state view would keep in mind these and many other elements of modern society, recognizing the virtually unavoidable tendency to confuse religious convictions with cultural norms. This applies not only to contemporary cultures, but to past cultures as well. A witness against the inclinations of modern culture may seem noble, but not when based on the political concepts of the sixteenth century or the living habits of the rural seventeenth. At any rate, recognition of the inescapable relationship between religion and culture in church-state views as in other religious expressions provides a fulcrum for criticism. But two other even more subtle elements contribute to the partiality of Protestant perspectives.

One, explicable by the Christian view of man as creature, points to the limited character of all theological symbols. Christian theology at its best has always realized that its statements did not really describe, but only pointed to the ultimate reality it purported to describe. To speak of God as sovereign, ruling in two regiments through love and wrath, is to use in nearly every word symbolic rather than literal statements. Theology, including church-state theology, is conditioned by language and the finite position of man. This is true even of the Bible, which reflects Semitic and Hellenistic thought forms. Theological symbols demand constant reassessment to guarantee their continued relevance and communicability, but at best their descriptive accuracy cannot cross the chasm between the finite and God. All church-state theologies will reflect the conditioned perspective of their originators.

The other element which contributes to the relative character of man's view, one with special relevance for both theory and practice in the area of church and state, is self-interest. This study has suggested at a number of points that institutional or personal self-interest has helped determine the way in which traditions during their development have handled problems. Because of the theoretical orientation of this study, detailed examination of practical applications has been impossible, but it would not be cynical to say that the voices of religious institutions seldom follow other courses than self-interest, despite a façade of commitment to religious or social ideals. Protestants have often used the slogans of preserving freedom and church-state separation to advance their interests or oppose actions by other religious groups.

Recognition of these significant influences upon church-state theory should give a degree of tentativeness to Protestant formulations. Loyalty to Protestantism as well as to a specific denomination or tradition should produce humility about one's claims in the light of an analysis of the varieties of Protestantism. Self-criticism begins by recognizing how views may be perverted and by questioning whether political loyalties, secularism, American culture, human finitude, and self-interest have not unduly influenced them, even on the highest theoretical level. Unfortunately, such humility is a rarity. Kenneth Underwood's study of Protestant-Catholic relations in a New England city indicated that the Protestant churches were rarely able to achieve unanimity on issues, but that in a few instances church-state issues provided the sense of certitude to engage in "crusades" whose actual ambivalence Underwood notes. Man's actions are so ironic that church-state problems, which should be rigorously examined because of the temptations they offer to the churches, become a channel for their least critical, most self-righteous expressions.

Protestantism and the Christian Political Motifs

The five Protestant perspectives all represent in *some* form the Christian motifs of the dualism of church and state, the sovereignty of God, and the moral ambivalence of government. To be sure, some of the traditions only imply them, for their particular concerns have not necessitated explicit definitions. The Quakers may serve as an illustration here, because in modern times they have preferred to emphasize individual responsibility for the state rather than the nature of church and state. Although they do not hold as sharp a distinction between the character and methods of church and state as other Protestant perspectives, the Quakers certainly recognize a difference between the noncoercive way of reaching decisions and acting within the religious congregation, and the regrettable use of force and power in society and government. The Christian ethic, which is actualized in the church and individual relations, is at best a hope and vision for government in the future. The church represents a leavening influence working to better and hopefully to perfect an egoistic and coercive world. Secondly, Quakers at least implicitly believe in the sovereignty of God over both church and state, though they may lack the sense of his dynamic involvement that Lutherans have. But God's will is achieved through men who act in both church and state, and ethically Quakers bind life in church and state more closely together than any other Protestants. Finally, government can and does serve both Christian and non-Christian purposes through its policies. One can evaluate governments by their commitment to peace, justice, and international welfare, and their recognition of the dignity of man in pursuing these ends. The moral ambivalence of government reveals itself in its ability to contribute to or detract from human welfare, and existent governments manifest both tendencies.

Despite the consistency of these motifs in all Protestants positions, a number of issues are unsolved and may remain unsolved because the truth does not lie in any one or in a compromise. The following are only illustrations and do not exhaust the disputed areas.

Dualism in Protestant history has appeared especially in the quest for noninterference by the church in the affairs of the state or the reverse, although freedom for both is upheld by all Protestant groups on the assumption that church and state have dif-

ferent purposes and means. The overriding problem of dualism
is the degree and form of these differences, ranging on a spectrum
from Quakers to Mennonites, from a relative correspondence between aims and methods of church and state to a radical difference. One might indicate the following issues for Protestants to
discuss in the future:

1. What is the nature of the church? Is it an association of
men united for religious purposes, or does it represent an institution ordained by God? Who speaks for it? What ethical demands
does it make upon its members which are compatible or incompatible with political responsibilities? What weight do evangelical, pastoral, and ethical functions have in the life of the church?

2. What is the nature of the state? To what degree is it beneficial or destructive to God's intentions? To what extent can the
state be bettered or perfected in accordance with Christian
norms? Are war and coercion inevitable within the state? Are
there forms of government more consistent with Christianity
than others? What is the relationship between society and the
state? Does government have certain inescapable obligations to
the citizenry?

3. What does independence of church and state mean? To
what extent is the state free from the influence of the churches?
What does religious liberty mean? When does a state become totalitarian toward religion? Are there forms of church-state relation which correspond more to Christian concerns than others?
Does the American system of church-state separation represent a
Christian ideal? Would relations between church and state differ
in a pluralistic society from those in a society predominantly
Protestant? What causes a breakdown of a normative relationship
between church and state? Does church-state separation deny the
use of religious symbols by government or political symbols by
the churches?

The sovereignty of God over both church and state raises a
new set of questions, pointing toward the relationship between
the two institutions rather than their separation.

1. How can one speak of the relationship between church and
state? How are the two united in God's creation? What symbols
can describe this relation? What institutional relations would be
presumed between the two? How does the Christian reconcile his
responsibilites to both church and state?

2. What obligations does the state have toward the churches?
Must it give concrete benefits such as tax exemption or indirect

support? Must it support religious schools and religious education in public schools? Must it acknowledge its dependence on God through support of religion and use of religious symbols? Can the church demand concessions from the state? Can the church influence the state? How?

3. What obligations do the church and Christians have toward the state? To what extent does the church support the aims of government? Is patriotism a Christian virtue? Can Christians hold office? Engage in war and coercion? Take an oath? How do Christians exercise their right of ballot in free societies? Must Christians support even a tyrannical government?

The moral ambivalence of government highlights the ethical problems of the Christian as citizen. It invites his response to the beneficence of government and his criticism and perhaps disobedience to its violations.

1. How can one speak of the moral ambivalence of government? Does the symbol of the demonic have any relevance today? What causes the moral ambivalence of government?

2. How do Christians and the churches respond to the virtues of government? What is the role of order, peace, and welfare in God's intentions? How virtuous can government be? How does Christianity enhance this virtue?

3. How do Christians and the churches react to moral degeneration in government? On what grounds can Christians refuse to co-operate? Is there justification for resistance? Nonviolent resistance? Criticism? Civil disobedience? Revolution?

Consideration of such questions may not lead to a Protestant consensus, but may at least clarify some of the problems. Few of them have attracted the attention of Protestant-wide bodies except religious liberty, the nature of the church, and Christian social and political responsibility. Even within single denominations, attention to these questions might broaden perspectives and mitigate the tendency to persist in unreflective denominational traditions.

Vocation

Along with relativism, dualism, divine sovereignty, and the moral duality of the political order, one other Protestant motif has relevance for a developed doctrine of church and state. This is *vocation*. It has appeared in the discussion on Lutheranism, but does not contradict the other traditions. It was used by Luther to give the natural functions of life—family, work, and politics—an evaluation equal to the specifically religious vocation. It presumes a relationship with God, and for Luther defined structurally how the love of man for man as response to the love of God was channeled.

Unfortunately, American churchmen misunderstand vocation, thinking of it fundamentally as a job in which one earns a living, and often detaching it from its religious roots. Even Lutherans have understood vocation to refer to the unpleasant responsibility of man in a world of sin to earn his livelihood through toil.

Vocation provides a category for examining individual responsibilities for social and political action and for church-state problems, whereas the previous themes have pointed principally to the relationship of God to church and state. Properly conceived, vocation recognizes that men, despite their uniqueness, do not live alone, but are members of groups as well, and that Christian faith can bear on the problems encountered within these groups. Later Lutheranism defined responsibilities very easily, for the authorities commanded, and those who were subservient obeyed. Wingren's significant study indicates that for Luther, however, vocation was an expression of the love of the Christian for his neighbor in response to the love of God. The form of this love varies, depending on the circumstances. The father must discipline and exercise authority over his child, even though love motivates him. Or the Mennonite loves God and man in the political order by ordinarily obeying authority and avoiding situations where he might have to coerce.

Vocation may serve as an agent for various explanations of Christian ethics, as well as a justification for diverse forms of action in different corporate structures. Love as a basis of Christian ethics underlies Luther's thought, but other Protestants might see their response to God in broader terms, as obedience, faith, duty, or without specification. However one defines the core of Christian response, he acts differently in the situations he faces. One of the great problems in Christian views of the state has been to reconcile the responsibilities of a citizen or ruler with the rather nonpolitical outlook of the New Testament, though the same problem exists in a number of other relationships involving authority and power of various kinds. How does one act in situations of power when he takes seriously the New Testament disinterest in power? To avoid it in Mennonite fashion might represent one expression of Christian vocation, but other Christians might see their vocation within worldly, even political contexts, on the assumption that God can act even through instruments that seem to compromise his will. Vocation provides a framework by which Christian response in personal relations, family, work, social organizations, church, and political life can be articulated.

The concept of vocation seems distinctly Protestant rather than Roman Catholic for at least two reasons. In the first place it recognizes the equal sanctity of nonreligious and religious activities. Roman Catholicism accepts the goodness of family, work, and political responsibility on the natural level, but sees religious ordination and life in the church as a higher good. The Mennonites, more than any other Protestant tradition, lean toward this Roman Catholic evaluation of the Church, which has led Hans Hillerbrand to wonder if the Anabaptists were not a Roman Catholic rather than a Protestant sect. Without doing violence to the integrity of the Mennonites, one might note that their twentieth-century writers have not distinguished as sharply between church and world as their forebears, that their criticism of participation in secular institutions has not so much turned on their essential nature, but on the methods they use. Mennonites act in secular institutions as long as they do not have to coerce. Vocation is Protestant, secondly, because it associates life in nonreligious groups with a religious rather than a natural law ethic. The classical Reformation objected to the Catholic definition of two ethics, one for the clergy and a lesser one for the laity. But in trying to solve the problem to their satisfaction, Protestants wavered between perfectionist indifference to the secular world and conformity to cultural and political patterns. Vocation, seen as the concretization of an ultimate religious response to the world and a framework for considering Christian actions in various corporate groups, links the religious impulse of ethics with the social and cultural world. Such an ethic does not spring from a rational determination of rights and duties in family, state, and other groups, but is a religiously grounded ethic in the fullest sense.

Church-State Problems as Ethical Problems:
A Protestant Perspective

If vocation applies to church-state theology, then it would seem that the issues called church-state problems really are problems of social and political ethics. The two traditions, separationist and transformationist, that have acted most vigorously on church-state problems, have not sufficiently realized this, though the transformationists are beginning to acknowledge it. Failure to relate these issues to ethics accounts for the strange sterility of church-state actions in most denominations, reflected in their inclination to base positions on legal arguments, slogans, anti-Catholicism, or self-interest. The Lutherans, Mennonites, and Quakers have dealt with church-state problems within a religio-ethical framework, which has probably tempered their involvement in them. They have acted only on the issues which they could reconcile with their ethic, such matters as secularism, non-resistance, or world peace. But other, often nonethical presuppositions govern the unrestrained response of the major denominations to the most obscure types of church-state problems. Many transformationists now hesitate to become involved in certain problems, because they no longer seem so important when considered from an ethical perspective.

What are church-state problems? The political aspects of Christian ethics usually refer to the justification and method of Christian influence on society and the state. Church-state problems, on the other hand, seem to arise from a conflict between the concerns of the church and the state to exercise responsibilities in society. The state, in maintaining its integrity, social peace, and the common good, makes demands upon Christians and the churches. These may include support of war for the survival of society, required attendance at school to guarantee an educated citizenry, and the defense of religious liberty on the assumption that all citizens have equal rights. The churches, on the other hand, have evangelical, pastoral, educational, and ethical concerns. Against the decisions of the state, a church may insist that its members cannot coerce, that they must have a religious education without undue financial discrimination by the state, or that it be free to proselytize wherever it wishes. Many church-state problems arise because Protestants disagree with Roman Catholic attempts to protect society from immoral or irreligious influence, to gain for Catholic parents some recompense for sending their children to religious schools, or to enable nuns to teach in public schools. Correspondingly, Catholics may object to the refusal of certain Protestant groups to defend their country, aspects of Protestant morality such as prohibition, or the Protestant espousal of radical church-state separation. When the state tries to decide such conflicts in a manner consistent with tradition and the common good, it frequently disturbs the religious groups involved.

In the coming decades Protestants must bring such problems within an ethical context, rather than leaving their determination to nonreligious, nonethical norms. The responsibility of a church for society as a whole may not correspond to its own self-interest; compromise may be necessary between institutional concerns and the equally valid responsibility of the church for a just society in which the interests of all groups and of the total society gain partial satisfaction. It is reasonable that what is good for Protestantism is *not* necessarily good for all of society.

Nor can an ethical approach to church-state problems rest satisfied with legal interpretations of American church-state separation, for the American system assumes that its constituent groups can change laws, constitutions, and promote interpretations of the law in unsettled areas. Nor does opposition to Roman Catholicism offer much hope for subsumption of church-state issues under an ethical perspective. Protestants have at times succeeded in overcoming their emotions and prejudices to deal with certain ethical issues, but strangely they have rarely been able to approach church-state issues without bringing along some anti-Catholic feelings. In political ethics they have transcended national loyalties; in economics they no longer follow the middle-class line; on race they have rejected paternalism and remarkably empathized with their brethren of other races. But on a far lesser scale have they achieved objectivity about Roman Catholicism on church-state problems.

A church-state theory provides a perspective for dealing with a range of problems, but it by no means solves the problems. In fact, one of the most trying aspects of this kind of problem is the need of considering other elements, such as the nature of the American church-state structure, social changes that suggest modification of older solutions, and the character of Roman Catholicism. The perspective must interact with these elements, rather than letting the perspective be determined by them. But it is one of the peculiarities of church-state problems that without consideration of these elements, a theological approach would be quite ineffective.

Solutions to church-state problems take place within the context of particular church-state structures. The issues faced by the East German or Swedish churches are not those of the American churches. To base one's strategy on approximating the American system of church-state independence in Sweden smacks of irrelevance. Responsible action deals with the problems in a given context. A major shortcoming of Protestant churches—once established—is their failure to grasp fully the American context in which they now exist, while many denominations have so grown up with the American system that they cannot envision action in any other context.

An adequate church-state perspective should be able to deal with problems in many countries, because such a perspective would be abstracted from contingencies. The perspective suggested here does give a point of view from which to deal with Communist oppression of the churches in East Germany or "public piety" in America; but the application of the perspective takes place within the legal framework of each country. Discussion of even so general an issue as religious liberty has been inhibited in larger ecumenical groups like the World Council of Churches because churches with different relations to the state have brought different conceptions to the forum. The tendency to confuse particular applications with perspectives points to the need to differentiate between the two. Many alternatives open to the churches of East Germany are not those open to the churches of America, even though they might have similar theological perspectives on church and state. The alternatives and possibilities for changes of church-state systems are defined by the legal systems of the respective countries.

American Protestantism, to be effective in church-state matters, must give much more attention to the nature of church-state independence or separation. It needs to shed slogans like the "wall of separation" or its opposite, "co-operation," for a thorough examination of concluded and unresolved aspects of constitutional law in this area. An unfortunate schism prevails between religious writers who often see things in terms of what is desirable and what is not, and legal experts who use as their guides what is constitutional and what is not. One finds little awareness in most religious writing on church-state matters of the complex history of adjudication or of elemental matters like the distinction between state and national jurisdiction on particular matters. The sole major agency that has acted for the religious groups in the legal field, Protestants and Other Americans United for Separation of Church and State, adheres to a dubious and doctrinaire understanding of American separation, and while pretending to uphold past legal decisions, is actually trying to reverse decisions that contradict its perspective.

Many Protestant denominational leaders are trying to rectify this lack of information, and the studies proposed for the next few years have blocked out areas where further legal information is needed. The denominations actually seem to sense a greater need for legal information than they do for a religious perspective by which to evaluate it. Absolute certitude on all problems is impossible, for the law continues to be debatable, but the churches should know more about the issues than they presently do. This book has suggested that the transformationists, by extricating themselves from the evangelical Protestant commitment to a "wall of separation," probably stand on a firmer interpretation of the American church-state arrangement, though much more research needs to be done.

The two chief problems lie in the interpretations of pluralism and church-state independence. The truth, if one can speak of truth in this area, lies in a tension between somewhat contradictory inclinations. Pluralism allows for influence by religious and other groups on society and the state, but seeks at the same time to preserve the rights of minorities from a tyranny of the majority. And while guaranteeing the right of groups to express their opinions, government retains a certain freedom of action in deciding the common good from a broader perspective than individual groups ordinarily have.

American church-state independence, furthermore, is neither co-operation nor separation, but a free functioning of religious groups with which the government does not ordinarily interfere unless the welfare of society, religious freedom, or nonestablishment seem threatened or violated. Whereas no real separation lies between church and state as far as the influence of the churches on the state is concerned, one can genuinely speak of separation, but not a "wall," with respect to the influence on or support of the churches by the state. In modern times the American federal and state governments have not engaged in a general support of religion, but in certain instances they have indirectly done so where their quest for education, health, and other forms of welfare necessitated it. Today, some features of the arrangement such as tax exemption of religious institutions, religious symbols in public life, and Sunday as a holiday indicate at most that the government does not hold a negative attitude toward religion.

A major issue with respect to the American church-state arrangement concerns the attitudes of the churches, as constituent groups, toward it. To be realistic, they must recognize that as long as nonestablishment and religious liberty as interpreted by the courts continue, they are legally subject to these definitions unless particular issues are so important that they suggest some form of disobedience. In some Southern states, for example, despite the *McCollum* decision, religious instruction has continued under Protestant auspices in the public schools, sanctioned by community consensus. Or a few Mormons have consciously defied the decision of the Supreme Court that religious liberty is not so unlimited as to allow for polygamy on religious grounds.

Protestants must decide whether the present American system is the context in which they wish to function. All of the groups that have been considered seem willing to accept it, though to varying degrees. Most have criticized some features of it. That religious pacifism is not a constitutional right tends to disturb Mennonites and Quakers. Others have expressed a concern about the secular implications of separation of church and state. The separationists disagree with the *Everson* case which permitted states to provide bus transportation for parochial school students.

There are two levels of understanding of the American church-state relationship. One is an intelligent grasp of its present status. The other is a recognition of how Protestants can change it if they wish. To suggest changes or reinterpretations of church-state separation is not a form of subversion, but a phenomenon taking place frequently through legislation, action by the courts, and amendments to state and federal constitutions. In wartime, for example, legislative action usually allows for conscientious objection not guaranteed by the Constitution, and pacifist groups consciously seek it. When Protestant agencies represent before the courts positions on Bible reading in the public schools or indirect aid to religious schools, they are either defending an existing practice or proposing a change. And during the nineteenth century Protestants and others succeeded in passing amendments to several state constitutions forbidding public payments to religious institutions. All of these represent legitimate activities by religious groups within the American system of pluralism, and to accuse Roman Catholics or others who act in this manner of unconstitutional procedures reflects lack of knowledge or prejudice. On the other hand, Protestants have every right to attempt such changes, but they must know when they represent settled conclusions about the American church-state arrangement, and when they are seeking innovations or clarification of unsolved questions. This would mitigate the tendency of religious groups to describe their own position as defense of American church-state independence, while castigating their opponents as subverters of it. It is in this complex context that Protestants must bring their perspectives to bear on church-state problems.

Protestants must be aware, furthermore, of social changes that make old church-state policies irrelevant and demand new and creative solutions to contemporary problems. The most obvious example of this is the change of American society from a quasi-Protestant to a pluralistic status. In the colonial period and the early years of the Republic, though only a small percentage of the populace belonged to churches, public control lay in the hands of people who sought to indicate the religious, even Protestant, character of society by symbols and a correspondence between a Protestant ethic and public law. That some of their actions discriminated against Roman Catholics, Jews, and the non-religious has become clear especially in the twentieth century when these groups have effectively challenged them. A great deal of Protestant energy on church-state matters presently goes to maintain such things as laws forbidding business activity on Sunday, upholding a certain standard of personal morality, or Bible reading and prayers in public schools. These have become church-state issues because individuals and groups who do not agree with them have seen them as infringements on their religious liberty and symbols of an unofficial Protestant "establishment."

Given these protests by conscientious groups within American society, it behooves Protestants to reconsider whether they really want to support such measures any longer, whether a sensitivity for the rights of non-Protestant citizens does not suggest actual measures to remove them. Protestantism draws to itself criticism and misunderstanding when it compels people by law to conform to its particular view of morality and religion. American society is quite different from what it was when everyone seemingly accepted religious symbols in the public schools and church attendance legally facilitated by a holiday on Sunday. Christians must now cultivate their religious and moral practices among their constituencies alone. The only justification for moral action of a legislative sort would seem to be the common good of all groups in American society. The common good is served by ending racial segregation in the name of justice, but not by preventing Jewish merchants from operating on Sunday or by requiring nonbelievers to say the Lord's Prayer. Protestants should not even argue for a religious consensus to maintain some of these symbols, for this overlooks a conscious secular minority and an unconsciously secular group within the churches who belie public religious symbols.

Protestants must reconcile their traditional quest for religious and moral symbolism with the fact that society today is highly secular. Lutheran writers and many others want the nation to symbolize its acknowledgment of God, but the danger is at least equally great that these symbols may be manipulated for rather ungodly purposes. The symbols not only hide this pervasive secularism and do little to alleviate it, but they corrupt Christianity by leading people to equate the values and policies of the United States with Christian norms. They intensify the self-righteousness and lack of self-criticism that plague the American people, and offer a convenient façade to which one can pay lip service while pursuing his own interests.

Finally, a church-state perspective must reassess its attitude toward Roman Catholicism. The chapter on separationism traced the origins of Protestant anti-Catholicism and suggested more adequate ways of dealing with Protestant-Catholic issues. The problem does not lie in misinformation alone, but in perspectives. Information will not change the views of someone who thinks that Roman Catholicism is systematically undercutting democracy and church-state separation. Such a point of view is not supported, however, by a relatively objective scrutiny of Roman Catholicism. Rather, Roman Catholicism is a religious institution that shares many theological ideas with Protestantism and differs with it on others. Believing in the truth of what it represents, Catholicism engages in society to convert men, nourish its members, advance its interests, and express its moral concerns where it can. Like Protestantism, it has tried to relate its outlook to the American church-state system. Its analysis of problems of religious liberty, and church and state, is probably the most significant expression of American Catholic thought, and

Protestants would learn much by acquainting themselves with the writings of John Courtney Murray, Gustave Weigel, and others.

Because the forebears of most Catholics came to America as immigrants in a time of Protestant dominance, contemporary Catholics sometimes suffer from a feeling of injustice and even resentment against Protestants. Most Catholics feel, for example, that some public support of aspects of their parochial school program would be more just. Like most religious groups they also have moral convictions—on such matters as birth control and pornography—which they seek to express in society. With its hierarchical system of church government the Catholic Church is often able to pursue its aims more effectively than most Protestant churches.

Protestants need to sense the concerns and feelings of Roman Catholics in American society. Catholics can further this enterprise by discussing their views wherever possible with sensitivity to traditional Protestant feelings about Roman Catholicism. Protestants, when facing church-state problems, must always ask themselves whether anti-Catholicism is governing their actions and whether they might not inform themselves before they act. Indubitably Protestants will disagree with Catholics on many social issues, because the two differ in their interests and conceptions of the common good for society. But objectivity about Roman Catholicism is an indispensable necessity for a mature handling of church-state problems.

The rich theological resources and creative actions of the Protestant past provide a common outlook which can preserve the contributions of its constituent denominations and traditions. Such an historical perspective is an absolute necessity if American Protestantism is to deal creatively with the church-state problems that will face the nation in the coming decades. There will be new and perplexing legal decisions, disturbing social changes, debatable actions taken by various Protestant and non-Protestant groups: to all of these American Protestantism must speak with integrity rather than confusion, with the wholeness of its total tradition.

Notes

Introduction

1 Harold J. Laski, *The Foundations of Sovereignty* (New York: Harcourt, 1921); Ernest Barker, *Principles of Social and Political Theory* (London: Oxford, 1951); John N. Figgis, *Churches in the Modern State* (New York: Longmans, 1913). Cf. Henry M. Magid, *English Political Pluralism* (New York: Columbia University Press, 1941). Pluralism is probably the most accurate philosophical expression of the American system of society and state.

2 The most thorough study of American church-state relations is by Anson Phelps Stokes, *Church and State in the United States* (New York: Harper & Row, 1950), 3 vols. Canon Stokes recognizes the role of religious theories of the state in influencing American church-state structure and the continuing problems posed by these theories within American society, e.g., I, 65-222; III, 454-552, *et passim*. A recent, suggestive work is Loren P. Beth, *The American Theory of Church and State* (Gainesville: University of Florida Press, 1958). Cf. Carl Zollman, *American Civil Church Law* (New York: Columbia University Press, 1917) and William C. Torpey, *Judicial Doctrines of Religious Rights in America* (Chapel Hill: University of North Carolina Press, 1948).

3 Besides expositions of religious attitudes by thinkers representing particular Protestant traditions, one finds two studies of Protestant church-state views as a whole. In a preparatory volume for the Oxford Conference, Nils Ehrenström, *Christian Faith and the Modern State* (New York: Willett, Clark, 1937), examined Roman Catholic and Eastern Orthodox as well as Protestant views. He focuses on Continental European Protestantism, especially Lutheranism and Calvinism, and is particularly concerned with the attitudes of theologians toward Nazi totalitarianism. He is thus limited in his awareness of the variety of Protestant expressions, especially in America, and although his exposition is excellent, it is dated. The same problem is found in William Adams Brown, *Church and State in Contemporary America* (New York: Scribner, 1936), especially pp. 83-96, 133-80. Although he deals with many Protestant groups, he tends to analyze them in terms of denominations rather than positions, which in many cases cross denominational lines.

4 Cf. Jacques Maritain, *Man and the State* (Chicago: University of Chicago Press, 1951) and John Courtney Murray, *We Hold These Truths* (New York: Sheed & Ward, 1960), as well as Murray's articles in *Theological Studies*, 1945-1954. For a non-Roman Catholic evaluation, *vide* A. F. Carrillo de Albornoz, *Roman Catholicism and Religious Liberty* (Geneva: World Council of Churches, 1959).

5 John C. Bennett, *Christians and the State* (New York: Scribner, 1958), p. 205.

6   Cf. Paul Tillich, *The Protestant Era*, abridged edition (Chicago: University of Chicago Press, 1957), pp. ix-xxv; John Dillenberger and Claude Welch, *Protestant Christianity* (New York: Scribner, 1954), pp. 313-15.

7   H. Richard Niebuhr, *Christ and Culture* (New York: Harper & Row, 1951), pp. 39-44.

8   Kenneth S. Latourette, *A History of the Expansion of Christianity: The Great Century* (New York: Harper & Row, 1941), IV, 428.

9   Oscar Cullmann, *The State in the New Testament* (New York: Scribner, 1956).

10   Augustine, *De Civ. Dei*, XVIII, 49; In Ps. LXIV, 2; Reinhold Niebuhr, *Christian Realism and Political Problems* (New York: Scribner, 1953), pp. 124-38; John N. Figgis, *Political Aspects of S. Augustine's 'City of God'* (London: Longmans, 1921), pp. 51-67.

11   J. P. Migne (ed.), *Patrilogiae Latinae*, LVI, 634.

12   The classical distinction between "church" and "sect" may be found in Ernst Troeltsch, *The Social Teachings of the Christian Churches* (New York: Macmillan, 1931), I, 331-43. The association of Protestant dualistic symbols with church and sect may help clarify the differences between the two types in the period of the Reformation, though there are exceptions, as there are in all of the characteristics Troeltsch used in defining the two types. For example, the Evangelical Anabaptists envisioned the relation of church and state through the symbols of the two kingdoms and separation.

13   Herbert Butterfield, *Christianity and History* (London: G. Bell, 1949), p. 34.

14   Augustine, *De Civ. Dei*, XIX, 12.

15   Cf. the analysis of Roman Catholic political thought in J. W. Allen, *A History of Political Thought in the Sixteenth Century* (New York: Barnes & Noble, 1928), pp. 343-66.

16   "The . . . *Erastian plan* . . . was one by which the State determined the policy of the Church and virtually controlled its conduct. This plan, advocated by Hugo Grotius . . . grew out of the decline of the power of the papacy in Western Europe. . . . It . . . developed in Germany and most other European states after the revolt of Luther, and had in it the seeds of State absolutism." Stokes, *Church and State in the United States*, I, 41.

17   For an account of disestablishment in Connecticut and Massachusetts, *vide ibid.*, I, 408-26.

18   James H. Nichols, *Democracy and the Churches* (Philadelphia: Westminster, 1951). The thesis of this book is that one tradition of Christianity, left-wing Puritanism, contributed significantly to Anglo-Saxon democracy, whereas other Protestant and Roman Catholic groups contributed little or not at all. Unfortunately Nichols' study, despite thought-provoking insights, is marred by lack of sympathy for Roman Catholic contributions and should be corrected by A. J. Carlyle, *The Influence of Christianity upon Social and Political Ideas* (London: Mowbray, 1912), *passim*, where equality, human interdependence, popular assent to rulers and laws, the limitation of political authority by law and justice, and the independence of spiritual authority are correctly ascribed to the Middle Ages.

19 Tillich, *The Protestant Era*, p. xii.

20 In America, as well, the early labor movement discerned hostility by the churches to its aims. Terence Powderly, for example, said that "it cannot be wondered at that many who strove to better the condition of the toiler lost all respect for religion when they saw that those who affected to be the most devout worshipers at the foot of the heavenly throne, were the most tyrannical of task-masters when dealing with the poor and the lowly . . ." Cited by Henry F. May, *Protestant Churches and Industrial America* (New York: Harper & Row, 1949), p. 218.

21 Democracy and church-state separation can lead to oppression or freedom for individual and church, depending on the systems to which these terms refer. J. L. Talmon, *The Origins of Totalitarian Democracy* (London: Secker and Warburg, 1952), calls "totalitarian" both French Revolutionary and Communist forms of democracy and church-state separation. He asserts that they suppressed dissent in the name of the popular will (democracy) and their view of separation forbade the church to influence social morality or public policy. In speaking of democracy and church-state separation, therefore, one must make clear which of several political systems he means.

22 Cf. the essays by Karl Barth and Johannes Hamel in *How to Serve God in a Marxist Land* (New York: Association Press, 1959); Günter Jacob and Christian Berg, *Evangelische Kirche jenseits der Zonengrenze* (Berlin: Lettner, 1957).

23 Note the centrality of the problem of sovereignty in Maritain, *Man and the State*, pp. 28-53. Maritain denies its validity as a political concept.

24 Christopher Dawson, *Religion and the Modern State* (New York: Sheed & Ward, 1936), p. 57.

25 Some recent discussions of this problem in the American context are Will Herberg, *Protestant-Catholic-Jew* (Garden City: Doubleday, 1955), pp. 85-104; Martin E. Marty, *The New Shape of American Religion* (New York: Harper & Row, 1958); A. Roy Eckardt, *The Surge of Piety in America* (New York: Association Press, 1958).

I God's Regiments and Man's Vocation: Luther and Lutheranism

1 Perhaps the most influential Reformed theologian whose thought reflects strong Lutheran influence is Emil Brunner. Cf. his *The Divine Imperative* (Philadelphia: Westminster, 1947), Bk. III, Sec. 4.

2 Cf. the influential criticism by Reinhold Niebuhr in *The Nature and Destiny of Man* (New York: Scribner, 1941), II, 191-97. Wilhelm Pauck has questioned Niebuhr's treatment of Luther in *The Heritage of the Reformation* (Glencoe: Free Press, 1950), pp. 11-14.

3 The following studies of Luther, which have helped structure this chapter, reflect not only an interest in what Luther himself thought but also his contemporary relevance: Edgar M. Carlson, "Luther's Conception of Government," *Church History*, XV (December, 1946), 257-70; Gunnar Hillerdal, *Gehorsam gegen Gott und Menschen: Luthers Lehre von der Obrigkeit und die moderne evangelische Staatsethik* (Stockholm: SKDB, 1955); Franz Lau, "Luthers Lehre von den beiden Reichen," *Luthertum*, VIII (Berlin: Lutherisches Verlagshaus, 1953); Gordon

Rupp, *The Righteousness of God* (London: Hodder, 1953), Ch. XIII; Gustaf Törnvall, *Andligt och världsligt regemente hos Luther* (Lund: Ohlsson, 1940); Gustaf Wingren, *Luther on Vocation* (Philadelphia: Muhlenberg, 1957).

4 Eivind Berggrav, *Man and State* (Philadelphia: Muhlenberg, 1951), p. 276.

5 The most significant work of this sort, one whose influence is reflected among many American Lutherans, is Edgar M. Carlson, *The Reinterpretation of Luther* (Philadelphia: Muhlenberg, 1948). This is an analysis of Swedish Luther research.

6 This is especially clear in A. D. Mattson, *Christian Social Consciousness* (Rock Island: Augustana Book Concern, 1953) and O. Frederick Nolde, *Christian World Action* (Philadelphia: Muhlenberg, 1942).

7 Most studies of Luther's political thought are deficient because they do not correlate it with his theology. "No teaching of Luther has been more misrepresented than his teaching about the nature, extent, and limits of temporal power. Partly this has been due to an attempt to bypass Luther's theology." Rupp, *The Righteousness of God*, p. 287.

8 In the struggle between the papacy and the political forces of the sixteenth century, Luther, like the other Protestants, strongly favored the political side. Today, historical perspective enables one to see more clearly the struggle for the freedom of the church from national exploitation and the destructive consequences of national absolutism. Cf. Lau, *Luthertum*, VIII, 67-68.

9 One of the major contributions of twentieth-century Luther research has been to show the theocentric unity of Lutheran thought. This is especially noteworthy in the Swedish school, e.g., Hillerdal, *Gehorsam gegen Gott und Menschen;* Törnvall, *Andligt och världsligt regemente hos Luther;* and Wingren, *Luther on Vocation.*

10 "On Secular Authority," *Works of Martin Luther* (Philadelphia: Muhlenberg, 1930), III, 234, 236.

11 *Ibid.*, p. 235. This contradiction in Luther may also be explained historically. According to a perceptive study by F. Edward Cranz, *An Essay on the Development of Luther's Thought on Justice, Law, and Society* (Cambridge: Harvard University Press, 1959), p. 169, Luther's political views undergo development. Whereas in "On Secular Authority" he divided men into two exclusive groups, he dropped this concept in "Whether Soldiers, Too, Can Be Saved" (1526). Cranz points to 1520-1521 as the period of change in Luther's thought on the two regiments as well. Before this date he interpreted politics legalistically as part of the Fourth Commandment, in terms of command and obedience, and he directed his polemic against the combination of the two powers in pope or clergy. But this rather traditional approach had to be modified by new distinctions between the two realms, to show how God brings about both religious and civil justice. Pp. 160-61.

12 Törnvall, *Andligt och världsligt regemente hos Luther*, pp. ix-x.

13 "Whether Soldiers, Too, Can Be Saved," *Works*, V, 39.

14 Here Luther reflects the influence of Augustine, who likewise felt that the earthly city was based on disorientation from God, but nevertheless mediated divine blessings through the peace and order accomplished by the temporal authorities.

15 The church, too, is an order.

16 Törnvall, *Andligt och världsligt regemente hos Luther*, pp. 169-72.
17 *Martin Luthers Werke* (Weimar: H. Böhlau, 1883), XXXVI, 385.
18 Törnvall, *Andligt och världsligt regemente hos Luther*, pp. 99-100.
19 "On Secular Authority," *Works*, III, 236.
20 Cf. Carlson, *The Reinterpretation of Luther*, pp. 48-57; Ragnar Bring, *Dualismen hos Luther* (Stockholm: SKDB, 1929).
21 Gustaf Aulén, *The Faith of the Christian Church*, revised ed. (Philadelphia: Muhlenberg, 1960), p. 244.
22 In his treatise "On War Against the Turk," Luther described the Turk as "God's rod and the devil's servant," *Works*, V, 88. Luther's emphasis on the dualistic tension between God and Satan is complicated almost to the point of insolubility by the dualism in the activity of God himself, who rules not only in love and blessing, but also in wrath and punishment. Hence, it is often impossible to discern in the event of war or disorder whether it is the activity of the devil or the wrath of God which appears. Luther seemed to feel that God's sovereignty takes precedence, but this is tenuous at best. At times the devil himself becomes an instrument of the wrath of God, as God punishes his people by allowing the devil to exercise his pernicious influence. "For since the Turk is the rod of the wrath of the Lord our God and the servant of the raging devil, the first thing to be done is to smite the devil, his lord, and take the rod out of God's hand, so that the Turk may be found in his own strength only, all by himself, without the devil's help and without God's hand." *Ibid.*, V, 88-89.
23 Hillerdal, *Gehorsam gegen Gott und Menschen*, pp. 30-31.
24 "Whether Soldiers, Too, Can Be Saved," *Works*, V, 55.
25 *Works*, V, 79-123, especially the opening pages.
26 "On Secular Authority," *Works*, III, 236-38.
27 *Ibid.*, III, 242. Here Luther cites the Old Testament to support coercion by government. The New Testament ethic of Jesus does not apply in the temporal institutions of the world. The emphasis on the Old Testament distinguishes Luther from the Anabaptists, who held that the Christian ethic was determinatively established by Jesus, who abrogated the old covenant.
28 "A Treatise on Christian Liberty," *Works*, II, 335-36.
29 *Ibid.*, II, 337-38.
30 According to Gustaf Wingren, "As far as we can determine Luther does not use *Beruf* or *vocatio* in reference to the work of a non-Christian. All have station (*Stand*) and office; but *Beruf* is the Christian's earthly or spiritual work," *Luther on Vocation*, p. 2.
31 "On Secular Authority," *Works*, III, 229.
32 *Ibid.*, III, 258.
33 *Ibid.*, III, 258.
34 *Ibid.*, III, 249.
35 *Ibid.*, III, 241.
36 "Eighty-second Psalm," *Works*, IV, 298. This should be contrasted, however, with another comment by Luther, that "the temporal power is a very small thing in God's sight, and far too slightly regarded by Him, that for its sake, whether it do right or wrong, we should resist, become disobedient and quarrel. On the other hand, the spiritual power is an exceeding great blessing. . . ." *Works*, I, 264.
37 "On Secular Authority," *Works*, III, 242.

38 "Eighty-second Psalm," *Works*, IV, 299-306.
39 "On Secular Authority," *Works*, III, 240. Cf. *ibid.*, III, 248-49.
40 "Whether Soldiers, Too, Can Be Saved," *Works*, V, 45.
41 For eschatological elements in Luther related to his political thought, see "Against the Robbing and Murdering Hordes of Peasants," *Works*, IV, 253, and "On War Against the Turk," *Works*, V, 118: "And so, I think, now that the Roman Empire is almost gone, Christ's coming is at the door, and the Turk is the Empire's token of farewell, a parting gift to the Roman Empire. . . ."
42 "Whether Soldiers, Too, Can Be Saved," *Works*, V, 38-39.
43 "On Secular Authority," *Works*, III, 269-70.
44 *Ibid.*, III, 246.
45 Cf. Thomas Aquinas, *Summa Theologica*, IIaIIae, q. 40, a. 1.
46 "Whether Soldiers, Too, Can Be Saved," *Works*, V, 59-60.
47 *Ibid.*, V, 68; "Treatise on Good Works," *Works*, I, 271; "On Secular Authority," *Works*, III, 270.
48 "Whether Soldiers, Too, Can Be Saved," *Works*, V, 44.
49 Hillerdal, *Gehorsam gegen Gott und Menschen*, pp. 79-80.
50 "When I have time and occasion to do so, I shall attack the princes and lords, too, for in my office of teacher, a prince is just the same to me as a peasant." "Concerning the Hard Book Against the Peasants," *Works*, IV, 271.
51 Harold J. Grimm, *The Reformation Era* (New York: Macmillan, 1954), pp. 171-72.
52 "An Admonition to Peace: A Reply to the Twelve Articles of the Peasants in Swabia," *Works*, IV, 220.
53 *Ibid.*, IV, 224.
54 *Ibid.*, IV, 231.
55 *Ibid.*, IV, 224-36.
56 "Against the Robbing and Murdering Hordes of Peasants," *Works*, IV, 248-54.
57 This is a fatuous claim by Luther, denying the patent meaning of the treatise "Against the Robbing and Murdering Hordes of Peasants," where the mercy of which he speaks refers to the mercy of the lords in killing the peasants and freeing society from their satanic threat.
58 "Concerning the Hard Book Against the Peasants," *Works*, IV, 280.
59 *Ibid.*, IV, 266.
60 Cf. H. Richard Klann, "Luther on War and Revolution," *Concordia Theological Monthly*, XXV (May, 1954), 353-66; Lowell C. Green, "Resistance to Authority and Luther," *Lutheran Quarterly*, VI (November, 1954), 338-48.
61 "On Secular Authority," *Works*, III, 228.
62 Cf. "An Open Letter to the Christian Nobility of the German Nation Concerning the Reform of the Christian Estate," *Works*, III, 66-73.
63 Particularly helpful discussions of this aspect of Luther's thought are found in Törnvall, *Andligt och världsligt regemente hos Luther*, pp. 113-28; Hillerdal, *Gehorsam gegen Gott und Menschen*, pp. 107-12; and Lau, *Luthertum*, VIII, 74-78.
64 "Eighty-second Psalm," *Works*, IV, 295.
65 *Ibid.*, IV, 297-98.
66 Cited by Berggrav, *Man and State*, p. 312. Cf. *Tischrede*, V.33.28.

67 Cited by Carl S. Mundiger, "Some of the Contributions of Lutheranism, with Special Reference to the Past and European Countries, to Theory and Practice of Government and Society," *The Church and Modern Culture,* ed. John G. Kunstmann (Valparaiso, Indiana: Valparaiso University Press, 1953), pp. 61-62.

68 "On Secular Authority," *Works,* III, 257.

69 "Treatise on Good Works," *Works,* I, 217-18.

70 "Whether Soldiers, Too, Can Be Saved," *Works,* V, 44; "An Admonition to Peace . . . ," *Works,* IV, 238.

71 "On Secular Authority," *Works,* III, 249-50.

72 "Whether Soldiers, Too, Can Be Saved," *Works,* V, 48-49.

73 Thomas Aquinas, *Summa Theologica,* IIaIIae, q. 10, a. 11, concl. (Jews); IIaIIae, q. 11, a. 3, concl. (heretics).

74 For Luther's policy toward the Jews, cf. Heinrich Bornkamm, *Luther's World of Thought* (St. Louis: Concordia, 1958), pp. 227-32.

75 Roland Bainton, "The Development and Consistency of Luther's Attitude to Religious Liberty," *Harvard Theological Review,* XXII (April, 1929), 107-49.

76 "On Secular Authority," *Works,* III, 259.

77 "Eighty-second Psalm," *Works,* IV, 309-12. In the Formula of Concord (1576) a somewhat different classification of Anabaptists appears: 1) Those who cannot be endured in the church, who deny for example that Christ assumed flesh and blood of the Virgin Mary or that infants should be baptized; 2) Those who are intolerable in the commonwealth, by denying to Christians magistracy and the oath; 3) Those who are intolerable in daily life, by denying the possession of property and giving all to the community. Philip Schaff, *The Creeds of Christendom* (New York: Harper & Row, 1877), III, 173-77.

78 Troeltsch, *The Social Teaching of the Christian Churches,* p. 698. In the Augsburg Confession, article XVI, "Of Civil Affairs," "Christians are necessarily bound to obey their own magistrates and laws, save only when commanded to sin, for then they ought to obey God rather than men (Acts 5:29)." The latter part of this article was neglected in Germany after Luther's death.

79 In "An Open Letter to the Christian Nobility of the German Nation Concerning the Reform of the Christian Estate," *Works,* II, 61-65.

80 For these developments cf. Grimm, *The Reformation Era,* pp. 153-58, 225-26. It is important to note that these tendencies in Germany toward political control of religious life were not unusual, but paralleled similar measures by governments, both Protestant and Roman Catholic, throughout Western Europe.

81 Troeltsch, *The Social Teaching of the Christian Churches,* p. 575.

82 *Ibid.,* p. 563.

83 E. Theodore Bachmann, "The Church and the Rise of Modern Society," *Christian Social Responsibility,* ed. Harold C. Letts (Philadelphia: Muhlenberg, 1957), II, 100. The great chancellor Bismarck typified this radical separation between personal piety and political interests. He called himself a "soldier of the Lord" and claimed to act daily "with genuine penitence," while on December 3, 1850, he said that "the only sound foundation for a great state, which therewith is essentially differentiated from a small state, is its state egotism and not romanticism.

It is unworthy of a great state to battle for a cause which is not within the sphere of its own interest." At the same time he argued that Germany was a "Christian" state, and he was proud of his social legislation which made Germany the most progressive country in that respect in his day. Salo W. Baron, *Modern Nationalism and Religion* (New York: Harper & Row, 1947), pp. 142-43.

84 Cited by Carlson, *The Reinterpretation of Luther*, p. 24.

85 Bachmann, *Christian Social Responsibility*, ed. Letts, II, 132.

86 Cf. R. K. Buehrle, "The Church, the State, and the Public Schools," *Lutheran Church Review*, XXI (January, 1902), 56-65; H. Douglass Spaeth, "Cooperation of Church and State in Religious Education," *ibid.*, XXXIII (July, 1914), 423-39.

87 Robert R. Durst, "The Duties of the Christian to his Government," *ibid.*, XXIV (January, 1905), 69-81.

88 Theodore E. Schmauk, "Politics and the Church," *ibid.*, XXXIX (January, 1920), 42. For other Lutheran discussion of the Social Gospel, cf. George W. Sandt, "The Church and Social Service," *ibid.*, XXXIV (October, 1915), 511-20; George Hodges, "The Function of the Church in the World of Today," *ibid.*, XXXVIII (April, 1919), 151-59; Franklin K. Fretz, "The Church and her Approach to Social Problems," *ibid.*, XLI (July, 1922), 253-57.

89 Otto Dibelius, "Die Kirche und das heutige Staatsproblem," *World Lutheranism of Today*, ed. Yngve Brilioth (Stockholm: SKDB, 1950), p. 70.

90 Taito A. Kantonen, "Christian Faith and the Political Order," *Christian Social Responsibility*, ed. Letts, III, 120-27; Elston Ruff, *The Dilemma of Church and State* (Philadelphia: Muhlenberg, 1954), pp. 84-86.

91 Lau, *Luthertum*, VIII, 13 n. For an account of the struggle in the German Church, cf. Arthur Frey, *Cross and Swastika* (London: SCM Press, 1938).

92 Berggrav, *Man and State*, especially the lecture, "Luther on the Duty of Disobedience," pp. 300-19. Cf. Berggrav, "The Task of the Church in the Field of International Affairs," *Ecumenical Review*, II (Summer, 1950), 333-41; Berggrav, "State and Church, The Lutheran View," *Lutheran Quarterly*, IV (November, 1952), 363-76. On the relationship of Lutheran thought to the Norwegian resistance, cf. Arne Fjellbu, "Luther as a Resource of Arms in the Fight for Democracy," *World Lutheranism of Today*, ed. Brilioth, pp. 81-97.

93 Berggrav, *Man and State*, pp. 277-78.

94 *Ibid.*, p. 314.

95 *Ibid.*, p. 283.

96 Hillerdal, like Berggrav, advocates rethinking the traditional Lutheran aversion to resisting political authority, but he correctly recognizes that here the Lutheran ethic must go beyond Luther. *Gehorsam gegen Gott und Menschen*, pp. 295-96.

97 George Hall, "Church and State," *What Lutherans are Thinking*, ed. E. C. Fendt (Columbus: Wartburg Press, 1947), p. 513.

98 Hillerdal, *Gehorsam gegen Gott und Menschen*, p. 295.

99 "In vain do we look to Luther for a completed doctrine of the state. But he has given that which is still better. He has shown the Chris-

tian way of regarding the state and its task. In these days, so full of the lust for power and the deification of the state—often accompanied with a feignedly Christian concept of the state—we have special need for understanding of the divine intention for the power of this world. In this we could find no better guidance than that supplied by the New Testament and its greatest interpreter, Martin Luther." Anders Nygren, "The State and the Church," *This is the Church,* ed. Anders Nygren (Philadelphia: Muhlenberg, 1952), pp. 305-06.

100   Ehrenström, *Christian Faith and the Modern State,* pp. 61-112.
101   Cf. his *The Christian Ethos* (Philadelphia: Muhlenberg, 1957).
102   *Ibid.,* pp. 120-22, 385.
103   Hillerdal, *Gehorsam gegen Gott und Menschen,* p. 298.
104   E.g. Dietrich Bonhoeffer, *Ethics* (New York: Macmillan, 1955); Joseph Sittler, *The Structure of Christian Ethics* (Baton Rouge: Louisiana State University Press, 1958); and George W. Forell, *Ethics of Decision* (Philadelphia: Muhlenberg, 1955).
105   This correlation is best expressed in Wingren, *Luther on Vocation, passim.*
106   Cf. Karl Barth, "The Christian Community and the Civil Community," *Against the Stream* (London: SCM Press, 1954), pp. 15-50.
107   Bonhoeffer, *Ethics,* pp. 302-03.
108   Hillerdal, *Gehorsam gegen Gott und Menschen,* pp. 270-71.
109   Törnvall, *Andligt och världsligt regemente hos Luther,* pp. 169-72.
110   Gustaf Aulén, *Church, Law and Society* (New York: Scribner, 1948), pp. 44-45.
111   Carlson, *The Reinterpretation of Luther,* p. 103.
112   Bonhoeffer, *Ethics,* p. 277.
113   *Ibid.,* p. 306.
114   Cited by Carlson, *The Reinterpretation of Luther,* p. 109.
115   Ruff, *The Dilemma of Church and State,* p. 50.
116   Conrad Bergendoff, "Religion and Culture," *The Church and Modern Culture,* ed. Kunstmann, p. 34.
117   Kantonen, *Christian Social Responsibility,* ed. Letts, III, 118.
118   Edgar M. Carlson, *The Church and the Public Conscience* (Philadelphia: Muhlenberg, 1956), pp. 73-74.
119   Ruff, *The Dilemma of Church and State,* p. 68; Kantonen, *Christian Social Responsibility,* ed. Letts, III, 120-22.
120   *Ibid.*
121   Cf. Barth's letter, *How to Serve God in a Marxist Land,* ed. Brown, pp. 45-80. "In the East there is arbitrary rule of the almighty party, propaganda, and police, but in the West we are surrounded by an equally tyrannous press, systems of private enterprise, snobbish presumption, and public opinion." P. 52.
122   Kantonen, *Christian Social Responsibility,* ed. Letts, III, 123.
123   *Ibid.,* pp. 124-25.
124   Ruff, *The Dilemma of Church and State,* pp. 101-103.
125   *Ibid.,* p. 88.
126   *Ibid.,* p. 30.
127   *Ibid.,* p. 62.
128   *Ibid.*
129   Scholarly studies have shown the changed attitude toward social prob-

lems in two Lutheran groups: Robert L. Anderson, "The Awakening Social Consciousness of the Lutheran Church in America since World War I, with Special Reference to the Augustana Lutheran Church," (S.T.M. thesis, Union Theological Seminary, 1959); Harold Haas, "The Social Thinking of the United Lutheran Church in America, 1918-1948," (Ph.D. dissertation, Drew University, 1953). Both authors discover increased attention to social problems with each decade, though the perspectives represent a conscious attempt to preserve the essentials of Lutheran theology. Anderson has insight into nonreligious factors influencing these changes such as the American "gospel of wealth," immigration patterns, and the rural nature of the Lutheran Church which is now becoming more urbanized. Pp. 33-50.

130   Bonhoeffer's *Ethics* has been the most important influence, along with Sittler's *The Structure of Christian Ethics*, and George W. Forell, *Faith Active in Love* (New York: American Book, 1954), among the American Lutheran writers. Among non-Lutherans who hold similar views may be found Alexander Miller, *The Renewal of Man* (Garden City: Doubleday, 1955) and Paul Lehmann, "The Foundation and Pattern of Christian Behavior," *Christian Faith and Social Action*, ed. John A. Hutchison (New York: Scribner, 1953), pp. 93-116.

131   Hall, "Church and State," *What Lutherans are Thinking*, ed. Fendt, p. 517.

132   Edgar M. Carlson, "Free for Service in the World," *Messages of the Third Assembly, The Lutheran World Federation* (Minneapolis: Augsburg, 1957), pp. 69-83. Cf. his *The Church and the Public Conscience*.

133   Carlson, *The Church and the Public Conscience*, p. 68.

134   Carlson, *Messages of the Third Assembly . . .* , pp. 79-80.

135   Mattson, *Christian Social Consciousness*, p. 163.

136   Mattson, "The Church and Society," *What Lutherans are Thinking*, ed. Fendt, p. 462.

137   Franklin Sherman, "Christian Love and Public Policy Today," *The Lutheran Quarterly*, XIII (August, 1961), 235-36.

138   Haas, *The Social Thinking of the United Lutheran Church . . .* , p. 160.

139   *New York Times* (November 6, 1960).

140   Fredrik A. Schiotz, *Lutheran Herald*, XLVII (November 22, 1960), 10.

141   Cf. his fair and perceptive study of the principal differences between Evangelical Lutheranism and Roman Catholicism, *One in Christ* (Philadelphia: Muhlenberg, 1957).

142   Theodore Hoyer, "Church and State," *The Abiding Word*, ed. Theodore Laetsch (St. Louis: Concordia Publishing House, 1947), II, 562-607. Similar to Hoyer is P. F. Siegel, "Civil Government," *ibid.*, I, 508-21.

143   *Ibid.*, II, 590.

144   *Ibid.*, II, 566.

145   *Ibid.*, II, 606.

146   Alan H. Jahsmann, *What's Lutheran in Education?* (St. Louis: Concordia Publishing House, 1960), p. 143.

147   *Ibid.*, p. 146. *McCollum v. Board of Education*, 333 U.S. 203 (1948) invalidated a system of released-time religious instruction in Champaign, Illinois, because of alleged sectarian use of public school buildings and resources, and implied compulsion for students to attend such classes.

148   This policy was established in 1944 and reaffirmed in 1953. The schools

of the denomination may accept and even request social service or welfare benefits from government, but not federal or state funds for support of the teaching program. *Ibid.*, p. 155.

149 Ernest B. Koenker, "The Two Realms and the 'Separation of Church and State' in American Society," *The Concordia Theological Monthly,* XXVII (January, 1956), 1-12. For revisionist tendencies in the Missouri Synod cf. especially the essays in *The Church and Modern Culture,* ed. Mundiger.

150 A. M. Rehwinkel, "The Christian and Government, III," *The Concordia Theological Monthly,* XXI (July, 1950), 496-508.

II Christian Life Without Political Compromise: The Anabaptists and Mennonites

1 George H. Williams and Angel M. Mergal, *Spiritual and Anabaptist Writers* (Philadelphia: Westminster, 1957), p. 19.

2 H. Richard Niebuhr, *The Social Sources of Denominationalism* (New York: Holt, Rinehart and Winston, Inc., 1929), p. 39.

3 Williams and Mergal, *Spiritual and Anabaptist Writers,* p. 80. Cf. Harold S. Bender, "Thomas Müntzer, the Zwickau Prophets, and the Anabaptists," *Mennonite Quarterly Review,* XXVII (January, 1953), 3-16.

4 Franklin H. Littell, *The Anabaptist View of the Church* (Boston: Beacon Press, 1952), p. xv.

5 Cited by John C. Wenger, *The Doctrines of the Mennonites* (Scottdale, Pa.: Mennonite Publishing House, 1952), pp. 17-18. Article II of the Dordrecht Confession (1632) emphasizes the sin of men who "can neither help themselves nor be helped by any of their descendents, nor by angels, nor by any other creature in heaven or on earth, nor be redeemed, or reconciled to God. . . ." *Ibid.*, p. 78.

6 The contemporary Anabaptist emphasis on discipleship traces its origin to the analysis of Johannes Kühn, *Toleranz und Offenbarung* (Leipzig: Meiner, 1923). Kühn distinguished five types of Protestantism, one of which emphasized *Nachfolge* and included the Anabaptists. The leading recent exponent of this interpretation has been Harold S. Bender. Cf. his "The Anabaptist Theology of Discipleship," *MQR,* XXIV (January, 1950), 25-32. The correlation of discipleship with justification has led Hans J. Hillerbrand, "Anabaptism and the Reformation: Another Look," *Church History,* XXIX (December, 1960), 404-23, to argue that Anabaptism may be closer in spirit to Roman Catholicism than to Reformation Protestantism, especially Luther and Calvin. If this is so, then a great many other Protestant movements, such as Pietism and Methodism, could likewise be termed Catholic in spirit. This would confirm the thesis of Louis Bouyer, *The Spirit and Forms of Protestantism* (Westminster: The Newman Press, 1957), especially pp. 177-92, that *sola gratia* is an inadequate interpretation of Christianity and leads to supplementation in all periods of Protestant history by an emphasis on human cooperation or effort in salvation.

7 John C. Wenger (ed.), "Why I Do Not Cease Teaching and Writing," *The Complete Writings of Menno Simons* (Scottdale, Pa.: Herald Press,

1956), p. 300. This is concretely expressed in the 1702 Catechism of Gerrit Roosen, quest. 69: "But as the question is here more particularly asked, whether such faith alone is sufficient to salvation, we must again say that a mere oral confession that we have such faith is not sufficient to salvation; but rather a faith whereby we willingly take upon ourselves the cross of Christ, and thereby show by the fruits of our faith that we have a 'faith which worketh by love.'"

8   "Reply to False Accusations," *ibid.*, pp. 563-66.

9   "Christian Baptism," *ibid.*, p. 265.

10 Cf. Dordrecht Confession, Art. VIII. "We believe in and confess a visible Church of God, consisting of those, who, as before remarked, have truly repented, and rightly believed; who are rightly baptized, united with God in heaven, and incorporated into the communion of the saints on earth." Wenger, *Doctrines . . .* , p. 81. Franklin Littell has argued that the view of the church is the central doctrine of the Anabaptists. His *The Anabaptist View of the Church* has helped bring out this important element of Anabaptist thought, but along with Bender and others this study regards the concept of the church as an aspect of discipleship.

11 Robert Friedmann, "The Doctrine of the Two Worlds," *The Recovery of the Anabaptist Vision*, ed. Guy F. Hershberger (Scottdale: Herald Press, 1957), p. 113.

12 The ban appears as a distinguishing characteristic of the Anabaptists as early as the Schleitheim Confession (1527), Art. II. The ban may be used as an admonition for those "who slip sometimes and fall into error and sin, being inadvertently overtaken" or as a form of expulsion or discipline after three violations. Harry E. Fosdick, *Great Voices of the Reformation* (New York: Random House, 1952), p. 288. The use of the ban and other communitarian characteristics of Anabaptism refute the supposition that the Protestant left wing was individualistic. If anything, the Anabaptists were covenant or church centered. The authority was not the individual conscience, but the Bible, and this was studied, discussed, and interpreted according to congregational norms, with expulsion the result of radical disagreement.

13 Fosdick, *Great Voices of the Reformation*, p. 289.

14 Harold S. Bender, "The Pacifism of the Sixteenth Century Anabaptists," *MQR*, XXX (January, 1956), 15.

15 Harold S. Bender, *Conrad Grebel* (Scottdale: Herald Press, 1950). In addition to this book, helpful studies of the beginning of Anabaptism in Zürich are John Horsch, "The Rise and Early History of the Swiss Brethren Church," *MQR*, VI (October, 1932), 227-49; and John Howard Yoder, "The Turning Point in the Zwinglian Reformation," *MQR*, XXXII (April, 1958), 128-40.

16 Littell, *The Anabaptist View of the Church, passim;* "The Anabaptist Doctrine of the Restitution of the True Church," *MQR*, XXIV (January, 1950), 33-52.

17 Cited in Littell, *The Anabaptist View of the Church*, p. 77.

18 Hans J. Hillerbrand, "The Anabaptist View of the State," *MQR*, XXXII (April, 1958), 84. This article, a condensation of the author's doctoral dissertation at Erlangen University, "Die politische Ethik des Oberdeutschen Täufertums," has valuable documentation in the footnotes.

19 Cited by Littell, *The Anabaptist View of the Church*, p. 106. Cf. Dordrecht Confession, Art. XIII: "We also believe and confess, that God has

instituted civil government, for the punishment of the wicked and the protection of the pious; and also further, for the purpose of governing the world. . . ." Wenger, *Doctrines* . . . , p. 83.

20 "Reply to False Accusations," *The Complete Writings* . . . , p. 549.
21 Hillerbrand, *MQR*, XXXII, 86-87.
22 "The Cross of the Saints," *The Complete Writings* . . . , p. 604.
23 Fosdick, *Great Voices of the Reformation*, p. 291.
24 *Ibid.*, p. 292.
25 Hillerbrand, *MQR*, XXXII, 109.
26 "Foundation of Christian Doctrine," *The Complete Writings* . . . , p. 159. Not to have upheld the authority of the Old Testament in principle would have led to the charge of Marcionism against the Anabaptists.
27 Cited by John Horsch, *The Principle of Nonresistance as Held by the Mennonite Church* (Scottdale: Mennonite Publishing House, 1940), pp. 22-23.
28 Hans Pfistermeyer. Cited by Guy F. Hershberger, *War, Peace, and Non-resistance* (Scottdale: Herald Press, 1944), pp. 22-23.
29 Paul Peachey, *Die soziale Herkunft der Schweizer Täufer in der Reformationszeit* (Karlsruhe: Schneider, 1954), p. 35.
30 Harold S. Bender, "State," *The Mennonite Encyclopedia* (Scottdale: Mennonite Publishing House, 1955-1959), IV, 614.
31 "Foundation of Christian Doctrine," *The Complete Writings* . . . , p. 200.
32 "Epistle to Micron," *ibid.*, p. 922.
33 "Reply to False Accusations," *ibid.*, p. 549.
34 *Ibid.*, pp. 550-52.
35 Peachey, *Die soziale Herkunft* . . . , pp. 22-35.
36 Cited by Horsch, *The Principle of Nonresistance* . . . , p. 18.
37 Williams and Mergel, *Spiritual and Anabaptist Writers*, p. 80, 84.
38 "Reply to Gellius Faber," *The Complete Writings* . . . , p. 779.
39 The correspondence between the political thought of the early Luther and the Anabaptists has been emphasized by Harold H. Schaff, "The Anabaptists, the Reformers, and the Civil Government," *Church History*, I (March, 1932), 27-46.
40 "The Cross of the Saints," *The Complete Writings* . . . , p. 620. The concept of the suffering church receives such emphasis among the Anabaptists that it can be said that they upheld a martyr theology. It has been noted as a major motif by Ethelbert Stauffer, "The Anabaptist Theology of Martyrdom," *MQR*, XIX (July, 1945), 179-214. Cf. Thieleman J. van Braght, *The Bloody Theater or Martyrs Mirror* . . . , (Scottdale: Mennonite Publishing House, 1951). In the later Mennonite Confessions, flight to another place became an established feature of articles on nonresistance, when persecution became intolerably severe. E.g., Dordrecht Confession, Art. XIV; Roosen's Catechism, quest. 136.
41 "The Cross of the Saints," *The Complete Writings* . . . , p. 615.
42 William Klassen, "Oath," *The Mennonite Encyclopedia*, IV, 7.
43 Fosdick, *Great Voices of the Reformation*, pp. 283-84.
44 Robert Kreider, "The Anabaptists and the Civil Authorities of Strassburg, 1525-1555," *Church History*, XXIV (June, 1955), 99-118.
45 "A Pathetic Supplication to all Magistrates," *The Complete Writings* . . . , p. 526.
46 One finds some eschatological references in Simons, e.g. *ibid.*, pp. 205,

528, as well as in other Anabaptist writers. But the theme is not as strong as might be expected from a group under persecution.

47 Simons complained that he and his associates were classed with those of Münster "who contrary to God's word and every evangelical Scripture . . . set up a new kingdom, incited turmoil, introduced polygamy, etc., matters which we oppose vehemently with God's Word. . . ." *Ibid.*, p. 526.

48 Cited by Bender, *MQR*, XXIX, 89.

49 Troeltsch, *The Social Teaching of the Christian Churches*, p. 805.

50 Harold S. Bender, "State," *The Mennonite Encyclopedia*, IV, 614.

51 Hershberger, *War, Peace and Nonresistance*, pp. 78-79.

52 A short account of this experiment in government is found in Harold S. Bender, "Church and State in Mennonite History," *MQR*, XIII (April, 1939), pp. 92-93.

53 For a study of the effects of social change on Canadian Mennonites, cf. E. K. Francis, *In Search of Utopia* (Glencoe, Ill.: Free Press, 1955).

54 Hershberger, *War, Peace and Nonresistance*, p. 189.

55 Edward Yoder, "Christianity and the State," *MQR*, XI (July, 1937), 172.

56 Guy F. Hershberger, *The Way of the Cross in Human Relations* (Scottdale: Herald Press, 1958), p. 20; *War, Peace and Nonresistance*, pp. 17-22.

57 Hershberger, *War, Peace and Nonresistance*, pp. 192-93.

58 *Ibid.*, pp. 194-95.

59 Cf. Archie Penner, *The Christian, the State, and the New Testament* (Scottdale: Herald Press, 1959), p. 13.

60 Hershberger, *War, Peace and Nonresistance*, p. 195.

61 Yoder, *MQR*, XI, 182.

62 Hershberger, *War, Peace and Nonresistance*, p. 159.

63 Guy F. Hershberger, *The Mennonite Church in the Second World War* (Scottdale: Mennonite Publishing House, 1951), p. 39.

64 *Ibid.*, pp. 49-63. For an account of the Mennonite Civilian Public Service, cf. Melvin Gingerich, *Service for Peace* (Akron, Pa.: Mennonite Central Committee, 1949).

65 This is printed in full in Hershberger, *War, Peace and Nonresistance*, pp. 373-77.

66 Luke E. Ebersole, *Church Lobbying in the Nation's Capitol* (New York: Macmillan, 1951), p. 41.

67 Hershberger, *War, Peace and Nonresistance*, p. 115.

68 *Ibid.*, p. 157.

69 Hershberger, *The Mennonite Church in the Second World War*, p. 5.

70 Hershberger, *War, Peace and Nonresistance*, p. 376.

71 Reinhold Niebuhr, "Why the Christian Church is not Pacifist," *Christianity and Power Politics* (New York: Scribner, 1940), pp. 1-32.

72 Hershberger, *War, Peace and Nonresistance*, pp. 213-14. Cf. Don E. Smucker, "A Mennonite Critique of the Pacifist Movement," *MQR*, XX (January, 1946), 81-88.

73 For a Mennonite analysis and criticism, though with appreciation, of the Social Gospel prophet, Walter Rauschenbusch, cf. Guy F. Hershberger, "The Modern Social Gospel and the Way of the Cross," *MQR*, XXX (April, 1956), 83-103.

74 Harold S. Bender, "Pacifism," *The Mennonite Encyclopedia*, IV, 104-05.

75 Don E. Smucker, "The Theological Basis for Christian Pacifism," *MQR*, XXVII (July, 1952), 183.

76 Hershberger, *War, Peace and Nonresistance*, p. 225. "The Sermon on the Mount is not a piece of legislation for a secular state in a sinful society. It is a set of principles to govern the sons of the kingdom of heaven." *Ibid.*, p. 49.

77 E.g. Wenger, *The Doctrines of the Mennonites*, pp. 40-43.

78 Hershberger, *War, Peace and Nonresistance*, p. 16.

79 Smucker, *MQR*, XXVII, 178.

80 *Ibid.*, 177.

81 Bender, "State," *The Mennonite Encyclopedia*, IV, 617.

82 Cf. Harley J. Stucky, "Should Mennonites Participate in Government?" *Mennonite Life*, XIV (January, 1959), 34-38.

83 Cf. Yoder, *MQR*, XI, 194-95.

84 Elmer Ediger, "A Christian's Political Responsibility," *Mennonite Life*, XI (July, 1956), 144.

85 J. Winfield Fretz, "Should Mennonites Participate in Politics?" *Mennonite Life*, XI (July, 1956), 139-40. Cf. Esko Loewen, "Church and State," *Mennonite Life*, XI (July, 1956), 141-42, who takes a position similar to that of Fretz, but emphasizes the limits of political activity.

86 Elmer Neufeld, "Christian Responsibility in the Political Situation," *MQR*, XXXII (April, 1958), 141-62.

87 Hershberger, *War, Peace and Nonresistance*, p. 198.

88 Smucker, *MQR*, XX, 88.

89 Hershberger, *War, Peace and Nonresistance*, p. 379.

90 John C. Wenger, *Introduction to Theology* (Scottdale: Herald Press, 1954), p. 406.

91 Hershberger, *The Way of the Cross in Human Relations*, p. 20.

III From Theocracy to Pacifism: The Quakers

1 E.g. Isaac Sharpless, *Quakerism and Politics* (Philadelphia: Ferris and Leach, 1905), pp. 105-06; Wilmer A. Cooper, "The Ethical Implications of Quaker Participation in Politics," (unpublished M.A. thesis, Haverford College, 1948), p. 51.

2 Cf. the description of the Fellowship of Reconciliation by Reinhold Niebuhr as "a kind of Quaker conventicle inside of the traditional church." "Why I Leave the F.O.R." *Christian Century*, LI (January 3, 1934), 17. There is considerable evidence that many, perhaps a majority, of American Protestant ministers were pacifists in the 1930's.

3 Frederick B. Tolles, *Meeting House and Counting House* (Chapel Hill: The University of North Carolina Press, 1948), p. 52.

4 E.g. William C. Braithwaite, *The Beginnings of Quakerism* (London: Macmillan, 1912), pp. 33-35, and the introduction by Rufus Jones, pp. xxxiv-xlii.

5 Goeffrey F. Nuttall, *The Holy Spirit in Puritan Faith and Experience* (Oxford: Blackwell, 1946).

6 Hugh S. Barbour, "The Early Quaker Outlook upon 'the World' and Society, 1647-1662," (unpublished Ph.D. dissertation, Yale University, 1952).

7 W.A. Cole, "The Quakers and Politics," (unpublished D.Phil. dissertation, Cambridge University, 1955).

8   Nuttall, *The Holy Spirit in Puritan Faith and Experience*, pp. 155-59.

9   George Fox, *The Journal of George Fox* (London: Cambridge, 1952), pp. 33, 34.

10   The Holy Spirit (*to pneuma hagion*) in the New Testament makes holy (*hagios*) the saints (*hagioi*). The term *hagios* does not originally carry a moralistic, but rather a numinous meaning; but very early in Christian history holiness began to convey moral rather than charismatic connotations. Cf. Rudolph Otto, *The Idea of the Holy* (New York: Oxford, 1923), especially pp. 82-93.

11   E.g. Rufus Jones, *The Later Periods of Quakerism* (London: Macmillan, 1921), pp. 59-60.

12   Fox, *Journal*, p. 19.

13   *Ibid.*, p. 12.

14   Nuttall, *The Holy Spirit in Puritan Faith and Experience*, pp. 158-59.

15   Robert Barclay, *An Apology for the True Christian Divinity* (Glasgow: Murdoch, 1886), Proposition II.

16   *Ibid.*, Proposition VII.

17   Cited in Rufus Jones, *The Quakers in the American Colonies* (London: Macmillan, 1911), p. 33.

18   Cotton Mather, *Magnalia Christi Americana* (Hartford: Andrus, 1853), II, 523.

19   Cited by Barbour, "The Early Quaker Outlook . . . ," pp. 330-31.

20   *Ibid.*, p. 253.

21   Fox, *Journal*, p. 444.

22   Barbour, "The Early Quaker Outlook . . . ," p. 355.

23   *Ibid.*, p. 360.

24   *Ibid.*, p. 474. Cf. George Fox, "To the Parliament of the Commonwealth of England" (London, 1659).

25   Braithwaite, *The Beginnings of Quakerism*, pp. 180, 435.

26   Barbour, "The Early Quaker Outlook . . . ," pp. 324-26.

27   *Ibid.*, p. 375.

28   E.g., George Fox, "To all the Magistrates in London &c.," *The Works of George Fox* (New York: Isaac T. Hopper, 1831), IV, 135-37.

29   Fox, "A Warning to all the Merchants in London and such as Buy and Sell," *ibid.*, IV, 160-63.

30   Fox, "To Both Houses of Parliament," *ibid.*, IV, 264-66.

31   Cole, "The Quakers and Politics," *passim*. Cf. James F. Maclear, "Quakerism and the End of the Interregnum: A Chapter in the Domestication of Radical Puritanism," *Church History*, XIX (December, 1950), 240-70.

32   Cole, "The Quakers and Politics," p. 65.

33   *Ibid.*, p. 35.

34   Braithwaite, *The Beginnings of Quakerism*, pp. 434-41.

35   Cited by Barbour, "The Early Quaker Outlook . . . ," p. 326.

36   Margaret E. Hirst, *The Quakers in Peace and War* (London: Swarthmore, 1923), p. 48.

37   Cole, "The Quakers and Politics," p. 137.

38   Maclear, *Church History*, XIX, 259.

39   Fox, *Journal*, p. 357.

40   Isaac Penington, *The Works of Isaac Penington* (Philadelphia: Friends Book-store, 1863), II, 168-69.

41   Fox, *Journal*, p. 65.

42 Cited by Cole, "The Quakers and Politics," p. 69.

43 Fox, "To the Councill of Officers" (London: 1659), p. 6.

44 Cited by Braithwaite, *The Beginnings of Quakerism*, p. 440.

45 Edward Burrough, "A Visitation and Warning Proclaimed" (London: Simmons, 1659), p. 29.

46 Fox, "To the Councill of Officers," p. 8.

47 Cole, "The Quakers and Politics," p. 284.

48 Fox, *Journal*, pp. 399-400.

49 Arnold Lloyd, *Quaker Social History, 1669-1738* (London: Longmans, 1950), pp. 92-93.

50 William C. Braithwaite, *The Second Period of Quakerism* (London: Cambridge, 1961), p. 98.

51 Cited in Ethyn W. Kirby, "The Quakers' Efforts to Secure Civil and Religious Liberty, 1660-96," *The Journal of Modern History*, VII (December, 1935), 413.

52 Rufus Jones, *The Quakers in the American Colonies*, p. xiv-xv.

53 William Penn, *The Rise and Progress of the People Called Quakers* (Philadelphia: Friends Book-store, 1870), pp. 26-27.

54 Barclay, *Apology*, Proposition XV.

55 Frederick B. Tolles, *The Witness of William Penn* (New York: Macmillan, 1957), p. 145.

56 Guy F. Hershberger, "The Pennsylvania Quaker Experiment in Politics, 1682-1756," *MQR*, X (October, 1936), 197.

57 Jones, *The Quakers in the American Colonies*, p. 462.

58 *Ibid.*, pp. 171-212.

59 From a letter to James Harrison (August 25, 1681). Cited in Braithwaite, *The Second Period of Quakerism*, p. 399.

60 Jones, *The Quakers in the American Colonies*, p. 476. For a discussion of the moral interests of early Pennsylvania Quakers, cf. Albert C. Applegarth, *Quakers in Pennsylvania* (Baltimore: The Johns Hopkins Press, 1892), pp. 30-49.

61 *Minutes of the Provincial Council of Pennsylvania* (Philadelphia: Severns, 1852), I, 23-24.

62 *Ibid.*, p. 30.

63 *Ibid.*, pp. 29-30.

64 *Ibid.*, p. 31.

65 Hershberger, *MQR*, X, 221. Cf. Hershberger, "Pacifism and the State in Colonial Pennsylvania," *Church History*, VIII (March, 1939), 54-74.

66 *Ibid.*, X, 198-99.

67 Cf. Benjamin Franklin's comments on the Quakers: "My being many years in the Assembly, a majority of which were constantly Quakers, gave me frequent opportunity of seeing the embarrassment given them by their principles against war, whenever application was made to them, by order of the crown, to grant aids for military purposes. They were unwilling to offend the government on the one hand, by direct refusal; and their friends, the body of Quakers, on the other, by a compliance contrary to their principles; using a variety of evasions to avoid complying, and modes of disguising the compliance, when it became unavoidable. The common mode at last was, to grant money under the phrase of its being *for the King's use* and never to inquire how it was applied." Cited in Applegarth, *Quakers in Pennsylvania*, p. 41.

68   Hershberger, *MQR*, X, 211-13.
69   *Ibid.*, X, 214-17.
70   *Ibid.*, X, 217-18.
71   Jones, *The Quakers in the American Colonies*, p. 493.
72   Daniel J. Boorstin, *The Americans: The Colonial Experience* (New York: Random House, 1958), pp. 63-69.
73   Barbour, "The Early Quaker Outlook . . . ," pp. 521-22. In "The Great Case of Liberty of Conscience," William Penn argued his case on the laws of God, of nature, and of England. Tolles, *The Witness of William Penn*, pp. 83-84.
74   *Extracts from the Minutes and Advices of the Yearly Meeting of Friends Held in London from its First Institution* (London: Phillips, 1783), p. 19.
75   Cited by Frederick B. Tolles, *Quakers and the Atlantic Culture* (New York: Macmillan, 1960), p. 45.
76   Cited by Walter C. Woodward, "The Individual and the State," *Beyond Dilemmas*, ed. S. B. Laughlin (Philadelphia: Lippincott, 1937), p. 214.
77   Jones, *The Later Periods of Quakerism*, pp. 36-37.
78   Boorstin, *The Americans: The Colonial Experience*, p. 41.
79   Barbour, "The Early Quaker Outlook . . . ," pp. 529-30.
80   Jones, *The Later Periods of Quakerism*, p. 715.
81   *Ibid.*, pp. 729-30. Cf. A.J.H. Duganne, *The Fighting Quakers* (New York: Robens, 1866).
82   Erica Martineau, "Quakerism and Public Service Chiefly between 1832 and 1867," (unpublished D.Phil. dissertation, Oxford University, 1938).
83   Leroy C. Ferguson, "The Quakers in Midwestern Politics." *Papers of the Michigan Academy of Science, Arts and Letters* (Ann Arbor, 1948).
84   Martineau, "Quakerism and Public Service . . . ," p. 237.
85   *Ibid.*, p. 9.
86   *Ibid.*, p. 33.
87   *Ibid.*, pp. 74-76.
88   Ferguson, "The Quakers in Midwestern Politics," pp. 415-16.
89   *Ibid.*, p. 420.
90   C. Stanley Lowell, "Changing Climate of Church and State," *Friends Journal*, III (February 9, 1957), 87-88.
91   "Washington Newsletter of the Friends Committee on National Legislation," No. 177 (June, 1958).
92   *Christian Discipline of the Religious Society of Friends of London Yearly Meeting* (London: Headley, 1911), II, 126.
93   Quakerism lacks any systematic study of its views on the state, or any thorough theological presentation examining the implications of Quaker suppositions for the state. At the 1937 Friends World Conference a great deal of attention was given to the topic, "The Individual and the State," but the results were generalized and not well grounded theologically. Cf. the study outlines and report of that meeting, *Report of Commission II: The Individual and the State, Friends World Conference, 1937*. Related presentations are Henry J. Cadbury, "The Individual Christian and the State." *Friends World Conference: Official Report* (Philadelphia: Friends World Conference Committee, 1937), pp. 29-36; Woodward, "The Individual and the State," *Beyond Dilemmas*, ed. Laughlin, pp. 205-27; Thomas E. Harvey, "The Christian Citizen and the State" (London: Friends Book Centre, 1939). The focus on the individual and the

state reflects the individualism and prominence of ethical interests in the Quaker attitude toward the state.

94 *Friends World Conference: Official Report (1937)*, p. 33.
95 *The Message of Christ for Today Through Friends: Commission Statements for the Five Years Meeting of Friends in America* (Richmond, Indiana: 1945), p. 13.
96 *Faith and Practice* (Philadelphia: Friends Central Bureau, 1955), p. 41.
97 *Friends World Conference: Official Report (1937)*, p. 28.
98 *Faith and Practice*, p. 42.
99 *Study Outline of Friends World Conference, 1937*, p. 19.
100 Robert O. Byrd, *Quaker Ways in Foreign Policy* (London: Oxford, 1960), p. 31.
101 Friends Committee on National Legislation, "Statement on Policy" (January 29, 1944), no pp.
102 *Ibid.*
103 Friends Committee on National Legislation, "1961-1962 Statement of Legislative Policy," *passim.*
104 Tolles, "Quakers and the Atlantic Culture," p. 53.
105 *Speak Truth to Power* (Philadelphia: American Friends Service Committee, 1955), p. iv.
106 Cited in William W. Comfort, *Just Among Friends* (New York: Macmillan, 1941), p. 184.
107 Richard B. Gregg, *The Power of Non-Violence* (Philadelphia: Lippincott, 1934).
108 *Speak Truth to Power*, pp. v, 57.
109 Reinhold Niebuhr, *Christianity and Power Politics*, pp. 10-12.
110 Byrd, *Quaker Ways in Foreign Policy*, p. 11.
111 *Ibid.*, pp. 36-37.
112 An early expression of this outlook was Cooper, "The Ethical Implications of Quaker Participation in Politics."
113 Mulford Q. Sibley, *The Political Theories of Modern Pacifism* (Philadelphia: Pacifist Research Bureau, 1944), p. 52.
114 *Ibid.*, pp. 8-9.
115 *Ibid.*, pp. 55-56.
116 Richard K. Ullman, *Between God and History* (London: G. Allen, 1959).
117 *Ibid.*, pp. 156-57.
118 *Ibid.*, p. 181.
119 *Ibid.*, p. 193.
120 *Ibid.*, p. 84.

IV Separationism: Defenders of the Wall

1 Paul Blanshard, *American Freedom and Catholic Power* (Boston: Beacon Press, 1949). This work was followed by several others which continued during the 1950's to focus attention on the relationship of Roman Catholicism to American church-state relations, e.g., *Communism, Democracy and Catholic Power* (1951); *The Irish and Catholic Power: An American Interpretation* (1953); and *The Right to Read: The Battle Against Censorship* (1955).
2 *The New York Times* (January 12, 1948).

3 *McCollum* v. *Board of Education*, 333 U.S. 203 (1948).

4 *Zorach* v. *Clauson*, 343 U.S. 306 (1952).

5 333 U.S. at 210-11. This *dictum* was originally set forth in *Everson* v. *Board of Education*, 330 U.S. 1 (1947).

6 343 U.S. at 312-13.

7 *Everson* v. *Board of Education*, 330 U.S. 1 (1947).

8 Stokes, *Church and State in the United States*, II, 750. Cf. pp. 744-58 for a detailed discussion of this controversy.

9 Protestant positions tend to change as they move through history, so that tracing a continuous religious and social pattern presents severe problems. The separationism of the seventeenth-century Puritan sects does not correspond to that of the twentieth-century Baptists and evangelicals, but in general a persistent but changing perspective can be discerned between the two periods, carried by denominations with sectarian characteristics and interested in revivalism or conversion, with the Baptists being the best example.

10 The chapters on the transformationists and separationists ascribe the origin of both to Calvinism. Religious energy is primarily directed by the transformationists toward the alteration of society in accordance with the divine will, and by the separationists toward maintaining the religious integrity of the local congregation. Both aims appear in both movements, but here the two positions represent different emphases. In the seventeenth century, transformationism tended to be strong among "churches," separationism among "sects."

11 Cf. the discussion on Anabaptist influence on sixteenth-century England in Champlin Burrage, *The Early English Dissenters in the Light of Recent Research* (London: Cambridge, 1912) I, 41-67.

12 Browne is usually regarded as the first English Congregationalist, though he returned to Anglicanism in 1585. Furthermore, his separationism was only a temporary measure, for he hoped that the magistrates would eventually bestow church property and official status on the separated congregations, while suppressing other religious groups. For an account of his career, see Burrage, *The Early English Dissenters . . .* , I, 94-117. His three major treatises are all part of one book entitled *A Booke Which Sheweth the Life and Manners of all true Christians* (1582).

13 Robert Browne, "A True and Short Declaration . . . ," *The Writings of Robert Harrison and Robert Browne*, ed. Albert Peel and Leland H. Carlson (London: G. Allen, 1953), p. 404.

14 Browne, "A Book Which Sheweth . . . ," *ibid.*, p. 227.

15 Cited in Perry Miller, *Orthodoxy in Massachusetts, 1630-1650* (Boston: Beacon Press, 1959), p. 139.

16 Browne, "A Treatise of reformation without tarying for anie," *The Writings of Robert Harrison and Robert Browne*, ed. Peel and Carlson, p. 164.

17 From the Confession of 1596, *The Creeds and Platforms of Congregationalism*, ed. Williston Walker (New York: Scribner, 1893), pp. 71-72. Cf. the comment of W. K. Jordan: "The theological system of the Separatists permitted the extension of their plea for toleration beyond the limits of their own group to the inclusion of all men. First, however, the chastening rod of repression had to weaken their resolute desire to impose their system upon other men before the inherent principle of

toleration could strongly manifest itself. . . . The early leaders of the movement had given expression to the first tolerant theory of religious practice in England. But when the Separatist viewed the sin and false worship of the nation and when he envisioned his party in control of the public opinion of the nation he was motivated by those principles of persecution which had for so many centuries impeded the progress of religious freedom. The magistrate in a Congregational community was reduced to the onerous duty of executing the sentences of the godly." *The Development of Religious Toleration in England* (Cambridge: Harvard University Press, 1932), I, 291-92.

18 On the early relation between Anabaptists and Baptists cf. Winthrop S. Hudson, "Baptists were not Anabaptists," *The Chronicle*, XVI (October, 1953), 171-79; James D. Mosteller, "Baptists and Anabaptists, II. John Smyth and the Dutch Mennonites," *The Chronicle*, XX (July, 1957), 100-114. Mosteller's article argues for a minimal connection between the two groups through the influence of John Smyth. On Smyth's career, see Burrage, *The Early English Dissenters . . .* , I, 221-50.

19 Edward B. Underhill, *Confessions of Faith and Other Public Documents Illustrative of the History of the Baptist Churches of England in the Seventeenth Century* (London: Hanserd Knollys, 1854), pp. 6-7. The political articles of the seventeenth-century Baptist confessions are chiefly concerned with distinguishing them from the Anabaptists. The 1646 and 1660 confessions refer to their authors as those "falsely called Anabaptists." In 1624 English Baptist congregations sought union with the Dutch Waterland Mennonites, but were rejected because of their refusal to adopt the Mennonite views on the oath and officeholding.

20 Thomas Helwys, *A Short Declaration of the Mistery of Iniquity* (London: Baptist Historical Society, 1935), p. 69.

21 On the implications of Baptist thought for religious freedom cf. Jordan, *The Development of Religious Toleration in England*, II, 258-62.

22 E.g. *ibid.*, II, 261-62; R.E.E. Harkness, "British, American, and Canadian Baptists and Church and State," *The Chronicle*, XIX (July, 1956), 130.

23 Jordan, *The Development of Religious Toleration in England*, II, 242.

24 *Ibid.*, II, 247.

25 The two best sources for information on this period are the introduction and documents in A.S.P. Woodhouse (ed.), *Puritanism and Liberty* (London: Dent, 1938) and William Haller, *Liberty and Reformation in the Puritan Revolution* (New York: Columbia University Press, 1955). For further insights cf. Joseph Frank, *The Levellers* (Cambridge: Harvard University Press, 1955) and James F. Maclear, "The Birth of the Free Church Tradition," *Church History*, XXVI (June, 1957), 99-131.

26 Reinhold Niebuhr, "A Note on Pluralism," *Religion in America*, ed. John Cogley (New York: Meridian, 1958), p. 42.

27 William Haller, *The Rise of Puritanism* (New York: Harper & Row, 1957), p. 215.

28 Woodhouse, *Puritanism and Liberty*, pp. 443-45.

29 *Ibid.*, p. 444.

30 *Ibid.*, p. 66.

31 *Ibid.*, p. 67.

32 *Ibid.*, p. 444.

33 *Ibid.*

34   *Ibid.,* p. 445.

35   *Ibid.,* p. 444.

36   Raymond G. Cowherd, *The Politics of English Dissent* (New York: New York University Press, 1956), p. 8.

37   Urian Oakes. Cited by Barbour, "The Early Quaker Outlook . . . ," p. 31.

38   Woodhouse, *Puritanism and Liberty,* pp. 319, 322.

39   Woodhouse, in his introduction, holds that the left wing contained two theories, but the biblicism of Roger Williams and the rationalism of some of the Leveller leaders, along with millenarianism, suggest the likelihood of three theories.

40   Cf. Thomas Collier, "A Discovery of the New Creation," *Puritanism and Liberty,* ed. Woodhouse, pp. 390-96.

41   *Ibid.,* p. 245.

42   *Ibid.,* pp. 233-41.

43   Excellent abridged editions of Williams' writings may be found in Perry Miller, *Roger Williams* (New York: Bobbs-Merrill, 1953). The thesis about Williams' contributions may be found on pp. 26-38.

44   "Queries of Highest Consideration," *ibid.,* p. 82.

45   Separation of church and state in Williams' thought proceeds from his sense of a radical contradiction between religion and cultural institutions. Because Williams was also strongly Calvinist in orientation, one finds in him both the impulse toward social change and the emphasis on separation of religious life from the rest of society.

46   "Letter to the Town of Providence" (January, 1655), *Roger Williams,* ed. Miller, pp. 225-26. This metaphor and other examples that Williams uses, such as corporations and companies within a city, indicate an understanding of the government as the noninterfering guardian of a pluralistic society.

47   "The Bloudy Tenant," *ibid.,* p. 139.

48   "The Bloudy Tenant," *Puritanism and Liberty,* ed. Woodhouse, p. 285.

49   Woodhouse, *Puritanism and Liberty,* p. 108.

50   *Ibid.,* pp. 87 ff.

51   Two helpful studies of the eighteenth-century revivals are Edwin S. Gaustad, *The Great Awakening in New England* (New York: Harper & Row, 1957) and Wesley M. Gewehr, *The Great Awakening in Virginia, 1740-1790* (Durham: Duke University Press, 1930). Cf. Gaustad, "The Baptist and the Great Awakening in New England," *The Chronicle,* XV (January, 1952), 41-48.

52   Gewehr, *The Great Awakening in Virginia, 1740-1790,* p. 187.

53   Boorstin, *The Americans: The Colonial Experience,* p. 136.

54   Cf. Isaac Backus, *A History of New England with Particular Reference to the Denomination of Christians Called Baptists,* (2nd ed.; Newton: Backus Historical Society, 1871); Alvah Hovey, *A Memoir of the Life and Times of the Rev. Isaac Backus, A.M.* (Boston: Gould and Lincoln, 1858).

55   John Leland, *The Writings of the Late Elder John Leland* (New York: G. W. Wood, 1845).

56   Robert G. Torbet, *A History of the Baptists* (Philadelphia: Judson Press, 1950), pp. 253-54.

57   Sidney Mead has brilliantly analyzed the development and decline of

the revivalist-rationalist alliance in "American Protestantism During the Revolutionary Epoch," *Church History*, XXII (December, 1953), 279-97. The discussion in the following pages strongly reflects the insights of Mead's article.

58   H. Shelton Smith, Lefferts A. Loetscher, and Robert T. Handy (eds.), *American Christianity* (New York: Scribner, 1960), I, 386.

59   Stokes, *Church and State in the United States*, I, 218.

60   John Leland, who often wavered between religious and political motivations, gives five arguments against religious establishments, three of which seem religious, while two point to the welfare of the nation. 1. Fallible men make their opinions tests of orthodoxy, which promotes religious hypocrisy in stimulating men to embrace the sanctioned religion while treating with contempt and persecution those who do not. 2. "These establishments metamorphose the church into a creature, and religion into a principle of state which has a natural tendency to make men conclude that *Bible religion* is nothing but a *trick of state*. . . ." 3. The fact that no two states establish the same creed and forms proves the questionable nature of establishments. 4. It discourages immigration and promotes social strife. 5. It keeps the best men from public office, for good men cannot follow what they do not believe. "The Rights of Conscience Inalienable" (1791), *The Writings of the Late Elder John Leland*, pp. 182-83.

61   Cf. Benjamin Franklin's religious and moral views in Smith, Loetscher, and Handy, *American Christianity*, I, 395-98.

62   Mead, *Church History*, XXII, 282.

63   Stokes, *Church and State in the United States*, I, 373.

64   *Ibid.*, I, 378.

65   *Ibid.*, I, 392-93.

66   Mead, *Church History*, XXII, 282.

67   *Ibid.*, XXII, 293.

68   John R. Bodo, *The Protestant Clergy and Public Issues, 1812-1848* (Princeton: Princeton University Press, 1954).

69   Charles C. Cole, *The Social Ideas of the Northern Evangelists, 1826-1860* (New York: Columbia University Press, 1954).

70   Timothy Smith, *Revivalism and Social Reform in Mid-Nineteenth Century America* (Nashville: Abingdon, 1957).

71   Winthrop S. Hudson, *The Great Tradition of the American Churches* (New York: Harper & Row, 1953).

72   Cited by Herbert W. Schneider, *The Puritan Mind* (New York: Holt, Rinehart and Winston, Inc., 1930), p. 207.

73   Bodo, *The Protestant Clergy and Public Issues, 1812-1848*, p. 26.

74   Hovey, *A Memoir of the Life and Times of the Rev. Isaac Backus, A.M.*, p. 210.

75   For an illustration of the theocentric thrust of seventeenth-century Baptist confessions, cf. Art. XLVI, "Of Liberty of Conscience," in a General Baptist Creed of 1678. "The Lord Jesus Christ, who is King of kings, and Lord of all by purchase, and is judge of quick and dead, is the only lord of conscience, having a peculiar right so to be; he having died for that end, to take away the guilt, and to destroy the filth of sin, that keeps the consciences of all men in thraldom and bondage, till they are set free by his special grace. And therefore he would not have the

consciences of men in bondage to or imposed upon by any usurpation, tyranny, or command whatsoever, contrary to his revealed will . . . which is the only rule he hath left for the consciences of all men to be ruled, and regulated, and guided by, through the assistance of his Spirit." Underhill, *Confessions of Faith* . . . , pp. 164-65.

76   Cited in Edwin S. Gaustad, "The Backus-Leland Tradition," *Baptist Concepts of the Church,* ed. Winthrop S. Hudson (Chicago: Judson Press, 1959), p. 113. This article is a contemporary Baptist critique of the replacement of religious by political and individualistic principles in this period of Baptist history.

77   Cf. Leland, *The Writings of the Late Elder John Leland, passim.*

78   Bodo, *The Protestant Clergy and Public Issues, 1812-1848,* p. 33 n.

79   *Ibid.,* p. 57.

80   *Ibid.,* p. 79.

81   *Ibid.,* p. 56.

82   Francis X. Curran has pointed out that only these three denominations unreservedly supported public education instead of trying to develop religious schools. *The Churches and the Schools* (Chicago: Loyola University Press, 1954), p. 123.

83   Philip Schaff, *America* (Cambridge: Harvard University Press, 1961), p. 76.

84   This point has been newly and helpfully emphasized in Smith, *Revivalism and Social Reform in Mid-Nineteenth Century America.*

85   Daniel D. Williams, "The Mystery of the Baptists," *Foundations,* I (January, 1958), 8.

86   The chief source of information on P.O.A.U. is its journal, *Church and State Review,* plus pamphlets. A critical study of the organization, Lawrence P. Creedon and William D. Falcon, *United for Separation* (Milwaukee: Bruce, 1959), is marred by polemical and journalistic techniques. A thorough study of the historical role and relation to Protestantism of this significant organization has yet to be written.

87   The National Association of Evangelicals can best be studied through its journal, *United Evangelical Action.* The widely circulated magazine, *Christianity Today,* represents the outlook of many leaders of the N.A.E. An official history is James D. Murch, *Cooperation without Compromise* (Grand Rapids: Eerdmans, 1956).

88   Cf. Dawson's *Separate Church and State Now* (New York: Richard R. Smith, 1948) and *America's Way in Church, State and Society* (New York: Macmillan, 1953).

89   Mullins' *The Axioms of Religion* (Philadelphia: American Baptist Publication Society, 1908) gives in a concise form his theological position. According to Mullins, "The sufficient statement of the historical significance of the Baptists is this: the competency of the soul in religion." *Ibid.,* p. 53. Cf. his discussion of this doctrine on pp. 53-69.

90   Walter P. Binns, "Christ and Freedom," *Official Report: Baptist World Alliance* (London: Carey Kingsgate Press, 1955), p. 123.

91   Edward H. Pruden. Cited by Paul M. Harrison, *Authority and Power in the Free Church Tradition* (Princeton: Princeton University Press, 1959), p. 25.

92   Cited by Rufus W. Weaver, *Champions of Religious Liberty* (Nashville: Sunday School Board of Southern Baptist Convention, 1946), p. 141.

93 Joseph M. Dawson, "The Church and Religious Liberty," *Review and Expositor*, L (April, 1953), 148.
94 Hudson, *The Great Tradition of the American Churches*, pp. 42-62.
95 Paul Blanshard's *God and Man in Washington* (Boston: Beacon Press, 1960), pp. 210-21, has a chapter on "Pluralism and the Good Society." For him pluralism seems to mean almost the opposite of the usual understanding; for he points out that through the public school America's "ethnic divisions [may] be softened and neutralized in the amalgam of a cultural institution that includes all creeds—as well as all races" (p. 219). Blanshard seems to regard pluralism as something undesirable, to be overcome through measures for promoting national unity. The same basic concern for national unity is reflected in Dawson, *Separate Church and State Now*, pp. 92-105, where the divisiveness is seen as a serious problem.
96 Weaver, *Champions of Religious Liberty*, p. 143.
97 Ernest A. Payne, *The Baptist Union: A Short History* (London: Carey Kingsgate, 1958), p. 290.
98 Binns, *Official Report: Baptist World Alliance* (1955), pp. 122-23.
99 Francesco Ruffini, *Religious Liberty* (London: Williams & Norgate, 1912), p. 513.
100 Harkness, *The Chronicle*, XIX, 135.
101 Gunnar Westin, "The Meaning of Religious Liberty," *Review and Expositor*, L (April, 1953), 160-66; "Why Fight for Religious Liberty," *Minutes of the Baptist World Alliance Meeting* (1955), p. 325.
102 Westin, *Review and Expositor*, L, 161.
103 *Ibid.*, L, 164.
104 *Ibid.*, L, 166.
105 Walfred H. Peterson, " 'Report from the Capital'—A Content Analysis," *Foundations* IV (April, 1961), 160-63.
106 Stokes, *Church and State in the United States*, II, 277.
107 E.g. Robert T. Miller, "The Development in Constitutional Law of the Principle of Religious Liberty and Separation of Church and State," *A Journal of Church and State*, I (1959), 145.
108 Dawson, *America's Way in Church, State and Society*, pp. 25-26.
109 Dawson, *Separate Church and State Now*, p. 53.
110 *Ibid.*, p. 50.
111 Dawson, *America's Way in Church, State and Society*, p. 167.
112 Murch, *Cooperation without Compromise*, p. 140.
113 Dawson, *Separate Church and State Now*, p. 90.
114 Murch, *Cooperation without Compromise*, pp. 151-52.
115 Conrad H. Moehlman, *The Wall of Separation between Church and State* (Boston: Beacon Press, 1951), pp. 55-57.
116 Murray, *We Hold These Truths*, p. 48.
117 Dawson, *Separate Church and State Now*, pp. 97-98.
118 For an historical account that reveals the dubious character of Protestant anti-Catholicism in the early nineteenth century, cf. Ray A. Billington, *The Protestant Crusade* (New York: Macmillan, 1938).
119 Thomas G. Sanders, "A Comparison of Two Current American Catholic Theories of the American Political System with Particular Reference to the Problem of Religious Liberty" (unpublished Ph.D. dissertation, Columbia University, 1958), pp. 374-419.

120 Cf. John A. Ryan and Francis J. Boland, *Catholic Principles of Politics* (New York: Macmillan, 1940), especially pp. 308-42.

121 Blanshard, *God and Man in Washington,* p. 43.

122 C. Emanuel Carlson, "The Meaning of the Baptist Position" (unpublished discussion material for the 1958 Religious Liberty Conference, Washington, D.C.), p. 13.

123 *Ibid.,* pp. 18-19.

124 *Ibid.,* p. 18.

125 C. Emanuel Carlson, "Approaches to our Public Relations Problems" (unpublished material for the Joint Promotion Conference, Nashville Tenn., 1960), p. 8.

126 Carlson, "The Meaning of the Baptist Position," pp. 4-5.

127 Hudson, *The Great Tradition of the American Churches.*

128 Franklin H. Littell, *From State Church to Pluralism* (Garden City: Doubleday, 1962).

129 Dean M. Kelley, "America as Heathen" (a review of Littell's *From State Church to Pluralism*), *Christian Century,* LXXIX (March 14, 1962), 330-31; "Beyond Separation of Church and State" (unpublished address, National Council of Churches, New York, 1962).

130 Herberg, *Protestant-Catholic-Jew.*

131 Peter L. Berger, *The Noise of Solemn Assemblies* (Garden City: Doubleday, 1961).

132 Hudson, *The Great Tradition of the American Churches,* p. 17.

V Moderation and Pragmatism: The Transformationists

1 This was the position of the influential Protestant journal, *The Christian Century.* "The Champaign Case," *The Christian Century,* LXV (April 7, 1948), 308-09.

2 "Statement on Church and State," *Christianity and Crisis,* VIII (July 5, 1948), 90.

3 Wayne H. Cowan, "POAU's Holy War," *Christianity and Crisis,* XXI (June 26, 1961), 111.

4 Cf. John Courtney Murray, "St. Robert Bellarmine on the Indirect Power," *Theological Studies,* IX (December, 1948), 491-535; "Church and State in the Light of History," *Theological Studies,* X (June, 1949), 177-234.

5 Wilhelm Niesel, *The Theology of Calvin* (Philadelphia: Westminster, 1956), p. 230.

6 Christopher Dawson, *The Judgment of the Nations* (New York: Sheed & Ward, Inc., 1942), pp. 45, 53.

7 For an account of the application of Calvin's theories to Geneva, cf. John T. McNeill, *The History and Character of Calvinism* (New York: Oxford, 1954), pp. 159-200.

8 John Calvin, *Institutes,* IV, 20, i.

9 *Ibid.,* IV, 20, ii.

10 *Ibid.,* IV, 20, ii.

11 *Ibid.,* IV, 20, ix.

12 A. M. Hunter, *The Teaching of Calvin* (London: J. Clarke, 1950), p. 222.

13 Calvin, *Institutes,* IV, 20, xxii.

14 *Ibid.,* IV, 20, xxiii.

15 *Ibid.*, IV, 20, xxxi.

16 *Ibid.*, IV, 20, xxxii.

17 *Ibid.*, IV, 20, viii. Cf. Thomas Aquinas, *Summa Theologica*, IaIIae, q. 105, a. 1, concl., where Aquinas expresses his preference for a monarchy "wherein one is given the power to preside over all." Aquinas also envisions the need of checks, by insisting that all should have some share in government.

18 Ernest Barker, *Church, State and Study* (London: Methuen, 1930), p. 76.

19 *Ibid.*, pp. 78-102.

20 G. P. Gooch, *English Democratic Ideas in the Seventeenth Century* (London: Cambridge, 1927), pp. 10-12.

21 John Knox, "History of the Reformation in Scotland," in Fosdick (ed.), *Great Voices of the Reformation*, pp. 268-69.

22 George Buchanan, "De Jure Regni apud Scotos," in *The Presbyterian's Armoury* (Edinburgh: Oliver & Boyd, 1846), III, 235-83.

23 Samuel Rutherford, "Lex, Rex," *ibid.*, III, 1-234.

24 *Ibid.*, p. 6.

25 Haller, *The Rise of Puritanism*, p. 7.

26 For a thoughtful exposition of the church-state theories of early Puritanism, cf. A. F. Scott-Pearson, *Church and State: Political Aspects of Sixteenth Century Puritanism* (London: Cambridge, 1928).

27 John R. Green, *A Short History of the English People* (New York: Macmillan, 1889), pp. 460, 462.

28 Haller, *Liberty and Reformation in the Puritan Revolution*, p. 107.

29 Jordan, *The Development of Religious Toleration in England*, I, 261.

30 *Ibid.*, I, 82-99.

31 Jordan correctly sees the significant role of Roman Catholicism in the development of governmental and Puritan attitudes in the early seventeenth century. In fact, the events of the time are inexplicable without taking them into strong consideration. From 1618 to 1648 Central Europe was decimated by the Protestant-Catholic struggle called the Thirty Years' War. The Puritans felt that the future of English Protestantism lay in a counterattack against the catholizing tendencies of the Anglican Church. *Ibid.*, especially vol. II.

32 Robert V. Carlyle and Alexander J. Carlyle, *Mediaeval Political Theory in the West* (Edinburgh: Blackwood, 1909-1936), VI, 437-40, for an analysis of James I's "The True Law of Free Monarchies."

33 Perry Miller, *Orthodoxy in Massachusetts, 1630-1650* p. 12.

34 The best account of the events of this period, one which takes seriously the influence of religious impulses and significant religious thinkers, is Haller, *Liberty and Reformation in the Puritan Revolution*.

35 Mather, *Magnalia Christi Americana*, I, 362.

36 Miller, *Orthodoxy in Massachusetts*, pp. xiv-xv. Cf. Burrage, *The Early English Dissenters* . . . , I, 281-311.

37 Miller, *Orthodoxy in Massachusetts*, Chs. VI-VII.

38 John Cotton, "Copy of a Letter from Mr. Cotton to Lord Say and Seal in the Year 1636," *The Puritans*, ed. Perry Miller and Thomas H. Johnson (New York: American Book, 1938), p. 209.

39 *Ibid.*, pp. 212-14.

40 *Ibid.*, p. 213.

41 Robert Baird, *Religion in America* (New York: Harper & Row, 1856), p. 178.

42 William W. Sweet, *Religion in Colonial America* (New York: Scribner, 1942), p. 89.

43 *Cambridge Platform*, XVII, 3. Cf. Henry W. Foote (ed.), *The Cambridge Platform of 1648* (Boston: Beacon Press, 1949).

44 *Ibid.*, XVII, 8.

45 William Bradford, *History of Plymouth Plantation*, ed. William T. Davis (New York: Scribner, 1908), p. 382.

46 Cited in Miller, *Orthodoxy in Massachusetts*, p. 167.

47 *Cambridge Platform*, XVII, 9.

48 Bodo, *The Protestant Clergy and Public Issues, 1812-1848;* Jerald C. Brauer, "The Rule of the Saints in American Politics," *Church History*, XXVII (September, 1958), 240-55; James F. Maclear, " 'The True American Union' of Church and State: The Reconstruction of the Theocratic Tradition," *Church History*, XXVIII (March, 1959), 41-62.

49 Maclear, *Church History*, XXVIII, 41-50. Maclear stresses the gradualness of the breakdown of the older order.

50 Hudson, *The Great Tradition of the American Churches*, pp. 64-65.

51 Cited in Brauer, *Church History*, XXVII, 252.

52 *Ibid.*

53 Maclear, *Church History*, XXVIII, 54-55.

54 *Ibid.*, XXVIII, 49.

55 Hudson, *The Great Tradition of the American Churches*, p. 80.

56 Bodo, *The Protestant Clergy and Public Issues, 1812-1848*, p. 9.

57 *Ibid.*, pp. 52-53, 60.

58 *Ibid.*, pp. 61-82.

59 Stokes, *Church and State in the United States*, II, 57.

60 Cf. Lewis J. Sherrill, *Presbyterian Parochial Schools, 1846-1870* (New Haven: Yale University Press, 1932).

61 Curran, *The Churches and the Schools*, pp. 32-33.

62 Cited in William E. Hocking, *Man and the State* (New Haven: Yale University Press, 1926), pp. 435-36.

63 Luther A. Weigle, "The American Tradition of Religious Freedom," *Social Action*, XIII (November 15, 1947), 12-13.

64 Bennett, *Christians and the State*, p. 5.

65 *Zorach* v. *Clauson* (1952), 343 U.S. at 313.

66 Cf. Merrimon Cuninggim, *Freedom's Holy Light* (New York: Harper & Row, 1955), pp. 122-23, where the author criticizes the use of "co-operation" by Wilfred Parsons, *Tne First Freedom* (New York: McMullen, 1948).

67 Bennett, *Christians and the State*, p. 238.

68 One of the most important statements which reflects a concern for some inclusion of religion in education is Henry P. Van Dusen, *God in Education* (New York: Scribner, 1951).

69 An influential discussion of the difference between freedom and separation was F. Ernest Johnson, "Some Crucial Contemporary Issues," *Social Action*, XIII (November 15, 1947), 15. "I am emphasizing this distinction between principle and policy because I believe the tendency in Protestant circles to make the separation of church and state a religious principle is the cause of much of our present difficulty. It blurs the

fact that this separation, inevitable as it is in a society like ours, supports a trend toward the secularization of life by making it very difficult to bring religious sanctions to bear upon political action."

70 General Council of the Congregational-Christian Churches of the United States, *Minutes* (1948), p. 67.

71 Forrest L. Knapp (ed.), "Relations between Church and State and Interfaith Relations as they Bear on Church and State" (Boston: Massachusetts Council of Churches, n.d.), pp. 25-27.

72 *Ibid.*, p. 26.

73 *Ibid.*

74 *Ibid.* Cf. Dean M. Kelley (ed.), "Questions of Church and State" (New York: Board of Social and Economic Relations, The Methodist Church, 1960), pp. 39-44; Robert M. Brown, "Rules for the Dialogue," *Christian Century* LXXVII (February 17, 1960), 183-85.

75 E.g. John Courtney Murray, *We Hold These Truths.*

76 Bennett, *Christians and the State*, pp. 252-68.

77 *Ibid.*, p. 252.

78 *Ibid.*, p. 254.

79 *Ibid.*, p. 258.

80 *Ibid.*, p. 268.

81 General Council of the Congregational-Christian Churches of the United States, *Minutes* (1950), pp. 46-48.

82 *Ibid.*, p. 46.

83 *Ibid.*, p. 48.

84 Bennett, *Christians and the State*, p. 9.

85 *Ibid.*, p. 11.

86 *Ibid.*, p. 15.

87 *Social Progress,* LI (December, 1960), 5. Italics mine.

88 Kelley, "Questions of Church and State."

89 "Preliminary Proposal for Church-State Studies: 1961-1964" (Department of Religious Liberty, National Council of Churches), p. 3. (Mimeographed.)

90 *Ibid.*, pp. 3-4.

91 Cuninggim, *Freedom's Holy Light*, p. 100.

92 *Ibid.*, p. 119.

93 *Ibid.*, pp. 26-30.

94 *Girouard* v. *U.S.*, 328 US 61 (1946).

95 Bennett, *Christians and the State*, p. 35.

96 *Ibid.*, pp. 57-61.

97 *Ibid.*, p. 67.

98 *Ibid.*, pp. 68-74.

99 *Ibid.*, pp. 96, 98.

100 John C. Bennett, *Christian Ethics and Social Policy* (New York: Scribner, 1946), pp. 76-85.

101 Bennett, *Christians and the State*, pp. 146-62.

102 Reinhold Niebuhr, *The Children of Light and the Children of Darkness* (New York: Scribner, 1944), p. xiii.

Index

Act for Establishing Religious Freedom, 188, 189

"Agreement of the People, An," 174–176, 177

Allen, Ethan, 186

Ambivalence, moral, 10–12, 287, 289

American Friends Service Committee, 114, 148–49, 151

American Protestant Association, 253

Amish, 75, 94, 107

Anabaptists, 11, 19–20, 21, 29, 31, 32–33, 75–94, 119, 124, 126, 137, 166, 168, 172, 218, 220, 225–26, 228, 230

"Appeal to Parliament, An," 178

Anastasius I, 7

Andover Seminary, 248

Anglican Church, 75, 116, 127, 168, 169, 171, 173, 177, 183, 187, 188, 205, 213, 234–40

Anti-Catholicism, 66, 69, 71, 73, 127, 162, 165, 190, 197–98, 204, 210, 211–16, 217, 219–20, 221–22, 223, 224, 239, 252, 262–63, 270, 276, 277, 293, 297, 298–99, 302

Antichrist, 32, 73, 127, 225

Anti-theocrats, 192–94

Apostles' Creed, 78

Archdale, John, 130

Aristocracy, 232, 252

Aristotle, 1

Arminianism, 172, 173, 194

Articles of Confederation (New England), 246

Augsburg, Peace of, 48

Augustine, 2, 6–7, 9, 10, 11, 27, 80

Aulén, Gustaf, 30, 59

Authority (religious), 4, 55–56

Backus, Isaac, 185, 192–93, 195, 197, 248

Baillie, Robert, 241

Bainton, Roland, 47

Balby, 125

Baptism, 77, 92, 170, 171, 216

Baptist Church
General Baptists, 174
in America, 2, 3, 21, 182, 183, 184, 185, 187–88, 190, 192, 194, 195–96, 198–218, 247, 248
in England, 165–66, 170–73, 193, 202–03, 204–05, 241
Particular Baptists, 173

Baptist Historical Association, 201

Baptist Joint Committee on Public Affairs, 199, 206, 216–17

Baptist World Alliance, 199–200

Barbour, Hugh S., 105, 120, 122, 137, 139

Barclay, Robert, 117–18, 131

Barden, Graham A., 164

Barker, Ernest, 2, 233

Barmen Declaration, 53

Barth, Karl, 57, 61

Beecher, Lyman, 249–50

Bender, Harold S., 82, 103, 105

Benezet, Anthony, 139

Bennett, John C., 2, 21, 258, 259, 265, 268, 269, 273–76, 279

Berger, Peter, 219

Berggrav, Eivind, 24, 53–54, 60, 70

Bern, 227

Bismark, Otto von, 307–08

Black, Hugo, 163

Blanshard, Mary, 198
Blanshard, Paul, 61–62, 161, 165, 198, 208, 215
Bodo, John, 191–93, 252
Bonhoeffer, Dietrich, 11, 53, 57, 58, 156
Boniface VIII, 224
Book of Common Prayer, 240
Boorstin, Daniel, 139
Brethren, Church of, 101, 148
Bright, John, 142
Browne, Robert, 167–69
Buchanan, George, 122, 180, 234
Bunyan, John, 205
Burrage, Champlin, 243
Burrough, Edward, 114, 119–20, 127, 128
Busher, Leonard, 172
Butterfield, Herbert, 10

Calvin, 5, 75, 78, 187, **225–32,** 243
Calvinism 21, 22, 23, 54, 62, 75, 94, 116, 118, 166, 167, 168, 170, 181, 186, 193, 223, 224, **225–35,** 238, 251, 270, 277
Cambridge Platform, 246, 247
Cambridge University, 238
Carlson, C. Emanuel, 206, **216–17**
Carlson, Edgar M., 50, 58, 64
Cartwright, Peter, 192
Cartwright, Thomas, 236
Castelberger, Andreas, 88
Celsus, 1
Censorship, 165
Chalcedonian Creed, 78
Channing, William E., 11, 252
Charles I, 127, 239–40
Charles II, 128
Chauncy, Charles, 185–86
Christian Social Responsibility, 63
Christianity and Crisis, 21, 223, 255
Christology, 225–26
Church, doctrine of, 18, 29–30 (Luther); 79-81 (Anabaptist); 110, 119 (Quaker); 167–68 (Browne); 179–80 (Williams); 193 (Baptist); 218–19 (modern separationist)
Church and State Review, 21
Churchman, The, 255
Civilian Public Service, 100
Clark, Mark W., 164

Coercion, 17, 30, 33, 36, 72, 87, 96, 98, 102–03, 105, 108, 109, 123, **125–28,** 131, 133, 135, 137, 147, 218, 230, 274, 288, 289, 291
Coffin, Levi, 242–43
Cole, Charles C., 191
Cole, W. A., 115, 123, 128
Coligny, Gaspard de, 233
Collegiants, 95
Collier, Thomas, 178
Commodus, 2
Communism, 2, 16, 52, 59, 61, 72, 154, 210, 285
Concordia Theological Monthly, 69
Confessing Church, 53
Confession of 1611, 171
Congregational Church, 184, 187, 192, 196, 249, 254–55, 262, 266
Congregational polity, 113, 167, 171, 175, 178, 185, 194, 237–38, 242, 243–44
Connecticut, 190, 248, 249
Connecticut Moral Society, 250
Conscience, 111, 114, 120, 133, 137, 139, 144, 147, 190, 217, 238
Consistory, 49, 229
Constantine, 67, 83, 218, 292
Contraception, 165, 299
Conversion, 86, 117, 184, 194
Cooper, Wilmer A., 145
Corn Laws, 142
Corpus Christianum, 7, 225, 226
Cotton, John, 244, 245, 248
Counter-Reformation, 226, 282
Covenant (church), 86–87, 89, 167, 170, 179
Cowan, Wayne H., 223
Cranmer, Thomas, 235
Creation, doctrine of, 8–9
Cromwell, Oliver, 120, 121, 123, 124, 127, 128, 129, 132, 176, 182, 241–242, 247
Cuius regio, eius religio, 48, 51
Cullmann, Oscar, 6
Cuninggim, Merrimon, 272–73

Davies, Samuel, 188
Dawson, Christopher, 16, 226
Dawson, Joseph M., 199, 201, 206, 208–09, 210, 211
Declaration of Independence, 258

Deists, 189
Demarchi, 230–31
Democracy, 11, 16, 17, 60, 105–06, 146, 174, 176, 185, 221, 232, 274–76
Denck, Hans, 76
Denny, Henry, 174
Devil (demonic), 7, 9, 17, 18, 20, 25, 30–31, 40, 42, 43, 45, 54, 57–58, 64, 71, 72, 79, 81, 82, 84, 87, 90, 103, 138, 155, 289, 305
Dibelius, Otto, 52
Diet of Speyer, 47
Diggers, 241, 242
Discipleship, 20, 78–81, 104, 107, 311
Discipline, church, 229
Disobedience, political, 18, 39, 45–46, 54, 70, 98–99, 122, 153, 154
Divine right of kings, 210
Donatists, 77
Dordrecht Confession, 100
Douglas, William O., 163, 258
Dualism, 6–8, 27, 85–86, 287–88
Dwight, Theodore, 196

East Germany, 72, 293, 294
Eastern Orthodoxy, 6, 283
Ecumenism, 24, 63, 67, 220, 263–64, 267
Ediger, Elmer, 105–06
Edwards, Jonathan, 183, 196, 247
Election, doctrine of, 167–68, 173, 232, 251
Elector of Saxony, 43, 49
Elert, Werner, 56
Elizabeth I, 168, 169, 170, 235–38, 239
Ephori, 230–31
Episcopal Church, 3, 254–55, 261
Equality, political, 175
Erasmus, 88
Erastianism, 12, 13, 93, 168, 180, 186, 204, 226, 227, 235–36, 246, 302
Eschatology, 25, 37, 76, 93, 125, 136, 137
Everson v. *Board of Education,* 163–164, 165, 207, 208, 296
Excommunication (ban), 81, 227, 229, 312

Farel, Willam, 227
Federal Council of Churches, 51, 64, 257

Federalist Party, 190, 192, 252
Ferguson, Leroy, 141
Fifth Monarchy Men, 124, 128, 178, 243
Figgis, John N., 2
Finney, Charles G., 253
Five Years Meeting, 113
Fothergill, Samuel, 135
Foundations, 201
Fox, George, 114, 116–17, 118, 122–23, 124, 125, 126, 127, 128, 131, 158
Fox, George (the Younger), 127
France, 232–34
Franck, Sebastian, 76
Franklin, Benjamin, 186
Free Quakers, 141
French Revolution, 61, 189, 250, 251, 252
Fretz, J. Winfield, 106
Friedmann, Robert, 80
Friendly persuasion, 139, 151
Friends Committee on National Legislation, 145, 148–49
Friends War Problems Committee, 148
Friends World Conference, 113, 146
Fundamentalism, 197

Gandhi, 103, 152
Gelasius I, 7
General Court (Mass.), 244
Geneva, 168, 226–27, 234, 236, 237, 246, 249
Gerhard, Johann, 51
Germantown, 95–96, 100
Germany, 52–54, 60, 73
Gewehr, Wesley M., 184
Girouard v. *United States,* 273
Glimpse of Sion's Glory, A., 179
Gnosticism, 9
Gooch, G. P., 234
Goodwin, Thomas, 241
Graham, Billy, 196
Great Awakenings, 183, 184
Grebel, Conrad, 76, 82, 88–89
Greene, Nathanael, 133
Gregg, Richard, 152
Gregorian Reform, 226
Grotius, Hugo, 302
Gustavus Adolphus, 239

Hass, Harold, 66
Haller, William, 174, 237–38
Hampton Court Conference, 236
Hanover Presbytery, 188
Harvard University, 196
Helwys, Thomas, 170–72, 174
Henry VIII, 235
Herberg, Will, 16, 219, 267
Heresy, 45, 47–48, 88
Hershberger, Guy F., 97, 98, 100, 102–103, 106–07, 109, 134, 136
Higginson, Francis, 243
Hillerbrand, Hans, 86, 291
Hillerdal, Gunnar, 56
History of the Reformation in Scotland, 233
Hitler, 53
Hobbes, Thomas, 2
Holy Roman Empire, 12, 13, 24, 43, 88
Holy Spirit, 79, 115–19, 120–21, 125, 137, 138, 177, 178
Hooker, Thomas, 245, 247
Hoover, Herbert, 150
Hopkinsianism, 248, 253
Hopper, Isaac T., 242
Howgill, Francis, 127
Hoyer, Theodore, 67–68
Hubmaier, Balthasar, 87, 93
Hudson, Winthrop S., 191, 201, 218–220, 250
Huguenots, 233, 239
Hut, Hans, 91
Hutchinson, Anne, 247
Hutterites, 75, 81, 84, 87, 91, 93, 99, 100, 107

Idolatry, 1, 52, 92, 121, 231, 268
Independents, 182, 241
India, 104, 153
Indiana Yearly Meeting, 143
Indians (American), 135–36, 140
Individualism, 18, 56, 73, 110, 190, 192–93, 199–203, 209, 251, 289
Inner Light, 115–19, 126, 131, 138, 147
Innocent III, 224
Insurrection (revolution), 11, 37–38, 39, 40–43, 44, 54, 230–31, 233–34, 274–75
Ireton, John, 175

Italy, 204
Iustitia civilis, 28, 29, 58–59

Jackson, Andrew, 192, 194, 252, 253
Jacob, Henry, 168, 243
Jahsmann, Alan, 69
James I, 170, 236–40
James II, 130
Jefferson, Thomas, 60, 71, 186, 189, 190, 192, 193, 195, 207, 208, 252
Jehovah's Witnesses, 260
Jeremiah, 9
Jesuits, 12, 240
Jews, 14, 46–47, 80, 121, 154, 172, 195, 260, 267–68, 297
John of Salisbury, 231
Johnson, F. Ernest, 279
Jones, Rufus, 138, 144
Jordan, Wilbur K., 238
Jurisdictionalism, 204
Justice, 36, 44–45, 46, 48, 55, 58–59, 62, 64, 65, 109, 123, 158, 159, 181
Justification, doctrine of, 8, 20, 25, 33, 58, 63, 78, 167, 200

Kantonen, T. A., 60, 61
Keehn, Thomas B., 262, 279
Kelley, Dean M., 218–20
Kennedy, John F., 66, 165, 212, 214
King William's War, 135
Knollys, Hanserd, 174, 178–79
Knox, John, 122, 233–34, 235, 237
Koenker, Ernest, 69–70
Koinonia, 80

Laski, Harold, 2
Latitudinarianism, 243
Latourette, Kenneth S., 5
Laud, William, 239–40, 243
Law, 27, 29, 54, 62, 274–75, 293, 295
Leland, John, 185, 192–94, 195, 197, 252, 323
Levellers, 174–76, 180–82, 190, 204, 211, 241, 242
Liberalism (Protestant), 97, 102–03, 105–06, 114–15, 144, 150, 198
Liechtenstein, Leonhard von, 87
Lindbeck, George, 67
Littell, Franklin, 83, 218–20
Liturgy, 213

Lobbying, 101, 108, 149
Locke, John, 186
Logan, James, 135
London Yearly Meeting, 135, 136, 137–38, 142, 145–46, 152
Lord's Supper, 92, 168
Love, 33–34, 35, 36, 46, 56–57, 59, 64, 65, 71, 72, 104, 105, 108–09, 111, 118, 131, 137, 150–51, 290
Luther, 5, 8, 9, 14, 20, 23–74, 75, 78, 79, 81, 82, 83, 84, 85, 89, 93, 200, 225–26, 228, 229, 230, 231, 277, 282
Lutheran Church
  Augustana Synod, 51, 65
  Evangelical Lutheran Church, 66
  General Council, 51
  General Synod, 51
  Missouri Synod 67–70, 73–74
  United Lutheran Church, 65, 66, 70
Lutheran Church Review, 51–52
Lutheranism, 19–20, 21, 22, 23, 48–74, 75, 110, 144, 168, 225, 226, 254, 270, 273, 274, 280, 281, 283, 284, 285, 290, 292, 298
Lutheran World Federation, 64, 66

McCollum v. Board of Education, 69, 162, 163, 165, 209, 223, 260, 279, 296
Machiavelli, 2
Mackay, John, 162
Madison, James, 60, 71, 186, 189, 208
Manichaeism, 9
Mann, Horace, 254
Manz, Felix, 88
Marcionism, 9
Marpeck, Pilgram, 88
Marquardt, Hans, 86
Martineau, Erica, 141–42
Martyrdom, theology of, 90
Marx, Karl, 2
Mary of Scotland, 233–34
Mary Tudor, 233, 235, 239
Mason, George, 186, 189
Massachusetts, 13, 190, 254, 270
Massachusetts Council of Churches, 263–64
Mather, Cotton, 119, 247
Mattson, A. D., 64–65
Mayhew, Jonathan, 185

Mead, Sidney, 187, 190
Medici, Catherine de, 233
Meeting for Sufferings, 130
Melanchthon, Philip, 48, 49
"Memorial and Remonstrance," 189
Mennonite Central Committee, 101
Mennonite Church (Old), 96, 99
Mennonite General Conference, 96, 100, 101, 108
Mennonites, 19, 21, 75, 94–112, 137, 138, 144, 148, 153, 159, 166, 179, 199, 221, 270, 273, 274, 280, 281, 285, 288, 291, 292, 296
Methodist Church, 194, 195–96, 271
Middle Ages, 7, 12, 15, 24, 36, 38, 46, 70, 176, 225, 226, 228
Middle Axioms, 275
Millenarians, 20, 119–20, 125–26, 178, 179, 182, 242–43
Miller, Perry, 179, 243
Minister, as social critic, 43–44
Missions, 190, 191, 199, 248, 249
Moehlman, Conrad H., 211
Monasticism, 34, 58, 84
Monk, Maria, Awful Disclosures of, 253
Mormons, 273, 296
Mornay, Philippe du Plessis, 233
Moses, 9
Münster radicals, 76, 93
Müntzer, Thomas, 76, 88–89, 91
Mullins, Edgar Y., 199–200
Murch, James D., 109
Murray, John C., 211, 258, 264, 298
Murton, John, 172
Muslims, 31

National Association of Evangelicals, 199, 209–10
National Council of Churches, 267, 271, 276
National Lutheran Council, 65–66, 70
National Service Board for Religious Objectors, 101
Natural law, 41, 45, 55, 176, 181, 182, 185, 224, 226, 275, 291
Natural rights, 181
Nazism, 2, 16, 24, 52–54, 56, 59, 72, 154
Neo-Orthodoxy, 63, 255, 268

Nero, 1
Neufeld, Elmer, 106
New Haven Theology, 248
New Testament, 1, 6, 73, 83, 86, 103–
    104, 194, 256, 273, 290
Newton, Louis D., 162
Niebuhr, H. Richard, 4, 19, 21, 76,
    159
Niebuhr, Reinhold, 21, 102, 153, 154,
    158, 174, 209, 276, 279
Niesel, Wilhelm, 225
Nikolsburg (Moravia), 87
Nixon, Richard M., 150
Nonestablishment clause, 145, 163,
    207, 248, 295
Nonresistance, 76, **88–90**, 91, 94, **99–
    104**, 108, 171
Nonviolent resistance, 103–04, **152–
    154**
Norway, 24, 52–54, 59
Notbischof, 49
Nuttall, Geoffrey F., 115

Oath, 84–85, 90–91, 114, 126, 129, 130,
    136, 171, 230, 289
Obedience (political), 28, 36, 38, 39,
    43, 45, 50, 51, 54, 68, 72, 84, 147
Officeholding, 17, 34–35, 51, 84, **85–
    88**, 91, 94, **104–07**, 124–25, 131,
    131, 132–33, 136, 138, **150–51**, 171,
    191, 197, 228, 230, 245–46, 249,
    252, 268–69, 289
Old Calvinists, 191
Old Testament, 1, 9, 62, 86, 179, 181,
    194, 228, 230, 251, 256
O'Neill, James M., 272
Optimism, 105, 193–94, 255
"Orders," 28, 33, 34, 56–57
Osborne, Charles, 142–43
Overton, Richard, 174
Oxford Conference, 56
Oxnam, G. Bromley, 162

Pacifism, 20, 88, 95, 96, 102–04, 128–
    129, 133, 135, 136, 150, 154, 155,
    159, 273, 296
Paine, Thomas, 190, 250
Papacy, 11, 12, 13, 29, 31–32, 39, 45,
    127, 128, 130
Paraguay, Mennonite colonies in,
    104–05

Parliament, English, 121, 123, 130,
    142, 175, 237, 239–40
Parsons, Wilfred, 272
Pastorius, 96
Paul, 1, 8, 37, 54, 84
Peasants' Revolt, 40–42, 46, 91
Penington, Isaac, 124, 125–26
Penn, William, 114, 130, 131, **132–
    135**, 146
Pennsylvania experiment, 114, **132–
    137**, 147, 159
Perfection, 117–18, 131, 150
Persecution, religious, 75, 82, 89–90,
    91–92, 96, 99, 129–30, 180
I Peter, 1, 84
Philadelphia Yearly Meeting, 113,
    136, 147, 154
Philip II, 239
Phillips, Dirck, 78
Pietism, 49
Pilate, Pontius, 45
Pilgrims, 173
Pliny, 1
Pluralism, 2, 16, 17, 98–99, 110, 202,
    219, 267–68, 271, 278, 288, 295,
    297, 301, 325
Political absolutism, 12–14, 16, 37, 49,
    52, 55, 62, 98–99
Polygamy, 273, 296
Ponet, John, 235
Poteat, Edwin M., 162
Powderly, Terence, 303
Predestination, 170, 172
Presbyterian Church, 188, 270–71
Presbyterian Church, New Side, 188–
    189
Presbyterian Church, Old School,
    254–55
Presbyterian polity, 167, 178, 236, 237,
    240, 243
Prohibition, 143, 197, 210, 268
Prophetism, 1, 8–9, 45, 122, 268, 277,
    278, 283
Protestant principle, 3
Protestants and Other Americans
    United for Separation of Church
    and State, 21, 62, 73, 145, **161–
    162**, 164, 165, 198–99, 206, 208,
    215, 216, 222, 223, 263, 267, 271,
    272, 276, 279, 295, 324

Public schools, 162, 253–55
  religious practices in, 69, 162, 165,
    195, 205–06, 207, 209, 210, 219,
    253–55, 258, **259–62**, 263, 297
Pupil benefits, 162, 164
Puritanism, 11, 20, 62, 133, 138, 140,
    158, 165, 167, 169, 171, 173, 177,
    181, 182, 185, 187, 190, 193, 201,
    203, 211, 218, 224, **234–50**, 277
Puritans, Massachusetts, 168, 179, 223,
    241, **243–48**
  relation of Quakers to, 115, 116–28
Putney Debates, 175, 181, 242

Quaker Act, 129
Quakers, 19–20, 21, 95–96, 101, **113–
    160**, 199, 241, 243, 247, 281–82,
    283, 285, 287, 292, 296
Quietism, 114, **130–32**, **137–42**

Rainborowe, Thomas, 181
Rationalism, 61, 71, 76, 137, 140, 141,
    181, **185–87**, 189–90, 200, 201, 207–
    208, 211, 220, 251
Rauschenbusch, Walter, 11
Regiments, **26–29**, 42, 43, 54, 72
Rehwinkel, A. M., 70
Relativism, 20–21, 114, 263, 283–84
Released time, 162, 163, 210
Religious Liberty, 7–8, 12, 13, 92–94,
    110, 121, 137, 145, 182, 190, 201,
    203–05, 216, 261, 263, 265, 273,
    288, 292, 295
Religious schools, public support for,
    17, 66, 69, 161, 162, 164, 165, 212,
    214, 262, 266, 289, 299
Religious symbols, public, 17, 144,
    209, 263, 278, 288, 296, 298
Remonstrants, 95
Revelation, 1
Revivalism, 14, 141, 143, 183–84, 185–
    187, 189–90, 195, 196–97, 199, 201,
    209, 249, 253
Rhode Island, Quakers in, 133–34,
    159
Roberts, Oral, 196
Robinson, John, 173
Roman Catholicism, 4, 5, 6, 12, 15,
    20–21, 25, 48, 61, 62, 68, 77, 80,
    84, 116, 144, 162, 172, 190, 194,
    195, 204, 206, 207, 223, 226, 235,
    241, 254–55, 260, 261, 267–68, 272,
    278, 279, 283, 291, 292, 293, 297,
    298
  views on church and state, 2, 7, 29,
    213–14, 221, 224, 231, 264–66, 301
  transformationist attitude toward,
    262–67
Roman Empire, 1, 6, 7, 9, 230
Roosevelt, Franklin D., 164
Roosevelt, Mrs. Franklin D., 164–65
Rudbeckius, Johannes, 50
Ruff, G. Elston, 59–60, 61
Ruffini, Francesco, 204
Rutherford, Samuel, 180, 234
Rulers, 26–27, 28, 34–35, 39, 40, 41, 43,
    55, 84, 87, 98, 131

Sacraments, 25, 200, 213
Saints, rule of, 124–25, 232, 246, 249
Samson, 46
Sanctification, 167, 168, 232
Satyagraha, **152–53**, 159
Schaff, Philip, 196
Schiotz, Fredrik A., 66
Schleitheim Confession, 81, 85, 91
Schmalkald League, 54
Scholastics, 24
Scotland, 233–34, 235, 236, 240
Scott, Samuel, 138
Sectarianism, 7, 13, 21, 95, 109, 182,
    254, 302
Sects, English, 21, 116, 121, 165–66,
    173, 174, 176, 178, 235, 241–42, 282
Secularism, **14–15**, 52, 60, 62, 70, 195–
    196, 259, 260–61, 262, 264, 268,
    284–85, 298
Separationists, 21, 144, **161–222**, 281–
    282, 292
Separation of church and state, 6, 7–8,
    11, 12, 13, 16, 55, 67–68, 81, 93,
    99, 121, 172, 177, 179–80, 182, 183,
    186, 188–89, 190, 194, 204, 216,
    221, 223, 257–59, 261, 264, 273,
    288, 295–96
  wall of, 20, 162, 163, 198, **205–12**,
    214, 216–17, 219, 221, 257, 270,
    271, 282, 294, 295
Sermon on the Mount, 26, 31, 34, 35,
    39, 78, 85, 103, 104, 112, 153
Servetus, Michael, 76, 229
Seventh Day Adventists, 273

Shakespeare, 237
Sharpless, Isaac, 144
Shepard, Thomas, 247
Sherman, Franklin, 65
Shillitoe, Thomas, 138
Short Declaration of the Mistery of Iniquity, A, 172
Sibley, Mulford Q., 155
Simons, Menno, 76, 78, 79, 84, 85, 86, 87–88, 89, 92, 93, 102
Sin, doctrine of, 10, 20, 27, 30, 55, 61, 63, 65, 78, 84, 97–98, 99, 102–03, 117–18, 137, 155, 156–57, 232, 245, 251–52, 273–74, 275–76, 277
Skydsgaard, K. E., 67
Slavery, 139, 140, 141, **142–43,** 196, 253
Smith, Alfred E., 161
Smith, Timothy, 191
Smucker, Don E., 104, 106–07
Smyth, John, 166, 170, 172, 174
Social ethics, 48, 50, 51, 58, **63–66,** 68, 70, **105–09,** 111, 122–23, 140, 142–143, 145–46, **147–50,** 210, 223, 249–251, **255–57,** 266–67, 277, 282, 292–93
Social Gospel, 51–52, 63, 102–03, 107, 114–15, 196–97, 209, 255–57
Socialism, 14
Socinianism, 95
Socinus, Faustus, 76
Sovereignty
  divine, 3, **8–10,** 11, 20, 60, 119, 287–289
  popular, 55, 233–34
Soul-competency, **199–200,** 203, 218
Spain, 239
Spellman, Francis Cardinal, 164–65
Spiritualism (mysticism), 20, 76, 119, 138, 139, 153, 154
Stahl, Friedrich Julius, 50
Stewardship, 218
Strassburg, 92, 227
Stumpf, Simon, 82
Subjectivism, 241
Sunday closing laws, 165, 193, 250, 268, 297, 298
Sweden, 50–51, 53, 54, 57, 64, 205, 293
Sweet, William W., 246
Switzerland, 76, 86

Taylor, Clyde, 162
Taylor, Myron C., 164
Theocentrism, 10, 24–26, 71, 72, 126, 136, 156–57, 171, 193, 200, 203, 216–17, 220, 277, 284, 323–24
Theocracy, **119–24,** 132, 136, 140, 144, 179, 181, **243–48**
"Theocrats," 192, 193, **248–53,** 266
Thomas Aquinas, 46
Tillich, Paul, 3, 14
Tinkham, George H., 256–57
Tithes, 121, 124, 129, 178, 182, 242
Törnvall, Gustaf, 27, 29, 58
Toleration, 13, 47–48, 93–94, 95, 120–122, 131, 169, 171, 172, 174, 177, 180, 204, 205, 235, 238, 241–43, 246–47
Tolles, Frederick B., 115, 151
Tradition, 5
Transformationists, 21, 22, 144, **223–280,** 282, 283, 292, 295
Trinity, doctrine of, 218
Troeltsch, Ernst, 48, 49, 50, 94, 95, 173
Truman, Harry S., 164
Turks, 9, 31–32, 38, 121, 127
"Twelve Articles," 40–41
Tyrannicide, 39, 231
Tyranny, 230

Ullman, Richard K., 155–57
Underwood, Kenneth W., 286
Unitarianism, 189, 191, 194, 198
United States Supreme Court, 162, 208
Utopianism, 33, 228, 253

Vatican ambassador, 66, 161, 162, **164,** 212, 263, 278
Vindiciae Contra Tyrannos, 233
Virginia, 183, 184, 188–89
Vocation, 9, 25, **34–36,** 55, 63, 64, 71, 72, 228, **290–91**
Volkskirche, 77, 80–81
Voluntaryism, 82, 93, 202, 211, 213, 218, 220, 248–49
Voting, problem of, 105–07

War, problem of, 17, 38, 84–85, 89, 99–104, 123, 126, 159, 230, 256, 288, 289, 292
Warren Association, 185

Washington, George, 186, 188
Waterlander Mennonites, 94, 166, 170–71
Weaver, Rufus W., 206
Webster, Daniel, 249
Weigel, Gustave, 298
Weigle, Luther A., 257–58
Welfare function of government, 55, 65, 98, 99, 106, 134, 147
Wesley, John, 176
Westin, Gunnar, 205–06
Westminster, 240
What Lutherans Are Thinking, 63
Whig Party, 192, 252
Wilberforce, William, 11
Wildman, John, 175, 181
Williams, Daniel D., 197–98
Williams, Roger, **179–80**, 182, 205, 247

Wilson, E. Raymond, 145
Wilson, Woodrow, 101
Wingren, Gustaf, 290
Wise, John, 185
Witzel, Georg, 83
Woodhouse, A. S. P., 181
Woolman, John, 139
World Council of Churches, 294
World War II, 52
Wunderleute, 46

Yost, Frank, 162

Zorach v. *Clauson*, 163, 207, 208, 258
Zurich, 82, 88
Zwickau prophets, 91
Zwingli, 20, 75, 82, 88, 91, 93, 168